The **Rough Guide** to

Melbourne

written and researched by

Stephen Townshend

with additional contributions by

George Dunford

**ROUGH
GUIDES**

NEW YORK • LONDON • DELHI

www.roughguides.com

△ View from Brighton beach

Introduction to
Melbourne

Australia's second-largest city and capital of the state of Victoria, Melbourne prides itself on being a place that knows how to live well. It may lag behind Sydney in terms of population and prestige, but its less brazen charms offer a quality of life which other Australian cities find difficult to match. Magnificent landscaped gardens and parklands have made the city one of the greenest in the world, while beneath the skyscrapers of the arresting Central Business District (CBD), elegant Victorian-era facades present Melbourne on an agreeably human scale.

Often topping lists as the world's most liveable big city, it's an enjoyable place to visit too. Residents and tourists alike can take pleasure in its successfully multi-ethnic society; its revitalized city centre, housing some of Australia's coolest cafés and bars; and in its leading role in Australian cultural and sporting life. For close on a century a rather staid, Anglo-Celtic city, postwar immigration has shaken up Melbourne's old ways for good. Reminders of former conservatism linger on in the city's uniform layout and relentless suburbanization, but the influx of people from Lebanon, Turkey, Greece, Vietnam, China and more recently Eastern Europe has enriched and energized the city's formerly inward-looking and parochial character.

In the last decade, Melbourne has also undergone a remarkable renaissance in everything from architecture and design to fashion, food and literature, thanks to forward-thinking state governments and massive

△ Luna Park entrance

private investment. The "Postcode 3000" campaign has reinvented the Central Business District as a place to live and socialize, not just to work. A key indicator of the campaign's success has been the rise in CBD residents – in 1982, a mere 700 lived here, now it's almost 10,000. Melbourne has also become a major cultural and architectural laboratory, with the redevelopment and creation of public spaces such as Federation Square, the National Gallery of Victoria and Docklands testament to the city's bold and experimental approach to art and design.

△ Bolte Bridge

Not all the changes have been positive – older buildings have been demolished to make way for Manhattan-style high-rises and apartments, and there's an increasing number of homeless people and drug addicts on the streets – but, despite these problems, this regenerated Melbourne is today, more than at any other time in its history, comfortable with its mantle of Australia's second city and looking forward to a confident and prosperous future.

What to see

Melbourne straddles the Yarra River, just before it flows into Port Phillip Bay. On the northern banks of the river and about five kilometres from the bay, the **Central Business District (CBD)** is the main focus of the city. A large, flat rectangle, with wide blocks laid out in a grid pattern, it boasts a lively and cosmopolitan atmosphere, and is easy to get around on foot. The main north–south artery is bustling **Swanston Street**, site of the massive Queen Victoria residential and shopping development. The most important east–west streets are **Collins** and **Bourke**.

The half of the CBD east of Swanston Street contains an attractive architectural legacy from the goldrush era, with many of the city's finest civic buildings, including the mammoth **Parliament House** and the magnificent cathedrals of **St Patrick** and **St Paul**. At the eastern edge of the district, the fashionable shops and cafés of the **"Paris End"** of Collins Street offer style and culture of a more contemporary kind, as does

△ Flinders Street Station clocks

v

△ Rowers on the Yarra River

atmospheric **Chinatown**, still home to the longest established of the city's many ethnic communities. Down by the riverfront, relative newcomer **Federation Square** forms a bold link between the CBD and the river.

West of Swanston Street, the other half of the CBD is home to bustling **Bourke Street Mall**, a pedestrian-only strip flanked by shops, department stores and the classical-style General Post Office. The area is also the location of a large and fascinating network of arcades and passageways, teeming with stylish boutiques, antique shops and innumerable cafés and restaurants. Southwest on Collins Street is Melbourne's tallest building, the **Rialto Towers**, while to the north, **Queen Victoria Market** is a popular venue for shopping and socializing.

South of the CBD, across the city's principal axis, the **Yarra River**, are many of Melbourne's newest and glitziest buildings, including the enormous leisure complexes of **Southgate** and the **Crown Casino**, the **Melbourne Exhibition** Centre and the **Victorian Arts Centre** with its distinctive spire, not to mention myriad skyscrapers and, further south, the refurbished **National Gallery of Victoria**. Opposite here, the beautifully tended

Melbourne prides itself on being a place that knows how to live well

Royal Botanic Gardens present a therapeutic respite from the pace of city life.

Rubbing shoulders just north of the CBD, the inner suburbs of **Carlton** and **Fitzroy** are at the heart of Melbourne's vibrant ethnic and alternative cultures. To the east, **Richmond** is famed for

△ Café scene

its Greek and Vietnamese eateries, as well as its bargain shopping, while **Collingwood** has gone from an industrial no-go area to a fashionable hotspot, with cafés, restaurants and trendy stores galore. South of the CBD, the main thoroughfare is St Kilda Road, a busy, tree-lined boulevard that runs past the exclusive, style-conscious suburbs of **South Yarra**, **Prahran** and **Toorak** before reaching the seafront at **St Kilda**, the perfect place for kicking back over coffee and newspapers. Heading west, the bayside suburbs of **South Melbourne** and **Albert Park** are worth visiting for their food markets, delis, upmarket stores and elegant nineteenth-century streetscapes. Beyond these, the city's sprawling outer suburbs hold fewer points of interest for the visitor, although **Williamstown**, on a promontory southwest of the city, warrants a trip for its maritime leanings and lively weekend coffee trade. Further afield, in the northeastern suburbs of Bulleen and Eltham, the artist retreats of the

△ Public art, Brunswick Street

△ Graffiti, Richmond

Museum of Modern Art at Heide and **Montsalvat** are two notable places of bohemian creativity.

Outside Melbourne, and easily accessible by public transport or car, are a host of rewarding day-trips. Nearby on the coast is **Phillip Island**, with its famous penguins, and the bucolic backdrops and beach resorts of the **Bellarine** and **Mornington peninsulas**, the latter including Wilson's Promontory, a magnificent national park. Inland, the scenic **Dandenong Ranges** and the prestigious wineries of the **Yarra Valley** are convenient escapes from the urban bustle, while the salubrious spa towns of **Daylesford** and **Hepburn Springs** and the grandiose architecture of the former gold-mining town of **Ballarat** – Victoria's largest inland city – offer reminders of the area's nineteenth-century heritage. Heading west along the coast, the magnificent **Great Ocean Road** winds 300km along some of Australia's most spectacular coastal scenery.

When to go

A feature of Melbourne's climate is its changeability, particularly during spring and summer when dramatic falls in temperature sometimes occur within a few minutes. In general the city's weather is warm to hot in summer (Dec–Feb), mild in autumn (March–May), cold and damp in winter (June–Aug), and cool in spring (Sept–Nov). January and February usually see the best weather, with clear blue skies tempting locals and visitors alike to enjoy some outdoor eating and drinking, though extreme hot spells – when temperatures can climb into the forties – and hiked up prices and crowded beaches are the downside. Wintery June and July, when night frosts sometimes occur, are not entirely unpleasant and are a great time to check out the inner-city pubs, or enjoy some of the excellent galleries and museums.

Melbourne's climate

	Average daily temp °F		Average daily temp °C		Average monthly rainfall	
	Max	Min	Max	Min	Inches	mm
January	79	59	26	15	1.8	48
February	79	60	26	16	1.9	50
March	75	57	24	14	2.1	54
April	70	53	21	12	2.3	59
May	63	50	17	10	2.2	58
June	57	44	14	7	1.9	50
July	57	44	14	7	1.8	48
August	59	44	15	7	1.9	50
September	63	48	17	9	2.2	58
October	68	50	20	10	2.6	67
November	71	53	22	12	2.3	59
December	75	57	24	14	2.2	58

things not to miss

It's not possible to see everything that Melbourne has to offer in one visit, and we don't suggest you try. What follows is a selective taste of the city's highlights, from outstanding museums and cosmopolitan bars to beautiful parks and unforgettable road-trips, arranged in five colour-coded categories. All highlights have a page reference to take you straight into the guide, where you can find out more.

01 Melbourne Museum Page **71** • Excellent museum complex, characterized by cutting-edge design and a variety of exhibition spaces including a kitchen set from *Neighbours* and a towering indoor rainforest.

02 Melbourne nightlife Page **121** • From sleek clubs and cutting-edge bars to traditional boozers, there are plenty of options for a great night out in Melbourne.

03 Royal Botanic Gardens Page **63** • Established in 1846, the Royal Botanic Gardens are an inviting oasis amid the clamour and bustle of Melbourne.

04 Federation Square Page **65** • Wander the galleries and exhibition spaces at stupendous Federation Square, an ambitious public monument in the heart of the city.

05 **The Great Ocean Road** Page **206** • Renowned coastal highway famous for its jaw-dropping scenery and picturesque seaside communities.

06 **Chinatown** Page **38** • Small and atmospheric, Melbourne's Chinatown is the real deal, complete with cheap eating houses, languid tea parlours and garish souvenir shops.

07 Scenic railway-roller Coaster Page **90** • Take a ride on the world's oldest operating roller-coaster at Luna Park.

08 Melbourne's arcades and passageways Page **40 & 49** • Australia's most extensive network of arcades and lanes is crammed with stores selling everything from funky glassware to edgy clothing, while cosy cafés provide the perfect pit stop.

09 Collins Street Page **51** • Melbourne's Parisian-style boulevard is lined with goldrush architecture and full of expensive boutiques.

10 French Island Page **175** • The pristine landscapes of this undeveloped island are home to a rich diversity of wildlife – including the country's largest population of koalas.

11 Docklands Page **53** • Melbourne's up-and-coming new waterfront precinct features buzzing cafés and restaurants, and some of the most conspicuous buildings and public art in the city – including the graceful Webb Bridge.

13 National Gallery of Victoria Page **58** • The revamped NGV contains the most comprehensive collection of international art in Australia, including the world's largest stained-glass ceiling.

12 Melbourne's cafés Page **112** • Experience Melbourne's passion for coffee at one of its ubiquitous cafés.

14 City Circle Tram Page 21

• Hop-on, hop-off free tram service circuiting the CBD and passing some of Melbourne's major attractions.

15 Phillip Island penguins Page 174 • Beat a path to the hugely popular Penguin Parade to see thousands of these cute aquatic birds emerge from the surf and waddle ashore.

16 Melbourne Cup Page 147 • One of the top sporting events in the calendar, the Melbourne Cup horse race is also a revered Australian tradition.

17 Wilsons Promontory National Park Page **176** • Magnificent national park with plenty of camping spots and some of Victoria's finest surfing beaches, wetlands and bushwalks.

18 Melbourne Cricket Ground Page **64** • Scream your heart out watching the footy or cricket at the venerable MCG.

19 Chapel Street Page **76** • With its wall-to-wall boutiques and plenty of cool cafés, exclusive Chapel Street is the place to come to see and be seen.

20 Yarra River cruise Page **21** • Take a leisurely cruise down the Yarra for a wonderful view of Melbourne from the water.

Contents

Using this Rough Guide

We've tried to make this Rough Guide a good read and easy to use. The book is divided into eight main sections, and you should be able to find whatever you want in one of them.

Colour section

The front **colour section** offers a quick tour of Melbourne and the surrounding area. The **introduction** aims to give you a feel for the place, with suggestions on where to head for and when to go. Next, the author rounds up his favourite aspects of Melbourne in the **things not to miss** section – whether it's amazing museums, great day-trips or a unique neighbourhood. Right after this comes the Rough Guide's full **contents** list.

Basics

The basics section covers all the pre-departure nitty-gritty to help you plan your trip. This is where to find out which airlines fly to your destination, what paperwork you'll need, what to do about money and insurance, about Internet access, food, public transport – in fact just about every piece of **general practical information** you might need.

The City

This is the heart of the Rough Guide, divided into user-friendly chapters, each of which covers a city district. Every chapter starts with an **introduction** that helps you to decide where to go, followed by an extensive tour of the sights.

Listings

This section contains all the consumer information you need to make the most of your stay, with chapters on **accommodation**, places to **eat** and **drink**, **nightlife**, **shopping**, **festivals** and more.

Beyond the city

These chapters describe attractions **further out of the city**, with all the accommodation, eating and practical details you'll need for both day-trips and longer stays.

Contexts

Read Contexts to get a deeper understanding of what makes Melbourne tick. We include a brief **history**, and a detailed further reading section that reviews dozens of **books** relating to the city.

small print + Index

Apart from a **full index**, which includes maps as well as places, this section covers publishing information and credits, and also has our contact details in case you want to send in updates and corrections to the book – or suggestions as to how we might improve it.

Colour maps

The **back colour section** contains detailed maps to give you an overview of the city and help you explore.

Map and chapter list

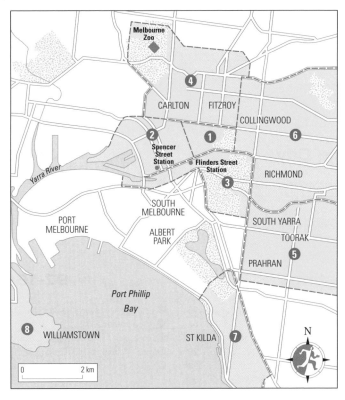

Contents

Beyond the city

Contexts

small print and Index

Basics

Basics

Getting there

Melbourne's airport – the second busiest in Australia – services all the major international airlines. Airfares depend on the season, with the weeks around Christmas generally being the busiest, and most expensive, time to travel.

Booking flights online

Many airlines and discount travel websites offer you the opportunity to book your tickets online, cutting out the costs of agents and middlemen; these are worth going for, as long as you don't mind the inflexibility of non-refundable, non-changeable deals. There are some bargains to be had on auction sites too, if you're prepared to bid keenly.

Online booking agents

Ⓦ **www.cheapflights.co.uk** (in UK & Ireland), Ⓦ **www.cheapflights.com** (in US), Ⓦ **www .cheapflights.ca** (in Canada). Flight deals, travel agents, plus links to other travel sites.
Ⓦ **www.ebookers.com** Efficient, easy to use flight finder, with competitive fares.
Ⓦ **www.expedia.co.uk** (in UK), Ⓦ **www .expedia.com** (in US), Ⓦ **www.expedia.ca** (in Canada). Discount airfares, all-airline search engine and daily deals.
Ⓦ **www.flyaow.com** "Airlines of the Web" – online air travel info and reservations.
Ⓦ **www.hotwire.com** Bookings from the US only. Last-minute savings of up to forty percent on regular published fares. Travellers must be at least 18 and there are no refunds, transfers or changes allowed. Log-in required.
Ⓦ **www.lastminute.com** (in UK), Ⓦ **www .lastminute.com.au** (in Australia), Ⓦ **www .lastminute.co.nz** (in New Zealand), Ⓦ **www .orbitz.com** Comprehensive web travel source, with the usual flight, car hire and hotel deals but also great follow-up customer service.
Ⓦ **www.priceline.co.uk** (in UK), Ⓦ **www .priceline.com** (in US). Name-your-own-price website that has deals at around forty percent off standard fares.
Ⓦ **www.skyauction.com** Bookings from the US only. Auctions tickets and travel packages to destinations worldwide.
Ⓦ **www.travelocity.co.uk** (in UK), Ⓦ **www**

.travelocity.com (in US), Ⓦ **www.travelocity.ca** (in Canada). Hot fares, plus great deals for car rental and lodging.

From the UK and Ireland

The quickest way to get to Melbourne from the UK is to fly direct with British Airways or Qantas from London Heathrow, with a **flying time** of around 21 hours. Plenty of other airlines have indirect flights to Melbourne (involving at least one change of plane), taking longer but costing significantly less. There are no direct flights from **regional airports** in the UK or from Ireland, but plenty of connections to London or flights via other European capitals.

Fares are most expensive from mid-June to mid-August and in the two weeks before Christmas, and cheapest from April to mid-June. The cheapest published scheduled fares **from the UK** start at around £600 return during low season, rising to around £1000 return at peak periods – to stand a chance of getting one of the cheaper tickets at these times, aim to book anything up to six months in advance. In the first instance it's always worth checking with the discount flight agents listed on p.10, which have many special offers, particularly for students and under-26s. Flying **from Ireland**, most of the cheaper routings involve a stop in London. Fares start at around €1000 in low season, increasing to around €1700 over Christmas.

Making one or more **stopovers** en route is one way of breaking up the long flight to Australia. You'll usually have to pay a supplement, although these are sometimes included in the price of the ticket. Alternatively, **round-the-world (RTW)** tickets offer a good way of including Australia as part of a longer journey. The routing permutations are endless, but fares normally reflect the length of the route chosen and the number of stops to be made; London–Bangkok–Melbourne–Los Angeles–London, for example, would cost around £900.

Airlines

Air New Zealand UK ☎0800/028 4149, ⓦwww .airnz.co.uk.

Austrian Airlines UK ☎0845/601 0948, Republic of Ireland ☎1800/509 142, ⓦwww.aua.com.

British Airways UK ☎0870/850 9850, Republic of Ireland ☎1800/626 747, ⓦwww.ba.com.

Cathay Pacific UK ☎020/8834 8888, ⓦwww .cathaypacific.com/uk.

Emirates UK ☎0870/243 2222, ⓦwww.emirates .com.

KLM (Royal Dutch Airlines) UK ☎0870/507 4074, ⓦwww.klm.com.

Malaysia Airlines UK ☎0870/607 9090, Republic of Ireland ☎01/676 2131, ⓦwww .malaysia-airlines.com.

Qantas UK ☎0845/774 7767, Republic of Ireland ☎01/407 3278, ⓦwww.qantas.co.uk.

Singapore Airlines UK ☎0870/608 8886, Republic of Ireland ☎01/671 0722, ⓦwww .singaporeair.com.

Thai Airways UK ☎0870/606 0911, ⓦwww .thaiair.com.

United Airlines UK ☎0845/844 4777, ⓦwww .unitedairlines.co.uk.

Discount agents in Britain and Ireland

Austravel UK ☎0870/166 2020, ⓦwww .austravel.net. Australia travel specialists, also issue ETAs (see p.12) and traditional visas.

Bridge the World UK ☎0870/443 2399, ⓦwww .bridgetheworld.com. Specialists in long-haul travel, with good-value flight deals, round-the-world tickets and tailor-made packages, all aimed at the backpacker market.

ebookers UK ☎0870/010 7000, ⓦwww .ebookers.com, Republic of Ireland ☎01/241 5689, ⓦwww.ebookers.ie. Low fares on an extensive selection of scheduled flights and package deals.

Flightcentre UK ☎0870/890 8099, ⓦwww .flightcentre.co.uk. Rock-bottom fares worldwide.

North South Travel UK ☎01245/608 291, ⓦwww.northsouthtravel.co.uk. Friendly, competitive travel agency, offering discounted fares worldwide. Profits are used to support projects in the developing world, especially the promotion of sustainable tourism.

STA Travel UK ☎0870/160 0599, ⓦwww .statravel.co.uk. Worldwide specialists in low-cost flights, overland and holiday deals. Good discounts for students and under-26s.

Trailfinders UK ☎020/7938 3939, ⓦwww .trailfinders.com, Republic of Ireland ☎01/677 7888, ⓦwww.trailfinders.ie. One of the best-informed and most efficient agents for independent travellers.

Travel Bag UK ☎0870/890 1456, ⓦwww .travelbag.co.uk. Discount deals worldwide.

Travel Care UK ☎0870/112 0085, ⓦwww .travelcare.co.uk. Flights and holiday around the world.

World Travel Centre Republic of Ireland ☎01/416 7007, ⓦwww.worldtravel.ie. Excellent fares worldwide.

From North America

There are no non-stop flights from North America to Melbourne, but plenty of one-stop services, usually routed via Sydney. The **flying time** to Melbourne, excluding stopovers, is approximately fifteen hours from Los Angeles; twenty hours from New York or Chicago. From Canada, most flights connect through Los Angeles. Flying time from Vancouver to Melbourne is approximately eighteen hours; from Toronto or Montréal it's about twenty.

Fares are highest from December to February and lowest from April to August. Typical scheduled fares to Melbourne from the west coast of the US are around US$900/1500 (low/high season); from the east coast US$1200/1900. From Vancouver, expect to pay CAN$1800/2000 (low/high season); CAN$1900/2500 from Montréal or Toronto. Fares depend upon how far in advance you purchase your tickets, as well as how many seats are available on a particular flight. Booking through a discount travel agent (see opposite) can knock dollars off published fares.

Another possibility are the **charter flights** offered by some companies. Fares are usually slightly cheaper than on scheduled flights, but generally come with various restrictions – check conditions carefully before booking. Charter flights can only be booked through a travel agent, not directly with the airline.

Round-the-world (RTW) and **Circle-Pacific** tickets can be very good value. Booked through a discount agent or consolidator, a typical Circle Pacific itinerary from Los Angeles via Tokyo, Hong Kong,

Bangkok, Singapore, Jakarta, Bali, Cairns and Melbourne costs about US$2500. A sample RTW ticket from Los Angeles via Melbourne, Bangkok, Delhi, Mumbai (Bombay) and London is a similar price.

Airlines

Air New Zealand US ☎1-800/262-1234, Canada ☎1-800/663-5494 or 604/606-0150, ⓦwww .airnz.com.
Air Canada ☎1-888/247-2262, ⓦwww .aircanada.com.
Cathay Pacific ☎1-800/233-2742, ⓦwww .cathay-usa.com.
JAL (Japan Air Lines) ☎1-800/525-3663, ⓦwww.japanair.com.
Malaysia Airlines ☎1-800/552-9264, ⓦwww .malaysia-airlines.com.
Qantas Airways ☎1-800/227-4500, ⓦwww .qantas.com.
Singapore Airlines US ☎1-800/742-3333, Canada %1-800/387-8039 or 663-3046, ⓦwww .singaporeair.com.
United Airlines ☎1-800/538-2929, ⓦwww .united.com.

Discount agents and consolidators

Air Brokers International ☎1-800/883-3273, ⓦwww.airbrokers.com. Consolidator and specialist in round-the-world and Circle Pacific tickets.
Air Courier Association ☎1-800/282-1202, ⓦwww.aircourier.org. Courier flight broker. Membership (US$35 for a year) also entitles you to twenty percent discount on travel insurance and name-your-own-price non-courier flights.
Airtech ☎212/219-7000, ⓦwww.airtech.com. Standby seat broker; also deals in consolidator fares.
Flightcentre US ☎1-866/WORLD-51, ⓦwww .flightcentre.us, Canada ☎1-888/WORLD-55, ⓦwww.flightcentre.ca. Rock-bottom fares worldwide.
International Association of Air Travel Couriers ☎308/632-3273, ⓦwww.courier.org. Courier flight broker. One year's membership costs US$45 in the US or Canada.
STA Travel US ☎1-800/329-9537, Canada ☎1-888/427-5639, ⓦwww.statravel.com. Worldwide specialists in independent travel; also student IDs, travel insurance, car rental, and more.
Travel Avenue ☎1-800/333-3335, ⓦwww .travelavenue.com. Full-service travel agent that offers discounts in the form of rebates.
Travel Cuts US ☎1-800/592-CUTS, Canada ☎1-888/246-9762, ⓦwww.travelcuts.com.

Popular, long-established student-travel organization, with worldwide offers.

From New Zealand

There's a good choice of flights to Melbourne from New Zealand: routes are busy and competition is fierce, resulting in an ever-changing range of deals and special offers. It's a relatively short hop across the Tasman Sea, with a flying time from Auckland to Melbourne of around three and a half hours.

Fares depend on how much flexibility you want: many of the cheapest deals are hedged with restrictions – typically, they must be booked at least seven days in advance, with a maximum stay of thirty days. Return tickets with the major airlines cost NZ$500–800 for a thirty-day ticket, and rise in price by several hundred dollars for longer stays of up to six months. Flying at peak times (primarily December to mid-January) can also add substantially to the price. Whatever kind of ticket you're after, your first call should be to one of the specialist travel agents listed below; staff can fill you in on all the latest fares and special offers.

Alternatively, the New Zealand web-based Freedom Air specialises in **no-frills**, low-cost trans-Tasman air travel, with one-way flights from Hamilton, Palmerston North and Dunedan to Melbourne starting at NZ$190.

Package deals can be a hassle-free way of getting a taste of Melbourne. There's a huge variety of holidays and tours to Australia available in New Zealand; call any of the travel agents listed below. Subsidiaries of airlines such as Air New Zealand and Qantas package short city-breaks (flight and accommodation) and fly-drive deals for little more than the cost of the regular airfare.

Airlines

Aerolineas Argentinas Australia ☎02/9317 3018, New Zealand ☎09/275 9914, ⓦwww .aerolineas.com.
Air New Zealand Australia ☎13 24 76, ⓦwww .airnz.com.au, New Zealand ☎0800/737 000, ⓦwww.airnz.co.nz.
Freedom Air ☎0800/600 500, ⓦwww.freedom .co.nz.

Malaysia Airlines Australia ☎13 26 27, New Zealand ☎0800/777 747, ⓦwww.malaysia -airlines.com.

Polynesian Airlines Australia ☎1300/653 737, New Zealand ☎0800/800 993, ⓦwww .polynesianairlines.com.

Qantas Australia ☎13 13 13, New Zealand ☎0800/808 767 or 09/357 8900, ⓦwww.qantas .com.

Thai Airways Australia ☎1300/651 960, New Zealand ☎09/377 3886, ⓦwww.thaiair.com.

Discount agents

Flight Centre Australia ☎13 31 33, ⓦwww .flightcentre.com.au, New Zealand ☎0800/243

544, ⓦwww.flightcentre.co.nz. Rock-bottom fares worldwide.

Holiday Shoppe New Zealand ☎0800/808 480, ⓦwww.holidayshoppe.co.nz. Great deals on flights, hotels and holidays.

STA Travel Australia ☎1300/733 035, New Zealand ☎0508/782 872, ⓦwww.statravel. com. Worldwide specialists in low-cost flights and holiday deals. Good discounts for students and under-26s.

Student Uni Travel Australia ☎02/9232 8444, ⓦwww.sut.com.au, New Zealand ☎09/379 4224, ⓦwww.sut.co.nz. Great deals for students.

Trailfinders Australia ☎02/9247 7666, ⓦwww .trailfinders.com.au. One of the best-informed and most efficient agents for independent travellers.

Red tape and visas

All visitors to Australia require a visa or Electronic Travel Authority (ETA) and a valid passport, except New Zealanders, who need only a passport and are issued with a visa on arrival. You can get visa application forms from Australian High Commissions, embassies or consulates listed opposite. ETAs can be applied for online or through travel agents and airlines for a small fee.

Three-month tourist visas (valid for multiple entries over one year) are issued free and either processed over the counter or returned within three weeks by mail. You may be asked to show proof that you have sufficient funds – at least AUS $1000 per month – to support yourself during your stay. The computerized ETA system (ⓦwww.eta.immi.gov.au) is speedier for those from participating countries (including the UK, Ireland, the US and most of Europe) and saves queuing or standing in line.

Longer visas, working visas and extensions

Six-month visas incur a fee: £25, US$36 and CAN$55 in the UK, US and Canada respectively. If you think you might stay more than three months, it's best to get the six-month visa in advance, since once you're in Australia extensions cost A$170, and are non-refundable. Once issued, a visa

usually allows multiple entries so long as your passport remains valid. To extend your visa in Melbourne, contact the Department of Immigration and Multicultural Affairs at 2 Lonsdale St (☎13 18 81). Make sure to apply at least a month before your visa expires, as the process can take some time.

Citizens of the UK, Canada, Holland, Japan and Korea aged between 18 and 25, can apply for a working holiday visa, which grants a twelve-month stay and allows the holder to work for up to three months with the same employer. You'll need to apply in your home country several months in advance and be able to show evidence of sufficient funds. For further information, visit the Department of Immigration and Multicultural and Indigenous Affairs website at ⓦwww.immi.gov.au/allforms/working.htm or contact your local embassy or consulate (see opposite).

Australian embassies and consulates

Canada Australian High Commission, Suite 710, 50 O'Connor St, Ottawa, Ontario K1P 6L2 ☎613/236-0841, ⓦwww.ahc-ottawa.org.
Ireland Australian Embassy, Fitzwilton House, Wilton Terrace, Dublin 2 ☎01/664 5300, ⓦwww.australianembassy.ie.
New Zealand Australian High Commission, 72–78 Hobson St, Thorndon, Wellington ☎04/473 6411, ⓦwww.australia.org.nz; Australian Consulate-General, 186–194 Quay St, Auckland 1 ☎09/303 2429, ⓕ377 0798.
UK Australian High Commission, Australia House, Strand, London WC2B 4LA ☎020/7379 4334, ⓦwww.australia.org.uk.
US Australian Embassy, 1601 Massachusetts Ave NW, Washington DC 20036 ☎202/797-3000, ⓕ797-3168; Australian Consulate-General, International Building, 150 East 42nd St, 34th floor, New York, NY 10017-5612 ☎212/351-6500, ⓕ351-6501; for more consulate addresses consult ⓦwww.austemb.org.

Customs

Prior to landing in Australia you'll be handed an immigration form to fill out, as well as Customs and Agriculture declaration forms. Australia has particularly strict **quarantine laws** to protect native flora and fauna, and to prevent the introduction of exotic pests and diseases. You must declare all goods of animal or plant origin, and you can't bring fresh fruit or vegetables into the country. As well as drugs and firearms, Australian customs officials are strict about anabolic steroids, pornographic material, protected wildlife and associated products. If you've been snacking on the flight, throw any leftovers in the amnesty quarantine bins available in the arrival area or on the way to the luggage collection bay.

To find out more about specific goods that are prohibited in Australia before you travel, visit the Australian Government Guide to Visiting Australia at ⓦwww.immi.gov.au/visitors.

Those aged over 18 have a **duty-free allowance** on entry of AUS$400 worth of goods, 1125ml of alcohol and 250 cigarettes/250g of tobacco.

Insurance

You'd do well to take out an insurance policy before travelling to cover against theft, loss and illness or injury. Before paying for a new policy, however, it's worth checking whether you are already covered: some all-risks home insurance policies may cover your possessions when overseas, and many private medical schemes include cover when abroad. In Canada, provincial health plans usually provide partial cover for medical mishaps overseas, while holders of official student/teacher/youth cards in Canada and the US are entitled to meagre accident coverage and hospital inpatient benefits. Students will often find that their student health coverage extends during the vacations and for one term beyond the date of last enrolment.

After checking out the possibilities above, you might want to contact a specialist travel insurance company, or consider the travel insurance deal Rough Guides offer. A typical travel insurance policy usually provides cover for the loss of baggage, tickets and – up to a certain limit – cash or cheques, as well as cancellation or curtailment of your journey. Most of them exclude so-called dangerous sports unless an extra premium is paid:

Rough Guides travel insurance

Rough Guides Ltd offers a low-cost travel insurance policy, especially customized for our statistically low-risk readers by a leading British broker, provided by the American International Group (AIG) and registered with the British regulatory body, GISC (the General Insurance Standards Council). There are five main Rough Guides insurance plans: **No Frills** for the bare minimum for secure travel; **Essential**, which provides decent all-round cover; **Premier** for comprehensive cover with a wide range of benefits; **Extended Stay** for cover lasting four months to a year; and Annual Multi-Trip, a cost-effective way of getting Premier cover if you travel more than once a year. Premier, **Annual Multi-Trip** and Extended Stay policies can be supplemented by a "Hazardous Pursuits Extension" if you plan to indulge in sports considered dangerous, such as scuba diving or trekking. For a policy quote, call the **Rough Guides Insurance Line**: toll-free in the UK ☎0800/015 09 06 or ☎+44 1392 314 665 from elsewhere. Alternatively, get an **online quote** at ⊛www.roughguides.com/insurance.

in Australia this can mean anything from scuba diving and surfing to trekking, though probably not kayaking or jeep safaris. Many policies can be chopped and changed to exclude coverage you don't need – for example, sickness and accident benefits can often be excluded or included at will. If you need to make a claim, you should keep receipts for medicines and medical treatment, and in the event you have anything stolen, you must obtain an official statement from the police.

Information, websites and maps

Information on Melbourne is easy to get hold of, either from Australian Tourist Commission (ATC) offices, via the Internet (⊛www.australia.com), or, after arrival, from any of the city's tourist offices. Also check out the online resources for Tourism Victoria and the City of Melbourne in the list of useful websites on p.16. Once in Melbourne, you'll find a wealth of information available from tourist offices and kiosks conveniently located in the city centre.

Australian Tourist Commission Offices abroad

UK Gemini House, 10–18 Putney Hill, Putney, London SW15 6AA; Aussie Helpline ☎0990/022 000.
US Suite 1920, 2049 Century Park East, Los Angeles; Aussie helpline ☎805/775 2000.
New Zealand Level 3, 125 The Strand, Parnell, Auckland; ☎ 09 915 2826.

Tourist information offices

Melbourne's main **tourist office** is the Melbourne Visitor Information Centre in

Federation Square, on the corner of Swanston and Flinders streets (daily 9am–6pm; ☎9658 9658). The centre has information on events, advice on the best things to see and do, multilingual facilities, Internet access, and an accommodation and tour booking service. There are free pamphlets galore, although some attract a small charge.

In the same location, the **Melbourne Greeter Service** (same contact details) is a free half-day walking orientation of the city. Visitors are matched with volunteer "greeters" according to language (thirty languages are available), age and interests. The service, which is available daily, should be booked at least three working days in advance. Also in Federation Square, the Best Of Victoria stores sells "My Tour Guide", an audio pack designed to give visitors an insight into the city with a two-and-a-half-hour **self-guided walking tour** ($24.95). The pack also includes discount vouchers to some of Melbourne's most popular attractions like the Melbourne Observation Deck, Melbourne Aquarium and Melbourne Zoo.

Other good sources of tourist information are the volunteer-staffed **visitor information booth** at Bourke St Mall (Mon–Thurs 9am–5pm, Fri 9am–7pm, Sat 10am–4pm, Sun 11am–4pm); Tourism Victoria (daily 8am–6pm; ☎13 28 42, ⓦwww.visitvictoria.com), a phone- and Internet-only service providing information on attractions, accommodation and upcoming events; **Information Victoria** at 356 Collins St (Mon–Fri 8.30am–5.30pm; ☎1300 366 356, ⓦwww.infovic.vic.gov .au/index.html), which has free maps and brochures, a noticeboard of city events and a shop selling the city's largest range of local maps; and, on Collins St outside the Sportsgirl Centre (between Swanston and Elizabeth streets), an interactive touch-screen terminal, where you can look up anything from a cab phone number to a Chinese restaurant. And dressed in distinctive red uniforms, Melbourne's award-winning city ambassadors rove the retail centre of the city, dispensing directions or simply lending visitors a hand.

Outside Melbourne, regional Visitor Information Centres are thick on the ground – look out for the distinctive blue and yellow "i" sign. Providing reliable information on attractions, activities and events, the centres can also help you make reservations for accommodation or sightseeing tours, or give up-to-the-minute advice on travel in the area.

Budget traveller information

Hostel **noticeboards** are an excellent means of obtaining information – you can find everything from flatmates wanted and car shares to tours, weekend soccer matches and general advice. Specialist organizations such as the Backpacker Travel Centre at Shop 1, 250 Flinders St (Mon–Fri 10.30am–5.30pm; ☎9654 8477; ⓦ www.backpackerstravel.com.au/index .php) are also good value, as they help budget travellers find low-cost travel and accommodation deals. Most of these organizations charge a smallish fee to sign up with them.

National park and heritage information

For information on **national parks** and conservation areas in Victoria, contact the NRE Information Centre at 8 Nicholson St, East Melbourne, run by the Department of Natural Resources and Environment (Mon–Fri 9am–5.30pm; ☎9637 8080, ⓦwww.nre .vic.gov.au), or Parks Victoria (☎13 19 63, ⓦwww.parkweb.vic.gov.au). The **National Trust** in Tasma Terrace, 6 Parliament Place (Mon–Fri 9am–5pm; ☎9654 4711), is where you can buy guides for walking tours and National Trust properties.

Publications

In most of the information centres you can pick up a range of free brochures and publications, plus a copy of *Melbourne Events*, a particularly good source of city-wide information. Other freebies are *Beat* and *Inpress*, two indie music and entertainment magazines out each Wednesday, and available from record shops, bars and fashion outlets. There is also the popular *MX* newspaper, available each afternoon from Monday to Friday, which offers a gushy mix of entertainment, sport and juicy gossip. You'll find it on railway platforms and outside stations.

To keep abreast of local news and events, read *The Age* (the Sunday edition is called *The Sunday Age*) and *Herald Sun* newspapers; for national newspapers the *Australian* and the *Australian Financial Review* are widely distributed throughout regional Victoria. Among an array of publications aimed at budget and independent travellers, *TNT Magazine* and *The Word* provide comprehensive coverage of local attractions, activities, events, transport, work, nightlife and entertainment.

Both are available from the Backpackers Travel Centre (see previous page) and Backpackers World Travel at 161 Franklin St (Mon–Fri 8.30am–7pm, Sat 9am–6pm, Sun 10.30am–6pm, ☎9329 1990, Ⓦwww .backpackers-world.com.au).

Useful websites

While relevant websites are provided throughout the guide, some general sites are listed below. For information on Internet access in Melbourne, see p.26 & p.164.

Ⓦ **www.visitvictoria.com** Tourism Victoria website containing details on the city and the state's key attractions, accommodation, shopping, sports, arts, events, food and drinking, with mapping and customization services. Tourism Victoria's other site, Ⓦwww.backpackvictoria.com, provides similar information for independent and budget travellers.

Ⓦ **www.cityofmelbourne.com** Website with visitor information on arts and culture, history, walking tours and sights from the City of Melbourne council.

Ⓦ **www.thatsmelbourne.com.au** Another of the City of Melbourne council's sites, this time focusing on the latest "it" places around town, tourism services, and festivals and events.

Ⓦ **www.melbourne.citysearch.com.au** Easily digestible Melbourne guide covering a wide range of topics, including entertainment, events, eating, drinking, shopping, sports, travel and recreation.

Ⓦ **www.theage.com.au** Online edition of Melbourne's prestigious daily, *The Age*, has breaking news, business and sports info, special reports, and weather and flight details.

Ⓦ **www.afl.com.au** Official AFL site including player profiles, loads of statistics, and news and features by football writers from *The Age*.

Ⓦ **www.beat.com.au** Modish online magazine of the free street paper Beat. Showcasing Melbourne's music and entertainment scene, it has profiles of upcoming bands, reviews, gig and club guides, and links to music and arts sites.

Ⓦ **www.getoutoftown.com.au** This site has everything you need to plan your itinerary outside Melbourne. Choose the type of "getaway" you want

– romantic, adventurous, sporty, relaxed – then make a booking.

Ⓦ **www.parkweb.vic.gov.au** Good site providing information on Victoria's many parks, as well as tour operators offering everything from walking and cycling to camel riding. Also includes downloadable publications and an impressive array of links to related sites.

Ⓦ **www.victrip.com.au** This is the best place to get details on Melbourne's public transport.

Ⓦ **www.haunted.com.au/ghosttour.html** Take a virtual tour of some of Melbourne's scariest streets and alleyways. You'll learn about botched hangings, the fifty or so ghosts lurking about the CBD, the thousands of bodies lying under the Queen Victoria Market and the "lady in white" who has caused a rapid succession of managers to leave a popular CBD pub.

Maps

To help you navigate your way around the centre of Melbourne, the maps in this book should be sufficient, but if you need greater detail, or are staying in the suburbs, or are driving, you might like to buy something more comprehensive. The best place to buy maps in Melbourne is Mapland, 372 Little Bourke St (Mon–Thurs 9am–5.30pm, Fri 9am–6pm, Sat 9.30am–4pm; ☎9670 4383, Ⓦwww.mapland.com.au) and Information Victoria, 356 Collins St (see previous page). If you've rented a car, make sure the rental company has provided a Melbourne street directory before you head off. Melbourne's best street directory is Melway, available from bookshops and newsagents. It's also good for getting out of Melbourne.

Victoria's motoring organization, the Royal Automobile Club of Victoria (RACV), 360 Bourke Street, City (☎9790 2121, Ⓦwww.racv.com.au), publishes road maps of Melbourne and the state. The maps are free to members of associated overseas motoring organizations.

Costs, money and banks

Prices in Melbourne are pretty much on a par with Europe or North America, if anything a little cheaper. Australia is well set up for budget and independent travellers, offering plenty of low-end accommodation and eating options, and with a student, YHA or backpackers' card you can get discounts on travel, nightlife and entertainment.

Currency

The currency is the **Australian dollar** (or buck), which is divided into 100 cents. Notes are available in denominations of $100, $50, $20, $10 and $5, while coins come in values of $2, $1, 50c, 20c, 10c and 5c. Exchange rates fluctuate at around AUS$2.50 for £1; AUS$1.50 for US$1; AUS$1.20 for CAN$1; and AUS$0.90 for NZ$1.

Costs

The absolute minimum **daily budget** is around $50 a day for food, board and transport if you stay in hostels, travel on buses and eat and drink frugally. On the other hand, if you're staying in hotels or B&Bs, and eating out regularly, reckon on $100; extras such as clubbing, car rental and tours will all add to your costs.

Youth and student cards

Once obtained, various official and quasi-official **youth/student ID cards** soon pay for themselves in savings. Full-time students are eligible for the International Student ID Card (ISIC, @www.isiccard .com), which entitles the bearer to special air, rail and bus fares and discounts at museums, theatres and other attractions. For Americans there's also a health benefit, providing up to US$3000 in emergency medical coverage and US$100 a day for sixty days in hospital, plus a 24-hour hotline to call in the event of a medical, legal or financial emergency. The card costs US$22 for Americans; CAN$16 for Canadians; NZ$21 for New Zealanders; and £7 in the UK. If you're no longer a student, but are 26 or younger, you still qualify for the International Youth Travel Card, which costs the same price and carries the same benefits, while teachers qualify for the International Teacher Card (same price and benefits). All these cards are available from your local student travel agent in the US, Canada, the UK and New Zealand, and in Australia itself, or you can download an application from the website. Once you are in Australia, purchasing either an **International YHA Card** or **Backpacker Resorts VIP Card** will give you discounts on not just the relevant hostel accommodation, but a host of transport, tours, services, entry fees and even meals; they're worth getting even if you're not planning to stay in hostels.

Banks and foreign exchange

The major banks (Australia's "big four"), with branches countrywide, are the National Australia Bank (@www.national .com.au), the Commonwealth (@www .commbank.com.au), Westpac (@www .westpac.com.au), and ANZ (@www.anz .com); their head branches, all with foreign currency counters, are in the CBD along Bourke and Collins streets. In general, Melbourne's **banking hours** are Monday to Thursday 9.30am–4pm and Friday 9.30am–5pm, although some branches of the Bank of Melbourne, including one at 142 Elizabeth St, are open on Saturday from 9am to noon.

Automatic Teller Machines (ATMs), which are usually located outside banks but also in front of ordinary shops, are often open 24 hours and allow international access for cards in the Cirrus-Maestro network (including Visa and Mastercard). **Bureaux de change** are found in both the domestic and international airport terminals, and throughout the city centre; only a few in the city are open at the weekend, and solely the ones at the airport late at night, so try to arrange your currency during the week. If you're going to spend a weekend in one of Victoria's smaller towns, plan on bringing along enough money to cover your stay.

Foreign exchange offices

American Express outlets include 233-239 Collins St (Mon–Fri 8.30am–5.30pm, Sat 9am–noon, ☎ 1300 139 060) and 360 Collins St (Mon–Fri 9am–5pm, ☎ 9600 2962).
Singapore Exchange and Finance Shop 3, 43–53 Elizabeth St (Mon–Fri 8.30am–5.30pm, ☎ 9620 1433) and Shop P08, Southgate shopping complex (Mon–Fri 8.30am–5.30pm, ☎ 9699 2322)
Thomas Cook 13 Floor, 257 Collins St (Mon–Fri 8.45am–5.15pm, Sat 9am–5pm, ☎ 9282 0282), another branch is at 188 Swanston St (Mon–Fri 9am–5.30pm, Sat 9am–5pm, ☎ 9652 3277).
The Thomas Cook desks at the international and domestic terminals of Melbourne Airport are open 24hr.

Wiring money

Having **money wired from home** is never convenient or cheap, and should be considered a last resort. It's also possible to have money wired directly from a bank in your home country to a bank in Australia, although this is somewhat less reliable because it involves two separate institutions. If you go down this route, your home bank will need the address of the branch bank where you want to pick up the money and the address and telex number of the head office, which will act as the clearing house; money wired this way normally takes two working days to arrive, and costs around £25/US$40 per transaction. Otherwise, to have money wired from home fast, arrangements can be made with TravelersExpress MoneyGram (ⓦwww .moneygram.com), through Thomas Cook foreign exchange outlets and Western Union (ⓦwww.westernunion.com) through American Express; see outlet addresses opposite. There is also a Western Union office within Travelex, 37–49 Pitt St, near Central Station (☎02/9241 5722).

Arrival

Melbourne's main point of arrival is Melbourne Airport (or Tullamarine Airport; international flight times ☎13 12 23, ⓦwww.melbourne-airport.com.au), 22km northwest of the city – about a 30min drive, depending on traffic. Australia's second busiest airport, it's open 24hrs, servicing all the major international airlines. The airport's international terminal has baggage lockers (24hr; $5–10), a 24-hour Thomas Cook foreign exchange desk with reasonable rates, and various ATMs. There are two travellers' information service desks on the ground and first floors (daily 5am–last flight), which can help you with accommodation; rooms can also be booked through the interactive video unit on the ground floor.

The modern **Skybus Super Shuttle** ($13 one-way, $22 return; ☎9335 3066, ⓦwww.skybus.com.au) runs daily every 15mins between 6.30am and 7.30pm from the Qantas domestic terminal and Virgin Blue terminal to the city centre, stopping en route at the Melbourne Transit Centre (Greyhound Pioneer Bus Terminal), Spencer Street Station and Bus Terminal, Melbourne Town Hall and Exhibition Street. The journey takes approximately twenty minutes and the buses are adapted for mobility-impaired passengers. Tickets can be purchased on board, or from the ticketing desk at the Qantas domestic terminal and Virgin Blue terminal. Skybus run a hotel connection service (Mon–Fri 6am–7pm, Sat & Sun 8am–6pm, ☎9670 7992; for hotel pick-ups, book at least 3hr in advance). There is also an airport shuttle service for southern suburbs (☎9783 1199) with a pickup point at the *Novotel St Kilda* (see p.105) in St Kilda.

A **taxi** from the airport costs around $35–40 to the city centre, $45–50 to St Kilda. Car rental desks are located in the car park opposite the airport. Most hotels advertise on noticeboards near the information desks;

there's a freephone line for reservations, and many of them will refund your bus fare. Some hotels and guesthouses also offer a free pick-up service from the airport on request.

Avalon is a secondary airport at Geelong (☎5227 9100; ⊕www.avalonairport.co.au) where you might arrive if flying with Jetstar, the domestic budget arm of Quantas. Sunbus connect all arrivals and departures with central Melbourne as well as various suburbs and towns in the area. The journey to Franklin Street or Spencer Street in central Melbourne takes about fifty to sixty minutes depending on the time of day. See the airport website for more details.

City transport

Melbourne has an efficient public transport system of trains, trams and buses, making getting around simple and convenient. The city also has ferry services travelling up and down the Yarra River and plenty of licensed taxis. Outside Melbourne, bus and train services reach all major cities and most towns. There's also regular ferry services linking the popular beachside spots of Queenscliff and Sorrento (see p.171). Alternatively, a network of good roads means it is easy to reach your destination by car, motorbike or bicycle.

Melbourne's public transport network, formerly known as **The Met**, operates Monday to Saturday from 5am until midnight, and Sunday from 8am until 11pm, supplemented in the early hours of Saturday and Sunday by NightRider buses (see overleaf). For public transport information, routes, timetables and fares, call ☎13 16 38 or visit ⊕www.victrip.com.au. If you have a ticketing enquiry, call the Metcard helpline on ☎1800 652 313.

Travel passes

A range of tickets valid on all trains, trams and buses is available through the Metcard automated ticketing system. Unless you're going on a day-trip to the outer suburbs, you can get anywhere you need to, including St Kilda and Williamstown, on a

zone 1 ticket, which costs $3 and is valid for unlimited travel within the zone for two hours (or all night if bought after 7pm) on any form of transport. A day ticket ($5.80 for zone 1; $9.40 for zones 1 & 2; $12.30 for zones 1, 2 & 3) is better value if you're making several trips, while for longer stays a weekly ticket ($25) or a ten-by-two-hour ticket ($26) is even more economical. You can also buy two-hour tickets ($3), which allow travel on a particular section of the bus or tram route.

You need to validate your ticket in a machine every time you board a new vehicle. Two-hour and day tickets are available from vending machines found at train stations, on board trams, on a limited selection of buses, from the Metlink Shop at the Melbourne Town Hall, near the corner of Swanston and Little Collins streets (Mon–Fri 8.30am–5.30pm, Sat 9am–1pm; ☎13 16 38), the

Melbourne Information Centre at Federation Square and other selected shops displaying the Metcard symbol (most newsagents, some milk bars and pharmacies).

Make sure you buy a ticket – Melbourne transport staff will slap you with a $100 fine if you don't have one. For further information, call Metlink (daily 6am–midnight; ☎13 16 38 or the Metcard helpline on ☎1800 652 313; for a range of public transport information including timetables and disability services, visit ⓦwww.victrip.com.au).

Buses

Melbourne's bus network is reasonably good, with the usual downside that buses can get caught in traffic during peak periods. Tickets can be pre-purchased from train stations and stores displaying a Metcard symbol and are interchangeable for use on all metropolitan public transport. You can also purchase tickets from the bus driver on selected services. Fares are based on duration and distance, with metropolitan Melbourne divided into three zones.

The red double-decker **Gray Line Explorer** (runs hourly 10am–4pm; ☎1300 85 86 87, ⓦwww.grayline.com.au), tickets for which should be bought on board (day ticket $24.50, 2-day ticket $38.50), does circuits of the city, starting from Melbourne Town Hall and running past the Rialto Observation Deck and the Polly Woodside Maritime Museum, to the Arts Centre south of the CBD, then back up the eastern side of the city to Lygon Street, the Zoo, Queen Victoria Market and Melbourne Central. Passengers can stay on the bus and use it as a sightseeing tour, or jump off and re-board later.

Probably the most useful service is the special after midnight **NightRider buses**, which are run by private transport operators and travel to the outer suburbs (Dandenong, Eltham, Franston, St Albans and Werribee, among others) on Saturday and Sunday mornings, or after major events such as the Australian Grand Prix and New Year's Eve. NightRider buses depart from the City Square (in front of the *Westin Hotel*) on Swanston Street, the Crown Casino or any other NightRider stops along one of its nine routes hourly between 12.30am and 4.30am ($6; except Mornington $8 and Melton $8.20).

Note that Metcards cannot be used on a NightRider service. For more information, visit ⓦwww.victrip.com.au/nightrider.

Buses also travel to outlying regions, including the Dandenong Ranges, Yarra Valley and Melbourne's bays and peninsulas, but you'll need to buy individual tickets for these journeys. For **long-distance** trips, tickets can be purchased from V/Line (☎13 61 96, ⓦwww.vlinepassenger.com.au) at the Spencer Street Bus Terminal, just west of the CBD.

Trains

Melbourne has a fast, efficient and user-friendly **train system**, with frequent services and coverage to most destinations. Flinders Street Station, on the corner of Flinders and Swanston streets, is the hub of Melbourne's train system, and all trains begin or end their journey there. Melbourne also enjoys an underground train system, known as the City Loop, with five stations servicing the CBD: Spencer Street, Flagstaff, Melbourne Central, Parliament and Flinders Street. See the "Greater Melbourne" colour map at the end of this book for the main routes. As well, there are sixteen different train lines servicing the outer suburbs – these lines are all linked to bus and tram services.

Services run from 5am until midnight. You can pick up train route maps at any City Loop station. Bicycles can be carried free except during rush hours (Mon–Fri 7–9.30am & 4–6pm), when an extra adult concession fee has to be paid. You'll also have to purchase a concession fare if you carry a surfboard on a train. Trains and train stations are fully accessible for people using wheelchairs or with limited mobility, and there are lifts at all City Loop stations. Security guards patrol the train network daily after 5pm, but if the train is deserted, sit in the front carriage nearest the driver. New and refurbished trains have a Passenger Emergency Intercom system that can be used to contact train staff (emergency use only), and all stations have a red emergency button – when pushed, a central operator can see the platform on a monitor via closed circuit television (CCTV).

Trams

Melbourne's famous **trams** and light rail service gives the city a distinctive character

Tramcar restaurant

The **Colonial Tramcar Restaurant** (☎9696 4000) is a converted 1927 tram offering traditional silver service as you trundle around Melbourne. Operating daily from Normandy Rd in South Melbourne, the restaurant (nonsmoking) offers a three-course early dinner (5.45–7.15pm; $66) and a five-course dinner (Mon–Thurs & Sun $93.50; Fri & Sat $104.50), plus a four-course lunch (Sun 1–3pm & other days subject to demand; $71.50); all drinks are included. Make reservations as early as possible – Friday and Saturday evenings can be booked up two months in advance.

and provide a scenic way to explore the city and inner suburbs. Travelling along most of the city's major thoroughfares and extending out into the suburbs, trams run down the centre of the road, stopping at every CBD intersection and then every two or three blocks once in the suburbs. See the map overleaf for the main routes. Passengers can board trams at signposted stops on the side of the road and from central islands in the CBD. These spots often have a map with route numbers and times – the route number is displayed at the front of the tram. Although motorists are prohibited from passing trams that are stationary at stops, always look left to see if there are any vehicles approaching. The introduction of a swish new fleet of modern, low-floor trams fusing European technology with Australian manufacturing expertise has meant CBD tram stops (known as "Superstops") have been widened and fitted with wheelchair-friendly ramps and audio clues advising passengers of stops.

Services run regularly from 5am until midnight Monday to Saturday and from 8am to 11pm on Sundays. At weekends and public holidays, services are reduced. **Tickets** can be pre-purchased from train stations and stores displaying a Metcard symbol and are interchangeable for use on all metropolitan public transport. As well, a limited selection of Metcards can be purchased from onboard coin-only ticket machines.

Ferries and cruises

Travelling by **boat** around Melbourne is probably the most civilized and scenic form of transport, although you tend to pay more for the service. In Melbourne, there's an abundance of vessels cruising up and down the Yarra River, travelling sightseeing and less commercial routes. Operators include Melbourne River Cruises (☎9614 1215), Southgate River Tours (☎9682 5711) and Williamstown Bay and River Cruises (☎9506 4144 or 9686 4664). One-way fares from

Useful tram routes

In the city centre, **useful trams** include the #1 and #22, which travel north–south along Swanston Street, and the #19, #57 and #59, which run along Elizabeth Street. Trams #11 and #12 run east–west along Collins Street; #86 and #96 along Bourke Street.

A free and particularly convenient way to get around town is the burgundy-and-cream **City Circle Trams,** which run in a loop (look for the specially marked stops) around Flinders, Spring and La Trobe streets, as well as Harbour Esplanade.

Routes #1 and #22 continue north of the city centre to Carlton; route #11 goes to Fitzroy. Other useful services include #57 for North Melbourne and #86 for Collingwood. East of the city centre, tram #75 serves East Melbourne, Richmond and Hawthorn.

Heading south of the city, **tram #8** runs from Swanston Street via South Yarra to Toorak; **tram #6** to Prahran. **Tram #1** runs through South Melbourne and Albert Park, while **tram #96** runs from Bourke Street through South Melbourne and Albert Park to St Kilda – the latter is served by a number of other routes. See map overleaf for details.

Southgate to Williamstown are around $10 one-way, double that to return.

Regular **ferries** link Sorrento in the Mornington Peninsula to Queenscliff in the Bellarine Peninsula. From Sorrento, ferries depart every hour from 7am to 6pm, returning from Queenscliff at the same hours. Tickets for passengers only are $8 one-way and can be purchased from the passenger lounges at Sorrento and Queenscliff. There is

also a ferry service between Phillip Island and French Island (8.30am and 4.15pm, returning at 9.30am and 4.30pm, $8.50 one-way).

Taxis

Melbourne **taxis** are reasonably numerous and easy to spot – they are uniformly yellow. Cabs ranks are clearly signposted at central locations like major hotels in the CBD, or busy spots such as Flinders and Spencer

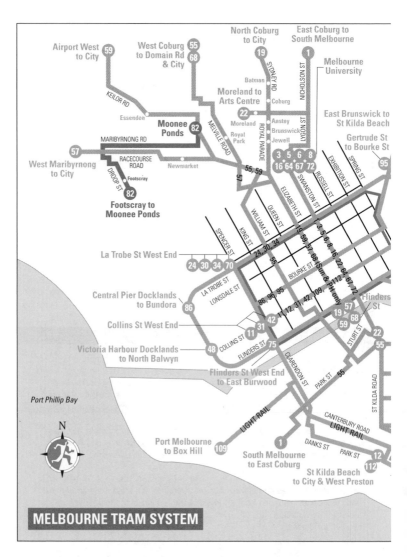

MELBOURNE TRAM SYSTEM

Street stations. You can also hail a taxi in the street if the rooftop light is illuminated, or book by telephone. In general, taxi meters are clearly visible so you can keep check of your fare. Fares begin with a $2.80 flagfall, and there's an additional $1.07 for every kilometre. Cabs also attract additional charges like a late-night surcharge from midnight to 6am, a fee for phone bookings, and a fee for airport pickups.

Finding a taxi late at night is difficult, especially at weekends, so if you know you'll need one, book it. Melbourne's major taxi companies include Arrow (☏13 22 11); Black Cabs Combined (☏13 22 27); Embassy Taxis (☏13 17 55); Silver Top Taxis (☏13 10 08); and Yellow Cabs (☏13 19 24). Black Cabs Combined and Silver Top Taxis also coordinate and despatch wheelchair-accessible taxis.

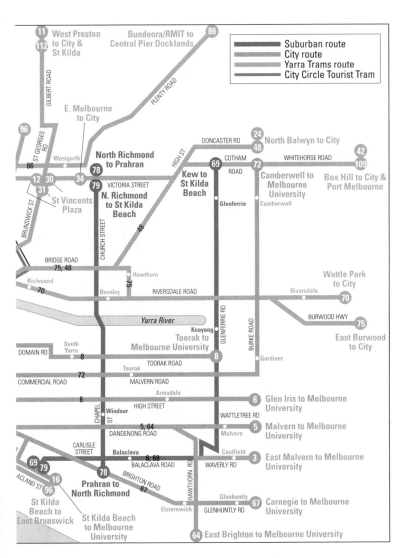

Driving and vehicle rental

Melbourne is a relatively easy city to drive in due to its wide thoroughfares and simple, well-signposted grid plan. The city's three major freeways – the West Gate, Monash and the Tullamarine – are conveniently linked by CityLink, a nonstop expressway. Really, the only thing you have to watch out for is trams, which share the roads with cars, and which can only be overtaken on the left. You also have to stop and wait behind them while passengers are getting off, as they usually step directly into the road (there's no need to stop, however, if there's a central pedestrian island).

Melbourne also has a peculiar road rule known as the **hook turn**, which accommodates trams at major intersections in the city centre: when turning right, you pull over to the left-hand lane (leaving the right-hand lane free for through-traffic and the tram tracks clear for trams) and wait for the lights to change to amber before turning. Black-and-white signs overhead indicate when this rule applies.

In Australia, driving is on the left-hand side of the road and, by law, you must wear a seatbelt. A **driver's licence** from home will suffice for up to three months in Australia, as long as it has photo ID and it's for the same class of vehicle you intend to drive. If you're staying more than three months, you'll need to get a Victorian licence; you can be fined if you don't have your licence with you when you're driving.

In Melbourne, the **speed limit** ranges from 40kmph in metropolitan shopping strips and school zones to 110 kmph outside built-up areas and in some sections of freeway. Whatever you do, don't drink alcohol and drive – random breath tests are common, even in rural areas, and especially on Friday and Saturday nights and during the Christmas season. For more information on road rules and driving safely in Melbourne, contact VicRoads (Mon–Fri 8.30am–5pm, ☏13 11 74, ⓦ www.vicroads.vic.gov.au).

Parking is relatively straightforward with a choice of commercial car parks and on-street parking although the expense can mount up. Coin-operated meters are the norm (there are hefty fines if you let the meter expire); for parking lots, expect to pay around $6 an hour, or $15–20 daily, although some offer discounts to moviegoers and shoppers.

Vehicle rental and purchase

Melbourne has a plethora of local and international car rental firms, offering a variety of deals and a wide range of cars, Multinational operators such as Hertz, Avis, Budget, Delta Europcar and Thrifty have offices in Melbourne, although local firms almost always offer better value, with "rent-a-bomb" agencies going as low as $12 a day; however, these places often have restrictions on how far away from Melbourne you're allowed to go. In general, a city-based non-multinational rental agency will supply new cars for around $50 a day with unlimited kilometres.

Rental companies

Avis ☏ 9663 6366, ⓦ www.avis.com
Budget ☏ 13 27 27, ⓦ www.budget.com
Hertz ☏ 9663 6244, ⓦ www.hertz.com
National ☏ 9329 5000, ⓦ www.nationalcar.com
Thrifty ☏ 9663 5200, ⓦ www.thrifty.com
Rent-A-Bomb ☏ 9428 0088, ⓦ www.rentabomb.com.au
Ugly Duckling ☏ 9525 4010 or 1800 335 908

Campervans

Britz Australia ☏ 9483 1888
ⓦ www.britz.com
Koala Campervan Rentals ☏ 9415 8140
NQ Australia Campervan Rentals ☏ 1800 079 529 ⓦ www.nqrentals.com.au

Opening hours and public holidays

Opening times and business hours of shops and post offices are generally Monday to Friday 9am to 5pm. Shops and services usually open Monday to Saturday 9am to 5.30pm, and until 7pm or 9pm on Thursday and Friday nights. The major retailers and shopping malls in the city and suburban areas are also open on Sunday between noon and 5pm, and big supermarkets generally open seven days from 8am until 9pm, though some close around 5pm on Sunday. There are several 24-hour convenience stores/supermarkets in the inner city and suburbs, and an all-night Coles Express on Elizabeth Street near Flinders Street Station. Shopping hours are also extended by up to two hours during daylight-saving months (November to March).

Tourist attractions – museums, galleries and historic monuments – are usually open between 10am and 5pm. All close on Christmas Day and Good Friday, as do virtually all banks, post offices and businesses, but otherwise specific opening hours are given throughout this Guide.

Public holidays

When an official holiday falls on a Saturday or Sunday, there may be an extra day off immediately before or after. Many bars, restaurants and cafés also observe public holidays, and there is limited public transport.

New Year's Day (Jan 1)
Australia Day (Jan 26)
Good Friday
Easter Monday
Labour Day (March 14)
Anzac Day (April 25)
Queen's Birthday (June 13)
Melbourne Cup Day (First Tues in Nov)
Christmas Day (Dec 25)
Boxing Day (Dec 26)

School holidays

The school year is divided into four terms with one long six-week holiday from mid-December to mid-January and three more fortnights spread through the year. You can roughly depend on them being around Easter, late June to early July and late September to early October. Prices rise during these periods, accommodation gets booked up and attractions are generally a lot busier.

Post, phones and email

Melbourne is well equipped to provide efficient postal, information technology and telecommunications services, with an efficient postal system, a good telephone network and plenty of places in the city centre and surrounding suburbs to go online and check email.

Post

Post offices are generally open Monday to Friday 9am to 5pm but a branch on the northeastern corner of Little Bourke and Elizabeth streets in the city has longer hours (Mon–Fri 8.15am–5.30pm & Sat 10am–3pm). There are red post boxes throughout the city. Stamps for overseas are sold at post offices with standard postcards costing $1 to the US, Canada and Europe; regular letters start at $1.65 to the US, Canada and Europe.

You can receive mail at any post office in or around Melbourne: address the letter to Poste Restante followed by the town or suburb, state of Victoria and post code. You'll need a passport or other ID to collect your mail, which is kept for just one month.

Phones, phonecards and mobile phones

Melbourne is well stocked with public telephones. Local calls from a **payphone** cost a minimum of 40c. Some backpacker hostels and shops in the city sell discount phonecards (such as Phoneaway, Unidial, EZI Great Rate Card, One Card and AAPT) which can be used in any payphone for cheap international calls, and which can be purchased from Telstra shops, post offices, duty-free stores and newsagents. The official Telstra rate for a call from a public phone to the UK is $2 per minute Mon–Fri, $1.20 Sat & Sun. With one of the phonecards mentioned above, expect to pay about 39–55c per minute, plus a small connecting fee (less than $1). Melbourne's General Post Office has several payphones plus a range of directories, including White and Yellow Pages.

Internatonal calls can be made by dialling ☏0011 (the overseas access code), followed by the country code, area code and required number. The cheapest time to make overseas calls is at off-peak periods (Mon–Fri 6pm–midnight, all day Sat & Sun).

Internet

Public **Internet access** is widespread across Australia and keeping in touch via the Web is easy, fast and cheap in Melbourne. Most hostels have Internet access for reading email and surfing the Web, and usually charge around $5-10 an hour. Likewise, cybercafés offer similar rates, not to mention plenty of workstations and cheap food and drink. Most local libraries also provide free access, while public kiosks in some laundries and larger shopping malls will have you online for a small fee.

Brunswick Street in Fitzroy (see p.75), Fitzroy and Grey streets in St Kilda (see p.88) and Chapel Street in South Yarra (see p.76) are littered with cut-rate Internet places, with rates as low as $3 per hour. The chain Global Gossip has an office

---

Useful numbers

☏ **000** Emergencies
☏ **12455** Local, national and international operator services
☏ **12452** Directory enquiries
☏ **12550** Reverse-charge calls
☏ **1234** Call for price of interstate or international calls
☏ **13 or 1300** indicates a toll-free number
☏ **03** Melbourne area code
☏ **613**, then the number. If ringing from overseas, dial the international access code followed by the above.

(daily 8am–midnight; ☎9663 0511, ☯www
.globalgossip.com) in the city at 440 Elizabeth
St. Among a raft of good cybercafés, try
Café Wired, 363 Clarendon St, South
Melbourne (Mon–Fri 9am–9pm, Sat noon–
6pm), Cybernet Café, 812 Glenferrie Rd,
Hawthorn (Mon–Thurs & Sun 11am–10pm,
Fri & Sat 11am–11pm), and The Binary Bar,
243 Brunswick St, Fitzroy (daily 5pm–1am);
all charge around $5 per hour and there's
usually an extra charge for printing out
emails.

Melbourne is also a wireless Internet
hotspot, with low-power radio waves
bouncing across the CBD and inner-city
suburbs, including South Yarra and St
Kilda. Popular access points are usually
cafés in the Jam Factory (see p.76) and the
Como (see p.104), Hudsons Coffee outlets,
including one on the corner of Bourke and
King streets, and the Village Cinema Centre
in Bourke Street. Rates range from twelve
cents to twenty cents per minute, and
$11- 20 an hour.

Crime and personal safety

Melbourne scores highly for personal safety. But even though it was recognized
by the World Health Organisation in 2000 as a "Safe Community", one of only
three capital cities worldwide to achieve such an honour, that doesn't mean you
should throw caution to the wind. Observe the same precautions with your safety
and possessions as you would in any other country or at home: avoid badly lit
areas at night, inform friends and family where you're travelling to and when you
expect to return, keep items of value in a safe place. Importantly, talk to other
travellers about their experiences and get their advice.

On Friday and Saturday nights in the
city, especially after an AFL match at the
MCG or Telstra Dome, drunk males may
pose the usual problems. Train stations
are equipped with CCTV camera – as are
many of the busier areas of the city centre.
You should also be careful with belongings
in most major strips, including the Crown
Casino promenade, Spencer Street and
Russell Street, a prime area for theft and
muggings. Outside the city centre, the
popular beachfront suburb and red-light
district of St Kilda, though going upmarket,
is still a little rough around the edges, so
it's wise to be careful at night, particularly
in backstreets around Grey, Greeves and
Barkly streets.

You're more likely to fall victim to a fellow
traveller or an opportunist crime: **theft** is
not unusual in hostels and so many provide
lockable boxes; if you leave valuables lying
around, or on view in cars, you can expect
them to be stolen.

Police and the law

Victoria Police headquarters are at 637
Flinders St, City (☎9247 6666). If you have
any problems, or need to report a theft for
insurance purposes or any other crime,
you can call or drop in here or a local
police station. For emergencies, ☎000 is
a free number that summons the police,
ambulance or fire service.

The media

Although much of the control of media content has now shifted to Sydney, which has the overwhelming majority of newspapers, radio and televisions headquartered or networked from there, Melbourne still has a wide range of media and services for casual or serious consumption.

The press

Melbourne's premier daily broadsheet is *The Age* (◉www.theage.com.au), which began operation in 1854. The city's other daily, the tabloid, Murdoch-owned *Herald Sun* (◉www.heraldsun.news.com.au), has the highest readership. Both Melbourne dailies have more populist, multi-section Sunday versions, the *Sunday Age* and the *Sun Herald Sun*. But *The Age* is the paper to buy to find out what's on in Melbourne, especially Tuesday's "Epicure", which focuses on the city's bar, restaurant and wine scene; Thursday's "EG", a programme and review of the week's TV and radio; and Friday's "EG", the entertainment supplement that includes listings and film, art and music reviews. Friday's *The Age* also has "The Form", a weekly racing guide. There are employment and rental sections daily, but the big Saturday edition is the best for these. For a gushy mix of entertainment, sport and gossip, Melbourne's *MX*, a free newspaper geared towards commuters, is available each afternoon from Monday to Friday; you'll find it on railway platforms and outside stations.

The *Guardian Weekly* and the *International Herald Tribune* are widely available international papers. The State Library of Victoria on Swanston Street (Mon–Thurs 10am–9pm, Fri–Sun 10am–6pm) keeps a large selection of domestic and overseas newspapers. You can also find a good selection of international newspapers at McGills Newsagency at 187 Elizabeth St in the city.

TV

Australian **television** isn't particularly exciting unless you're into sport. Much of the local TV content originates from Victoria: series like *The Secret Life of Us*, *Neighbours* and *SeaChange* are filmed in the state, with *The Secret Life of Us* (recently axed in Australia due to poor ratings) attracting hordes of travellers to location shoots in St Kilda and around Melbourne.

Radio

Melbourne has a host of commercial and community **radio stations**. The best are on the various ABC stations, both local and national: Radio National (621 AM) offers a popular mix of arty intellectual topics; 3LO (774 FM), intelligent talkback radio; News Radio (1026 AM), 24-hour local and international news, current affairs, sports, science and finance, also utilizing a diverse range of foreign radio networks including the BBC World Service, the US's National Public Radio (NPR) and Germany's Radio Deutsche Welle; ABC Classic FM (105.9 FM), for classical music; and 2JJJ ("Triple J"; 107.5 FM), which supports local bands and alternative rock – aimed squarely at the nation's youth. You can listen to various ABC radio stations on the Web with live or on-demand audio (◉www.abc.net.au/streaming). Self-supporting community radio stations, such as 3RRR (102.7) and 3PBS (106.7), are Melbourne's "underground" alternatives, playing a regular diet of funk, reggae, death metal, techno, house and esoterica. Melbourne's gay and lesbian radio station is Joy Melbourne (90.7 FM).

Work and study

The availability of temporary working visas makes Australia a magnet for budget and independent travellers. Once you've got your visa (see p.12), there are plenty of opportunities for finding a job. There are a number of employment agencies matching people with a variety of roles – from banking and financial positions to call centre work, nannying, nursing, catering and fruit-picking. Seasonal and harvest work, in particular, is very popular with travellers across Victoria, especially in the peak season between November and April.

Australia-wide online employment websites include the JobSearch website at ⓦjobsearch.gov.au and the Seek website at ⓦwww.seek.com.au. The Saturday editions of *The Age* and *Herald Sun* newspapers also feature comprehensive job listings, while the online versions have jobs searchable by type and location, resumé builders, and tips and advice. Some Melbourne hostels have in-house employment agencies, while backpacker travel centres have a job notice board displaying current jobs. They also have daily Melbourne newspapers and a list of city-based agencies that you can contact for work. For something different, you can sign up to do voluntary work on organic farms – try Willing Workers on Organic Farms (WWOOF) at ⓦwww.wwoof .com.au, which offers everything from animal care to gardening and permaculture.

On arrival in Melbourne, register with a few agencies to ensure you get a good spread of the jobs on offer. Before you start work, open a bank account and get a Tax File Number (TFN), available from the Australian Taxation Office (ⓦwww.ato.gov.au); if you don't have a TFN, you'll be slugged a tax rate of 48.5 percent.

Study

Melbourne is often referred to as "Australia's student city" and in the last decade the city has become a major destination for overseas students. **Studying** in Melbourne and Victoria offers value for money as living expenses and tuition costs are much less than in the UK and USA. Australia's academic year runs from February to December, with applications for many tertiary courses closing the previous October. Most universities provide on-campus accommodation, and are equipped to help students find a place to live. If you're a full-time student you qualify for a range of concessions, including discounted travel and cut-price cinema tickets.

For details on educational opportunities in Melbourne and Victoria, links to Victorian institutions and comprehensive information about studying and living in Victoria, visit the Study in Melbourne website at ⓦwww .studymelbourne.vic.edu.au.

The City

The City

The Eastside

The Eastside – the area of the city centre bounded by Swanston, Flinders, Spring and Victoria streets – impressively captures the "Marvellous Melbourne" era which followed the discovery of gold in 1851. Replete with nineteenth-century civic landmarks, it also buzzes with designer shops and elegant watering holes, and continues to serve as the focal point of much of Melbourne's cultural and political life.

Many of Melbourne's best-known buildings were constructed in the three decades after gold was discovered in 1851, including the imposing **Parliament House** on Spring Street, book-ended by small and tranquil gardens to the north and south, and the handsome **Old Treasury Building** nearby. Melbourne's short but bounteous history is also reflected in two magnificent nineteenth-century cathedrals, **St Patrick's** and **St Paul's**, built to administer spiritual salvation to a rapidly expanding and increasingly diverse population, while to the north is probably the most interesting of all the city's sights, the **Old Melbourne Gaol**, which captures in grisly detail the fates of some of the early city's less fortunate souls. Civic monuments apart, there is plenty to enjoy, from the well-heeled boutiques and cafés at the "**Paris End**" of Collins Street to the characterful restaurants and stores of **Chinatown**, home to the large Chinese community that established itself in Melbourne in the 1880s and which – later augmented by waves of postwar Greek and Italian immigrants – has done much to give the Eastside precincts their cosmopolitan accent. A recent addition to the area, the much-hyped **Queen Victoria** retail and residential complex more than lives up to the splendour of its surroundings, boasting numerous food stalls and busy laneways that are home to many of the best fashion boutiques in the city.

Flinders Street Station and around

Located in the heart of the city on the corner of Flinders Street and St Kilda Road, the Neoclassical Flinders Street Station (1910) is the traditional gateway to the city for the 100,000-plus commuters who pass through it every day. The station's imposing bulk, complete with dome and clock tower, is reasonably eye-friendly, while the interior has been upgraded with the addition of a new concourse. Out front, the entrance acts as a landmark-cum-meeting place (Ava Gardner and Gregory Peck had a gloriously prolonged goodbye here in the film *On the Beach*), where people gather under the famous clocks, each of which indicates the next scheduled departure on a different suburban line.

Opposite the station, on the corner of Swanston and Flinders streets, the splendid **St Paul's Cathedral** (Mon–Fri 7am–5.45pm, Sat 8am–5pm, Sun

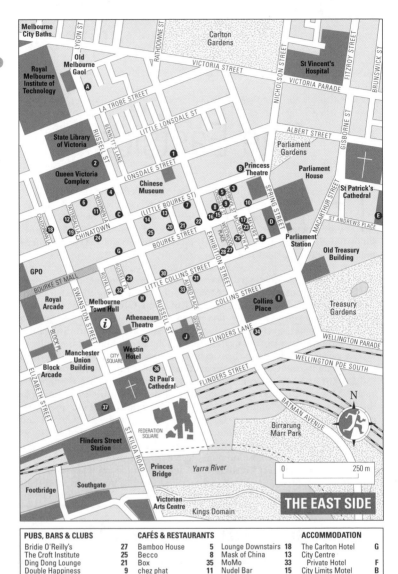

THE EAST SIDE

PUBS, BARS & CLUBS		CAFÉS & RESTAURANTS				ACCOMMODATION	
Bridie O'Reilly's	27	Bamboo House	5	Lounge Downstairs	18	The Carlton Hotel	G
The Croft Institute	25	Becco	8	Mask of China	13	City Centre	
Ding Dong Lounge	21	Box	35	MoMo	33	Private Hotel	F
Double Happiness	9	chez phat	11	Nudel Bar	15	City Limits Motel	B
The Elephant & Wheelbarrow	22	Chine on Paramount	7	Pellegrini's		Exford Hotel	C
Gin Palace	29	Flower Drum	20	Espresso Bar	15	Grand Hyatt	J
Hairy Canary	32	Grossi Florentino	16	Punch Lane	3	Park Hyatt Melbourne	E
Loop	26	Il Bacaro Cucina		Radii	E	Hotel Sofitel	I
Lounge	18	e Bar	30	Shark Fin House	14	Victoria Hall	A
Metro	10	Il Solito Posto	31	Stalactites	4	Victoria Hotel	H
Meyers Place	23	Kenzan	I	Supper Inn	12	Windsor Hotel	D
Pony	28	Kun Ming Café	19	Tsindos	6		
Purple Emerald	36	Langton's	34	West Lake	24		
Spleen	17	Le Restaurant	I				
Three Degrees Bar							
Brewery Brasserie	2						
Troika	1						
Young & Jackson's	37						

7.30am–7.30pm) was built between 1880 and 1891 on the site where the colony's first settlers had held ecumenical services in a tent pitched under a gum tree. Constructed in the Gothic Revival design of English architect William Butterfield – who never actually visited Australia – the cathedral's spire is the second-largest Anglican structure of its kind in the world, after England's Salisbury Cathedral. Inside, intricate tiled floors compete with carved woodwork, magnificent stained-glass windows and a beautiful pulpit bearing a representation of the head of Nellie Cain, daughter of lay canon William Cain, chairman of the committee which organized the building of the church. Unfortunately, crumbling spires, leaky roofs, exploding tiles and more than a century's worth of grime have gradually taken their toll, necessitating major refurbishment of the cathedral and car-park area in time for the 2006 Commonwealth Games.

Running up from the cathedral is central Melbourne's main north–south axis, **Swanston Street**. For years a drab and grotty stretch of low-rent shops, failed cinemas and fast-food joints, Swanston Street has been reborn in the last few years as the city's Southeast Asian and Chinese student area. A walk along the strip north of Bourke Street Mall to the State Library of Victoria (see p.41) is like taking a trip to Hong Kong, with students from nearby colleges and universities pouring into Hello Kitty boutiques, emporiums and photo-sticker arcades, and some of the city's liveliest eating spots selling everything from Vietnamese *pho* and Chinese noodles to Indonesian nasi goreng, Malaysian curries and bubble tea. If you need a recharging drink, the historic, restored **Young & Jackson's** pub is on the corner of Swanston and Flinders streets. The land on which the hotel stands was originally purchased by John Batman for £100, then used as a butcher's shop until licensed as a watering hole in 1861. Upstairs in "Chloe's Bar", patrons drink pots under the portrait of *Chloe,* a full-length nude by French artist Jules Lefebre (her lover) that seems tame today, but which drew thin-lipped disapproval from Melbourne society when it arrived from France. First exhibited at the Paris Salon of 1875, it was sent to the International Exhibition in Melbourne in 1880, then shown three years later at the National Gallery of Victoria, where it was taken down after only a few weeks following a public outcry. The painting was bought by the hotel in 1908, installed in the public bar, and has grudgingly gained respectability and iconic status over the years.

Melbourne Town Hall

Two blocks north of the cathedral is another civic icon: **Melbourne Town Hall** (free guided tours Mon–Fri 11am & 1pm & on the third Sat of the month hourly 10am–3pm), dating from 1870 (the portico was added in 1887; an adjacent administrative block in 1908). It's best known as the place where Australia's famous operatic soprano Dame Nellie Melba made her debut in 1884, but it's also played host to everything from public debates and waltzes to poultry shows and wrestling. Here the Queen sipped tea in the stately Melbourne Room in 1954; here, ten years later, the Beatles waved to their adoring fans from the balcony; and here, in 1997, Germaine Greer kicked off the annual Melbourne Writers' Festival by launching a stinging attack against "penetration culture" (old-fogey Melburnians are still recovering). The Town Hall can only be seen on a **tour**, when you can roam through rooms mired in syrupy nostalgia. There's also an excellent collection of rustic paintings by early Melbourne artists Tom Roberts and George Folingsby.

Facing Melbourne Town Hall, the new *Westin Hotel* (see p.101) squats on **City Square**, a beleaguered space that was created during the 1960s by clearing a number of nineteenth-century buildings. The square, which has been dogged by controversy ever since, has now been reduced to a desperately small strip of dusty land, and looks like it will never fulfil its intended purpose of providing Melbourne with an appealing and welcoming public space – it's now hoped that Federation Square (see p.65), further south by the Yarra, will achieve this. Apart from the hotel, the City Square is home to a canal, kiosk, a smattering of spindly gum trees, and a forty-ton statue of bewhiskered *Burke and Wills*, two of Australia's best-known explorers who perished on a transcontinental expedition in 1860. Like *Vault* (see p.59), another well-known public artwork, the statue of Burke and Wills was roundly scorned when it was first unveiled, largely because the artist has made the hapless pair too "heroic". Also worth a look from here is the neo-Gothic **Manchester Unity Building** (1932), on the corner of Collins and Swanston streets, inspired by the Chicago Tribune Building.

The "Paris End"

From City Square, **Collins Street** rises up past the pompous Athenaeum Theatre and the lovingly restored Regent Theatre (see p.136 & p.137) to **Scots Church**, whose Gothic Revival design merits a quick peek, though it's famous mainly as the place where Dame Nellie Melba first sang in the choir. Further up, the towering I.M. Pei-designed *Hotel Sofitel* dominates the upper part of the street, known as the "Paris End" (or "Top End"). While it has a nice ring to it, there's nothing especially Parisian about this end of Collins Street: alongside the exclusive boutiques and cafés, there are also the practices of over one hundred dentists and lawyers in the upper reaches of the street's imposing but corporate buildings whose large vacuous foyers are a throwback to the 1980s.

At no. 101 is one of Melbourne's more daring modern commercial buildings, inventively combining erotic sculptures with freestanding columns, while nearby Collins Place plays host to a dreary **arts-and-crafts market** every Sunday (9am–5pm). Opposite, at no. 36, is one of Australia's last bastions of male chauvinism, the snooty, men-only **Melbourne Club** (1858). In the early days, the club was frequented by Sir Redmond Barry, who created civic institutions like the State Library of Victoria (see p.41) and Melbourne University (see p.71).

At the top of Collins Street, on the junction with Spring and Macarthur streets, the superb **Old Treasury Building** (Mon–Fri 9am–5pm, Sat & Sun 10am–4pm; $8.50) is emblematic of Melbourne's goldrush prosperity, combining elegance with unbridled opulence in its graceful balconies and high-ceilinged rooms. Completed in 1862 to a design by 19-year-old John James Clark, who also designed the Melbourne City Baths (see p.43), its basement once held fortunes in gold, though today it houses nothing more valuable than an exhibition on the social and architectural history of Melbourne. The building is also used for special events such as exhibitions and live performances.

Adjoining the building are the small and beautiful **Treasury Gardens**, packed most weekdays with public servants from nearby offices. The gardens feature many fine examples of European trees, including elms, plane trees and Canary Island palm. An extensive pathway system runs through the park, and there's a large embankment offering a fine walk with extensive views. Also within the gardens is a striking memorial to former US President J.F. Kennedy. At night, the gardens are overrun with possums scrounging for food.

Fitzroy Gardens

A stone's throw east, **Fitzroy Gardens** stand on what was a swamp until the 1860s, when the land was reclaimed and turned into a garden laid out in the shape of the Union Jack – a jingoistic conceit later abandoned in favour of a more free-flowing design. Classified by the National Trust in 1974 and placed on the Victorian Heritage Register in 1999, the gardens derived their name from Sir Charles Augustus Fitzroy, Governor of New South Wales (1846–1851) and Governor-General of the Australian Colonies (1851–1855). They're best appreciated on weekdays, as weekends tend to attract cavalcades of bridal parties having their photographs taken. Hidden among the trees is the gardens' main attraction, **Captain Cook's Cottage**, the family home of Captain James Cook (daily 9am–5pm; $3.70), the English navigator who explored the southern hemisphere in three great voyages and first "discovered" the east coast of Australia. The two-storey brick cottage and its adjoining stable were purchased for £800 in 1933 by Russell Grimwade, a wealthy Melbourne businessman, who had it shipped over piece by piece from its original location in Whitby, North Yorkshire, and presented it as a gift to the state of Victoria for its 1934 centenary. Originally, Grimwade wanted to set up the cottage in front of the State Library of Victoria (p.41), but the idea "of a whole pile of rubbish cluttering up the lawn" was poo-pooed by the library authorities. Other locations were suggested – including the St Kilda foreshore – until its present position was agreed. The twee red-brick and creeper-covered cottage with period fittings attempts to re-create the atmosphere of eighteenth-century England, reinforced by worthy displays about the explorer himself. The only link with the cottage and its original inhabitants is the stone inscription "JCG 1755" for Cook's parent James and Grace above the main doorway. Elsewhere in the gardens, a tacky model **Tudor village** (free) continues the olde-worlde theme. Created by 77-year-old Edgar Wilson from England, the cringe-worthy "village" was presented to the people of Melbourne in 1948 in appreciation of food sent to Britain during World War II. The model apes typical Tudor Kent villages, complete with thatched cottages, school, hotel, barns, church, streets plus an incongruous scale model of the house in which William Shakespeare lived in Warwickshire. Also here, the conservatory's flower displays (daily 7am–5pm; free), changed five times each year, and the Fairies' Tree – an old gum tree sculpted with fairies, dwarfs, gnomes and koalas – are popular with visitors of all ages.

Parliament House and around

Returning to the Old Treasury Building and heading up Spring Street brings you to **Eastern Hill**, the area selected by Charles La Trobe, Victoria's first governor, for state use in the 1840s. Oozing authority at its summit is the colossal **Parliament House** (free 50min tours Mon–Fri 10am, 11am, noon, 2pm, 3pm & 3.45pm on days when parliament is not sitting; ☎9651 8568 for dates), built in stages between 1856 and 1930 on a grassy knoll known as Lovers' Lane. Following the federation of Australia's six colonies in 1901, the first Federal Parliament of Australia took over the building, forcing the

Victorian Government to find alternative accommodation in the Royal Exhibition Building (see p.70), where it remained until 1927. The Federal Parliament then shifted to Canberra, allowing the Victorian Government to reclaim its original home.

Through the main doors a vestibule leads into the elaborate Queen's Hall, used mainly for formal state functions, while doors to the right and left connect with the chambers of the Legislative Council and Legislative Assembly. Don't miss **Question Time** (2pm; arrive early to claim a seat), when you can sit in the Public Gallery and – depending on the subject of the debate – listen either to the members' heated exchanges or count the number who have fallen asleep.

Opposite Parliament House, the immaculately preserved **Windsor Hotel** began life as the *Grand Hotel* in 1883, before being taken over three years later by future Victorian premier James Munro, who established his moral credentials by immediately declaring the establishment teetotal. Check out the palatial interior, its rooms resonating with the hum of well-bred conversation, or indulge in a posh afternoon tea (daily 3.30–5.30pm) of tarts and lamingtons in the hotel's restaurant, 111 Spring Street. Just north on the same side of the street, the **Princess Theatre** is a sparky piece of nineteenth-century chic which opened in 1886 and was transformed a year later into one of Melbourne's most extravagant buildings, when tarted up in recognition of Queen Victoria's Golden Jubilee Year. Designed by William Pitt and later refurbished by Henry White in 1901 and David Marriner in 1987, the Princess is arguably Australia's most lavish theatre, notable for its flamboyant exterior topped off by a gilded trumpeting angel on the uppermost tower and the latest hi-tech stage equipment. Legend has it that the 38-year-old Italian-born Englishman Frederick Baker ("Federici") had a heart attack and fell to his death while playing Mephistopheles in the opera *Faust*, and his ghost haunts the theatre to this day. The Theatre Bar is named in his honour.

To the northeast looms **St Patrick's Cathedral**, designed by William Wardell, the architect responsible for some of Melbourne's finest nineteenth-century churches (Mon–Fri 8am–6pm, Sat 8am–7.30pm, Sun 8am–8pm). A more modest church stood on the site until 1850, when the Reverend J.A. Goold, Bishop of Melbourne, decided it was too small for the city's burgeoning population and had it demolished. Its replacement was still under construction when, in 1858, the ambitious Goold declared that a still grander cathedral was required, to be constructed on the proceeds of Victoria's booming pastoral industries. Work proceeded slowly, however, and was frequently suspended as labour vanished to the goldfields. Finally consecrated in 1897, the cathedral boasts one of the city's finest collections of stained-glass windows, and the beautifully proportioned interior is graced by an enormous marble crucifix.

Chinatown

Back towards the city centre, Melbourne's small but lively **Chinatown** revolves around the section of Little Bourke Street between Swanston and Exhibition streets. Australia's oldest permanent Chinese settlement, the area began as a few boarding houses in the 1850s, when the goldrushes attracted Chinese prospectors (mainly from the Pearl River Delta near Hong Kong), then grew as gold petered out and Chinese fortune-seekers returned from the backbreaking work of prospecting to settle in the city. Despite being spruced up in 1974 as a tourist attraction, Chinatown retains a low-rise, narrow-laned,

▲ Queen Victoria Complex

Queen Victoria Lanes

A series of **laneways** and arcades traverses the Queen Victoria development, crossing the block east-west from Russell to Swanston streets and stop at the State Library of Victoria's southern wall. The lanes, designed to extend the network north of the city, are named to reflect the site's medical history:

Shilling Lane named after Constance Stone's "Shilling Fund", which raised money from Victorian women to help pay for the original hospital building.

Albert Coates Lane named after a World War I stretcher-bearer, who became a leading surgeon at the hospital.

Artemis Lane named after the Greek goddess of fertility and childbirth, and a nod to the development's proximity to the Greek precinct in Lonsdale Street.

Jane Bell Lane named after the matron of the Melbourne Hospital from 1910–1934.

Red Cape Lane named for the red capes worn by nurses of the era.

Constance Stone Lane named after Australia's first woman registered as a doctor.

nineteenth-century character, with atmospheric cafés, restaurants and shops selling everything from chinoiserie to fungi lying cheek by jowl. Jackie Chan, the famous Hong Kong actor and director, made good use of the location when he shot several madcap scenes here for his Cantonese-language flick *Mr Nice Guy*, in which he played the part of a Melbourne TV chef. Chinatown is also close to some of Melbourne's best Italian restaurants like *Pellegrini's* (p.111) and the *Grossi Florentino* (p.109).

Established in 1985 in an old warehouse on Cohen Place, the **Chinese Museum** (daily 10am–5pm; $6.50) traces the experience of Chinese immigrants in Australia during the mid-nineteenth century, especially their role in the development of Melbourne. The museum is worth a visit for the 92-metre-long Dai Loong dragon alone, which is paraded each Chinese New Year and during the Moomba Festival (see p.140). There's also a good collection of antiques and artefacts relating to Chinatown's social history, together with an exhibition gallery on the top floor showcasing Chinese artists from Melbourne and elsewhere. The museum organizes two-hour guided tours of the building and Chinatown ($16 or $33 including lunch; ☎9662 2888); these require a minimum of four people, and should be booked two or three days in advance.

Queen Victoria Complex

North of Chinatown along Swanston Street, the new **Queen Victoria Complex** is one of the biggest ever developments in Melbourne's city centre. Having sat vacant and desolate in the city's heart for almost a decade, the former site of the Queen Victoria Women's Hospital – Victoria's first women's hospital – was skilfully transformed in late 2004 into a residential and shopping precinct comprising a public square, subterranean food court with cheap eats, edgy fashion boutiques, a medley of apartments and the slick corporate headquarters of global mining giant BHP Billiton. The original hospital, a smart brick building designed by the ubiquitous John James Clarke, looks a bit like a comfortably settled older house that's had a glassy modern neighbourhood grow up around it.

One of the main reasons to visit the $600 million development – bounded by Swanston, Lonsdale, Russell and Little Lonsdale streets – is the eighty-metre-long fashion strip, called **Albert Coates Lane**, running east from Swanston Street above the intersection with Lonsdale Street. Expected to rival Chapel Street in South Yarra (see p.76), it comprises about twenty-five shops showcasing clothes from top-shelf local and overseas designers including brands like Christensen Copenhagen, Cactus Jam, Guess, Nicola Finetti and Wayne Cooper. Various other lanes also enter at street level, taking visitors via boutiques, cafés and juice bars to the food court below. Modelled on older Asian cities where people live and work above the shops, the complex is already popular with international students who throng Swanston Street and the surrounding area. In the thick of the complex, a public square is home to the enormous *Three Degrees Bar Brewery Brasserie* (see p.124), which serves fantastic food (washed down with beer from the on-site micro-brewery) to a young crowd of hungry locals.

State Library of Victoria

A blink away just north of here is the **State Library of Victoria** (Mon–Thurs 10am–9pm, Fri–Sun 10am–6pm; free introductory tours Mon–Fri plus first & third Sat of the month 2pm; ☎9669 9888, ⊛www .slv.vic.gov.au). Australia's first public library and one of Victoria's grandest civic monuments, the "people's university" was completed in 1856 under the direction of the library's founder, dandy, womanizer and Melbourne philanthropist Sir Redmond Barry, the Anglo-Irish judge who sentenced Ned Kelly to hang (see overleaf), although construction of the portico, dome and reading room, which was modelled on the reading room of the British Museum, wasn't finished until 1913. The library houses a trove of rare and antiquarian books and newspapers, along with material such as the diaries of founding fathers Charles La Trobe and John Pascoe Fawkner (see p.216), the deed of land purchase by John Batman from the Dugitalla Aborigines, Ned Kelly's famous rage-filled Jerilderie letter which inspired Peter Carey's Booker Prize-winning novel *The True History of the Kelly Gang* (see p.223), and a leaf of the Gutenberg Bible, the first major work printed using moveable type in 1455. At the entrance of the library is a statue of Sir Redmond, which was "erected by a grateful public", and beyond, Petrus Spronks' "Architectural Fragment", one of Melbourne's more famous and friendlier public sculptures. Refurbishment has meant the venerable building has now been returned to its old grandeur, complemented by state-of-the-art storage facilities and information services.

Melbourne is home to a large Greek community and, just south of the State Library, **Lonsdale Street** is the city's Greek precinct. A walk along this brief stretch of the city is an opportunity to linger in cake shops and grocery stores, take in the New Age instrumentals of Yanni blasted from doorway speakers or watch the old men playing "tavli" in the outdoor cafes. There are also restaurants such as *Stalactites* (p.111) and *Tsindos* (p.112) serving tzatziki and traditional coffee and cakes.

RMIT

The **Royal Melbourne Institute of Technology** (RMIT), just across La Trobe Street, is a scene-stealer that mixes the shock of the new with the style and proportion of the old days. Constructed from the shell of an original Victorian building embellished with striking modern facades, its architectural surprises include Building 8, with a playful combination of colour, shapes and perforations, and Storey Hall's pick'n'mix facade of livid

Ned Kelly

Notorious bushranger, national hero and potent symbol of freedom and resistance to authority, **Ned Kelly** was hanged at Melbourne Gaol in 1880. It was the final curtain in one of the most colourful and controversial careers in Australia's history. Kelly was born in December 1854, near the town of Beveridge in Victoria. When he was 12, his Irish father John "Red" Kelly, an ex-convict, died of dropsy, forcing Kelly to leave school and become the family breadwinner. Soon after, his mother Ellen, a woman of frontier fire and fortitude, moved the family to a slab hut in the tiny Victorian community of Greta to be near her own family, the Quinns, who were squatters. Greta was something of a lawless outpost, and the young Kelly was soon in constant trouble with the police, who considered the whole family troublemakers.

Having served a brief apprenticeship with the infamous bushranger, Harry Power, Kelly formed a gang (Kelly, his brother Dan and mates Joe Byrne and Steve Hart) in 1878 and they fled to the countryside, roaming and living off their wits. At the time, bushrangers stole livestock to cash in on high meat prices, horses for transport, and gold and money as it was transported from the diggings. They robbed banks, businesses and private dwellings. And they lived in the bush, where many were born, hiding from a Victorian police force depleted in numbers from an exodus of officers to the goldfields.

One day, hearing that Dan had turned up at his mother's, a policeman set out, drunk and without a warrant, to arrest him. A scuffle ensued and the unsteady constable fell to the floor, hitting his head and allowing Dan to escape. The following day, warrants were issued for the arrest of Ned (who was in New South Wales at the time) and Dan for attempted murder; their mother was sentenced to three years' imprisonment. From this point on, the Kelly gang's crime spree accelerated and, following the death of three constables in a shoot-out at Stringybark Creek, the biggest manhunt in Australia's history began, with a £1000 reward offered for the gang's apprehension. On December 9, 1878, they robbed the bank at Euroa in Victoria's northeast, taking £2000, before moving on to Jerilderie in New South Wales.

After a year on the run, the gang formulated a grand plan: they executed Aaron Sherritt, a police informer, in Sebastopol, thus attracting a train-bound posse from nearby Beechworth. It was planned to derail this train at Glenrowan with as much bloodshed as possible before moving on to rob the bank at Benalla and barter hostages for the release of Kelly's mother. In the event, having already sabotaged the tracks, the gang commandeered the Glenrowan Inn and, in a moment of drunken candour, Kelly detailed his ambush to a schoolteacher who escaped, managing to save the special train.

As the armed troopers approached the inn, the gang prepared for their last stand. In a back room, the clanking sounds of Kelly donning his homemade iron armour, which has since become his motif, could be heard. The armour weighed ninety pounds. Police surrounded the hotel and at 3am opened fire. When the smoke had cleared, Dan Kelly, Joe Byrne and Steve Hart lay dead. Incredibly, Kelly escaped to the bush, only to reappear at sunrise out of the early morning mist to rescue his brother. This time, the police aimed low, where Kelly was vulnerable, taking out his legs in a volley of bullets. The inn was torched, while Ned himself was taken alive, tried by the same judge who had incarcerated his mother, and sentenced to hang.

Public sympathies lay strongly with Ned Kelly, and a crowd of five thousand gathered outside Melbourne Gaol on November 11, 1880 for his execution, believing that the 25-year-old bushranger would "die game". True to form, his last words are said to have been "Such is life".

Today, Ned Kelly is indelibly stamped on the nation's psyche – part villain, part folk hero, but also a man whose courage and defiance is uniquely Australian.

green and purple patterns, loosely arranged according to the principles of chaos theory. The interest continues inside Storey Hall, with terrific installations, including an auditorium in which the original Victorian fittings have been immersed in great panels of pink, purple, green and white. Designers have even built a replica of *Vault* (see p.59), plus there's a serene 1990s minimalist gallery, First Site (Mon–Fri 11am–5pm, Sat 2–5pm; free) which shows new works by students, and a subterranean café, called *re:Vault*.

Immediately north are the congenial red-brick **Melbourne City Baths**, which were constructed in 1860 so Melbourne's great unwashed could scrub themselves here rather than in Port Phillip Bay or the typhoid-stricken Yarra. It was a time when "germ theory", which argued that contagious diseases came from individuals rather than the environment, added impetus to the prevailing obsession with cleanliness. After winning a contract to redevelop the baths in 1901, John James Clark, who also designed the Old Treasury Building (see p.36) and many other great Melbourne landmarks, arrived at the present style, with its distinctive "blood and bandages" red-brick and cream facade, and the new baths were opened in 1904. Over the years, the heritage-listed building has survived numerous fires, termites and rising damp to play a leading role in Melbourne's social history, a place where Melburnians could wash, swim, gossip and work out. In one of the terrazzo-floored cubicles, you can still bathe in a grand claw-foot hot tub shipped over from England in the nineteenth century ($4), swim in the thirty-metre men's pool or fifteen-metre women's pool (the pool was segregated until 1947), relax in inviting lounges and open-air terraces after a swim, work out in an African drumming or yoga class, or sweat it out in a sauna (see p.146).

Old Melbourne Gaol

Behind the RMIT on Russell Street, the massive **Old Melbourne Gaol** (daily 9am–5pm; $12.50; ☎9663 7228; the guided "Melbourne Gaol Night Tour" Wed, Fri & Sun: April–Oct 7.30pm, Nov–March 8.30pm; $20; advance bookings required by calling Ticketmaster on ☎13 61 00) is the city's most popular sight, largely on account of its associations with Victorian bushranger Ned Kelly, who was hanged here on November 11, 1880. Opened in 1854, the gaol was modelled on Joshua Jebb's Pentonville Prison in London, with high-ceilinged brick cells and observation towers to prevent escape. Melbourne's general state of lawlessness during the goldrushes caused such overcrowding that the jail was continually expanded – later additions included the thick outer wall where, in 1880, thousands gathered to hear that Kelly had shuffled off this mortal coil. A mix of condemned men and women (segregation didn't exist until 1864), remand and short-sentence prisoners and "lunatics" (often, in fact, drunks) were housed here; long-term prisoners languished in hulks moored at Williamstown, or at the Pentridge Stockade. The jail was recommended for closure in 1870, but it wasn't until 1929 that it was shut for good, although it served as a detention barracks for AWOL soldiers during World War II. Much has been torn down since its closure, but the entrance and outer wall still survive, and it's worth walking round the outside of the building to take a look at the formidable arched brick portal on Franklin Street.

The gruesome collection of death masks on show in the tiny cells bears witness to the nineteenth-century obsession with phrenology, a wobbly branch of science which studied how people's characters were related to the size and shape of their skulls. Accompanying the masks are compelling case histories of the murderers and their victims. Most fascinating are the women: Martha Needle, who poisoned her husband and daughters (among others) with arsenic, and young Martha Knorr, the notorious "baby farmer", who advertised herself as a "kind motherly person, willing to adopt a child". After receiving a few dollars per child, she killed and buried them in her backyard. The jail serves up other macabre memorabilia, including the beam from which Kelly was hanged, a scaffold still in working order, various nooses, and a triangle on which malcontents were strapped to receive lashes with a cat-o'-nine-tails. Perhaps the ultimate rite of visitor passage is the "Art of Hanging", an interpretive display that's part educational tool and part setting for a medieval snuff movie.

The Westside

The **Westside** – bounded by Swanston Street to the east and Victoria Street to the West and stretching beyond Spencer Street to include the new Docklands development – was for centuries a favoured hunting ground for the local Aboriginal people, and later the area where John Pascoe Fawkner and John Batman founded the settlement of Melbourne in 1835. Docks were built, marshlands drained, and slaughterhouses and gasworks introduced, but development only really took off once vast numbers of fortune-seekers began pouring into Melbourne during the goldrush of the 1850s, when it became the centre of the city's daily life, its commercial heart, and the hub of its sea and rail transport.

Much has changed since the area's heyday, and it now has few obvious attractions, save for the **Rialto Towers** to the west and the multicultural melee of the **Queen Victoria Market** to the north. Here and there, however, are examples of goldrush architecture, glorious gardens, interesting museums and one of Melbourne's giant sporting venues, while a fascinating network of historical arcades, laneways and passageways conceals some of the city's finest cafés and speciality shops. As well, the evolution of Melbourne's cityscape has been given new impetus with **Docklands**, in which a thriving waterfront precinct is slowly rising from what was once a desolate eyesore. This massive redevelopment is the real key to the future of the city, which is also being given an exciting new dimension with the revitalization of Spencer Street – when finished in 2005, the $700 million facelift will provide a convenient gateway to both the Telstra Dome and surrounding area.

Queen Victoria Market

On the corner of Victoria and Elizabeth streets, the **Queen Victoria Market** (Tues & Thurs 6am–2pm, Fri 6am–6pm, Sat 6am–3pm, Sun 9am–4pm; Nov–Jan same hours plus Wed 6.30–10.30pm; guided "Foodies' Dream Tour" Tues & Thurs–Sat 10am; $25; heritage tours same days 10.30am; $16.50; ⓦwww .qvm.com.au) is at once historic landmark, popular shopping destination and much-loved city institution. Built on the site of Melbourne's first general cemetery, the market was officially opened in 1878. Its collection of huge, decorative sheds and high-roofed halls – regarded as only temporary when first built – remains, fronted along Victoria Street by restored shops, their original awnings held up by decorative iron posts.

Although quaint and tourist-friendly, the real appeal of the Queen Victoria Market lies in its rowdy, down-to-earth qualities. A stroll through the market, from the dozen stalls selling nothing but blood-red tomatoes to another dozen plying dodgy leather goods and souvenirs, is much more fun than loafing around the city's expensive designer shops. Amidst the potpourri of people and

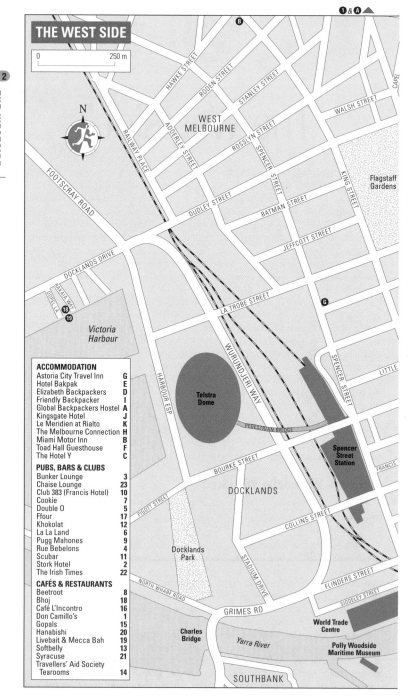

THE WEST SIDE

0   250 m

N

WEST
MELBOURNE

Flagstaff
Gardens

Victoria
Harbour

Telstra
Dome

Spencer
Street
Station

DOCKLANDS

Docklands
Park

Charles
Bridge

Yarra River

World Trade
Centre

Polly Woodside
Maritime Museum

SOUTHBANK

HAWKE STREET
RODEN STREET
STANLEY STREET
WALSH STREET
RAILWAY PLACE
ADDERLEY STREET
ROSSLYN STREET
SPENCER STREET
KING STREET
CAPEL
FOOTSCRAY ROAD
DUDLEY STREET
BATMAN STREET
JEFFCOTT STREET
DOCKLANDS DRIVE
BAKAIA WAY
DUDEI LA.
LA TROBE STREET
WURUNDJERI WAY
HARBOUR ESP
SPENCER STREET
LITTLE
PEDESTRIAN BRIDGE
BOURKE STREET
FRANCIS
PIGOTT STREET
COLLINS STREET
STADIUM DRIVE
FLINDERS STREET
NORTH WHARF ROAD
SIDDELEY STREET
GRIMES RD

ACCOMMODATION

Astoria City Travel Inn	**G**
Hotel Bakpak	**E**
Elizabeth Backpackers	**D**
Friendly Backpacker	**I**
Global Backpackers Hostel	**A**
Kingsgate Hotel	**J**
Le Meridien at Rialto	**K**
The Melbourne Connection	**H**
Miami Motor Inn	**B**
Toad Hall Guesthouse	**F**
The Hotel Y	**C**

PUBS, BARS & CLUBS

Bunker Lounge	**3**
Chaise Lounge	**23**
Club 383 (Francis Hotel)	**10**
Cookie	**7**
Double 0	**5**
Ffour	**17**
Khokolat	**12**
La La Land	**6**
Pugg Mahones	**9**
Rue Bebelons	**4**
Scubar	**11**
Stork Hotel	**2**
The Irish Times	**22**

CAFÉS & RESTAURANTS

Beetroot	**8**
Bhoj	**18**
Café L'Incontro	**16**
Don Camillo's	**1**
Gopals	**15**
Hanabishi	**20**
Livebait & Mecca Bah	**19**
Softbelly	**13**
Syracuse	**21**
Travellers' Aid Society Tearooms	**14**

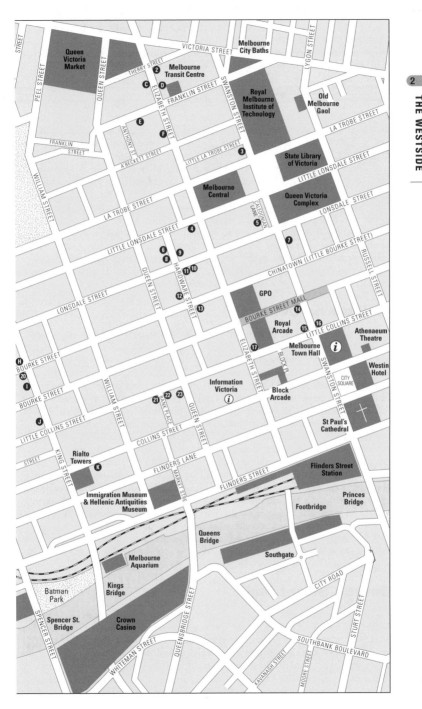

produce are food and deli halls – great for sampling Middle Eastern, Italian, Asian and seafood dishes – while vans outside dispense hot dogs, pies and ice cream. Saturday morning marks a weekly social ritual as Melbourne's foodies turn out for their groceries; Sunday is for clothing and shoe shopping; while Wednesday night's focus in summer is on live music, jugglers, alfresco eating and drinking, and shopping for jewellery and furniture.

Abutting Queen Victoria Market to the southwest are **Flagstaff Gardens**, originally known as Burial Hill by European settlers because it was the site of one of Melbourne's earliest burial grounds (a Gothic monument marks the graves of some of the town's pioneers). In 1840, an observatory incorporating a flagstaff and signal house was built, complete with a cannon which was fired to announce the arrival of important vessels in Port Phillip Bay. From this vantage point, the townsfolk would watch as passengers were ferried up the Yarra to the wharf at the foot of William Street. Indeed, it was here where thousands stood in 1880 when the standard was hoisted to greet the large fleet of tall ships gathered in the bay, their passengers having travelled to see the Melbourne International Exhibition. By then most of the structures had been torn down for the planting of shade-giving trees, lawns and flowerbeds, which today provide a welcome antidote to the hurly-burly of the city. Attesting to its historical and horticultural significance, the Flagstaff Gardens joined the Treasury, Royal Botanic, Carlton and Fitzroy gardens on the heritage protection register in 2004.

Melbourne Central

A couple of blocks east of Flagstaff Gardens, **Melbourne Central** shopping complex was opened in 1991 as a fillip to Melbourne's moribund retail scene. Unfortunately, consolidating several land titles into a single complex turned into a huge urban mistake, draining the life from important city streets, killing off several laneways and destroying many of the spaces used for public interactions. Inside the 55-storey steel-and-glass building is a minotauran maze that contained the upmarket Japanese department store Daimaru. The demise of the Japanese retailer in 2003 has meant better integration with the Melbourne Central train station, which has over 20 million travellers passing through it each year. The new environment has more diverse retailers – replacing the previous walled facade with appealing shopfronts.

Melbourne Central is also home to an ingenious cone-shaped glass dome enclosing a historic brick **shot tower** built on this site in 1889–90. Suspended from the dome is a hot-air balloon and a large fob watch that lets loose every hour with fascinatingly grotesque renditions of Australian songs. Mercifully, the creation of through streets and alleys has opened up the hitherto enclosed shot tower, which can now be seen from Swanston Street. Avoid the complex at midday, when there's a jam of office workers, students from the nearby RMIT, and commuters surfacing from the train station below.

Bourke Street Mall

The corner of Swanston and Bourke streets marks the start of **Bourke Street Mall**, Melbourne's bustling retail hub, which extends west to Elizabeth Street. The mall has been closed to traffic since 1972, although the odd tram trundling through makes for rather anarchic interactions with pedestrians. In desperate need of an overhaul (removing the trams would be a good start), this increasingly dishevelled pedestrian centre has some of the city's major department stores (including David Jones and Myer – see p.156), sundry food

Melbourne's laneways

Honeycombing the area bordered by Swanston, Queen, Lonsdale and Flinders streets is one of the city's highlights – a large and labyrinthine network of arcades and passageways, perfect for serendipitous exploring. Once tarred with scurrilous reputations, in recent years Melbourne's **laneways** have undergone a major renaissance and now pulsate with youthful energy, yet the bars, cafés, galleries, tarot readers, watchmakers and pie shops still remain hidden treasures, often only known to local or inner-city workers. Around them, laneways that had once been swallowed up by corporate developments in the 1970s and 1980s are being reinstated. These days the laneways play host to a range of public artworks and installations, ranging from graphic works to weather-sensitive instruments that are "played" by the wind. For more **information** about Melbourne's laneways, in particular how they came to be named, pick up a free copy of *Melbourne's Streets and Lanes*, available from the Royal Historical Society of Victoria in A'Beckett Street and at the Victoria Visitor Information Centre at Federation Square.

Block Place (Little Collins Street, between Swanston and Elizabeth streets). Narrow, dimly lit warren, where Asian takeaways, clothing and music stores jostle for space with umpteen cafés – some little more than holes in the wall – specializing in excellent coffee and pastries.

Degraves Street (Flinders Lane, between Swanston and Elizabeth streets). Cosmopolitan walkway that throbs with office workers at lunchtime and after five. The tables down the middle are great for people-watching, while Vespas anchored at the kerbside provide a nice European touch.

Hardware Street (Bourke Street, between Queen and Elizabeth streets). Home to the Campari restaurant (where musicians play Latino love songs to the gatherings outside), the fabulous *Khokolat* bar (see p.123), the Discurio music shop (see p.158) and the very spiffy *Segafredo*, where the coffee is exemplary even by Melbourne standards. Ranged around the street are old-fashioned barbershops, floral studios, camping and ski stores. In summer, the laid-back bustle, colourful awnings and footpath tables lend the street an ersatz Mediterranean ambience.

Howey Place (Little Collins Street, between Swanston and Elizabeth streets). Small but capacious arcade peopled by expensive women's boutiques and cosy cafés.

McKillop Street (Bourke Street, between Queen and Elizabeth streets). Opposite Hardware Street, this laneway was a haunt for gangsters in the 1920s, but now oozes a dated charm with browseable music, antique and secondhand stores amidst the quaint street lamps and benches.

and clothing shops, and is where you'll find an entrance to the lovely old Royal Arcade (see p.51). The state government and retailers have been asked to foot a $15 million bill to improve the mall by revitalizing facades, replacing awnings, adding more trees and improving the area's lighting. Even in the midst of this facelift it is still a major thoroughfare in the heart of the CBD.

The mall's western end is dominated by the **General Post Office** (GPO), a solid, porticoed pile with Doric, Ionic and Corinthian styles represented in the ground, first and second storeys respectively. Work began on the present GPO in 1859, taking twenty years to complete; the distinctive clock tower was added shortly afterwards. For most Melburnians, however, the GPO's most important architectural features are its broad bluestone steps, which are at their most useful during the Melbourne International Comedy Festival (see p.140), when they provide an excellent podium for watching clowns on unicycles or avant-garde troupes flailing themselves into insensibility. If the comics don't have you in convulsions, Melbourne's stab at public sculpture – a giant brown

▲ ANZ Bank

purse at the foot of the steps – will. However, the architecture and interiors of the grand old icon are being brought up to date and redeveloped into a luxury retail precinct.

The Block

The area south of Bourke Street Mall to Collins Street – known as **The Block** – was made fashionable in the 1890s by the aristocracy who came here to promenade or ride about in their carriages. It's still a draw for dedicated boulevardiers, lured by exclusive shops and cappuccino.

Running off Elizabeth Street (there are other entrances at Little Collins Street and Bourke Street Mall), the **Royal Arcade**, Melbourne's oldest, was opened in 1869 to connect Collins and Bourke streets. It's worth taking a look to see the haphazard mix of cafés and secondhand emporiums flanking the sunlit passageways. Perched at the arcade's entrance on Little Collins Street is a clock with two creepy, larger-than-life wooden figures – Gog and Magog, two mythological Ancient Britons – who strike the time each hour, while a dusty Father Time watches over the arcade's entrance at Bourke Street Mall. The arcade is currently undergoing renovations, which will introduce a new glass roof and return many of the shopfronts to their original 1890s lustre.

Across Little Collins Street and through Block Place is Melbourne's most illustrious arcade. Constructed in 1892 in emulation of Milan's Galleria Vittorio Emmanuele, the **Block Arcade** features intricate mosaic-tiled flooring, an enormous glass-domed roof and an eye-catching selection of shops and cafés. You can take a spin through the arcade's ground floor and upper rooms on an organized **tour** (Tues & Thurs 1pm; $9; ☎9654 5244), which winds up over free afternoon tea at the historic *Hopetoun Tea Rooms* (see p.110).

West along Collins Street

Leaving the Block and heading south down Elizabeth Street brings you back to **Collins Street**. West of here, at the intersection with Queen Street, the **English, Scottish and Australian Bank** (1887), designed by William Wardell, houses a sumptuous banking chamber, as well as the aptly named Cathedral Room, which often hosts exhibitions and performances. Below street level, the small but delightful **ANZ Banking Museum** (Mon–Fri 9am–4pm; free) spotlights the history of Melbourne's wealth during the goldrush era, and has displays of weights, scales, safes and adding machines, as well as changing displays illustrating the history of Australian banking.

Just before reaching the Rialto Towers, it's worth a diversion to the **Immigration Museum** (daily 10am–5pm; $6; ●www.immigration.vic.gov.au), situated on the corner of Flinders and William streets in the Old Customs House. Inside, a poignant collection of images and displays includes dolls brought by children from their home countries, and a detailed cross-section of a ship used to transport immigrants to Australia. In the **Tribute Garden**, the outdoor centrepiece of the museum, a film of water flows over polished granite on which are engraved the names of migrants to Victoria, symbolizing the passage over the seas to reach these faraway shores. The names of all the Koorie people living in Victoria prior to white settlement are listed separately at the entrance to the garden. On the second floor, the **Hellenic Antiquities Museum** (same hours; admission fee depends on the exhibition; min $6) is an exhibition space for antique treasures loaned by the government of Greece, most of them rarely seen outside their homeland, while out front a plaque marks the spot where John Batman founded Melbourne, with his famous words: "This will be the place for a village". The museum is also the starting point for the Golden Mile Heritage Walk.

Rialto Towers and around

On Collins Street, between King and William streets, the **Rialto Block** juxtaposes stylish nineteenth-century buildings, born out of the easy times of the 1880s land boom, and sleek modern office blocks, including the vertiginous **Rialto Towers**, Melbourne's tallest building. In the 1980s, the block was at the centre of a storm of vituperation as conservationists and developers fought over the planned Rialto Towers' evolution. Part of the controversy stemmed from the proposal to make it the tallest building in the city; part was caused by the planned demolition of some of the older sites fronting Collins Street to make way for the development. After protracted discussions, the heritage properties were spared, and construction of the new towers began.

The result is a skyscraper that has permanently broken up Melbourne's skyline – hairily high at 253m, covered with more than 13,000 windows reflecting a glassy, gridded city. On a clear day, take an elevator ride to the **observation deck** on the 55th floor (Mon–Thurs & Sun 10am–10pm, Fri & Sat 10am–11pm; $12.50, $10 for YHA members; ☎9629 8222, ⓦwww .ob.deck@rialto.com.au). As you make your way to the windows, a warts-and-all view awaits: Melbourne, both the city and its flat, limitless suburbs; the railyards with their spaghetti of tracks, grimy goods sheds and engineless carriages; the Melbourne Cricket Ground, near at hand, a perfect truncated doughnut; the higher and more distant ridge of the Dandenong Ranges; the ant-like life below. The night view is equally spectacular. Pity that the food from the licensed café doesn't match the view, and that Melbourne's answer to New York's Empire State Building is often crowded.

Back on street level and just to the right of the elevator, the **Rialto Vision Theatre** screens "Melbourne the Living City" (free with observation-deck admission), an audiovisual presentation that skilfully stretches two minutes of worthwhile material over twenty.

The **West End**, hugging the edges of the CBD around the Rialto Towers, is where Melbourne was first settled, and where the city's earliest industrial and commercial interests began. Its proximity to the Yarra meant it was the principal gateway to town: in the wake of the goldrush, the area heaved with merchant stores, seedy hotels, pawnshops and brothels. It's now rather subdued, consisting mostly of unkempt warehouses and wool stores from the 1850s – forlorn reminders of what happened when Melbourne expanded to the east – and newer office blocks of should-be-outlawed dreariness.

Recently, the West End was given a major lift with the opening of the **Telstra Dome** on Wurunndjeri Way (☎8625 7700). Immediately behind Spencer Street Station (currently undergoing a huge makeover transforming it into the "Southern Cross Station") this spanking new 52,000-seater has a giant sliding roof, which makes it an all-weather venue for AFL, international soccer, cricket and rugby union matches. Concerts by big-time performers, such as Barbara Streisand and Ricky Martin, or the dance-inspired concert Rumba that features the likes of Pink and Shaggy are all held at the stadium. TV station Channel 7 have their hi-tech headquarters here, and there are several bars, food outlets, retail stores and a nightclub to check out.

Docklands

From the area west of the Telstra Dome, a brand new city – complete with hotels, office buildings, luxury living spaces, department stores, marinas and other leisure facilities – is slowly rising. Formerly a run-down industrial area, **Docklands** fortunes are finally being reversed: in the last couple of years, yuppies have colonized the vast waterfront (almost the same size as Melbourne's CBD), bagging swanky apartments perched on the water's edge with stunning views of the city. When completed in fifteen years' time, this new face of Melbourne is expected to house 20,000 residents and 25,000 workers, and attract more than 20 million visitors a year.

Previously, the waterfront was amputated from the rest of the CBD by unused docks and abandoned goods sheds and warehouses. While the area's development has only just begun and there are still numerous building sites, it already has a good choice of convenient **public transport** options. Various trains and trams – including the free City Circle tram (see p.21) – cover the area and, apart from pedestrian links and a web of designated cycling paths, a weekend 45-minute ferry service connects Docklands to the CBD at NewQuay, stopping at various central locations en route.

Among the attractions, **Docklands Park**, the first new park to be created on the western side of the city for a hundred years, features public artworks and picnic spaces, while the wetlands attract native birdlife. Rejuvenation of the Docklands three waterways – the lower Yarra River, Moonee Ponds Creek and Victoria Harbour – has also created **Blue Park**, a home for boats, marine life, and skaters and rollerbladers attracted to the wide waterside promenade. At the **NewQuay** residential and restaurant precinct on Victoria Harbour, visitors come in their droves for the streets and promenades studded with buzzing cafes and eateries like *Bhoj* (see p.108), *Livebait* (p.110) and *Mecca Bah* (p.110), gourmet bakeries and shops. At weekends, the NewQuay tends to get swamped with families looking to while away their time before the kick-off at nearby Telstra Dome.

Docklands is also home to some of the most conspicuous buildings and public art in Melbourne. There's the **National Australia Bank's** head-turning twin-tower headquarters with their multicoloured panelling Meccanoed together into a giant Rubik's cube. A more natural-looking landmark is the slinky **Webb Bridge**, a pedestrian and cycle link to Southbank designed to resemble a Koori eel trap. Asserting Melbourne's cutting-edge credentials **Digital Harbour** is a $300 million technology-based development that's a mini-Silicon Valley for the city, while the film and television studios also take up prime real estate. Better understood by children than adult arts critics, Adrian Mauriks' *Silence* is a series of bulky white forms that kids love to crawl over. Perhaps most visually intriguing of them all is a remarkable 25-metre-high timber and aluminium sculpture known as **Bunjil**. Marking the gateway to the Docklands at the southern end of Wurundjeri Way, the sculpture is inspired by the eaglehawk, the totem animal of the Aboriginal Wurundjeri, who believe that it created all living things from the land.

The River District

Nowhere has the giddy transformation of Melbourne's urban spaces been more apparent in the last five years than in the River District, the area on either side of the Yarra from the Docklands in the west to the Melbourne Cricket Ground (MCG) in the east. The building boom – driven by a demand for inner-city accommodation and offices – has been on a scale not seen since the goldrush and "Marvellous Melbourne" era. As the city centre becomes ever more congested, so development has swept towards and embraced the river and the vast waterways of the Docklands, which are set to become Melbourne's next major commercial, residential and entertainment precinct, doubling the size of the CBD in the process.

Although Melbourne's brash plans to build the new 88-storey **Eureka Tower** on the Southgate site are unlikely to win any awards, the rest of the area's ferocious development remains as innovative as ever. Many of the city's cache of cultural spaces have been given fantastic facelifts by forward-thinking governments, while a building frenzy of apartments has attracted thousands of first-time residents, who have single-handedly revived the area. The **Yarra** itself, once the lifeblood of the infant settlement, is now being progressively reopened to the public, and is a popular focus of leisure activities, with the majority of the district's attractions stretching along its south bank and down St Kilda Road. Principal among them is the Victorian Arts Centre, home to some of Australia's leading performing-arts companies, while further west along the river are the two enormous leisure complexes of Southgate and Crown Casino. Nearby, the inventively designed Melbourne Exhibition Centre offers a possible clue as to what the future city will look like, while across the river the Melbourne Aquarium provides a fish-eye view of underwater life. Stretching down St Kilda Road beyond the Arts Centre is the newly opened **National Gallery of Victoria** (NGV), one of Melbourne's iconic landmarks containing the most comprehensive collection of international art in Australia, behind which stands an artfully rusted hillock housing the **Australian Centre for Contemporary Art** (ACCA), while across the road are the expansive parklands and gracious nineteenth-century buildings of **Kings Domain** and the **Royal Botanic Gardens**. On the opposite bank of the river lies the new heart of Melbourne and the city's answer – finally – to Sydney's Opera House: the jazzy **Federation Square**, built to celebrate the centenary of the Australian Federation and featuring the **Ian Potter Centre: NGV Australia**, home to an extensive collection of Australian indigenous and non-indigenous art. From here, Melbourne's new parkland of **Birrarung Marr** links Federation Square with the city's sporting precinct, **Yarra Park**, which contains various stadiums, principal among them the legendary MCG.

The Yarra River

Starting out as a series of soaks and swamps at the foot of the Great Dividing Range almost 250 kilometres to the east, and fed by myriad tributaries along the way, the **Yarra** swells into a broad, brown-stained stretch of water as it silently curves through Melbourne on its way to the sea. Only a few years after Melbourne's founding, the Yarra was ripe with effluent from wool washers, bone works, tanneries, soap makers and other suburban industries, which used the river as a major means of waste disposal. Indeed, so befouled was the waterway that during the 19th century it was occasionally seen to "run red with blood", while sharks were known to come as far up the river as Richmond to feed on the blood, offal and dead animals that were deposited in the river. Babies, unwanted by their mothers, were also abandoned along its banks. Typhoid was common, and the river was blamed as a major source of illness. But thanks to a number of improvement projects and stringent anti-pollution legislation, the Yarra today provides one of the purest water sources available to a city of this size anywhere on earth.

Now quiet and orderly, the Yarra was once an unruly river "choked with the trunks and branches of trees". In the nineteenth century, tidal movements of up to two metres often menaced the city with floods, a problem which was partly solved in 1888, when the river was deepened and widened to allow for the upgrading of Melbourne's port facilities, and its embankments raised. Only three years later, however, the river flooded to a new record, peaking at 13 metres. It wasn't until 1937, when parts of the river were lined with bluestone to curb erosion and trees were planted to create a flood-buffer zone, that a proper approach to land use was developed to stop the Yarra from bursting its banks.

Long reviled by Sydneysiders as "the river that flows upside down" (the mud is on the top), the Yarra is still nevertheless an essential part of Melbourne, its banks now dotted with barbecues and beautified by tree-lined boulevards and paths. A boat cruise is the best way to see the river, but it can also be explored on foot or by bike on the cycle paths which run along both riverbanks. **Bikes** can be rented from Hire a Bicycle (Mon–Fri from 11am, Sat & Sun

The city afloat

Natural disasters figure prominently in the development of Melbourne. In 1891, a "great flood" occurred after the city was pelted with exceptionally heavy rains over two days and nights. At one point, the Yarra swelled to be 305m wide and **flooding** was rampant. Over 3000 people, mostly living in the inner-city suburbs of Richmond and Collingwood, were evacuated from their homes, while two enormous lakes were formed on either side of Chapel Street in South Yarra. According to *The Age* newspaper at the time, the flood "rose so rapidly in the night that one resident reported plunging his arm into water as he stretched, awaking to the real danger of being drowned in his bed". In 1934, **storms** caused widespread destruction throughout the city, destroying houses, commercial and industrial buildings and private mansions. The economic loss was devastating, and the human toll was costly – eighteen people drowned and 6000 were left homeless. Thirty-eight years later, in 1972, flash flooding in the CBD resulted in Bourke and Elizabeth streets disappearing underwater. Apart from floods, the threat of **fire** was an ever-present danger. In 1897, raging fires ripped through the city. When the fires were finally extinguished, the entire block between Swanston and Elizabeth streets, and Flinders Street and Flinders Lane, was reportedly reduced to rubble.

from 10am, weather permitting; ☎0412 616 633) on the south side of Princes Bridge; prices range from $10 for a standard bike to $12 for a geared bike; helmets, locks, maps and backpacks are provided.

Yarra cruises

Cruising on the Yarra has been a popular pastime since Melbourne's earliest days, when steamers plied regularly up and down the river and out to the resorts of Queenscliff and Sorrento. Nowadays the choice of vessels on offer ranges from quaint sailing boats and steamships to gondolas and hi-tech motor launches, and you can go on short trips or longer journeys towards the sea and the bird colonies at Port Phillip Bay and Herring Island.

Melbourne River Cruises ($16.50, or combined up- and downriver cruise $30; bookings ☎9629 7233) make half-hourly departures from Princes Walk

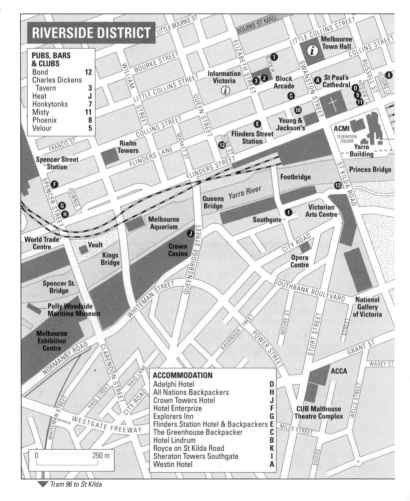

RIVERSIDE DISTRICT

PUBS, BARS & CLUBS
Bond	12
Charles Dickens Tavern	3
Heat	J
Honkytonks	7
Misty	11
Phoenix	8
Velour	5

ACCOMMODATION
Adelphi Hotel	D
All Nations Backpackers	H
Crown Towers Hotel	J
Hotel Enterprize	F
Explorers Inn	G
Flinders Station Hotel & Backpackers	E
The Greenhouse Backpacker	C
Hotel Lindrum	B
Royce on St Kilda Road	K
Sheraton Towers Southgate	I
Westin Hotel	A

0   250 m

▼ *Tram 96 to St Kilda*

below the northern end of Princes Bridge. Their Scenic River Garden Cruise (1hr 15min) will take you upriver past affluent South Yarra and industrial Richmond to Herring Island; the Port and Docklands Cruise (also 1hr 15min) runs downriver past the Crown Casino and the Melbourne Exhibition Centre – and then past shipping channels and docks to the Westgate bridge.

Southgate River Tours (bookings ☏9682 5711) offer daily trips on the hour from 11am up- or downriver. There are also daily departures to Williamstown at 10.45am, 12.45am, 2.45pm and 4.45pm. Both cruises cost $19.80 and depart from Berth 4 at Southgate.

Williamstown Bay and River Cruises ($14, or $25 return; for recorded information call ☏9506 4144; for bookings ☏9397 2255;) ply the lower section of the Yarra between Williamstown and Southgate in the west of the city, passing the Crown Casino, the Melbourne Exhibition Centre and the docks.

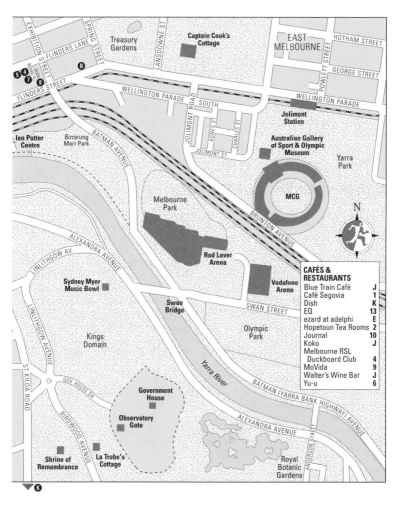

CAFÉS & RESTAURANTS

Blue Train Café	J
Café Segovia	1
Dish	K
EQ	13
ezard at adelphi	E
Hopetoun Tea Rooms	2
Journal	10
Koko	J
Melbourne RSL Duckboard Club	4
MoVida	9
Walter's Wine Bar	J
Yu-u	6

There are daily departures throughout the summer at 11am, 1pm, 3pm & 5pm, returning from Williamstown at noon, 2pm, 4pm & 6pm. Their cruises are pleasantly uncommercial, with no commentary or pressure to buy anything.

Victorian Arts Centre

At the southern end of Princes Bridge is the **Victorian Arts Centre** – home to Opera Australia, the Australian Ballet, the Melbourne Symphony Orchestra and the Melbourne Theatre Company. The centre comprises three main buildings: the National Gallery of Victoria (see below), the Hamer Hall and the Theatres Building, which is topped by one of Melbourne's most blatant landmarks – a 162-metre-high lattice spire which inspires love, hatred and every degree of feeling in between. Dull by day, by night it's transformed into a powerful rod of purple light.

The Theatres Building and the rather dull Hamer Hall – two separate buildings but linked to each other and the National Gallery of Victoria by covered walks – have worthwhile guided tours, during which you can view the permanent art collection (Mon–Sat noon & 2.30pm; $10; backstage tour Sun 12.15pm; $13.50; ⓦwww.vicartscentre.com.au). Tours begin from the souvenir shop, just to the left as you enter the Theatres Building. The highlight is the fun and accessible Performing Arts Museum in the Theatres Building (Mon–Sat 9am–11pm, Sun 10am–5pm; free), which covers everything from opera to rock'n'roll: you can see the hand-painted jackets worn by Neil and Tim Finn during Crowded House's Woodface tour, and Dame Edna Everage's frocks and spectacles. It also has splendid temporary exhibitions, normally focusing on popular culture.

On Sundays, a good **arts-and-crafts market** (10am–6pm) is held outside the Arts Centre on the paved promenade under Princes Bridge.

National Gallery of Victoria

After four and a half years of restoration, rebuilding and reorganizing, the **National Gallery of Victoria** (NGV; daily 10am–5pm; free; ☎8620 2222, ⓦwww.ngv.vic.gov.au) finally reopened in 2003. The late Sir Roy Grounds' resolutely grey slab of 1960s formalism – dubbed the "Kremlin of St Kilda Road" by a former gallery director – was completed in 1968, but has since undergone a $168 million transformation under the Baroque eye of Milanese industrial designer-turned-architect Mario Bellini (of Tokyo Design Centre fame) and local firm Metier 3 into a work of great skill and sensitivity. While the gallery has been radically renovated and expanded from the inside, including the introduction of newfangled escalators and angled mesh screens, the basic design of the exterior "palazzo" remains, as does the much-loved waterwall entry, which has been moved to allow untrammelled views across the central courtyard.

Also untouched is the gallery's most famous feature: the world's largest stained-glass ceiling in the Great Hall. Designed by artist Leonard French, who was invited by Grounds to make "the biggest ceiling in the world", it consists of hundreds of sculptured pieces of glass imported from Belgium and France. Taking five years to produce, French worked on the ceiling as if it was a giant jigsaw, cutting and chiselling each section of glass. To get a better look, visitors lie on their backs on the grey-checked carpet, looking up at the astonishingly vivid red-, blue- and green-coloured ceiling, while a public walkway on the second level brings people closer to the thick stained glass.

The central courtyard, hardly used previously, is now the gallery's principal gathering place, complete with obligatory café, bookshop, cloakroom and various galleries of antiquities. Maximizing the gallery's potential for interaction between art and public, large framed gateways, rich colour palettes on the walls and interconnecting gallery spaces ensure visitors are given open and inviting access to big draws such as Tiepolo's *Banquet of Cleopatra*, arguably Australia's greatest Old Master painting, Claude Lorrain's *Temple at Tivoli*, Cézanne's *The Uphill Road*, Rembrandt's self-portrait and Turner's seascapes, as well as decorative, sculpture, fashion, furniture and glassware exhibits over two levels above. While richly serving the gallery's large art collection, the opening of the NGV has alleviated only some of the hanging and holding problems, and only around six per cent of the collection can be aired at any one time.

Australian Centre for Contemporary Art (ACCA)

Behind the NGV, in the $10 million Malthouse Arts Complex, stands a dramatic sight: the Australian Centre for Contemporary Art (ACCA) (Tues–Sun 11am–6pm; free; ☎9697 9999, ✪www.accaonline.org.au). Looking like the urban equivalent of the sandstone monolith Uluru, or as one critic admiringly noted a "burnt out car body", the building rises on a stark linear landscape and is clad in nearly one thousand slabs of rust-coloured Cor-ten steel. Wood Marsh Architects have created a flexible and unpretentious building to replace the ACCA's former home in a quaint weatherboard cottage in the Royal Botanic Gardens. Squeezing every inch of space from its compact scale, the centre provides an excellent platform for creative talents, especially young and emerging local and overseas artists. Also here are the offices and rehearsal spaces of Chunky Move, Victoria's contemporary dance company, and the property and set facilities for the Malthouse Theatre next door.

Taking pride of place in the forecourt of the ACCA is Ron Robertson-Swann's 1980s abstract sculpture **Vault**, cruelly called "Yellow Peril". Misunderstood and much maligned, it is also one of Melbourne's most nomadic public artworks: shunted from site to site, it was originally erected as the crowning glory for the City Square in 1980 (where it was likened by one city councillor to a "broken-down barbecue" and, incredibly, thought to harbour sex offenders and its yellow colour to cause people to urinate), then banished to ankle-deep mud next to the Yarra opposite the Crown Casino, where it was used as a crashpad at night by the city's junkies and homeless, before relocating to its present sympathetic position in one of Melbourne's newest cultural precincts. At first glance, *Vault* resembles a wall that's collapsed and been hurriedly put back together again, but at close quarters it is an extraordinary fusion of art and engineering. Its author, Robertson-Swann, spent some time as an assistant to Henry Moore while living in London.

Southgate and Crown Casino

To the north of the ACCA, awash with swanky cafés, bars and shops, **Southgate**, one of the city's smartest food, drink and shopping complexes, lies on the riverbank opposite Flinders Street Station (to which it is linked by a beautifully engineered pedestrian bridge affording grand views of the river). Built on former industrial wasteland in the early 1990s, Southgate's three levels fizz with life, especially at lunchtimes and weekends, when it attracts hordes soaking up the views across the river.

West of Southgate, the enormous **Crown Casino** (☎9292 8888, ⊚www .crowncasino.com.au), stretching across 600m of riverfront, provides the focal point for the Yarra as it flows through the city centre. Australia's largest gambling and entertainment palace, the casino is crammed with a grim assortment of tacky gaming rooms, themed restaurants, cafés, bars, nightclubs, cinemas, shops and the luxury *Crown Towers* hotel. Equally egregious is the five-storey, black-marble atrium, which features "Seasons of Fortune", a sound-and-light show set amidst a waterworld of fountains and ponds. Outside, the only distinguishing feature, apart from eight granite-columned towers, which belch fire at night, is the promenade fountain, which provides a kind of assault course for children dodging the jets of water.

Melbourne Exhibition Centre

Directly across Clarendon Street, the striking **Melbourne Exhibition Centre** (Mon–Fri 8.30am–6pm, Sat & Sun 9am–1pm; free; ⊚www.mecc.com.au) is a whimsical example of the city's dynamic new architectural style. Opened in 1996 and known locally as "Jeff's Shed" (a reference to Jeff Kennett, the former state premier behind its construction), it was designed by Melbourne's hottest architectural practice, Denton Corker Marshall (DCM), collectively known as the "Blade Runners" and the team behind the distinctive Tullamarine Freeway gateway, the Melbourne Museum (see p.71), the Webb Bridge (see p.53) and just about every other construction project of note in Melbourne during the last ten years. Facing the river is an immense, 450-metre-long glass wall, while the street entrance has one of DCM's signature slicing "blades" – an awning resembling a ski jump propped up by wafer-thin staves, amongst which yellow and purple colours are craftily blended. Multi-dimensional in design, it allows organizers to hold events that require a high level of versatility – anything from trucking displays to the Melbourne International Music and Blues Festival (see p.140). Gliding over the water between here and the revamped Melbourne Convention Centre on the opposite side of the Yarra, a covered steel-and-glass footbridge provides pedestrians with an elegant, weatherproof route across the river.

Berthed in the wooden-walled Duke and Orr's dock next to the Melbourne Exhibition Centre, the **Polly Woodside** (daily 10am–4pm; $9.90) is a small barque-rigged sailing ship built in 1885 and described as "the prettiest vessel ever launched in Belfast". After a working life, most of it spent carrying coal and nitrate between Europe and South America, she was acquired by the National Trust in 1968. Now faithfully restored under her original name, you can climb on board and take the ropes, or explore the captain's quarters and storage holds below. Adjoining the ship are historic cargo sheds containing pumping engines and a museum of shipping relics relating to the history of the docks and Port Melbourne.

Melbourne Aquarium

Facing the Crown Casino, on the corner of Queenwharf Road and King Street, is **Melbourne Aquarium** (daily: Jan 9am–9pm; Feb–Dec 9.30am–6pm; last admission 5pm; $22; ⊚www.melbourneaquarium.com.au). Resembling a giant version of a Melbourne fish-and-chip shop, the aquarium harbours thousands of creatures from the Southern Ocean. Part of it is taken up by the Oceanarium tank, which rests seven metres below the Yarra, holding over two

▲ Shrine of Remembrance

million litres of water and containing 3200 animals from 150 species (there are over 550 species, or 4000 creatures, in the aquarium in total), a stingray-filled beach with a wave machine, a habitats area filled with starfish and eels among the mangroves and rockpools, a floor-to-ceiling coral atoll, and a fish bowl turned inside out where visitors stand in a glass room surrounded by shark-filled waters.

Education-wise, the curved, four-storey building also offers a variety of programmes suitable for children of all ages: a hands-on learning centre where children gain a glimpse of life underwater or dissect a fish via a computer screen, plus the "Blue Zoo" marine conservation programme, which includes interpretive displays and divers giving underwater presentations. The building also contains "Ride the Dive" platforms that simulate an underwater roller-coaster, lecture halls, an amphitheatre, cafés, a shop and a restaurant. And if you want to come nose-to-nose with a wild shark, the aquarium arranges "Dive With Sharks" experiences. Dives are provided by fully qualified instructors and prices are $124 (certified divers with own equipment), $184 (certified divers without own equipment) and $264 for non-divers (includes pre-dive briefing and practical dive). Bookings are essential on ☎9510 9081 or visit ⊕www.divingheadquarters.com.au.

Kings Domain

Returning to the Victorian Arts Centre and heading down St Kilda Road brings you to the grassy open spaces of **Kings Domain**. At the northern end of the domain lies the Sidney Myer Music Bowl, an outdoor shell which serves as a music arena for the Victorian Arts Centre. Built in 1958, "the Bowl" hosted everything from symphonies to the Seekers before falling into a state of disrepair. Now returned to its former glory, the Bowl has a new aluminium roof and an underground network of spaces equipped with performers' rooms, changing rooms and public toilets, while out front is fixed seating for over 2000 people and re-configured viewing lawns. Further south is the palatial **Government House**, official residence of the Governor of Victoria. The National Trust runs guided **tours** of the formal gardens and several of the rooms (Mon & Wed; $11; to book call ☎9654 4711, ⊕www.governor.vic.gov.au). Most spectacular is the enormous state ballroom, which includes a throne hung and canopied with velvet, brocade-covered benches and gilded chairs, all brilliantly lit by three massive crystal chandeliers.

Immediately south of Government House, the **Observatory Gate** precinct includes a number of Italianate buildings (originally built 1861–63), which have been painstakingly restored. The observatory performed a wide range of important functions for the fledgling colony of Victoria, providing scientific data essential for the running of businesses from shipping to farming. Also part of the precinct, the Visitors Centre (daily 10am–5pm) has a café and garden shop, where you can buy botanical books, maps and brochures. Guided tours start from here, including the Night Sky Experience tour, which allow visitors to track and chart the darkest reaches of space through huge old telescopes in the Observatory group of buildings (Tues 7.30–9pm; $15.50); and walks explaining the diversity of plant and animal life in the Royal Botanic Gardens (see opposite; Sun 8.30am; $10). If you're interested in investigating Melbourne's Aboriginal culture, the **Aboriginal Heritage Walk** (Thurs 11am & alternate Suns at 10.30am, $15.50) includes a smoking ceremony, in which permission is asked to enter the traditional lands of the Boon wurung and Woi wurrung people, guided walks (clapsticks and digging sticks in hand) through the native sections of the gardens, explanations of the different uses of plants and trees, and lessons on bush tucker. Bookings for tours are essential, and can be made by calling ☎9525 2429. Adjoining the precinct, the **Children's Garden** features sculptures from Norman Lindsay's story *The Magic Pudding* and is where children are encouraged to explore and learn more about nature in outdoor classrooms.

Nearby, on the corner of Birdwood Avenue and Dallas Brook Drive, **La Trobe's Cottage** (Mon, Wed, Sat & Sun 11am–4pm; $2.20) was bought in London by Victoria's first lieutenant governor, Charles La Trobe, who had it shipped over to Melbourne in 1863. The remains of the humble prefabricated house were re-erected on the present site in 1998. Small but elegantly furnished, it features the first governor's furniture and possessions, plus historical displays on the early days of the colony.

The **Shrine of Remembrance** (daily 10am–5pm; free; ⊕www.shrine .org.au), in the southwestern corner of the domain, was built in 1934 to commemorate those who served their country during various conflicts. It's a rather menacingly stolid mass whose architectural style is part Classical Greek, part Aztec pyramid. The strangeness continues when a disembodied voice booms out and calls you in to see the symbolic "Ray of Light", a shaft of sunlight that strikes the memorial stone each year at 11am on Remembrance Day (November 11) – an effect that's conveniently simulated every thirty minutes by an electric light. The Shrine's entrance and undercroft – the area under the shrine's walkway – has undergone a dramatic reworking to improve public access and reception facilities, and to provide educational displays on Australia's servicemen and women. A new **visitors centre** (daily 10am–4.30pm), an expressive and colourful array of spaces cut into the ground beneath the Shrine, features changing exhibitions, plus the forty-metre-long Gallery of Medals, commemorating the 40,000 Victorians who have served in military and peace-keeping campaigns. There's also a red wall bearing the message "Lest we forget", as well as other reminders of those who fell defending Australia. In the **Garden of Appreciation**, next to the Shrine, a bronzed statue carrying the words "Homage" and "Remembrance" commemorates the care given to the widows and children of soldiers killed in action, while directly behind the Shrine is also one of the city's most significant trees: a solitary Calabrian Pine, germinated from a seed brought by a young soldier who fought at Lone Pine in Gallipoli during World War I. Each year, the Shrine attracts over 50,000 visitors on Anzac Day, who make the very moving early-morning pilgrimage along St Kilda Road and past the Eternal Flame.

Heading east across Kings Domain from the Shrine of Remembrance brings you to the **Royal Botanic Gardens** (daily: April–Oct 7.30am–5.30pm; Nov–March 7.30am–8.30pm; free; ⊕www.rbg.vic.gov.au). Established in 1846, the gardens now contain twelve thousand types of plant and over fifty species of bird, not to mention great clumps of big bushy trees, rockeries, waterfalls, flowerbeds and pavilions. Highlights include the herbarium, shady walks through native rainforests, a large ornamental lake where you can feed the swans and eels, and various hothouses where exotic cacti and fascinating plants like the Venus flytrap thrive. The Terrace Tearooms and Conference Centre (daily 9.30am–5pm) by the lake serve refreshments and Devonshire teas.

Melbourne's much-maligned climate is perfect for horticulture: ideal for temperate trees and flowers, warm enough for palms and other subtropical species, and wet enough for anything else. It's also inviting for grey-headed flying foxes, which have long made the gardens their home, in the process damaging almost a third of the area by stripping the foliage off trees and harming plants with their droppings – their future has long been an annual source of debate and, in 2003, the state government eventually bowed to pressure and forced a colony of about 30,000 bats out of the gardens.

Circling Kings Domain is "The Tan", a 4km sand and crushed rock path that was once a horse-exercising track and is now a favourite route with couples and the city's joggers.

Melbourne Cricket Ground (MCG)

Opposite Kings Domain on the north bank of the Yarra (and connected to it by Swan Street Bridge) lies Melbourne's sporting precinct: **Yarra Park**. Within its wide, open spaces is an abundance of venues including the Rod Laver Arena (home of the Australian Open tennis championship); the "Glasshouse", or Melbourne Sports & Entertainment Centre; Olympic Park (where the Melbourne Storm rugby league team play their matches); and the Vodafone Arena, which can seat up to 10,500 people, and has a retractable roof and moveable seating that allows for fully enclosed events such as cycling, tennis, basketball and music concerts.

Taking pride of place, however, is the venerable **Melbourne Cricket Ground** (MCG), long known as "the people's ground". Originally built in 1838, but transformed to host the 1956 Olympic Games, the MCG (affectionately known as "the G") is Australia's oldest cricket ground and one of the country's biggest and most popular stadiums. Inspiring awe and reverence, the landmark is to Melbourne what the Opera House is to Sydney, the Eiffel Tower is to Paris and the Statue of Liberty is to New York. As well as being the spiritual home of AFL football, the arena accommodates cricket, international soccer and rugby union, rugby league, music concerts and other major events.

The present-day MCG has a capacity of 90,000 spectators (the attendance record is held by American evangelist Billy Graham, who in 1959 drew a crowd of 130,000 to his Melbourne crusade), which will be boosted with the development of the new Northern Stand, a massive piece of surgery that will see demolition of the historic Members Pavilion and Olympic and Ponsford stands in time for the 2006 Commonwealth Games, when it will host the opening and closing ceremonies, as well as the athletes programme. Eco-friendly, the new stand will feature solar panels and water storage facilities on the rooftop. The MCG really comes to life during the AFL season, when it regularly packs in footballing crowds for club games involving Melbourne sides, plus the AFL Grand Final itself. The siren blast that can be heard around the CBD at weekends signals the end of each quarter of AFL.

Despite potential competition from new venues such as the Telstra Dome and the Olympic Stadium in Sydney, the MCG's place as an icon among Australia's sporting stadiums is assured – annual pilgrimages to the AFL Grand Final continue to take place there as they have done for decades – while the Boxing Day cricket test match at the MCG is a tradition synonymous with Australian Christmases since 1968. For a greater understanding of the MCG's resonant place in Australia's sporting history, you can take a one-hour **tour** (daily from 10am–3pm; $10; no tours on event days; ⊚www.mcg.org.au) of the ground itself.

Federation Square

Federation Square (🕸www.federationsquare.com.au) lies just across the river from Southgate, opposite Flinders Street Station and the graceful St Paul's Cathedral. One of the most ambitious and complex projects ever undertaken in Victoria, it involved building across the Flinders Street railway yards, where work was limited to the early hours of the morning so trains would not be disrupted. Conceived as a tribute to the first 100 years of Australian nationhood, the Square – which links the CBD with the Yarra, fusing art, architecture, culture and hospitality into a distinct public space with crazy paving-style facades of geometric panels – opened in late 2002, almost two years after the centenary of federation.

Former Victorian Premier Jeff Kennett's most costly public monument, it was completed by the Bracks government bearing a price tag of almost $460 million (three times over budget). Often referred to as the city's "new heart", it's also been described by one Melbourne humorist as its "spleen", given that it was "odd, misshapen and nobody's really quite sure what it does". One thing everybody's in agreement about is its size: covering an entire block, its sheer enormity changes for the first time in over 150 years the famous grid of streets laid out by Hoddle (see p.217) by extending the CBD further towards the river. The Square includes an expansive plaza of 500,000 sandstone cobblestones from the Kimberleys in Western Australia, which affords commanding views of Melbourne's riverside and cityscape. There's also a soaring glass and metal Meccano-style atrium, evolved from the same triangular geometry as the building's facades, connecting galleries, an amphitheatre, the TV studios of multicultural broadcaster SBS, and a plethora of new plaza cafes, bars, shops and restaurants like *Chocolate Buddha* (see p.109) and *Reserve* (see p.111).

Eyeballing the stately bluestone NGV across the river the **Ian Potter Centre: NGV Australia** (Mon–Thurs 10am–5pm, Fri 10am–9pm, Sat & Sun 10am–6pm, free admission; ☎8662 1553, 🕸www.ngv.vic.gov.au) is the largest building in the Square. Built in an X shape and described as a "giant twisted worm", it

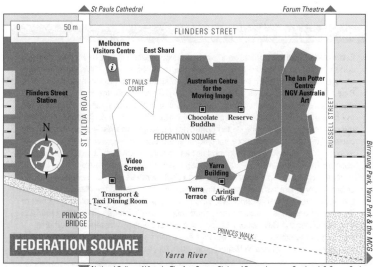

National Gallery of Victoria, The Arts Centre, Shrine of Rememberance, Southpark & Crown Casino

is home to a diverse collection of Australian indigenous and non-indigenous art from the colonial period to the present day. Despite its reputation as the little brother to the NGV behemoth, the Centre comprises over twenty highly theatrical galleries, with a collection including around 800 works (out of more than 20,000). There's highly regarded Aboriginal and Torres Strait Islander art such as Emily Kam Kngwarray's *Big Yam Dreaming* (Australia's answer to Jackson Pollock's *Blue Poles*) in a prominent ground-floor position. The Heidelberg School (see p.83) was particularly significant in Australian art as they showed the dry colours of the country in a non-European style, as illustrated in works such as Tom Roberts' *Shearing of the Rams* and Frederick McCubbin's *The Pioneer* on the first floor. More confronting contemporary works, installations and special exhibitions by artists such as Brett Whiteley are held on the second floor. The third floor is reserved for retrospective and temporary exhibitions (some may attract an additional fee; refer to the screens above the information desk for details). The centre is completed by austere industrial-type spaces that house cafés and bistros, a 109-seat lecture theatre and gallery shop selling impressive arts, architecture and design books.

Nearby, the glossy **Australian Centre for the Moving Image** (ACMI) (daily 10am–6pm; ☎8663 2200, ⊛www.acmi.net.au) is touted as "the first centre of its kind in the world", a mecca of screen culture charged with the lofty mission of helping visitors understand the moving image in all its forms. The four-storey complex features two state-of-the-art cinemas, a subterranean screen gallery incorporating up to 275 screens (reportedly the world's largest digital media art gallery), reception areas flush with plasma screens, hands-on activities and other examples of technical wizardry, but behind the scenes all has not been well – staff morale has been low, while budget blowouts have lead to a freeze on ACMI's superb lending collection, which contains works from directors such as Pasolini and Godard, as well as historic footage of the 1896 Melbourne Cup. Despite the challenges, the centre continues to present a range of interesting programmes for families and digital geeks, from cinema and educative events to hip-hop festivals. There's also a copy of *City Lights*, Charlie Chaplin's last silent film.

The case of the missing "shard"

Federation Square's complex and unique design, described by one Melbourne radio commentator as a "rancid lamington", is the result of an international architectural competition won in 1997 by Lab architecture studio of London in association with Bates Smart of Melbourne. The intent of the design, which draws on cutting-edge architecture and engineering, is to create visual harmony, whilst diffentiating between the square's civic, cultural and commercial buildings. Prior to completion, however, the development was embroiled in controversy over the **shards** – large, three-storey glass office towers – but more specifically the proposed western shard, which was to frame the Square's main plaza and act as its entrance. If built, it would have partly obscured the views of St Paul's Cathedral. But under pressure from the National Trust, the Heritage Council of Victoria and vocal members of a sometimes malicious public, Premier Bracks ruled against its development, much to the disappointment of the architects and their supporters, who believed its axing went against the spirit of the original design and would provide too much open frontage – something that has long bedevilled the City Square. Instead of a giant optimistic western shard, there now stands a single-storey building that looks like a fish tank, which acts as an entrance to the underground Melbourne Visitor Information Centre.

Just west of here, where the controversial "western shard" was to have stood, is the excellent **Melbourne Visitor Information Centre**. Over five times bigger than its predecessor in the Town Hall, it provides information on events, accommodation, transport, entertainment and a travel service for local and overseas visitors. See p.14 for contact details.

Outside, a giant video screen facing into the outdoor plaza from the three-level *Transport* pub (see p.124) features exhibits from ACMI and the Ian Potter Centre, and regularly attracts up to 15,000 people who come to watch major sporting events like the AFL Grand Final and the Australian Open Tennis Championship.

Birrarung Marr

Linking Federation Square to Melbourne's sporting precinct to the east, **Birrarung Marr** (birrarung means "river of mists" and marr is "side") is Melbourne's first new park since the city was originally laid out over one hundred years ago. Three times the size of Federation Square, the park forms a continuous green belt to Yarra Park, its wide, open spaces and sculptured terraces designed to host events and festivals throughout the year. Apart from a theatre-like space at the water's edge to accommodate large crowds, there are also rows of Red River gum trees, a gift from the Jewish National Fund of Australia, and the Federation Bells, a permanent installation comprising thirty-nine bells that are struck by computer-controlled hammers each day at 8am and 5pm.

4

Carlton and Fitzroy

With the goldrush of the 1850s, the settlement of Melbourne began to spread outwards, and by the decade's end, prosperous suburbs such as **Carlton** and **Fitzroy** had taken root. Carlton is still an elegant home to the city's thriving middle classes, who stock up on chic clothing and authentic victuals from the Italian precinct of Lygon Street. Southwest of here is the late nineteenth-century **Royal Exhibition Building**, home of Australia's first parliament, and the **Melbourne Museum**, the largest museum complex in the Southern Hemisphere, which draws on the latest technology to give an insight into Australia's flora, fauna and culture. Flanking Carlton's northwestern reaches, the small enclave of Parkville is home to the **city's university**, the popular **Melbourne Zoo** and, still under construction, the Athletes Village for the 2006 Commonwealth Games.

Bordering Carlton to the east, Fitzroy is now famed for its alternative and bohemian mood. In **Brunswick Street**, nominated for inclusion on the historic register of the National Trust, it has one of the city's most colourful arteries, with vibrant eating places and lifestyle stores. As for outstanding examples of residential colonial buildings, Fitzroy has them in spades.

Carlton

Carlton lies just north of the city, but in terms of looks and feel it could be a million miles away, with its café society based around the fashionable trattorias of **Lygon Street**. It was here, in the 1950s, that Melburnians sipped their first espressos and tasted spaghetti for the first time at exotic spots like the *University Café* and *Toto's* (see p.115), opened by some of the Italian immigrants who flooded into Melbourne in the postwar years. Lygon Street held an unconventional allure in staid Anglo-Saxon Melbourne, attracting the city's intelligentsia, who soon made the bars and pubs in this pretty, kilometre-long strip their home-from-home.

These days, however, Carlton's relevance as an intellectual and culinary milieu is on the wane. Its former bohemians have either left or aged ungracefully, while Lygon Street has gone upmarket, although the encroaching designer stores and tourist restaurants haven't yet completely displaced the arts centres, old-fashioned grocers and bookshops. Sustaining the street's heart and soul are a smattering of unpretentious ethnic cafés and restaurants, where students still congregate over tiny cups of bitter existential coffee. And in the Carlton Housing Estate, the high-rise project for low-income Australians between Rathdown and Lygon streets, live the suburb's new wave of immigrant children – this time more likely to be Somalian or Eritrean than Italian.

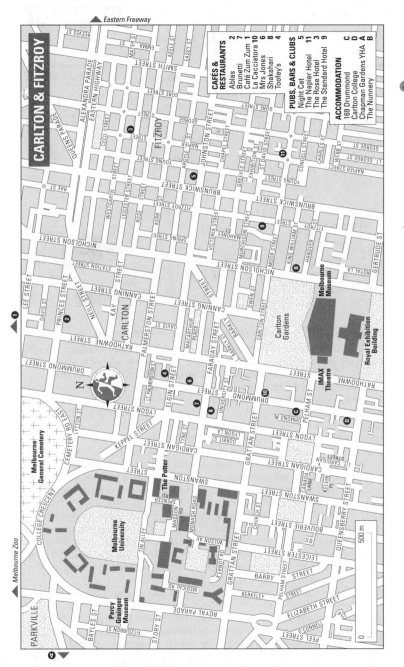

CARLTON & FITZROY

**CAFÉS &
RESTAURANTS**
Ablas   2
Brunetti   7
Café Zum Zum   1
La Cacciatora   10
Mrs Jones   6
Shakahari   8
Toofey's   4

PUBS, BARS & CLUBS
Night Cat   5
The Napier Hotel   11
The Rose Hotel   3
The Standard Hotel   9

ACCOMMODATION
169 Drummond   C
Carlton College   D
Chapman Gardens YHA   A
The Nunnery   B

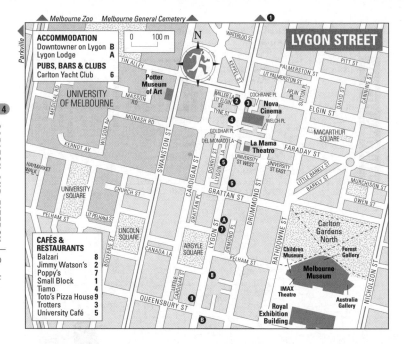

Map legend:

ACCOMMODATION
Downtowner on Lygon   B
Lygon Lodge   A

PUBS, BARS & CLUBS
Carlton Yacht Club   6

CAFÉS & RESTAURANTS
Balzari   8
Jimmy Watson's   2
Poppy's   7
Small Block   1
Tiamo   4
Toto's Pizza House   9
Trotters   3
University Café   5

0   100 m

N

LYGON STREET

Melbourne Zoo   Melbourne General Cemetery

Parkville

UNIVERSITY OF MELBOURNE

Potter Museum of Art

Nova Cinema

La Mama Theatre

MACARTHUR SQUARE

Carlton Gardens North

Children Museum

Forest Gallery

Melbourne Museum

IMAX Theatre

Australia Gallery

Royal Exhibition Building

Royal Exhibition Building and Melbourne Museum

At the CBD's northeast corner are the picturesque Carlton Gardens, home to plenty of fossicking possums and one of Melbourne's most significant historic landmarks, the **Royal Exhibition Building**. Conceived by ambitious former London shopkeeper Graham Berry, it was built by David Mitchell (father of Dame Nellie Melba) for the Melbourne International Exhibition of 1880–81, when everything from steam locomotives to lawnmowers were exhibited. Seven years later, in 1888, over two million people visited the Melbourne Centennial Exhibition to mark one hundred years of European settlement in Australia. The Royal Exhibition Building is also where Australia's first parliament sat in 1901 (the northern facade and majestic dome were restored to mark the centenary of the Federation in 2001) when the Duke of York opened proceedings to thousands of onlookers, and where the Victorian State Parliament resided from 1901 to 1927. Among its other incarnations, the building was used as an emergency hospital during the great flu pandemic of 1919, a barracks and training site during World War II, a sporting venue for the 1956 Melbourne Olympics and a migrant reception centre in the 1950s. In its prime, the Exhibition Building was a perfect symbol of Melbourne's vaulting ambition, with a dome higher than London's St Paul's Cathedral.

Buildings originally covered the whole of the park, but only the magnificent Neoclassical Main Hall remains, although this is still big enough to host the annual Melbourne International Flower and Garden Show (see p.140), plus everything from bridal shows to alpaca-lassoing exhibitions. Recognizing its unique place in Australia's history, the federal government recently sought World Heritage Listing for the Royal Exhibition Building as the best surviving "Palace of Industry", and it is the first landmark of national importance to be listed on a newly created National Heritage List. Guided **tours** of the Royal Exhibition Building (Sat & Sun 11.30am–noon; $4; ⊛www.museum.vic.gov.au) can be booked on ☎13 11 62.

Dwarfing the Exhibition Building and, at the same time, giving it a new lease of life, is the mammoth **Melbourne Museum** (daily 10am–5pm; $6; ☎8341 7777, ⊛www.melbourne.museum.vic.gov.au). Opened in October 2000, the state-of-the-art museum is in dramatic contrast to its nineteenth-century neighbour, with its geometric forms, vibrant colours, immense blade-like roof and a greenhouse accommodating a lush fern gully, flanked by a canopy of dozens of tall forest trees. The museum, which also houses a 400-seat amphitheatre, a touring hall for major exhibitions, an Info Zone study centre and a museum shop, has been designed with the Internet generation in mind: glass-covered display cabinets are few and far between and instead there is a greater emphasis on interactivity, with exhibition spaces exploring the way science and technology are shaping the future.

The **Science and Life Gallery** is a real highlight, exploring the plants and animals inhabiting the southern lands and seas. The **Bunjilaka Aboriginal Centre** showcases an extraordinary collection of Aboriginal culture: curving for 50m at the entrance is "Wurreka", a wall of over seventy zinc panels etched with Aboriginal artefacts, shells, plants and fish; while in the "Two Laws" section, traditional paintings depict the outline and anatomy of animals, symbolizing the relationship between external and "secret" internal knowledge. The **Australia Gallery** focuses on the social history of Melbourne and Victoria, ranging from the (now stuffed) legendary racehorse Phar Lap to the kitchen set of number 26 Ramsay Street from the TV show Neighbours. Also of interest is the **Evolution Gallery**, which looks at the earth's history and holds an assortment of dinosaur casts (including the first dinosaur bone found in Australia), and the **Children's Museum**, where the exhibition gallery "Big Box" is built in the shape of a giant tilted cube painted in brightly coloured squares. One of the most striking exhibits is the **Forest Gallery**, a living, breathing indoor rainforest containing over 8000 plants from more than 120 species, including 25-metre tall gums, as well as birds, insects, snakes, lizards and fish.

Also part of the museum is the **IMAX Melbourne**, which boasts the world's biggest movie screen. Up to seven different IMAX films (daily on the hour 10am–10pm; $16, 3D films $17; ☎9663 5454, ⊛www.imax.com.au), ranging from natural wonders to artificial marvels and spacewalks, are projected each day; for 3D action you need to don special liquid crystal glasses.

Melbourne University

Just west of Lygon Street in the adjacent suburb of Parkville, **Melbourne University** is worth a visit for its formidable art collection (Tues, Wed & Fri–Sun 10am–5pm, Thurs 10am–9pm; free). This is housed in **The Potter**, near the corner of Elgin and Swanston streets, a small but striking building adorned with Classical busts and reliefs and containing drawings, archeological exhibits, and nineteenth- and twentieth-century Australian art by the likes of Norman Lindsay, Joy Hester and Rupert Bunny. The life of Percy Grainger – composer, linguist, fashion maverick – is captured in the **Percy Grainger Museum** (Mon 10am–12.30pm, Tues–Fri 10am–5pm; free; ⊛www.lib.unimelb.edu.au/collections/grainger) at Gate 13, Royal Parade, in the southwestern corner of the university. Grainger designed the museum (opened in 1938) and stocked it with over 250,000 of his personal effects, including musical instruments and Bibles collected from his travels around

△ Facade of The Potter, Melbourne University

the world. His provocative and thoroughly interesting life – he regularly wore outfits made from terry towelling, favoured sadomasochistic sex and was unusually close to his mother, Rose (all major no-nos in the prim and proper Melbourne of the time) – was captured in the film *Passion* by Australian director Peter Duncan. Least known of the university's attractions is the **underground car park** beneath the South Lawn: a Gothic netherworld of concrete arches and columns, which was used for the police garage scenes in the film *Mad Max*.

Just north of the university, the **Melbourne General Cemetery**, established in 1853, is the oldest in the city, although most of its fine examples of funerary architecture have disappeared or fallen apart. Over half a million people are buried here, including Melbourne founder John Batman, explorers Burke and Wills, and Australian Prime Minister Sir Robert Menzies. For those who wish to be spooked, the National Trust organizes **full-moon tours** of the cemetery ($20; booking essential ☎9890 9288/9872 5452).

Melbourne Zoo

West from the cemetery, the green plenitude of Royal Park is home to the **Melbourne Zoo** (daily 9am–5pm; $18; ⊛www.zoo.org.au), opened in 1862 and the oldest in Australia. Some of its original features are still in evidence, including the landscaped gardens with their Australian and foreign trees, and a few restored Victorian-era cages, but almost all the animals have now been rehoused in more sympathetic enclosures. In winter, the enclosures are specially heated to keep the animals warm. The zoo is currently overseeing an $85 million revamp, which incorporates an upgrade to the orang-utan enclosure and several other projects aimed at providing even more appropriate contexts for the animals, promoting social and environmental issues, and placing zookeepers as a fundamental part of the attraction by becoming storytellers and educationalists. The easiest way to get to the zoo is to catch a tram from the city: tram #55 from William St; tram #68 from Elizabeth St.

The **Australian bush habitat**, densely planted with more than twenty thousand native plants, contains wombats, koalas, echidnas, monitor lizards and cockatoos, while a maze of underground enclosures allows you to observe dozing groups of wombats and includes a small tunnel where you can experience the burrowing lifestyle of these animals. The **Great Flight Aviary** (daily 10.30am–4.30pm) has areas of rainforest, wetland and a patch of scrub with a huge gum tree where many birds like the blue crane and bower bird nest, while the dark **Platypus Habitat** (daily 9.30am–4.30pm) is also worth a visit to see these notoriously elusive mammals. Other highlights include the newly developed Elephant Village, where visitors can pat resident elephants Mek Kapah and Bong Su, learn about the life of a "mahout" or elephant keeper, or eat nasi goreng at the Asian food stalls; the Butterfly House (daily 9.30am–4.30pm); the gorilla and small-ape enclosures; and the popular meerkats, to the right of the main entrance. For sustenance there's the *Lakeside Bistro* (daily 10.30am–4.30pm) and the Meerkat Kiosk (daily 9am–5pm), plus plenty of takeaway facilities.

One of the best ways to experience the zoo is to time your visit with an animal handler session or during feeding times. "**Meet the Keeper**" sessions are as follows: wombats (daily 11.15am), macaws (daily 1.15pm), seals (weekends & public holidays 2.15pm), pelicans (daily 2.30pm), tree kangaroos (daily 3.30pm), penguins (daily 3.30pm) and lorikeets (daily 3.45pm). **Feeding times** are: baboons (daily 9.45am), orang-utans (daily 1.10pm), otters (most days 1.15pm) and meerkats (most days 1.30pm). Free guided tours are available

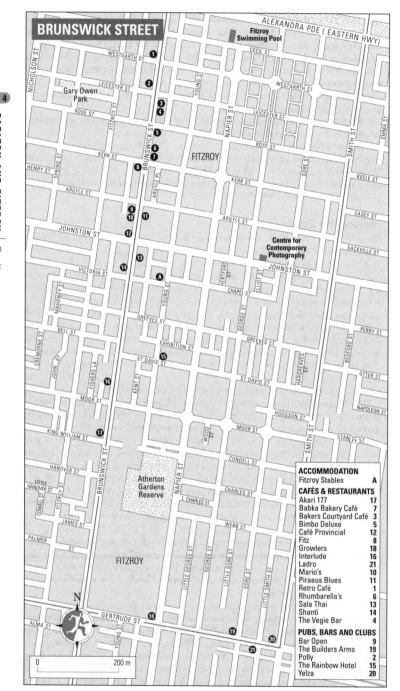

BRUNSWICK STREET

FITZROY

Fitzroy
Swimming Pool

Gary Owen
Park

Centre for
Contemporary
Photography

Atherton
Gardens
Reserve

FITZROY

N

ACCOMMODATION
Fitzroy Stables — A

CAFÉS & RESTAURANTS
Akari 177 — 17
Babka Bakery Café — 7
Bakers Courtyard Café — 3
Bimbo Deluxe — 5
Café Provincial — 12
Fitz — 8
Growlers — 18
Interlude — 16
Ladro — 21
Mario's — 10
Piraeus Blues — 11
Retro Café — 1
Rhumbarella's — 6
Sala Thai — 13
Shanti — 14
The Vegie Bar — 4

PUBS, BARS AND CLUBS
Bar Open — 9
The Builders Arms — 19
Polly — 2
The Rainbow Hotel — 15
Yelza — 20

0   200 m

daily 10am–3pm. During January (Thurs–Sun) and February (Fri–Sun) the zoo stays open until 9.30pm for meals, jazz concerts and twilight tours. The zoo also runs specialist events such as the very popular "Roar 'n' Snore" sleepover, when you pitch your tent next to an animal enclosure ($99 adults, $88 children; dinner, breakfast and snacks are provided, as are tents, but bring your own bedding – for more information call ☎9285 9335).

Construction is in process in Royal Park on the 2006 Commonwealth Games Athletes Village which will accommodate 6000 athletes and officials for the opening ceremony in March 2006. After the Games, ten per cent of the village will become public housing.

Fitzroy

Melbourne's first and Australia's smallest suburb, **Fitzroy** has had a varied and fluctuating history. In the early years of European settlement it was considered eminently desirable – high, dry and conveniently north of the city. Many colonial buildings remain intact, and, apart from the CBD, Fitzroy houses the city's finest collection of mid-nineteenth-century bluestone buildings (the best examples, like Royal Terrace, are in Nicholson Street opposite the Royal Exhibition Building, or on Victoria Parade further south). Gradually, however, the area's fortunes declined, and by the turn of the twentieth century Fitzroy was providing land and cheap labour for noxious trades such as tanning and soap and candle manufacturing. By the 1930s, even the factories had moved to the suburbs and Fitzroy had become a slum. Gradually, the suburb's fortunes were revived: first by the arrival of a mix of European, Middle Eastern and Asian immigrants in the postwar period; later by the young and sophisticated suburbanites who stumbled upon the area during the early 1970s, setting the fashion ever since for terrace-style living and louche gentility.

Fitzroy's focal point is **Brunswick Street**, where, in the shadow of Housing Commission high-rises, you can pick up clothes and accessories from funky shops at knock-down prices, eat at the area's abundance of ethnic restaurants, drink decaff with artists and actors, bury your head in Aussie "grunge" literature in one of the street's late-night bookshops, or down a VB at the many bars and live music venues sprinkling the strip. The fires of anti-fashion raging through the area have also left the street full of hotels with "raw" paint jobs and deliberately half-finished decor inside.

Also well worth a look is **Gertrude Street**, one of the first streets in Fitzroy. Once a transient, junkie stronghold, Gertrude Street is fast becoming a chic hub for Melbourne's artistic community, with its galleries and performance art spaces. Mixed in with the organic delis, eclectic clothing boutiques, and music stores specializing in dance and hip-hop, is a string of casual cafés and bars, where there's the chatter of numerous different languages.

Running at right angles across Brunswick Street is the centre of Melbourne's Spanish community, **Johnston Street**, a lively stretch of tapas bars and flamenco restaurants. Nearby, Fitzroy's fringe-art leanings are embodied in a number of local galleries, in particular monthly exhibitions at the **Centre for Contemporary Photography**, 205 Johnston St (Wed–Sat 11am–5pm), which has four gallery spaces showing mostly experimental works, and **200 Gertrude St** (Tues–Sat 10am–5.30pm), a converted warehouse that is now a state-funded gallery and studio space for emerging artists. Fitzroy also boasts its own **arts-and-crafts market** (third Sun of the month 10am–3.30pm) at the old Fitzroy Town Hall on the corner of Napier and Moor streets.

5

South Yarra, Prahran and Toorak

The trio of suburbs southeast of the city centre is one of Melbourne's premier destinations for food, shopping and promenading. Just south of the river, **South Yarra** has long been the haunt of fashion-conscious Melburnians, centred on exclusive **Chapel Street**, with its painfully cool cafés and label-proud shops. A few hours on the street and you'll be convinced it's the most vacuous plot in the world, but it's hard not to be drawn into the movements of the young and willowy bolting from one boutique or grazing spot to the next. Also in South Yarra, stately **Como House** provides an insight into the luxurious life of a nineteenth-century landowner.

Chapel Street continues south to the less salubrious but infinitely funkier environs of Prahran, boasting switched-on Greville Street and its surrounding markets. The gay strip of **Commercial Road** separates the two suburbs, combining bookshops, gift and clothes stores with gyms, cafés and restaurants. For a real blue-blood experience, head east from Prahran to the rich heart of Toorak, home to Melbourne's economic elite and boasting even glitzier designer boutiques than South Yarra, but few tourist attractions.

South Yarra

South Yarra is home to Melbourne's smart set, who browse the racks at designer stores, graze at chic hangouts, then boogie at nightclubs to work it all off. At the heart of the district is the strip of **Chapel Street** between Toorak and Commercial roads – the so-called "Golden Mile", or "right" end – where myriad shops and restaurants spill onto pavements with white linen napery and full-aproned waiters. At weekends, hotted-up cars and baby-boomers driving 4WDs make this a heavily trafficked strip to the pound of engine noise and subwoofer bravado.

Halfway down Chapel Street is the **Jam Factory**. Jam-making began here in 1885 and continued until the factory's closure in 1973. Six years later the building was overhauled and reopened as a monster cinema-and-entertainment centre. The brick-and-bluestone complex is quite comely for a former factory, and still has quaint machinery on display, but you'll have to look hard for it among kitsch Hollywood effigies of Marilyn Monroe, James Dean and R2-D2.

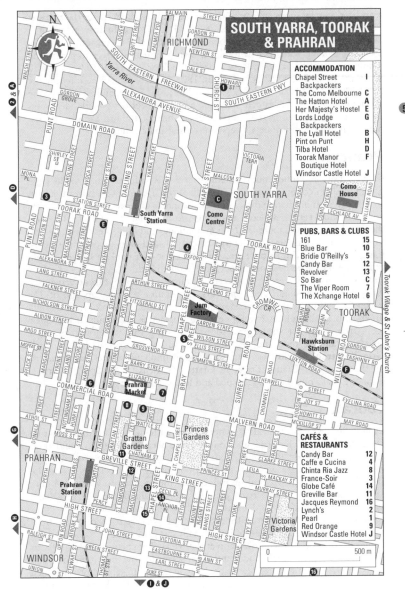

Map: South Yarra, Toorak & Prahran

ACCOMMODATION

Chapel Street	I
Backpackers	
The Como Melbourne	C
The Hatton Hotel	A
Her Majesty's Hostel	E
Lords Lodge	G
Backpackers	
The Lyall Hotel	B
Pint on Punt	H
Tilba Hotel	D
Toorak Manor	F
Boutique Hotel	
Windsor Castle Hotel	J

PUBS, BARS & CLUBS

161	15
Blue Bar	10
Bridie O'Reilly's	5
Candy Bar	12
Revolver	13
So Bar	C
The Viper Room	7
The Xchange Hotel	6

CAFÉS & RESTAURANTS

Candy Bar	12
Caffe e Cucina	4
Chinta Ria Jazz	8
France-Soir	3
Globe Café	14
Greville Bar	11
Jacques Reymond	16
Lynch's	2
Pearl	1
Red Orange	9
Windsor Castle Hotel	J

Toorak Village & St John's Church

Como House

To the north, overlooking the river from Como Avenue is **Como House** (daily 10am–5pm, tours every 30min from 10.15am to 4.15pm; $11; ☎9827 2500), a fine example of the townhouses built by the city's well-to-do nineteenth-century landowners. The site was originally bought by George and Alfred Langhorne in 1837 from the Woiworung Aboriginal people and used as a stock run. Nine years later, a single-storey villa was built on the banks of the Yarra for the barrister Edward Eyre Williams, who named it after Lake Como in Italy, where it is said he proposed to his wife. The house then enjoyed a succession of wealthy owners, including wine merchant John Brown (who added a second storey) and prominent graziers and Melbourne citizens the Armytage family, who extended the house by adding a ballroom wing in 1874. Now beautifully restored by the National Trust, many of the house's original furnishings remain intact, while the surrounding landscaped gardens and pine and cypress glades provide ideal spots for a picnic. Twilight tours of Como House are held on the first Saturday of each month ($69.50) and include a three-course meal and champagne.

Prahran

Chapel Street continues south to **Commercial Road**, renowned for its large gay and lesbian community (see "Gay Melbourne"), then into **Prahran** proper, an area given an interesting dimension by the influx of newcomers in the 1950s, especially shopkeepers, students, and emigrants from Italy and Greece. The further south you go, the more the fashion boutiques and upmarket cafés give way to secondhand clothing stores, tattooists and fish-and-chip shops. Some prefer this grungey area with its nose-rings and cockatoo-like punkish haircuts, while others like the slicker end of Chapel Street to the north.

Just off Chapel Street in the heart of Prahran, **Greville Street** remains a hip strip with late-night clubs and bars. The demise several years ago of *The Continental*, a hugely popular restaurant and nightclub, is still mourned by old-timers, but smaller places have appeared to replace it. Weekends in particular see a steady flow of young professionals enjoying the easy-going vibe, the generally fantastic food and spacious pubs and bars. Every Sunday the small **Greville Street Market** has arts, crafts and secondhand clothes and jewellery on the corner of Grattan Street in Grattan Gardens (noon–5pm), a former billabong that's now been landscaped and looks like an airport runway.

Toorak

East of South Yarra, **Toorak** is synonymous with money and born-to-rule pedigree. When Melbourne was founded, the wealthy chose to build their homes here, high on the banks of the Yarra, while the cottages of the poor were confined to narrow streets on the flood-prone areas below. During the 1950s and 1960s, old Melbourne money was joined by new, when an influx of European Jews – who arrived penniless in Australia during the 1930s and 1940s – celebrated their hard-earned wealth by moving to Toorak.

Snobbish and conservative, Toorak has little to see or do, apart from wandering around leafy streets of homes with vast gardens and box hedges. On Toorak Road, you can window-shop at the wickedly expensive Toorak Village, a higgledy-piggledy mock-Tudor mess that seems to have rewritten the book on bad 1970s architecture. Alternatively, pavement-café tables are unrivalled spots for watching late-model Range Rovers and 4WDs (known locally as "Toorak Tractors") idling past. If you're interested in early woodcarvings of Australian flora and fauna, you should make a pilgrimage to **St John's Church** (daily 8am–6pm), on the corner of Toorak and Clendon roads. Ornamental reliefs of kangaroos, dingos, wattles and ferns can be found on the arm ends and heads of pews on both the north and south side of the church. St John's also hosts B-list celebrity weddings, usually involving either a local footy star or a scion of Melbourne society.

Collingwood
and the east

The last decade has seen **Collingwood** and Richmond dramatically regenerated and gentrified. While both share a history of blue-collar culture, Irish Catholic-dominated municipal politics and fierce loyal support for their local football teams, Collingwood is the rising underdog of the two, a once-dreary industrial area whose revival of fortunes is largely due to an abundance of relatively cheap living space and a vibrant bar and café scene along **Smith Street**. Not much further down the road, the **Collingwood Children's Farm** is far less frenetic, and is a popular spot for families and school groups.

More on the tourist route, **Richmond** was once the hilly heart of nineteenth-century Melbourne, becoming a lively immigrant quarter after World War II and today a focus for bargain shopping, food, houseware and leisurely boozing. Despite its obvious urbanity, Richmond manages to retain something of a village atmosphere, with its tangle of genteel streets and iconic landmarks like Dimmeys, one of Australia's oldest retail stores.

Even further East there's the creative nexus that was once home to some of Australia's greatest visual artists, like the Boyd family home at **Museum of Modern Art at Heide** or **Montsalvat,** the home of architect and painter, Justus Jorgensen. If you prefer your culture a little more popular, there's always the chance to spot a new plot development on the real-life **Ramsay Street** of Pin Oak Court.

Collingwood

Right from the first subdivisions of land of 1838–39, **Collingwood** (named after Admiral Lord Collingwood, who led the British fleet to victory at Trafalgar) was a combination of residential and industrial properties. Settlement intensified after the goldrush with cottages built to house the workers from the nearby mills and slaughterhouses, which were fuelling the city's growth and polluting the Yarra River in Collingwood's east. The savage depression of the 1890s severely affected the suburb, and it slipped into decline and became a slum area subsisting in a miasma of rats and noxious fumes. In the 1950s, Greek, Italian and Lebanese migrants joined the neighbourhood of workers and indigenous people but in recent years students, artists, a large gay and lesbian community, and a wave of savvy entrepreneurs on the prowl for warehouse

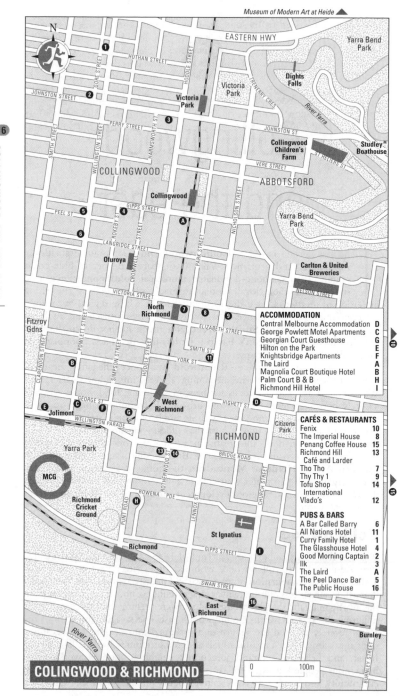

EASTERN HWY

Yarra Bend Park

HOTHAN STREET

Dights Falls

River Yarra

JOHNSTON STREET

Victoria Park

Victoria Park

TRENERRY CRES

PERRY STREET

JOHNSTON ST

Collingwood Children's Farm

ST HELIERS ST

Studley Boathouse

VERE STREET

COLLINGWOOD

ABBOTSFORD

Collingwood

PEEL ST

GIPPS STREET

Yarra Bend Park

LANGRIDGE STREET

Ofuroya

Carlton & United Breweries

VICTORIA STREET

NELSON STREET

North Richmond

ELIZABETH STREET

Fitzroy Gdns

ACCOMMODATION

Central Melbourne Accommodation	D
George Powlett Motel Apartments	C
Georgian Court Guesthouse	G
Hilton on the Park	E
Knightsbridge Apartments	F
The Laird	A
Magnolia Court Boutique Hotel	B
Palm Court B & B	H
Richmond Hill Hotel	I

SMITH ST

YORK ST

West Richmond

HIGHETT ST

Jolimont

WELLINGTON PARADE

GEORGE ST

Citizens Park

RICHMOND

CAFÉS & RESTAURANTS

Fenix	10
The Imperial House	8
Penang Coffee House	15
Richmond Hill Café and Larder	13
Tho Tho	7
Thy Thy 1	9
Tofu Shop International	14
Vlado's	12

Yarra Park

MCG

Richmond Cricket Ground

BRIDGE ROAD

ROWENA PDE

PONT ROAD

ROTHERWOOD ST

LENNOX ST

Richmond

St Ignatius

GIPPS STREET

PUBS & BARS

A Bar Called Barry	6
All Nations Hotel	11
Curry Family Hotel	1
The Glasshouse Hotel	4
Good Morning Captain	2
Ilk	3
The Laird	A
The Peel Dance Bar	5
The Public House	16

SWAN STREET

East Richmond

Burnley

BURNLEY STREET

River Yarra

COLLINGWOOD & RICHMOND

0   100m

space have also added to the mix. In 1892, Australia's most famous sporting institution – the Collingwood Football Club – was founded, and still continues to maintain tenacious support and a high level of club membership.

Collingwood had an iffy, after-dark reputation with outsiders especially in and around **Smith Street**, the main thoroughfare running from Victoria Parade and marking the boundary with Fitzroy. Today the street bulges with bright cafés and restaurants, offering all the caffeine and fusion cuisine you could hope for, plus designer boutiques, health food stores, alternative bookshops and gritty nightclubs. Local colour is a big part of the ambience, and amidst the swathes of untouched and unmodernized nineteenth-century buildings off the main drag you'll find gay-friendly pubs, hole-in-the-wall cafés, and yoga and meditation schools. A few minutes walk east of Smith Street, at 59 Cromwell Street, is the first traditional **Ofuroya** (or **Japanese Bath House**; Tues–Fri noon–9pm, Sat & Sun noon–6pm) in Australia, and further east in St Heliers Street, the **Collingwood Children's Farm** (see p.161) provides bucolic bliss in the form of paddocks, gardens, rustic buildings and animals, tucked away on a bend of the Yarra River.

Just east of Collingwood, Abbotsford was once part of the Collingwood municipality, and is now the location for the **Carlton and United Breweries** (CUB), on the corner of Nelson and Church streets. Guided tours of the brewery (Mon–Fri 10am & 2pm; $15; bookings essential ☎9420 6800, ☻www .fostersgroup.com) present the modern face of brewing, from raw materials through the unique filtration and fermentation process to one of Australia's fastest bottling plants, producing over 1.5 million bottles a day. After working up a thirst, visitors are given a complimentary tasting of the famous CUB draught beers.

Richmond

One of Melbourne's oldest industrial areas, **Richmond** began as a mix of villas, tanneries, wool-washing establishments, brickworks and watering holes. Made a municipality in 1855, the suburb experienced further industrial and residential growth in the 1870s and 1880s but by the turn of the twentieth century, Richmond's gentility had begun its retreat. Waves of postwar immigration to Australia made a huge impact on Richmond, and with the completion of a high-rise housing project in the 1960s, the area attracted large numbers of Italians, Greeks and Vietnamese, signalling full-scale transformation of the suburb. In recent years, nineteenth-century family cottages have been snapped up by new Richmond bohos pursuing retro-chic and CBD proximity, while the development of riverside parkland has led to a widespread "greening" of the suburb. Indeed, there is no better inner-city area to tackle by foot or bike as Richmond has a fantastic network of walking and cycling tracks fringing the riverbank.

Starting at the western city end marked by Punt Road, Richmond falls away from the area known as Richmond Hill to the east, with the Yarra River forming its eastern boundary. **Richmond Hill** is where most of the shops and restaurants are located, and adorning the highest point is the steeple of St Ignatius, a reminder of the area's early Irish Catholic heritage. This is where you'll find the larger, more palatial brick homes – as opposed to the weatherboard workers' cottages down on the flat.

Three main roads traverse Richmond on their way east from the city: Swan Street, Bridge Road and Victoria Street. Swan Street is the most unchanged of Richmond's thoroughfares, still boasting a number of solid and sober old shop facades and verandahs. Relatively speaking, the clock tower of **Dimmey's** – an icon of Melbourne budget shopping since 1853 – marks the centre of the strip, and amid its eclectic and eccentric mix of cut-price clothing and knick-knacks you'll be able to find just about anything. **Swan Street** was once the hub of Melbourne's thriving Greek food scene, and just over Church Street you can still test your tolerance for tzatziki and ouzo at one of the slightly kitsch Greek restaurants. Heading north and parallel to Swan Street, Bridge Road is renowned for its bargain shopping, and many of Australia's finest fashion designers have their factory seconds there. When you're done hunting down jeans, swimwear, trainers, and even surfboards at heavily reduced prices, around the corner at 64 Lennox Street, the *All Nations Hotel* (see p.127) is a popular local, serving some of the best pub grub in town. Further north, **Victoria Street** or "Little Saigon", is the bustling heart of Melbourne's well-established Vietnamese community, a kilometre-long stretch of bargain-priced restaurants, supermarkets, grocery stores, butchers and fishmongers. Traditional soup cafés serving steaming bowls of *pho*, either chicken- or beef-based broth with noodles and veg – are a great place for a delicious, inexpensive lunch.

Richmond is also the homeware and design hub of Melbourne, with switched-on shoppers like Kylie Minogue snapping up European and domestic furniture in the showrooms along Church and Victoria streets, or at the massive branch of furnishing giant IKEA, on the corner of Victoria and Burnley streets.

Nearby, in East Melbourne, French designer and architect Philippe Starck is helping redevelop the former Victoria Brewery site into a retail and residential complex known as **Tribeca East Melbourne**. Modelled on the trendy New York precinct Tribeca, the $240-million redevelopment of the historic site, which is listed with the National Trust, involves restoration of the facade, heritage walls and various buildings within the complex, including the brew towers and the bottling hall. The brewery was opened in 1854, with its distinctive facade designed by architect William Pitt around 1895 and extended by CUB in the early 1900s.

Eastern suburbs

One of the best ways to explore Melbourne's northeast is by **bicycle** (see p.163 for information on bike rental). A bicycle path runs beside the Yarra all the way from the city centre to Eltham, 24km inland. Starting at Southgate it passes through South Yarra and Toorak before reaching Yarra Bend and

Love thy Neighbours

Set in Melbourne's eastern suburbs is Pin Oak Court (aka "Ramsay Street"), former address of Kylie, Jason and co from the successful TV soap **Neighbours** (also alma mater of Hollywood darlings Guy Pierce and Russell Crowe). The interior set is closed, but you can star-spot in the street location and even spot an upcoming episode being filmed. To get there catch a train to Glen Waverley from Flinders Street Station, hop on a bus to Vermont (approx 1hr), and get out at Weeden Drive. There are also several tour companies that will take you onto the set. Ramsay Street Tours (☎9534 4755, $30) go daily to Pin Oak Court and past other locations. Most days you can get great photos of the houses, but on days when the soap is being filmed, no tours or tourists are allowed into the street. If the drive seems too far then there's always Monday nights' "Meet the Neighbours" at the *Elephant and Wheelbarrow* (see p.124) for a chance to play trivia with the stars of today.

Studley parks, with their prime riverside frontage, sandstone escarpments, golf courses, barbecue facilities, boathouses, playing fields, and untouched bushland which is home to many of the flying foxes forced out of the Royal Botanic Gardens (see p.63). From here there are great views of the city skyline and the massive CUB Brewery. Originally the land was occupied by the Aboriginal Wurundjeri, the traditional owners, who used it as a source of fish, eels, freshwater mussels and waterfowl.

After passing Collingwood Children's Farm (see p.161), nestled in the elbow of the river, and then riding under the Johnston Street Bridge, you'll catch a glimpse of Dight's Falls, the remains of Melbourne's first industrial site, a flour mill built by John Dight in 1841. It was also the site for a school set up for Aboriginal boys in 1845, although now closed. Just beyond here is the junction of the Yarra with Merri Creek, now a fordable stream that often became a mighty torrent in times of flood, from where you can continue along the river to Fairfield Boathouse – with its old-fashioned skiffs and well-fed ducks – or take the walking track to Kane's Bridge, which leads back to Studley Park Boathouse. Both places have cafés and rent out boats ($22 per hour).

If you're feeling energetic, you can continue on from Fairfield Boathouse to **Banksia Park**. In the late 1880s and 1890s this area was a magnet for a group of artists known as the **Heidelberg School**, who broke with European landscape conventions and charted a distinctive and more naturalistic depiction of local conditions "that captured something truthful about the Australian landscape…a land that Australians themselves recognised". For more information, contact the Banyule City Council (☎9490 4222) or the Museum of Modern Art at Heide (see below), who can also provide details on the **Heidelberg Artists Trail**, a six-kilometre path of information panels and reproductions located at the sites where Arthur Streeton, Tom Roberts and Frederick McCubbin once set up their easels beside the river.

Museum of Modern Art at Heide

Adjoining Banksia Park, the **Museum of Modern Art at Heide** (Tues–Fri 10am–5pm, Sat & Sun noon–5pm; $8; ☎9850 1500, ⊛www.heide.com.au) is set in bush property at 7 Templestowe Road in Bulleen. Heide was the home of urbane art patrons John and Sunday Reed, who bought this former dairy farm in 1934; it was also where Australia's second major indigenous art movement – Modernism – took off during the 1930s and 1940s. A volatile collection of artists such as Sidney Nolan, Joy Hester, Albert Tucker, Charles Blackman and Arthur Boyd flourished here with support from the Reeds. The iconographic Ned Kelly series, which was to make Sydney Nolan famous, was painted on Heide's dining table. The property has numerous sculptures by international artists such as Bruce Armstrong, Anthony Caro and Anish Kapoor, an exquisite kitchen garden and an airy courtyard café (Tues–Fri 11am–4pm, Sat & Sun 11am–5pm), while the gallery holds a collection of modern Australian art from the 1920s to the 1980s, plus temporary exhibitions of contemporary art. If you're **driving**, Heide is well marked off the Eastern Freeway (take the Bulleen Road turn-off). By public transport, take a Hurstbridge-line train from Flinders Street Station to Heidelberg Station, then bus #291; alternatively, catch bus #200 from Market Street, which will drop you at the front gate.

Montsalvat

Eltham, just east of Heide, cemented its reputation as a crafts centre in 1935 when the painter and architect Justus Jorgensen founded **Montsalvat** (daily

△ Collingwood football team at the MCG

9am–5pm; $6.50; ⓦwww.montsalvat.com.au), a European-style artists' colony complete with rustic buildings, tranquil gardens, galleries and studios. Built with the help of his students and followers, the colony's eclectic design was inspired by medieval European buildings, with wonderfully quirky results. Jorgensen died before it was completed, and it has deliberately been left unfinished, although he did live long enough to oversee the completion of the mud-brick Great Hall, whose influence is evident in other similar buildings around Eltham. Today the colony is still home to assorted painters, potters and craftspeople, while the galleries and grounds are often used for visual and performing arts, exhibitions, and jazz and classical concerts. You can get to Montsalvat by taking a Hurstbridge-line **train** from Flinders Street Station to Eltham Station, from where it's a 2km walk.

St Kilda

When the wealthy merchants and legislators of goldrush-era Melbourne sought refuge from the congested and polluted city, they settled upon a green bayside area 5km to the southeast. Within a decade the beach suburb of **St Kilda** had become the address of choice for Melbourne's moneyed. Then, in 1857, Victoria's second train line – running from the city to St Kilda – was opened, and suddenly the suburb's briny pleasures were accessible to the great unwashed. St Kilda's grandeur went to seed as the wealthy took flight to more exclusive areas like South Yarra and Toorak, while in the 1930s its substantial mansions were demolished or left to become a crumbling sea of dosshouses, apartment blocks, dance halls and tacky amusement arcades.

Epitomizing the boom and bust nature of Melbourne's real estate market, St Kilda underwent rejuvenation and renovation in the early 1990s, which again marked a turnaround in the fortunes of the suburb. At that time, residents finally grasped what fine real estate they had been sitting on, and what kind of fun and fantastic lives they could lead living in St Kilda. Property values have since skyrocketed, new shopping and residential complexes have sprung up, and trendy cafés and bars seem to open daily. For high-income earners and recreation-seekers intent on partying till dawn several nights a week, St Kilda offers the perfect lifestyle. Melbourne's most changeable suburb has also seen a new wave of transients come to the area – Australia's greatest concentration of backpackers, who arrive in their thousands to stay in the suburb's legal and not-so-legal lodges and hostels. While backpackers add a certain frisson to St Kilda, many of those who gave the suburb its raffish character – artists, actors, musicians and eccentrics – have been forced out by rising rents and gentrification.

Even so, there's still plenty to explore. Starting in Fitzroy Street, with its landmark hotels and eateries, it's only a short distance to the Upper **Esplanade** and **foreshore**, favourite places for strolling, chatting, seeing and being seen. Continuing along, you'll come to the tourist precinct of Acland Street, noted for its cake shops and sharp cafés, while beyond St Kilda are the excellent **Jewish Museum of Australia** and **Rippon Lea**, one of Melbourne's grand nineteenth-century estates, and the Jewish enclave of East St Kilda.

Trains no longer run to St Kilda, but the suburb is easily reached by any of three **tram routes**: the quickest routes are trams #96 from Bourke Street in the city to Barkly Street; #15 or #16 from Swanston Street to Barkly Street; or #10 or #12 from Collins Street to the intersection of Park and Fitzroy streets.

The best time to visit St Kilda is in February, when the fabulous **Midsumma Gay Festival** and the **St Kilda Festival** take place; both feature music, outdoor performances, exhibitions, sporting events and dancing.

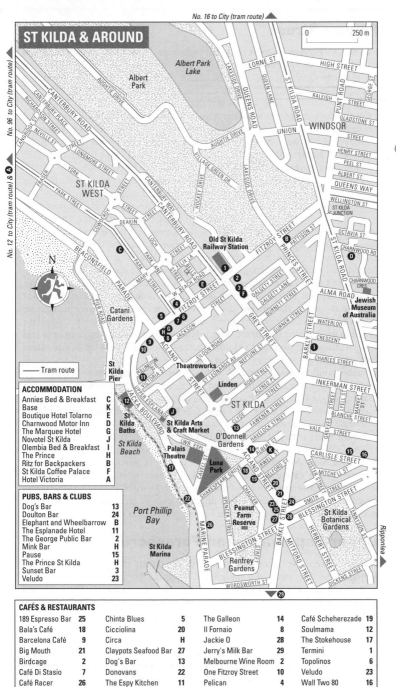

ST KILDA & AROUND

No. 16 to City (tram route)

0   250 m

No. 96 to City (tram route)

No. 12 to City (tram route) & N

Albert Park Lake

Albert Park

ST KILDA WEST

ST KILDA

WINDSOR

Old St Kilda Railway Station

Jewish Museum of Australia

Theatreworks

Linden

St Kilda Arts & Craft Market

O'Donnell Gardens

St Kilda Pier

St Kilda Baths

St Kilda Beach

Palais Theatre

Luna Park

Port Phillip Bay

St Kilda Marina

Peanut Farm Reserve

St Kilda Botanical Gardens

Renfrey Gardens

Catani Gardens

Jacka Boulevard

— Tram route

ACCOMMODATION

Annies Bed & Breakfast	C
Base	K
Boutique Hotel Tolarno	E
Charnwood Motor Inn	D
The Marquee Hotel	G
Novotel St Kilda	J
Olembia Bed & Breakfast	I
The Prince	H
Ritz for Backpackers	B
St Kilda Coffee Palace	F
Hotel Victoria	A

PUBS, BARS & CLUBS

Dog's Bar	13
Doulton Bar	24
Elephant and Wheelbarrow	B
The Esplanade Hotel	11
The George Public Bar	2
Mink Bar	H
Pause	15
The Prince St Kilda	H
Sunset Bar	3
Veludo	23

CAFÉS & RESTAURANTS

189 Espresso Bar	25	Chinta Blues	5	The Galleon	14	Café Scheherazade	19
Bala's Café	18	Cicciolina	20	Il Fornaio	8	Soulmama	12
Barcelona Café	9	Circa	H	Jackie O	28	The Stokehouse	17
Big Mouth	21	Claypots Seafood Bar	27	Jerry's Milk Bar	29	Termini	1
Birdcage	2	Dog's Bar	13	Melbourne Wine Room	2	Topolinos	6
Café Di Stasio	7	Donovans	22	One Fitzroy Street	10	Veludo	23
Café Racer	26	The Espy Kitchen	11	Pelican	4	Wall Two 80	16

7

ST KILDA

Ripponlea

87

Fitzroy Street

For years, **Fitzroy Street** was the focus of St Kilda's often overblown reputation as Melbourne's epicentre of drugs and sleaze. Recently, however, it has gone decidedly upmarket: most of the pawnshops, hamburger joints and adult bookstores have given way to cafés and bars, although **Grey Street** is still home to prostitutes, drug addicts and down-and-outs.

On the corner of Grey and Fitzroy streets, the Venetian-style **George Hotel** has been the barometer of St Kilda's fortunes since the days in the nineteenth century when it was one of Australia's finest hotels. Originally known as the *Terminus*, it was renamed the *George* after the *George Hotel* in Ballarat in 1868, when former governor of the Ballarat gaol, Charles Foster, took it over. By the end of the 1940s, the Depression and two world wars had taken their toll, but despite the chipped crockery and peeling paint, the hotel's permanent residents clung to the genteel rituals of its glory days. The writer Hal Porter, who worked as the hotel's assistant manager in 1949, described it as "the Titanic that missed the iceberg". By the late 1970s, the *George* had become seriously run-down, with syringe-littered floors and the hotel's Seaview Ballroom a venue for Melbourne's punk rock explosion – Melbourne's "Prince of Darkness", Nick Cave, used to regularly sing here – and nightclubs like *Sedition*. In the 1980s, the *George's* front bar was described by hotel inspectors as "the sleaziest, seamiest, seediest and most sordid hotel in Australia", and each night it was hosed out after a day of boozing, brawling and whoring. Eventually, after years of colourful neglect, the hotel was transformed in the early 1990s into a slick wine bar and restaurant, with adjoining bars, restaurants, a cinema and an apartment complex that is home to the glamorous local set of financiers, property tycoons and mega-wealthy residents.

Further south, where Fitzroy Street meets the water, the **Catani Gardens** are a palm-fringed expanse of manicured lawns, which look as if they have come straight out of Hollywood casting. This is where the action shots of the gang from the popular TV show *The Secret Life Of Us* playing soccer were filmed. Mercifully free of development, it's also where many come to escape the showier side of St Kilda with fish 'n' chips and a can or two of VB. Just off Fitzroy Street at 270 Canterbury Road is the former house of television bad boy and former AFL great **Sam Newman**, which bears the face of pneumatic nymph Pamela Anderson. The extraordinary image, taken from Anderson's famous *Playboy* shoot, covers the entire laminated glass facade of the three-level home. Newman, a well-known local womanizer, was once run over by an ex-flame and punched in the face by an irate plumber after he had pinched his girlfriend.

Upper Esplanade and Foreshore

Running from the western end of Fitzroy Street, the palm-lined **Upper Esplanade** is the work of a committee set up in 1906 to provide municipal entertainment that did not offend "good taste or sound morals". The split-level boulevard with its foreshore parkland is still pretty tame, even if the iced lollies and sea baths have been replaced by rollerbladers, *gelatis* and the odd topless bather. By Australian standards, the **beach** is small but beautifully formed, with a sweeping crescent of sand framed by gardens and walkways. Melbourne's busiest beach, the area can also get suffocatingly thick with bodies – after hot summer nights, it's often littered with cans, bottles and cigarette butts left behind by overnight campers or boozing revellers. Despite murky water, the swimming here is okay with not a wave in sight, so it can be a good family beach.

△ Acland Street, St Kilda

Taking pride of place on the Upper Esplanade is the *Esplanade Hotel* (or "Espy"), a famously beer-soaked corner of the city and one of Australia's best-known band venues, with fantastic views overlooking Port Phillip Bay. Each Sunday, the Upper Esplanade hosts the popular **St Kilda Arts and Craft Market** (see p.158), part of the ritual of going to St Kilda that includes taking a look at the beach, feeding your face, ambling into a few shops and listening to the buskers.

Across Jacka Boulevard (the Lower Esplanade), **St Kilda Pier**, built in 1904, is the departure point for boat trips across the bay to Williamstown (Sat, Sun & public holidays hourly from 11.30am to 3.30pm; $11 return; ☎9397 2255). An alternative is a daily ninety-minute penguin-watching cruise (daytime $25, sunrise and sunset cruise $35; bookings necessary ☎9645 0533), with a barbecue lunch or dinner thrown in. On the evening cruises – with a little luck – you'll catch a glimpse of little penguins coming ashore at a certain spot 4km from the mouth of the Yarra. As the exact location is not publicized, you can see them without the crowds that congregate on Phillip Island (see p.172). Until late 2003, St Kilda Pier boasted the first European-style pier pavilion in Australia, but it was burned down just before its centenary. Plans are under way to restore the pier with its legendary kiosk to its former glory by early 2005, though whether the replacement will be a replica of the old or a structure pointing to the future is dependent on the heritage requirements of the pier, the existing infrastructure and the perspectives of the local community.

Near the base of the pier are the **St Kilda Baths**, which date back to 1931. After decades of deterioration, it was decided to redevelop the historic site in the late 1990s. The completed work has renovated the existing building into a curious complex of a seawater pool, restaurants, food shops, and various health facilities like a spa and gym available to the public. It's a heroically bad mix of shopping complex and function centre with a Moorish twist and despite the runaway success of the *Soulmama* restaurant (see p.119), many of the retail spaces remain empty.

Dominating the southern end of the Upper Esplanade, the magnificent Rococo **Palais Theatre** hosts touring bands, while nearby is "Mr Moon", a laughing face whose gaping mouth serves as an entrance to St Kilda's most famous icon: Luna Park. When it opened in 1912, the attractions were circus performers, contortionists and "Big Ben", an enormous twelve-year-old boy who weighed almost 350 pounds. Later, during World War I, Luna Park screened propaganda movies – audiences were encouraged to throw objects at images of the Kaiser. Despite a couple of new attractions, there's still nothing too hi-tech about this amusement park: the Scenic Railway (the world's oldest operating roller-coaster) runs along wooden trestles, the dodgem cars could do with a lick of paint and the Ghost Train wouldn't spook a toddler, but that's half the fun. Rides are reasonably priced, ensuring **Luna Park** (Fri 7–11pm, Sat 11am–11pm, Sun 11am–6pm; admission free, rides $6.50, unlimited rides $29.95; ☎1300 888 272, ⊛www.lunapark.com.au) is still *the* place for local children's birthday bashes.

Acland Street and around

St Kilda has long had a strong Jewish presence. Following World War II, Central European Jews introduced **Acland Street** to *kugelhöpfs*, Wiener schnitzels and early-morning get-togethers, while Eastern European Jews have added their mark since the collapse of the former Soviet Union, particularly in the section of Carlisle Street east of St Kilda Road (see p.92). The leafy northern end of

Acland Street is predominantly residential, although there are a few cafés and bars. At no. 26, occupying a National Trust-listed mansion, **Linden** (Tues–Sun 1–6pm; free; ☎9209 6560, ⦿www.lindenarts.org) is probably the best community gallery in Australia as it offers a studio to new artists and displays the newest contemporary paintings, installations and video art all year round.

Once noted for its Jewishness and family-run restaurants, the southern end of Acland Street is now a melange of gift stores, bookshops, cafés, fast-food franchises, bars, florists, and continental cake shops. A single Jewish restaurant remains, the once legendary *Scheherazade* (see p.119), though several other good cake shops and eateries are worth checking out. Now a "tourist precinct", the main strip's widened footpaths can become busy at weekends with visitors staring at the strange assortment of buskers.

To escape the throng, head for the **St Kilda Botanical Gardens** – across Barkly Street and up nearby Blessington Street (sunrise–sunset; free) – which include a huge rose garden, an indigenous plant section, a duck pond and a conservatory.

Around St Kilda

As St Kilda has grown, rents in the area have swelled, pushing many of the original Jewish families into the surrounding suburbs. As St Kilda remains a popular address, real-estate agents have craftily invented **East St Kilda** (also called **Balaclava** by those who don't have property there). Still distinctively Jewish (some wryly refer to it as the "Bagel Belt"), Saturdays see residents dressed in their best buzzing along to worship and the area boasts the interesting **Jewish Museum of Australia**. A few kilometres away, the nineteenth-century house **Rippon Lea** makes for a relaxing break from the city, While further south around the bay lies pleasant **Brighton Beach**, with its colourful beach huts and great views back across the bay to the city centre.

The Jewish Museum

The best place to find out more about the Australian-Jewish experience is the rewarding **Jewish Museum of Australia** at 26 Alma Road (Tues–Thurs 10am–4pm, Sun 11am–5pm; $7; ⦿www.jewishmuseum.com.au). Opened in 1995, exhibitions display thousands of pieces of Judaica with four permanent exhibitions: the Australian Jewish History Gallery, documenting Jewish life in Australia since colonization 200 years ago; the Timeline of Jewish History, tracing the last four thousand years; and Jewish Year and Belief and Ritual, both dedicated to the culture of Judaism, with a focus on festivals and customs. Temporary exhibitions on a wide range of related topics are another feature of the museum.

East St Kilda

Up-and-coming **East St Kilda** (long-time locals know the area better as "the ghetto", in honour of the sizeable population of pre- and post-war Jewish émigrés) is a grungier alternative to its shiny neighbour, St Kilda. East St Kilda's appeal owes much to the immigrants – mostly from the Ukraine, Poland and Russia – who arrived here decades ago. Their presence can be immediately seen in the low-rise skyline of worker's cottages or Art Deco flats, dominated by synagogues and Jewish schools. In recent years, another wave of refugees have moved in: bohemians and hipsters fleeing the rocketing rents and the yuppification of St Kilda and Prahran further to the north. On **Carlisle Street**, the main thoroughfare, instead of trendy chains there are authentic European butchers, Asian grocers, $2 stores, the popular hole-in-the wall *Wall Two 80* café (see p.120), and funky but low-key clothing boutiques and eateries such as Hudson (see p.155) and *Pause* (see p.127).

On the corner of Carlisle Street and Nepean Highway, the restored **St Kilda Town Hall** (1890) was renovated in the 1960s to include a scaled down replica of architect Alvar Aalto's scalloped Finlandia Hall in Helsinki, while facing here, the **St Kilda Public Library** is the suburb's popular community hub, featuring an extension in the shape of an open book. The area's only parkland is the pleasant **Alma Park** on Alma Road, while the sprawling **St Kilda cemetery** further east on the same road serves as the final resting place of Australia's second prime minister, Alfred Deakin and Albert Jacka, the popular former mayor of St Kilda. To get to East St Kilda, take a Sandringham-line **train** from Flinders Street Station in the city and get off at Balaclava Station.

Rippon Lea

Rippon Lea, at 192 Hotham St in **Elsternwick** (Tues–Sun 10am–5pm; $11 full tour, $6 gardens only; tours on the half-hour from 10.30am, and estate tours daily at 2pm), is several kilometres southeast of St Kilda. Work on this nineteenth-century Romanesque mansion and its "pleasure gardens" was begun by Frederick Sargood, who made his fortune during the goldrush. The 33-room mansion has magnificent grounds complete with ornamental lake and fernery, and an over-the-top interior that combines opulent Victoriana with cod silent-era Hollywood style. The grounds are also popular for picnics at weekends. To get here, take a Sandringham-line **train** from Flinders Street Station in the city and get off at nearby Rippon Lea Station, or catch tram #67 from Swanston Street to stop no. 42.

Williamstown

Until the Yarra was widened in the 1880s to allow for the upgrading of Melbourne's port facilities, **Williamstown** was Port Phillip Bay's major seaport. Established in 1835, it saw scores of vessels unloading convicts, gold-diggers and farmers bound for the open plains of central Victoria. But as Melbourne's port facilities improved, Williamstown's maritime significance waned. Eventually, a band of industrial suburbs to the west of the centre isolated Williamstown from the city and the small seaside settlement withdrew into itself.

Then, with the opening of the Westgate Bridge near the mouth of the Yarra in 1978, "Willy" became more accessible, and its charms were rediscovered. At weekends it's every bit as frantic as St Kilda or Southgate, yet on weekdays it could be just another quiet country town. Most visitors beat a path to **Nelson Place**, Williamstown's historic precinct, ringed by stately bluestone buildings, cafés, pubs and galleries. From here it's a short stroll to the picturesque waterfront park of **Commonwealth Reserve** and **Gem Pier**, while further east, **Port Gellibrand** is where convicts from Britain were shipped ashore. There are also three small but excellent rail and maritime museums and some popular beaches. In the adjacent suburb of Spotswood, the **Scienceworks** deserves a visit for its fascinating array of interactive displays and exhibits and the hi-tech planetarium.

As the crow flies, Williamstown is only 5km southwest of the city. The easiest way to get there is to catch a Williamstown **train** from Flinders Street Station to the end of the line, from where it's a short walk along Ann Street to Nelson Place, the suburb's busy hub. By **boat**, Williamstown is connected to St Kilda Pier by the Williamstown Bay & River Cruises' *John Batman* ferry (see p.90), and to Southgate by the same company's *Williamstown Seeker* (see p.57).

If you're feeling energetic, you could always **cycle** to Williamstown: a bicycle path runs along the St Kilda foreshore to Port Melbourne and Eastbridge Park (under the Westgate Bridge), from where you can catch a punt (Mon & Fri–Sun; $3.50 one-way, $6 return) across the mouth of the Yarra to join up with the track, which then winds through Riverside Park and on to Williamstown, a total of around 10km each way. Once you're in Williamstown, the local council runs a free **bus** service in summer each Sunday between 11am and 7pm (☏9397 3791). The service, which operates every 15mins, is signposted at six park-and-ride stops around Williamstown – simply hail the bus as it approaches.

Around Nelson place

Ferries berth at **Gem Pier** and, as they pull in, you'd almost think you were coming ashore at a naval shipyard. The *HMAS Castlemaine*, a decommissioned World War II minesweeper, is permanently docked at the pier, and now houses

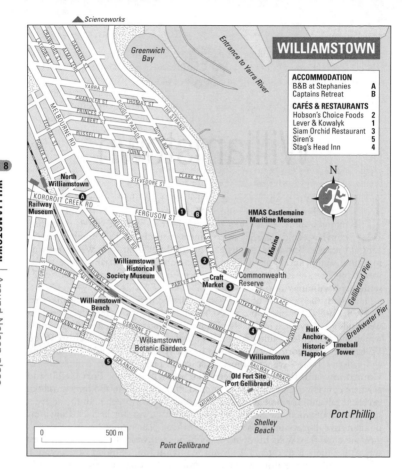

an interesting **maritime museum** (Sat & Sun noon–5pm; $5). Also here, the tall ship *Enterprize* runs a variety of cruises around the bay during the week and at weekends (prices range from $17.50 for 1hr trip to $390 for a weekend sail; for more information contact ☎9397 3477, ⓦwww.enterprize.com.au).

Next to Gem Pier, the small park of **Commonwealth Reserve** affords panoramic views of Melbourne's city skyline and houses a tourist office (Mon–Fri 10am–4pm, Sat & Sun 10am–5pm; ☎9397 3791), bandstand, tide-gauge house and a water fountain donated by one Reverend John Wilkinson to deter sailors from hitting the grog. Across the park is displayed an anchor from the nineteenth-century British warship *HMVS Nelson*, the first vessel to enter the nearby dockyards. On the third Sunday of each month, the popular **Williamstown Craft Market** is held in the reserve (7am–4pm). The section of **Nelson Place** opposite is lined with cafés, restaurants, ice-cream parlours and one of the highest concentrations of pubs anywhere in the southern hemisphere (hence the Reverend Wilkinson's water fountain).

Point Gellibrand

A twenty-minute walk along Nelson Place past the piers, dockyards and storage tanks brings you to **Point Gellibrand**, named after Joseph Tice Gellibrand, a member of Batman's original scouting party. Plans are afoot to turn a large chunk of this area into a historical park – a move applauded by locals, who are increasingly concerned that Willy is being imperilled by unrestrained development. Nearby, a copper ball in the convict-built **Timeball Tower** is lowered each day at 1pm – a time-check by which shipmasters used to calibrate their chronometers before taking to sea. Further southwest of the tower are the remains of **Fort Gellibrand**, a former defence battery that saw plenty of mock battles but never fired a shot in anger. Just behind the fort, and below an old railway embankment, mutineering convicts stoned the Inspector-General of Penal Establishments, John Price, to death in 1857. As there was no local morgue, Price was taken to the *Prince of Wales* hotel, on the corner of Nelson Place and Kanowna Street, where his body was laid out. Today the *Prince of Wales* is known as the **Titanic** and lives on as a reconditioned pub that re-enacts the sinking of the famous ocean-liner, offering dinner and the excitingly realistic re-enactments of Steerage Passage ($58) or First Class ($79) every Saturday (☏9397 5101, ⊛www.titanic.com.au).

In the nineteenth century, convicts were carried by barge ashore from prison hulks moored at sea and employed in chain gangs on public works, including the building of **Breakwater Pier** on the southeastern tip from bluestone extracted from quarries on Point Gellibrand. For a time, Ned Kelly (see p.42) languished in a yellow-daubed prison hulk anchored offshore – they were painted yellow to distinguish them from other vessels. The site where Price was brutally murdered, as well as work done by the convicts, can be seen on an excellent **tour** of the area (for bookings contact Williamstown Tours ☏9391 2011; $5.50).

Around the point and beyond the cricket ground, **Williamstown Beach** is one of Melbourne's best bayside swimming spots, while the lush botanical gardens, just back from the beach, are a good spot for a picnic. Following Giffard Street along the eastern side of the Botanical Gardens as far as Electra Street to no. 5 brings you to the small **Williamstown Historical Society Museum** (Sun 2–5pm; $3), a repository for a fine collection of maritime displays and some interesting artefacts from the suburb's early and somewhat grim development, including antique furnishings, detailed models of ships, convict leg irons and paintings of Price's murder. Williamstown's other museum is trainspotter heaven: the **Railway Museum** (Sat & Sun noon–5pm; $5.50) on Champion Road, which has an impressive collection of beautifully restored steam and diesel engines. The museum is next to North Williamstown Station, the second-to-last stop on the Williamstown line.

Scienceworks

In the neighbouring suburb of Spotswood, **Scienceworks**, at 2 Booker St (daily 10am–4.30pm; $6, or $12.30 for combined Scienceworks and Planetarium ticket; ☏9392 4800, ⊛scienceworks.museum.vic.gov.au), is an excellent hands-on science and technology museum. Inside the space-age building, set in a desolate wasteland, the tactile displays, exhibits and touring shows on themes such as *Star Trek* are ingenious, fun and highly interactive. Permanent highlights include Stayin' Alive, explaining how the human body can survive in extreme conditions, and Sports Works, which lets you work out how sporty or otherwise your body is.

Part of the exhibition consists of the original Spotswood Pumping Station, an unusually attractive industrial complex with working steam pumps. Protected by the National Trust, the station and its pumps helped nineteenth-century Melbourne get rid of its severe stench (satirists of the day called the city "Marvellous Smellbourne"). There's also a state-of-the-art **Planetarium** (Mon–Fri 2pm, Sat & Sun noon, 1pm, 2pm & 3pm, Thurs 8pm; bookings on ☏9392 4819), which uses the latest digital technology – Digistar II, a super computer and projection system – to re-create the night sky on the domed ceiling. You can recline in comfy chairs and listen to a narration by Leonard Nimoy (*Star Trek*'s Mr Spock) as he takes you on a simulated 3D journey through space and time. To get to Scienceworks, take a Williamstown- or Werribee-line train from Flinders Street Station to Spotswood Station, where it's a 10min walk. If you're cycling from the city, Scienceworks is just off the bicycle route west of Riverside Park.

Listings

Listings

Accommodation

Melbourne has a range of accommodation options, from multi-bed hostels, motel chains and cosy bed and breakfast establishments to luxury hotels and serviced apartments that allow you to spread out in style and comfort. The only time you're likely to have problems **finding a room** is during major sporting events such as the Grand Prix or the AFL Grand Final (see "Festivals and events", when rooms are often booked out a long time in advance – it's best at these times to reserve a couple of months ahead. Hostels, particularly those in the CBD and St Kilda, also fill up quickly from December to March, although student residences such as Carlton College (see p.103) are often an excellent alternative, just when cheap accommodation is at a premium. Again, plan on making a reservation, preferably not less than a week in advance.

If you fly in without a reservation, head for the **travellers information service desks** (daily 5am to last flight) at Melbourne Airport. Located on the ground and first floors of the international terminal, they provide a free booking service for all types of accommodation throught the city and suburbs. You can also use the interactive accommodation board near the information service desk on the ground floor. Bookings can be made downtown at the **Melbourne Visitor Information Centre** (daily 9am–6pm) in Federation Square on the corner of Swanston and Flinders streets. Again, there's no booking fee. Gay and lesbian visitors are unlikely to experience more than a sideways look booking into hotels in Melbourne, but for only **gay and lesbian accommodation**, see p.134.

When deciding which **area** to stay in, your basic choice is between the CBD, adjacent inner-city suburbs, and St Kilda. The **city centre** (particularly Collins

---

Accommodation prices

All accommodation listed in this book has been categorized according to the following price codes, which represent the **cheapest rate for a double** or twin room available (excluding special offers). Note that all accommodation is GST inclusive, and that rates generally increase during major sporting and cultural events, summer months (Dec–March) and peak holiday periods such as Christmas and Easter. For **hostels** providing dormitory accommodation, the code represents the per-person charge for a bed.

❶ under $25	❻ $100–130
❷ $25–40	❼ $130–160
❸ $40–55	❽ $160–200
❹ $55–80	❾ over $200
❺ $80–100	

Street) and the leisure precincts of Southgate and the Crown Casino are the domain of upmarket hotels, while a number of mid-range joints cluster around Spencer Street Station, although unfortunately the area is rather noisy and unattractive. For cheaper rooms, there's plenty of backpacker accommodation, especially along Elizabeth and King streets. **Inner-city suburbs** such as North and East Melbourne, Carlton, Richmond, South Yarra and South Melbourne offer good alternatives to the CBD in all price ranges, while seaside **St Kilda** ("backpacker central") has perhaps the best-value accommodation in Melbourne, with hostels by the bucketload and plenty of inexpensive hotels, lodges and motels.

For last-minute, **discounted accommodation** you can book through Ⓦwww.wotif.com. For places to stay outside Melbourne, check out Ⓦwww .greatplacestostay.com.au, where you can search for B&Bs, self-contained cottages and boutique hotels, get regional profiles and learn about upcoming events.

Our listings are grouped by **area**, subdivided into **type of accommodation** (hotels and motels, B&Bs, and hostels). The majority are easily accessible by tram, train or bus.

City Centre

We have divided the city centre up into three areas – for accommodation in the Eastside, see map p.34, for that in the Westside see map p.46 and for the Riverside District see map p.56.

Hotels and motels

Adelphi Hotel 187 Flinders Lane ☏9650 7555, Ⓦ www.adelphi.com.au. Boutique hotel *par excellence*, the 34-room Adelphi has slick service and an even slicker design. The ultra-modern, minimalist interior extends to the large rooms and bars, and is topped off with exquisite contemporary art and photography. Rounding out the experience are a sauna, a tiny fitness centre and, most strikingly, a glass-bottomed rooftop pool suspended above the street. In the same building is the superb *ezard at adelphi* restaurant (see p.109). ❾

Astoria City Travel Inn 288 Spencer St ☏9670 6801, Ⓦ www.astoriainternational.com. Pleasant motel three blocks north of Spencer Street Station, conveniently located on the City Circle tram route. Units are spacious and bright, and amenities include free videos, swimming pool and laundry (at a nominal charge). ❺

City Centre Private Hotel 22 Little Collins St ☏9654 5401, ℉9650 7256. Good position on a quiet street, 100m from Parliament station. Inexpensive doubles, singles and a few, mainly single-sex, four-bed dorms, all sharing bathrooms. Most rooms have fridges; other facilities include heating, basic kitchens, a TV lounge, laundry and car parking. Dorms, ❶ rooms. ❸

City Limits Motel 20 Little Bourke St ☏9662 2544, ☏1800 808 651, Ⓦwww .citylimits.com.au. Motel-style units with en-suite bathrooms and the usual mod cons, just around the corner from Parliament station. Rates include breakfast on the first morning. ❼

Crown Towers Hotel Level 2, Crown Casino, 8 Whiteman St, Southbank ☏9292 6868, ☏1800 811 653, Ⓦwww.crowntowers.com.au. This luxurious five-star hotel in Australia's largest casino is far and away the most opulent place to stay in Melbourne. Combining a central location with spacious and beautifully appointed rooms, it's the ideal destination for high-rollers and cashed-up travellers, although the glitzy tat surrounding the hotel is a real downer. ❾

Hotel Enterprize 44 Spencer St ☏9629 6991, Ⓦwww.hotelenterprize.com.au. Opposite Spencer Street Station, this solid, no-frills hotel has reasonably well-appointed en-suite rooms and a good restaurant downstairs. Room service and cover parking available. ❺

Explorers Inn Melbourne 16 Spencer St ☏9621 3333, ☏1800 816 168, Ⓦwww .explorersinn.com.au. Close to the Melbourne

Exhibition Centre and popular with cost-cutting business types and budget-minded travellers. Pleasant and well maintained, it offers en-suite rooms, bar, restaurant and other facilities, plus there's loads of tourist information and friendly, unstuffy staff. ❻

Grand Hyatt 123 Collins St ☏9657 1234, ⓦwww.melbourne.grand.hyatt.com. This over-the-top hotel has 547 rooms, 18 executive suites and a lobby big enough to land a plane in. If you're really flush, you can upgrade to the hotel's "Regency Club", where there's a butler on call and free breakfast and drinks. ❾

Kingsgate Hotel 131 King St ☏9629 4171, ☏1300 734 171, ⓦwww.kingsgatehotel.com.au. Huge, renovated old private hotel. En-suite rooms with colour TV, heating, air-con and telephone are good value; there are also inexpensive basic rooms with shared facilities, a few rooms for small groups or families (up to four beds), a laundry and a pleasant TV lounge, but no kitchen facilities. Bar, restaurant and café on premises. Cheap breakfast. ❹–❺

Le Meridien at Rialto 495 Collins St ☏9620 9111, ⓦwww.lemeridien.com. According to the brochure this hotel is "the soul of Europe in the heart of Melbourne", and once inside you'll see why. Behind an Italian Gothic facade and beneath the vertiginous Rialto Towers are 244 rooms stacked with romantic French furnishings and decor, while the hotel's eateries have excellent diverse food prepared by some of Melbourne's finest chefs. ❾

Hotel Lindrum 26 Flinders St ☏9668 1111, ⓦwww.hotellindrum.com.au. Named after the legendary Australian billiards player Walter Lindrum, this intimate five-storey boutique hotel has large comfy chairs, an open fireplace and books, and instead of a formal reception you register at the front bar. Apart from a billiard table and lots of Lindrum memorabilia, you'll find a back bar with a selection of wines and cigars, the classy Felt restaurant and rooms complete with huge beds, a fax, CD player and complimentary in-house movies. ❾

Miami Motor Inn 13 Hawke St ☏9321 2444, ☏1800 132 333, ⓦwww.themiami.com.au. A variety of rooms are on offer here – some en suite with TV and fan, some more simple with shared facilities. Good-value rates, TV lounge, pool table, laundry, free off-street parking but no kitchen. ❹–❻

Park Hyatt Melbourne 1 Parliament Square, off Parliament Place ☏9224 1234, ⓦwww.melbourne.park.hyatt.com. This opulent bunker for business travellers and Melbourne's junior moguls has deluxe rooms and suites with lush trimmings, such as open fireplaces and spa baths with TV. The service, naturally, is first class. ❾

Royce on St Kilda Road 379 St Kilda Rd ☏9677 9900, ☏1800 820 909, ⓦwww.roycehotels.com.au. This luxury, heritage-listed boutique establishment is usefully positioned within walking distance of the CBD, Royal Botanic Gardens, Shrine of Remembrance and Arts Centre. There's a variety of room types available, from mezzanines with a ground-level lounge, to deluxe spa rooms and rooms with balconies. All have the usual trimmings, plus data-port connections and ISDN availability. ❾

Sheraton Towers Southgate 1 Southgate Ave ☏8696 8888, Ⓕ9690 6581. Large, reasonable rooms, but the real attraction of this hotel is its height, affording great views over Southgate, the Yarra and the city centre. Includes a good fitness centre, while the elegant *Tisane Lounge* serves high tea (daily 2.30–5pm) and posh cocktails at night. ❾

Hotel Sofitel 25 Collins St ☏9653 0000, ⓦwww.sofitelmelbourne.com.au. I.M. Pei-designed hotel with marvellous views across Melbourne and surrounds. Gloriously comfortable rooms, which begin on the 36th floor, as well as a good spread of cafés and restaurants, including the airy and reasonably cheap *Café La* and *Le Restaurant* (see p.110). ❾

Stork Hotel 504 Elizabeth St ☏9663 6237, ⓦwww.storkhotel.com. Small goldrush-era hotel with simple but pleasant rooms and shared facilities. Central location opposite Queen Victoria Market. ❹

Victoria Hotel 215 Little Collins St ☏9653 0441, ☏1800 331 147, ⓦwww.victoriahotel.com.au. Huge, old refurbished hotel in an unbeatable central location, with its own café and bar; all rooms – with or without their own bathrooms – have telephones, heating and tea- and coffee-making facilities. Covered parking available ($6 per day). ❹

Westin Hotel 205 Collins St ☏9635 2222, ⓦwww.westin.com.au. Right on City Square, the hideous exterior of this monstrous 262-room hotel hides surprisingly glamorous interiors and rooms notable for their understated elegance. ❾

Windsor Hotel 103 Spring St ☎9633 6000,
☎1800 033 100, ⓦwww.thewindsor.com.au.
Built in 1883 opposite Parliament House,
this grand colonial pile has played host
to Sir Laurence Olivier, Vivien Leigh and
Muhammad Ali, as well as legions of
silverhairs who can't seem to keep away.
The prestigious suites are pure nineteenth-
century opulence. Service is excellent, and
don't leave without taking afternoon tea at
the hotel's *111 Spring Street* restaurant. ❾

Hostels

All Nations Backpackers Hostel & Bar
2 Spencer St ☎9620 1022, ⓦwww.allnations
.com.au. Friendly no-frills place primarily
catering to working backpackers, with bar,
in-house travel bureau and clean rooms.
Regular events include pool competitions,
games and soccer friendlies in the park
across the road. Dorms,❶ rooms. ❷
Hotel Bakpak 167 Franklin St ☎9329 7525,
☎1800 645 200, ⓦwww.bakpak.com.
Happening place with lots of activity
and information. Hundreds of beds in a
converted former school building brightened
up with colour-coordinated paintwork,
carpets and polished timber. Standard,
sometimes grubby facilities plus in-house
employment agency, travel shop, small
gym, basement bar, cable TV, Internet café,
cinema and a rooftop terrace with a tiny
pool and great views of the city. Dorms
with four to twelve beds (single-sex dorms
available on request), fans and lockers;
doubles are spartan. Dorms, ❶ doubles. ❹
The Carlton Hotel 197 Bourke St ☎9650 2734,
ⓦwww.carltonhotel.com.au. Reasonable
accommodation, given the price: non-dorm
rooms have TVs and bar-fridges. All have
shared toilets and showers. Also known as
Backpackers City Inn. Dorms, ❶ rooms. ❸
Elizabeth Backpackers 490 Elizabeth St
☎9663 1685, ⓦwww.elizabethhostel.com
.au. Centrally located above a pub, with
Internet, laundry, cable TV and large
kitchens. Provides a free pick-up service
from the airport. Dorms, ❶ doubles. ❸
Exford Hotel 199 Russell St ☎9663 2697,
ⓦwww.exfordhotel.com.au. In an extremely
central position above a refurbished pub,
this hostel is secure and clean, with friendly
and helpful staff. Usual amenities, plus
a tiny sundeck with barbecue. Two- to
four-bed dorms (separate for women on

request); twins and doubles are good value.
Dorms, ❶ rooms. ❹
Flinders Station Hotel & Backpackers 35 Elizabeth St ☎9620 5100, ⓦwww
.flindersbackpackers.com.au. Central hostel in
a former office block a few hundred metres
from Flinders Street Station. Basic twins
and doubles, and two en-suite doubles
for wheelchair users. Dorms have lockers
and four or ten beds (single-sex dorms on
request), and there are also TV, Internet and
reading rooms. Dorms, ❶ rooms. ❹
Friendly Backpacker 197 King St ☎9670 1111,
☎1800 671 115, ⓦwww.friendlygroup.com.au.
This hostel in a refurbished office building
lives up to its name and is also clean
and secure. Dorms are bright, offer air-
con and heating and are mainly four-bed
(some women-only); each floor has a cosy
sitting area with TV. Doubles available.
Good kitchen and common room in the
basement; rates include free breakfast and
Internet. Dorms, ❶ doubles. ❺
The Greenhouse Backpacker 228 Flinders Lane
☎9639 6400, ⓦwww.friendlygroup.com.au.
Superb location amidst the alleys of
Melbourne's CBD. Clean singles, doubles
and dorms, plus a range of free services
from pick-ups and employment assistance
to luggage storage, and as much tea and
coffee as you can drink. Rates include
free breakfast and Internet. Operated by
the same people who run *The Friendly
Backpacker*. Dorms, ❷ rooms. ❹
The Melbourne Connection 205 King St ☎9642
4464, ⓦwww.melbourneconnection.com.
Convenient though hard-to-find location
(look for the small sign) close to Spencer
Street Station and Queen Victoria Market.
Rooms and dorms are clean; facilities
include laundry, kitchen and lounge with
satellite TV. Dorms, ❶ doubles. ❹
Queensberry Hill YHA 78 Howard St
☎9329 8599, ⓦwww.yha.com.au. Excellent
value, purpose-built hostel with dorms (4–8
beds), single, double and family rooms, plus
apartment-style accommodation. Facilities
include a cafeteria, a huge, well-equipped
kitchen and free use of bicycles. It's a
10min walk from the Melbourne Transit
Centre, or the Skybus will drop you off on
request. Dorms, ❶ rooms. ❹
Toad Hall Guesthouse 441 Elizabeth St
☎9600 9010, ⓦwww.toadhall-hotel.com.au.
Historic Victorian building close to the
Melbourne Transit Centre providing cosy,

secure rooms and dorms with shared bathrooms and clean facilities. Parking available. Dorms, ❶ rooms. ❹
Victoria Hall 380 Russell St ☎9662 3888, ℉9639 0101. International student accommodation that accepts budget travellers when rooms (no dorms) are available – usually end of November to end of February. Top value, especially for single rooms, and great location near the Old Melbourne Gaol and Lygon Street. Breakfast and cheap dinner available on request. Book in advance. ❹
The Hotel Y 489 Elizabeth St ☎9329 5188, or central YWCA reservations free call ☎1800 468 359, ⓦwww.hotely.com.au. All en-suite rooms with fridge, telephone, TV and air-conditioning. Also has a small kitchen, laundry, a sinfully cheap but excellent licensed café, covered parking and a swimming pool. Near the Melbourne Transit Centre and Queen Victoria Market. Dorm, ❶ rooms. ❻

Carlton, Fitzroy and North Melbourne

Accommodation is marked on the maps on p.69, p.70 and p.74.

Hotels and motels

Downtowner on Lygon 66 Lygon St, Carlton ☎9663 5555, ☎1800 800 130, ⓦwww .downtowner.com.au. Attractively refurbished en-suite rooms, some with spas, plus a restaurant and covered parking. ❼
Lygon Lodge 220 Lygon St, Carlton ☎9663 6633, ☎1800 337 099, ⓦwww.lygonlodge.com. au. Good drive-in motel in a terrific location. Rooms are clean and attractive, and some have small kitchenettes. ❻

Hostels

Carlton College 101 Drummond St, Carlton ☎9664 0664, ☎1800 066 551, ⓦwww.carltoncollege.com.au. Student accommodation in Italianate terraces that turns into a backpackers' hostel from mid-December to mid-February. The small dorms, singles, twins and doubles are simple but good. Plenty of communal facilities like a games room, TV lounge, laundry and a kitchen/breakfast area. Rate includes breakfast. Dorms, ❶ rooms. ❸
Chapman Gardens YHA 76 Chapman St, North Melbourne ☎9328 3595, ⓦwww.yha.com.au.

More intimate than its sister hostel, the *Queensberry Hill YHA*, but further away from the city centre (3km), this hostel has mainly twin-share rooms with a few singles, plus self-catering kitchen, free car parking, free bike rental and personal lockers. Leafy setting and very friendly atmosphere. Dorms, ❶ rooms. ❹
Global Backpackers Hostel 238 Victoria St, North Melbourne ☎9328 3728, ℉9329 8966. Small, basic hostel with dorms and shared facilities, opposite Queen Victoria Market – preferably for people who don't mind loud music as *The Public Bar* next door features live indie and heavy-metal bands. Dorms, ❶ rooms. ❷
The Nunnery 116 Nicholson St, Fitzroy ☎9419 8637, ☎1800 032 635, ⓦwww .bakpak.com. This attractive guesthouse, in a former convent, is Fitzroy's only budget accommodation option. A small courtyard and a tiny rooftop are the only outdoor sitting areas, and the dorms are rather cramped, but the atmosphere is friendly if a little disorganized. There's also a big, cosy TV lounge, Internet facilities and a kitchen. Dorms, ❶–❷ rooms. ❺

East Melbourne and Richmond

For location of the following, please see map p.80.

Hotels and motels

George Powlett Motel Apartments Cnr Powlett and George streets, East Melbourne ☎9419 9488, ☎1800 689 948, ⓦwww.georgepowlett .com.au. Motel-style units off two central courtyards. All mod cons, including parking, in an excellent location. ❻

Hilton on the Park 192 Wellington Parade, East Melbourne ☎9419 2000, ☎1800 222 255, ⓦwww.hilton.com. Opposite the MCG, and popular with football and cricketing enthusiasts, the facilities here include the Hepburn Day spa, sauna, pool and second telephone lines that allow you to use the Internet. ❸–❾

Knightsbridge Apartments 101 George St, East Melbourne ☎9419 1333, ⓦwww .knightsbridgeapartments.com.au. Bright, self-catering studio apartments 1km from the centre, on a quiet street off the east side of Fitzroy Gardens. Laundry and off-street parking. Excellent value. ❼

Magnolia Court Boutique Hotel 101 Powlett St, East Melbourne ☎9419 4222, ⓦwww.magnolia -court.com.au. Elegant, small hotel in a quiet residential street, a hop, skip and jump from Fitzroy Gardens, the city, MCG and the Rod Laver Arena in Melbourne Park. Tastefully furnished range of rooms in two older, lovingly restored buildings and a newish motel section. Excellent breakfasts available in an airy room overlooking a courtyard garden. ❼

B&B

Georgian Court Guesthouse 21–25 George St, East Melbourne ☎9419 6353, ⓦwww

.georgiancourt.com.au. Cosy B&B with a mix of standard rooms sharing facilities, and en-suite rooms equipped with TV, fridge and radio; all bright, tastefully furnished and serviced daily. Rates include breakfast. Quiet, but central to the CBD, MCG and Richmond. ❺

Hostels

Central Melbourne Accommodation 21 Bromham Place, Richmond ☎9427 9826, ⓦwww.centralaccommodation.net. Small place, with four- and six-bed dorms (one women-only) plus a few single and double rooms, located close to the main drags of Church Street and Bridge Road. Owners have good employment contacts in the area. Dorms, ❶ doubles. ❹

Richmond Hill Hotel 353 Church St, Richmond ☎9428 6501, ☎1800 801 618, ⓦwww .richmondhillhotel.com.au. Clean and well-run ex-YWCA in a refurbished old mansion with cosy sitting rooms, large shared kitchen, courtyard and off-street parking. Accommodation consists of dorms (some women-only), and many pleasant private rooms, as well as some apartments; non-dorm rooms include continental breakfast ($8 otherwise). Dorms, ❶ rooms. ❺

South Yarra, Prahran, Toorak and Windsor

Find this accommodation on the map on p.77.

Hotels and motels

The Como Melbourne 630 Chapel St, South Yarra ☎9825 2222, ☎1800 033 400, ⓦwww .mirvachotels.com.au. Ultra-stylish hotel that often plays host to visiting celebs. Rooms are generously spacious, with some facing onto Japanese gardens, and feature the usual facilities, plus CD players and gigantic bathtubs that come with a complimentary companion – the hotel's signature rubber duck. *The Como's* elegant *So Bar* (see p.126) is also a great place for a drink. Special offers abound, such as bike and scooter rentals. ❾

The Hatton Hotel 65 Park St, South Yarra ☎9868 4800, ⓦwww.hatton.com.au. Modern boutique hotel, with each room immaculately and stylishly arranged, within walking distance of the Botanic Gardens. ❽

The Lyall Hotel 14 Murphy St, South Yarra ☎9868 8222, ☎1800 338 234, ⓦwww.thelyall .com. Luxury lifestyle bolthole that *Condé Nast Traveller* included in its fifty coolest new hotels in the world. Has a surprisingly relaxed feel and the suites, which are stylishly fitted out in a contemporary Oriental style, come with all one could ever need and more, including gourmet minibars, steam-free mirrors and velour robes. When you wish to emerge from your room, indulge in a spa treatment, perch at the *Champagne Bar*, or get yourself fitter at the fully equipped gym. ❾

B&Bs

Tilba Hotel 30 Toorak Rd, South Yarra ☎9867 8844, ⓦwww.thetilba.com.au. Small B&B in a sumptuous nineteenth-century mansion. Features include a grand staircase, a conservatory housing a giant wooden birdcage, and plenty of antique furnishings. ❼

Toorak Manor Boutique Hotel 220 Williams Rd, Toorak ☎9827 2689, ⓦwww.toorakmanor.net. Close to Chapel Street, this lovely old establishment has eighteen rooms replete with opulent Victoriana. A silver-service breakfast and free parking is included in the price. ❼

Hostels

Chapel Street Backpackers 22 Chapel St, Windsor ☎9533 6855, ☎1800 613 333, ⓦwww.csbackpackers.com.au. Offers small, clean dorms (4–8 beds; women-only available) and en-suite doubles. Tight security, Internet service and 24hr access. To get there, take the Sandringham line train from Flinders Street Station to Windsor Station; the hostel is across the road. Breakfast included. Dorms, ❶ rooms. ❹

Her Majesty's Hostel Level 1, 134 Toorak Rd, South Yarra ☎9866 8999, ☎1800 334 473. Above a bar in the heart of Toorak Road, *Her Majesty's* is a small and friendly hostel with a funky rooftop terrace, free linen, TV and video lounge, and a free drink on arrival. Dorms, ❶rooms. ❷–❹

Lords Lodge Backpackers 204 Punt Rd, Prahran ☎9510 5658, ⓦwww.lordslodge.com.au. Small, non-smoking hostel near the bars, cafés and retro shops of groovy Greville Street. Basic but reasonably clean singles and double rooms (all with heating), and medium-sized dorms (some women-only) with fridge and lockers. Pick-up from airport and bus terminals on request. Dorms, ❶ rooms. ❹

Pint on Punt 42 Punt Rd, Windsor ☎9510 4273/9510 3310, ⓦwww.pintonpunt.com.au. Hostel above a refurbished British-style pub in a central location, within walking distance of Chapel St and St Kilda nightlife. Clean dorms (4–6 beds), twins and doubles, all with shared facilities. Full kitchen, common room and cable TV; cheap pub dinners available and discounts on drinks. All rates include continental breakfast. Reception 7am–2pm and 4–7pm; check in at other times through the bar. Take train to Windsor Station (Sandringham line) or tram #3, #5, #16, #64 or #67 from Swanston St to St Kilda Junction. Dorms, ❶ rooms. ❸

St Kilda

St Kilda accommodation is marked on the map on p.87.

Hotels and motels

Boutique Hotel Tolarno 42 Fitzroy St ☎9537 0200, ☎1800 620 363, ⓦwww .hoteltolarno.com.au. Set in a restored building right in the thick of things. Pleasant rooms with 1950s and 60s retro furnishings, polished timber floors and all mod cons are good value for money. All rooms are en suite. ❻

Charnwood Motor Inn 3 Charnwood Rd ☎9525 4199, ☎1800 010 477, ⓦwww .charnwoodmotorinn.com. Secluded, quiet location 5–10min walk from Fitzroy Street. The plain rooms are simple but clean, en suite and with TV, and tea- and coffee-making facilities. ❺

Novotel St Kilda 16 The Esplanade ☎9525 5522, ☎1300 656 565, ⓦwww .novotelstkilda.com. This apricot-coloured eyesore has a bird's-eye view of the beach and Sunday market, plus heated pool, gym, spa, sauna, café and restaurant. Convenient for both Acland and Fitzroy streets. ❽

The Marquee Hotel 35 Fitzroy St ☎8539 8888, ⓦwww.rendezvoushotels.com. St Kilda's newest boutique hotel has a slick contemporary feel, and a bustling bar and bistro. Even the night owls who flock here will appreciate the double-glazed windows that keep the street noise at bay. ❼

The Prince 2 Acland St ☎9536 1111, ⓦwww .theprince.com.au. This forty-room boutique hotel housed within The Prince St Kilda complex is one of Melbourne's most elegant places to lay your head. Minimalist bedrooms include Loewe TVs and DVD players, Bose stereo radios, and a data connection for modem and fax, while the bathrooms are stocked with Aesop products. Away from your room you can relax in the Aurora spa and relaxation centre (see p.150), dine in the elegant *Circa* restaurant (see p.117), drink at *Mink* (see p.127), or dance in the club/band room. ❾

Hotel Victoria 123 Beaconsfield Parade, South Melbourne ☏9690 3666, ℱ9699 9570. This grand hotel, built in 1888, has been restored to its Victorian splendour. The upstairs accommodation is in a more modern style, while the bright front rooms have good views of the waterfront but suffer from traffic noise. Choose between stylish en-suite doubles and cheaper rooms with shared facilities. Great house music from some of Melbourne's best DJs every Sunday from 2pm till late in the downstairs area. ❹

B&Bs

Annies Bed and Breakfast 93 Park St ☏8500 3755, ⓦwww.anniesbedandbreakfast.com.au. Offering a traditional-style B&B in an Edwardian terrace house, with friendly service and all the comforts of home, *Annies* is conveniently located on a narrow strip of land between Port Phillip Bay beaches and Albert Park Lake. ❻–❼

Base 17 Carlisle Street ☏9536 6109, ⓦwww .basebackpackers.com. This funky new addition to St Kilda's hostel scene is slick and well managed. There's a good Thai restaurant and all rooms have their own bathroom – this is boutique backpacking. Dorms, ❶ rooms. ❸

Olembia Bed and Breakfast 96 Barkly St ☏9537 1412, ⓦwww.olembia.com.au. Old Edwardian building in a leafy setting provides a peaceful, nonsmoking retreat from the bustle of Barkly Street. Smallish singles, twins and doubles are spotlessly clean and appealing affairs, as are the dorms (some women-only). Book in advance. Dorms, ❶ rooms. ❹

Ritz for Backpackers 169 Fitzroy St ☏9525 3501, ☏1800 670 364, ⓦwww .backpackerscentre.com/ritz. Well-furnished and friendly hostel above the English-style *Elephant and Wheelbarrow* pub (see p.124), and within range of restaurants, cafés and milk bars. Rooms are simple and generally clean, and there are two TV lounges, a pool table, dining room, tiny kitchen and Internet kiosk. Lots of activities and tours and free breakfast. Dorms, ❶ rooms. ❸

St Kilda Coffee Palace 24 Grey St ☏9534 5283, ☏1800 654 098, ⓦwww.coffeepalace.com.au. Bustling hostel in large and rambling building popular with ravers and revellers. Some of the spacious dorms are women-only, and there's plenty of super-clean, motel-style accommodation with en-suite bathrooms on the top floor. The older part of the building is in desperate need of a makeover, however. Nice rooftop garden, plus good travel shop and work centre. Pick-up service from the airport, bus terminals and Tasmanian ferry. Dorms, ❶ rooms. ❸

Williamstown

See map p.94.

B&Bs

B&B at Stephanies 153–160 Ferguson St ☏9397 5587, ⓦwww.stephanies.biz. A comfy, large B&B with extras such as fireplaces and private courtyards. Be sure to get up for the hearty cooked breakfast in the morning (included in the price). Dorms, ❶ rooms. ❸

Captains Retreat 2 Ferguson Street ☏9397 0352, ℮captainsretreat@ozemail.com

.au. Set in a Victorian-era homestead, this B&B is conveniently located near the port and busy Ferguson Street. Views of the city and rooms with spas, a good selection of magazines and period furniture make this the best spot for even the most decadent captain to hang their hat. Singles, ❺ doubles & spa rooms. ❻

Eating

The rivalry between Melbourne and Sydney for the title of food capital of Australia is taken very seriously by both cities, although in truth the two are so different that each can be said to have its own distinctive style. Where Sydney is brash, fast-paced, alfresco and Asian-inspired, Melbourne is more relaxed and considered – café life is seen as a cultural activity, while dining out tends to be a serious, more classical affair driven by French and Italian influences. Service cultures also differ between the two cities: where Sydney's waiters are unfailingly chatty and familiar, Melbourne's are quietly professional and discreet. During the 1970s and early 1980s, Melbourne's restaurants lagged behind Sydney and Adelaide's more innovative approaches, but in the last decade a handful of newly arrived French and British chefs (brought, legend has it, to Melbourne by their homesick Australian girlfriends), along with locals such as Stephanie Alexander and the late Mietta O'Donnell, have been responsible for the development of a new wave of cooking in the city.

Melbourne is a melting pot of cultures, a fact reflected in its microcosmos of restaurants, cafés, bistros and bars. Fashionable, eclectic and eccentric, the city's dining spots offer a dizzying spread of the world's great cuisines, serving meals from the substantial and classic to the truly exotic. In the city, you can settle into the genteel surroundings of a nineteenth-century hotel, where afternoon tea can be enjoyed in a starched table-clothed timewarp reminiscent of bygone times, watch and be watched in buzzing laneway cafés and bars, or handpick a bottle of Yarra Valley Chardonnay at the latest über-chic hangout. Alternatively, head outside the city centre, where world cuisines are spreading to **suburbs** such as Fitzroy, South Melbourne, South Yarra, St Kilda, and the Vietnamese enclave of Richmond – affectionately known as "Little Saigon" – which is also a burgeoning destination for cheap and cheerful Burmese and Middle Eastern fare. In the past, the Italian eateries of Lygon Street in Carlton were among the city's culinary highlights – unfortunately, they've become something of a

Restaurant prices

In the following listings, prices are indicated by the terms:
cheap (under $25)
inexpensive ($25–35)
moderate ($35–50)
expensive ($55–80)
very expensive (over $80).
These refer to the cost of a starter, main course and dessert for one person, excluding drinks.

tourist trap and some are now best avoided (see pp.112–115 for those recommended). Further out are other specialist eating destinations: Footscray has | excellent Vietnamese cuisine, Brighton is renowned for its fine Italian restaurants and cafés, while Box Hill in Melbourne's outer suburbs has some of the city's best Chinese food. Of course, there are always **fast-food** outlets, with branches of *McDonald's*, *KFC*, *Pizza Hut* and Australian chains such as *Hungry Jacks* and *Lone Star* in virtually every neighbourhood. And if you're **self-catering**, Melbourne has a number of quality fruit, meat and veg markets in the city and surrounding suburbs. In the CBD, the Coles Express supermarket, on Elizabeth Street near Flinders Street Station, has good-value dinner-on-the-run meals.

The other major difference in dining between Melbourne and Sydney is **price**, with a main course at a top Melbourne restaurant costing around $15–20 less than its Sydney counterpart. Most restaurants and upmarket cafés offer special **lunchtime** set menus of three courses with wine for about half the cost of an equivalent evening meal. Pubs are also good value, and nowadays offer interesting food and beverages at reasonable prices, as do the **food halls** in major department stores, Southgate and the Crown Casino. In addition, some Melbourne eateries are **bring your own** (BYO), allowing you to supply your own drink, though the practice is slowly but gradually on the demise and a corkage fee of $5–7 per person often applies. Most places listed also accept payment by **credit card**.

Watch out for *Epicure*, an excellent pullout appearing each Tuesday in *The Age*, which features a lively mix of gossip, cheap eats, recipes from noted cookbook authors, café and restaurant reviews, and chef comings and goings. Two other indispensable **guides** to the city's restaurants are *The Age Cheap Eats in Melbourne* and *The Age Good Food Guide*, which are available from bookshops and major newsagents.

City Centre

Eating establishments are marked on the maps on p.34, p.46, p.56 and p.65.

Arintji Café/Bar Federation Square, Swanston St ☎9663 9900. Jacques Reymond's wonderful new addition to Federation Square offers flavoursome modern Australian food in a bright uptempo setting, with great outdoor seating and patrons rubbernecking at the local celebrities. Mon–Sun noon–late. Inexpensive.

Bamboo House 47 Little Bourke St ☎9662 1565. Much favoured by businessfolk and politicians, who come for the scampi, spicy Sichuan beef and tea-smoked duck, plus the deal-making and point-scoring that usually accompanies the meal. Mon–Fri noon–3pm & 5.30–11pm, Sat 5.30–11pm, Sun 6–10pm. Moderate to expensive.

Becco 11–25 Crossley St ☎9663 3000. If the pleasing Italian-style fare and interesting wine selection from the formal dining area don't whet your appetite, perhaps a quick drink, dessert or late supper at the bar will, or you can pick up a takeaway from the produce store (see p.156). Mon–Sat noon–

3pm & 6pm–11pm; bar Mon–Wed noon–1am, Thurs–Sat noon–3am. Expensive.

Beetroot 123 Hardware St ☎9600 0695 This stylish back-alley lunch room offers massive sandwiches, fajitas, bakes and pastas that are home-made daily. Staff are friendly and the menu has a vegetarian spin. Mon–Fri 7am–4pm. Cheap.

Bhoj Docklands 54 New Quay Promenade, Docklands. ☎9600 0884. Nestled in the glitz and glam of Docklands, *Bhoj* has a stylish timber and tiled interior, a decent wine-list and possibly the best Indian food in Melbourne, produced from very high-quality produce. Daily noon–3pm & 5.30–11pm. Inexpensive to moderate.

Blue Train Café Level 3, Southgate ☎9696 0111. Attracts a young, hip crowd and dishes out basic meals like wood-fired pizzas, pasta and salad. There's also full bar service and plenty of reading material if you're dining solo. Daily 7am–late. Cheap to inexpensive.

Box 189 Collins St ☎ 9663 0411. Next to the Regent Theatre, *Box* is a small space split over two levels, with a formal though cosy restaurant offering imaginative food one flight up. There's an affordable café serving snacks and a bar downstairs (inexpensive). Mon–Fri noon–3pm & 6pm–late, Sat 6pm–late. Expensive.

Café L'Incontro Cnr Little Collins and Swanston streets ☎ 9650 9603. The food from this smart-looking licensed café (mostly nachos, pasta and sweets) plays second fiddle to the alfresco setting in a prime location overlooking busy Swanston Street. Daily 24hr. Cheap.

Café Segovia 33 Block Place ☎ 9650 2373. Cute Spanish-style café serving good coffee and modern Australian food that satisfies rather than stupefies. A firm favourite among inner-city workers in the know. Mon–Fri 7am–late, Sat 7.30am–late, Sun 9am–5pm. Moderate.

chez phat Level 1, 7 Waratah Place ☎ 9663 0988. Arrive famished at this kitsch first-floor hideaway. Everything on the small but appetizing menu is flavoursome and well thought out, from baguettes, pizza, polenta and steak to apple pie, all of which can be enjoyed on a vast communal table or at simple separate plywood units. Tues–Sat 6pm–midnight, Sun 4–11pm. Inexpensive to moderate.

Chine on Paramount Shops 9 & 10, 101 Little Bourke St ☎ 9663 6556. Located in the Paramount Centre, *Chine* is a formal restaurant-cum-café with tables, booths and the ubiquitous fish tank. Mainly Cantonese dishes, including delicious soups, and has a good sprinkling of local and imported wines. Mon–Thur noon–3pm & 6–11pm, Fri & Sat noon–3pm & 6–11.30pm, Sun 6–11pm. Moderate to expensive.

Chocolate Buddha Federation Square, ☎ 9654 5688. A busy space inspired by Japanese canteens and serving organic modern Japanese food on weathered timber tables. The sake-based cocktails will surely kick-start your night – and if they don't, you can always look over the sandstone expanse and watch free movies on Federation Square's big screen. Daily noon–1am. Cheap to inexpensive.

Dish 379 St Kilda Rd ☎ 9677 9933. Hip, cavernous restaurant nestled in the *Royce on St Kilda Road* hotel (see p.101), a

few minutes from Melbourne's CBD. The modern Australian cuisine is expensive and modish, running from salmon fish cakes, risotto and lamb shanks to vegetable tarts and a reasonable choice of desserts. Mon–Fri 6–10.30am, noon–2.30pm & 6–10.30pm, Sat 6.30am–noon & 6–10.30pm, Sun 6.30am–noon. Moderate.

EQ Victorian Arts Centre, 100 St Kilda Rd ☎ 9645 0644. A firm favourite with the Arts Centre crowd and the creation of Dur-e Dara (of *Nudel Bar* fame – see p.111), this café/bar has a varied selection of snacky, down-to-earth but fantastically flavoured Mediterranean-style food such as fish cakes, meze platters and meatballs, using organic ingredients whenever possible. Meals are best enjoyed on the timber deck overlooking the Yarra. Tues–Sun 11am–1am. Moderate.

ezard at adelphi 187 Flinders Lane ☎ 9639 6811. Down a small flight of stairs, this hip, dimly lit place is one of Melbourne's hottest and most seductive eateries, with a tasty and moderately expensive range of East meets West favourites. Don't leave without trying the divine lamb cutlets. Mon–Fri noon–2.30pm, Mon–Sat 6–10.30pm. Expensive.

Flower Drum 17 Market Lane, off Bourke St ☎ 9662 3655. Quite simply the finest Chinese restaurant in Melbourne – if not Australia. Its capacious space, sophisticated cuisine (Peking duck, dumplings, Hainanese pork, *yi-meen* noodles) and discreet service from an army of waiting staff have garnered it a clutch of top awards. An essential Melbourne dining experience. Mon–Sat noon–3pm & 6–10pm, Sun 6–10pm. Expensive to very expensive.

Food Court Ground Level, Crown Casino, 8 Whiteman St, Southbank. Hugely popular food court, hawking everything from Singaporean noodles, Mexican nachos, salads and sandwiches to fish and chips. Some stalls are licensed. Daily 7am–late. Cheap.

Gopals 139 Swanston St ☎ 9650 1578. Typically wholesome, vegetarian food from the Hare Krishna organization. Even cheaper is their *Crossways Food for Life* at 123 Swanston St, which has all-you-can-eat lunch deals for next to nothing. Mon–Sat 11.30am–8.30pm. Cheap.

Grossi Florentino 80 Bourke St ☎ 9662 1811. A Melbourne institution, which divides loyalties between the cellar café-grill-restaurant (inexpensive), serving cheapish, home-style pasta dishes, drinks and good coffee, and upstairs the very pricey and elegant Italian-French restaurant that's been synonymous with fine dining for many years. Cellar bar Mon–Sat 7.30am–1am, restaurant Mon–Fri noon–3pm & 6–11pm, Sat 6–11pm. Inexpensive/expensive.

Hanabishi 187 King St. ☎9670 1167 In the middle of seedy King Street, this modest establishment serves up some of the city's best Japanese food, including great sushi and generous udon noodle dishes. Mon–Fri noon–2.30pm & 6pm–10.30pm. Moderate.

Hopetoun Tea Rooms Shop 2, Block Arcade, 282 Collins St ☎9650 2777. Food and drink have been served in these elegant surroundings for more than a century. The scones and cakes remain delicious, and are now served alongside more exotic treats such as focaccia with pesto sauce. Mon–Thurs 10am–5pm, Fri 9am–6pm, Sat 10am–3.30pm. Cheap.

Il Bacaro Cucina e Bar 168–170 Little Collins St ☎9654 6778. High prices and sometimes uninterested service mar an otherwise interesting menu of modern Italian favourites and intimate ambience. An award-winner when first started, *Il Bacaro* seems to be resting on its laurels. Mon–Sat noon–midnight. Expensive.

Il Solito Posto Basement, 113 Collins St, off George Parade ☎9654 4466. Charming basement location, casual atmosphere and fine no-fuss Italian food make for one of Melbourne's best dining experiences. Mon–Fri 7.30am–11pm, Sat 9am–11pm. Moderate to expensive.

Journal 1/253 Flinders Lane ☎9650 4399. Bookish types and students flock to this savvy, intellectual hangout that is crammed with books. It's a good spot to grab a coffee, snack or light pasta meal in warm surroundings with clever-and-cute waiting staff. Mon–Fri 7am–late, Sat 9am–5.30pm. Inexpensive.

Kenzan 45 Collins St ☎9654 8933. Epitome of Japanese food and style: great sushi selection and cool, elegant surroundings beneath the *Hotel Sofitel*. Mon–Fri noon–2.30pm & 6–10pm, Sat & Sun 6–10pm. Moderate to expensive.

Koko Level 3, Crown Casino, 8 Whiteman St, Southbank ☎9292 6886. Melbourne's premier Japanese restaurant, *Koko* inhabits a large and decorative space fitted out with tables, myriad grills, a tranquil water garden and,

in one corner, a sushi-sashimi bar perfect for pre-dinner drinks. Daily noon–3pm & 6–11pm. Expensive to very expensive.

Kun Ming Café 212 Little Bourke St ☎9663 1851. No-frills cooking, with such dishes as short soup and sweet-and-sour pork served on laminex tables with knives and forks. A bustling café, and you can't quibble with the prices. Daily 11.30am–3pm & 5.30–10pm. Cheap to inexpensive.

Langton's 61 Flinders Lane ☎9663 0222. Excellent place for a French-style breakfast or dinner, with some of the best regional wines and service in Melbourne. No expense has been spared on the stylish decor, which includes parquet floors, polished brass columns and a theatrical open kitchen dominated by a copper Bonnet stove. Restaurant Mon–Fri noon–2.30pm & 6–10.30pm, Sat 6–10.30pm; bar Mon–Sat 7.30am–11pm. Moderate to expensive.

Le Restaurant Level 35, Hotel Sofitel, 25 Collins St ☎9653 0000. Luxurious restaurant serving carefully prepared seasonal dishes. Apart from the food and superb table settings, you can admire the sublime views over Melbourne from the comfort of your chair. For a cheaper alternative, try the hotel's *Café La* (moderate). Tues–Sat 6.30–11pm. Very expensive.

Livebait 55b New Quay Promenade, Docklands. ☎9642 1500. Sparsely designed and unadorned, and boasting panoramic views of the city, Docklands and Bolte Bridge, *Livebait*'s emphasis is on super fresh Mediterranean-style seafood. Daily noon–3pm & 6–11pm. Moderate to expensive.

Lounge Downstairs 243 Swanston St ☎9662 9995. Sleek, pleasurable eating spot underneath *Lounge* (see p.123) with reasonably priced, stylishly presented Asian and Italian food in a retro setting. Mon–Thurs 7.30am–midnight, Fri 7.30am–late, Sat 5pm–late. Inexpensive to moderate.

Mask of China 115–117 Little Bourke St ☎9662 2116. Extensive menu and wine list with emphasis on Southern Chinese-style Chiu Chow dishes of seafood, poultry and fresh produce with no gluggy sauces in sight. Service is also good. Try the banquet menu, which changes every few weeks. Mon–Fri & Sun noon–3pm & 6–11pm, Sat 6–11pm. Expensive.

Mecca Bah 55a New Quay Promenade, Docklands. ☎9642 1300. Mouth-watering modern Middle Eastern treats and a killer spot on the harbour make this place a popular choice day or night. On still days the outdoor deck is perfect for sharing meze platters and watching the boats cruise by. Daily 11am–11pm. Inexpensive.

Melbourne RSL Duckboard Club 91 Flinders Lane ☎9654 5576. Good, honest tucker such as sausage, eggs and chips served with a can-do, no-prob Aussie attitude. Mon–Fri noon–2pm. Cheap to inexpensive.

MoMo Basement 115 Collins St (enter from George Pde) ☎9650 0660. Chef Greg Malouf's modern take on Middle Eastern cuisine makes a trip to this basement restaurant seem like a treasured visit to Aladdin's secret cave. Good wines by the glass. Mon–Fri noon–3pm, Mon–Sat 6–10.30pm. Expensive.

MoVida 1 Hosier Lane ☎9663 3038. Tables are scarce at this busy tapas bar/restaurant but grab a seat at the bar or couch and soak up the Spanish flavours. Spanish beers and wine complete the vibe. Mon–Fri noon–late, Sat 4pm–late, Sun 5pm–late. Inexpensive to moderate.

Nudel Bar 76 Bourke St ☎9662 9100. Wide-ranging menu covering mostly Asian and European noodle dishes such as *mee goreng*, and Hungarian goulash, with benches downstairs for quick meals when you're seriously pressed for time. The *tom yum* soup is a blinder. Mon–Thurs 11am–10.30pm, Fri 11am–11.30pm, Sat noon–11pm, Sun 5–10pm. Cheap to inexpensive.

Pellegrini's Espresso Bar 66 Bourke St ☎9662 1885. A Melbourne institution, *Pellegrini's* has hardly changed since it first opened in the 1950s, with its time-warp decor of chequered floors and mirrored walls. It's just the ticket for hearty Italian fare (risotto, meatballs, spag bol) presented at lightning speed. Also good for coffee and scrummy home-made cakes. Mon–Sat 8am–11.30pm, Sun noon–8pm. Cheap.

Punch Lane 43 Little Bourke St ☎9639 4944. An eclectic menu spanning antipasto to curries, comfortable seating in solid red-leather chairs, late suppers and good wines from the bar make this a classy haunt for Melbourne urbanites. Mon–Fri noon–11pm, Sat & Sun 5pm–11pm. Moderate.

Radii Park Hyatt Melbourne, 1 Parliament Square ☎9224 1211. Part of the swanky *Park Hyatt Melbourne*, this monstrously large and very expensive restaurant seats close to 150 souls. If you can take your

eyes off the opulent decor (all marble and mirrors), you'll discover enough waiters to serve a small island state, as well as a Mediterranean-style menu dreamt up by some of the most imaginative chefs in the city. Food fit for a king and an ideal place for marriage proposals and assorted special occasions. Mon–Thurs & Sun noon–2.30pm & 6–10.30pm, Fri & Sat noon–2.30pm & 6–11pm. Very expensive.

Reserve Upper Plaza, Federation Square. ☎9654 60002. Daring Modern European food in an over-the-top interior have earned *Reserve* a veritable swag of foodie honours. Be prepared: it's a notorious hangout for poseurs. Mon–Fri noon–3pm & 6–10pm, Sat 6–10pm. Expensive.

Shark Fin House 131 Little Bourke St ☎9663 1555. *Yum cha* specialists located in a converted three-storey warehouse that is the quintessential Chinese eating experience: preposterously loud, closely packed tables, adrenaline-charged waiters and queues of people waiting to be seated. Daily 11am–11pm. Cheap to inexpensive.

Softbelly 367 Little Bourke St ☎9670 4404. Sausages, mash, pasta dishes, pizza and salads dished up in another of Melbourne's retro-style eateries-cum-bars. Although the food is hardly first class, it's a convivial space in which to hang out with some of the city's more hip inhabitants. Mon–Thurs 9am–late, Fri 9am–midnight, Sat 7.30pm–1am. Inexpensive.

Stalactites 177 Lonsdale St ☎9663 3316. Operating for over twenty years, *Stalactites* serves so-so *giros*, *souvlaki*, moussaka and *saganaki* (traditional deep-fried cheese), all dished up in huge portions in a dimly lit dining area. For more upmarket Greek cuisine, try *Antipodes* (inexpensive to moderate) a few doors down. Daily 24hr. Cheap to inexpensive.

Supper Inn 15 Celestial Ave ☎9663 4759. The decor may be dated but the generous Cantonese food is worth the climb up those stairs. The menu is large, with plenty of unusual options and the kitchen stays open till very, very late, making it a favourite for those in the hospitality trade. Daily 5.30pm–2.30am. Cheap.

Syracuse 23 Bank Place ☎9670 1777. Come for the mouthwatering tapas (served from 3pm) and the lamb and leek sausages, then top it off with fantastic cheeses, *panforte* and coffee. Extensive, almost daunting wine

EATING | City Centre

list, good selection of cigars and seductive atmosphere. Mon–Fri 7.30am–11pm, Sat 6pm–late. Moderate to expensive.

Taxi Dining Room Upstairs, Federation Square ℡9654 8808. Above *Transport* (see p.124), the open windows of this eatery give a stunning perspective on the city and the Yarra. Staff wear zippy cab-driver uniforms, delivering nibbly sushi or mains such as organic rabbit with chorizo, soya beans and basil. You can alternatively just grab a beer or sake and watch the city lights blur. Mon–Sat noon–11pm. Moderate.

Travellers' Aid Society Tearooms 169 Swanston St ℡9654 2081. Located on the second floor, these tearooms are like a blast from the past: naff 1950s decor, Devonshire teas, crumpets, muffins, hearty quiches and classic milk shakes in big plastic cups straight out of grandma's parlour. Mon–Fri 8.30am–4.30pm. Cheap.

Tsindos 197 Lonsdale St ℡9663 3194. Established Greek café with all the classics, including taramasalata, moussaka and *souvlaki*. Leave some space for the incredibly sweet desserts. Mon–Thurs 11.30am–3pm & 5–10pm, Fri 11.30am–

3pm & 5–11pm, Sat 5–11pm, Sun 5–10pm. Cheap to inexpensive.

West Lake 189 Little Bourke St ℡9662 2048. This noisy and often messy restaurant speeds good *yum cha* and delicious desserts to your table. Mon–Fri 11am–2am, Sat & Sun 10am–2am. Cheap.

Walter's Wine Bar Level 3, Southgate ℡9690 9211. Award-winning restaurant-cum-wine bar, *Walter's* prepares excellent contemporary bistro food, and has knowledgeable staff, good Australian wines by the glass and superb views across the Yarra to the city. Opposite here, *Walter's Wine and Food Store* (Mon–Fri 8am–5.30pm, Sat & Sun 9am–5.30pm; inexpensive) is an affordable deli where you can sit down over a glass of wine and a sandwich. Daily noon–late. Moderate to expensive.

Yu-u 137 Flinders Lane ℡9639 7073. Hard to find, due to its small sign, this tiny Japanese-style bar serves delicious and very cheap meat and rice dishes, tempura and miso. So hip that the foot you're likely to stand on probably belongs to one of Melbourne's architectural or design elite. Mon–Fri noon–2.15pm & 6–9.15pm. Inexpensive.

Carlton and Fitzroy

For locations of the following establishments, see maps p.69, p.70 and p.74.

Café culture

Where to get the best coffee can be a topic of real debate in Melbourne. **Cafés** of every shape and size can be found throughout the CBD, from shoeboxes in Block Place to the wide-open spaces of *Lounge* (see p.123), which can seat over a hundred. The new emphasis on inner-city living, combined with a backlash against mega-corporate enterprises like Southgate and the Crown Casino, has seen a coterie of small cafés spring up, showing that with little more than an idea, a coffee machine and a place to put it, anything is possible. Human and intimate, these cafés are the perfect accompaniment to the European architectural style and feel of the area. And, judging by their popularity and Melbourne's clamour for coffee, there's plenty of scope for more. If you want to try something further out, high-tail it to the café-dominated strips of Fitzroy and Acland streets in St Kilda or Bridport Street in Albert Park.

Here's a few choice cafés that are distinctly "Melbourne" and well worth seeking out:

Babka Bakery Café 358 Brunswick St, Fitzroy ℡9416 0091.

Part bakery, part café, *Babka* serves simple Middle Eastern, Russian and Jewish food. The antithesis of *Caffe e Cucina* (see opposite) in style, it's unpretentious, bright and breezy with fresh white walls and large windows. The coffee will win over the most discerning caffeine addict, while a bowl of borscht with rye bread can do wonders for the soul. And don't leave without trying their justly famous "shoo fly buns", yeast buns with currants, eaten with butter. Tues–Sun 7am–7pm.

Ablas 109 Elgin St, Carlton ☏9347 0006.
A homely restaurant serving some of the
best Lebanese food in town. The thirteen-
course banquet (compulsory on Friday and
Saturday nights) is magnificent. Mon–Wed
& Sat 6–11pm Thurs & Fri noon–3pm &
6–11pm. Inexpensive to moderate.

Akari 177 177 Brunswick St, Fitzroy
☏9419 3786. A mainstay on Brunswick
Street for many years, *Akari 177* has a
deluge of Japanese-style goodies, with
wonderful beef sushi (regular sushi too) and
recommended daily specials. The owner
also sells beautiful Japanese ceramics. Mon
& Sat 6–10.30pm, Tues–Fri noon–3pm &
6–10.30pm. Cheap to inexpensive.

Bakers Courtyard Café 384 Brunswick St,
Fitzroy ☏9419 7437. The strip's longest-
running restaurant is not as trendy as
places such as *Mario's* (see overleaf), but
the food (pasta, eggs, focaccia) is always
tasty and filling. Mon 9am–4pm, Wed–Sat
9am–10pm, Sun 9am–5pm. Cheap.

Balzari 130 Lygon St, Carlton ☏9639 9383. A
welcome addition to Lygon Street, this laid-
back eatery serves simple Mediterranean/
European style food, perfect for sharing.
Mon–Sun noon–10.30pm. Inexpensive.

Bimbo Deluxe 376 Brunswick St, Fitzroy.
☏9419 8600. An endless procession of
super cheap and delicious simple pizzas
(only $3 at lunch), plus a few other favour-
ites, keep diners happy, while the cosy
rooms out back keep the drinkers and pool
sharks happy. Daily noon–3am. Cheap.

Brunetti 194–204 Faraday St, Carlton
☏9347 2801. After 30 years this Carlton icon
got a make-over and its many shopfronts
contain a café, restaurant, paninoteca,
pasticceria and gelateria. A steady stream
of customers file past an array of display
cases filled with a selection of cholesterol-
boosting chocolates, pastries, biscuits and
cakes to get their daily espresso in the café
section, or have pasta and meat dishes
in the licensed restaurant next door. Café
daily 7am–late; bistro Mon–Fri 7am–3pm &
6–10pm, Sat 8am–3pm & 6pm–late, Sun
8am–1pm. Moderate.

Café Provincial Cnr Brunswick & Johnston
streets, Fitzroy ☏9417 2228. One of
Melbourne's best grazing joints, this lovely
café is set within the *Provincial Hotel*.
Well-presented food, with a French-Italian
pedigree, plus good blackboard specials
and reasonably priced wines by the glass.
Daily noon–late. Inexpensive.

Café Zum Zum 645 Rathdowne St, Carlton
Nth. ☏9348 0455. This hidden nook (on the
western side of the street) serves outstanding
Middle Eastern food in a warm and cheerful
space. The tajines will satisfy even the most
ambitious appetite. Tues 6–10pm, Wed–Sun
noon–3pm & 6–10pm. Cheap.

Caffe e Cucina 581 Chapel St, South Yarra ☏9827 4139.
Became the benchmark for Melbourne's restaurant/café style when it opened in
1988, and has spawned a score of imitators with its wood panelling, cute little table
lamps and a creative menu written up on a central blackboard. Very Italian, dark,
and small enough to make a toilet cubicle look spacious, it's staffed by immaculately
dressed, theatrically aloof waiters serving sublime *al dente* pasta, mouthwatering
bigne pastries and some of the best coffee in town. Mon–Sat 7am–10.30pm, Sun
9am–10.30pm.

Don Camillo's 215 Victoria St, West Melbourne ☏9329 8883. Tram #109 from
Collins St.
Classic, unspoiled 1950s Italian café with a terrazzo floor and long bar. The walls are
covered with photographs of AFL and other sporting stars, many of whom form part
of the *Don's* clientele. Mon–Fri 10am–4pm, Sat 10am–2pm.

The Galleon 9 Carlisle St, St Kilda ☏9534 8934.
One of St Kilda's long-standing favourites, *The Galleon* was around long before
the area was transformed from a run-down and forgotten beach resort to the funky
place it is today. Large and grungy with lots of formica-topped tables, it's busy
and noisy, the menu rarely changes, the coffee's good and the fried breakfasts are
great. Thur–Fri 8am–11pm Sat–Sun 8am–6pm, Mon–Wed 8am–4.30pm.

Fitz 347 Brunswick St, Fitzroy ☏9417 5794.
Fitz has a deserved reputation for fuelling
locals with one of the best and biggest
breakfasts in town. The decor is simple, the
Asian and European cuisine feel-good and
down-to-earth, while the large outdoor area
is ideal for catching the sun. Daily 7am–late.
Cheap.

Growlers 153 Gertrude St, Fitzroy ☏9416 4116.
Cluttered with bohemian tat, *Growlers*
dishes up big servings of traditional fare
(steak, lamb shanks, mashed potatoes),
and has free bread and olives plonked on
each table. In winter, the open fires make
this spot an ideal proposition. Tues–Sat
6–11pm. Inexpensive.

Interlude 211 Brunswick St, Fitzroy
☏9415 7300. Fine European/modern
Australian cuisine that appeals to a food-
literate crowd in a stylish and sophisticated
setting. Tues 6.30pm–late, Wed & Thurs
noon–3pm & 6.30pm–late, Fri & Sat
6.30pm–late. Expensive.

Jimmy Watson's 333 Lygon St, Carlton
☏9347 3985. Designed by Robin Boyd in
1962, this place has survived the vagaries
of Melbourne's food and drinking trends,
and still attracts locals, academics,
students and anyone who loves a tipple.
Despite several minor renovations, not
much has changed and that includes
its reputation for pub grub in convivial,
atmospheric surroundings. Formerly a
wine saloon, *Jimmy's* continues to sport a
superb list of Australian vintage wines from
the cellar. Mon 10.30am–6pm, Tues–Sat
10.30am–late. Moderate to expensive.

Ladro 224 Gertrude St, Fitzroy ☏9415 7575.
Simple, authentic and inspired Italian fare,
plus some of the best pizza in town, means
Ladro is one of the toughest places in town
to get a table. But if you're prepared to
wait, you'll be rewarded. Wed–Sun 6pm–
late. Inexpensive to moderate.

La Cacciatora Cnr Grattan & Drummond sts
☏9663 6906. There's no shortage of good
pizza places in Carlton, but this out-of-the-
way spot is worth singling out from the
crowd. They slice up gourmet flavours such
as artichoke and sweet potato in either the
everday pie or in long rectangles "by the
metre" for big appetites. Dine in for platefuls
of pasta and an authentic Italian atmosphere.
Daily noon–11pm. Cheap to inexpensive.

Mario's 303 Brunswick St, Fitzroy ☏9417 3343.
Anyone who wants to get a true feel of

Brunswick Street should home in on this
European-style café, where you can eat
brekkie (until midnight), lunch and dinner or
just have a coffee or a drink. Although the
staff are dauntingly smart, *Mario's* is by no
means expensive or dressy. While waiting
for a seat (it gets very busy at weekends),
you can browse the bookstores down the
road. Mon–Wed & Sun 7am–midnight,
Thurs–Sat 7am–1am. Inexpensive to moderate.

Mrs Jones 312 Drummond St, Carlton
☏9347 3312, ⊛www.mrsjones.com.au. A tiny
fixed-price $38 menu offers an entrée and
main from an ever-changing and interesting
menu list posted on their website weekly.
Weekend brunch is à la carte and runs all
day. Tues–Fri 6pm–late, Sat & Sun 9am–
late. Moderate.

Piraeus Blues 310 Brunswick St, Fitzroy
☏9417 0222. Has gained a solid reputation
for serving flavoursome, homespun cooking
such as spicy sausages and spinach and
feta pie and offering a great ever-changing
specials board. A must for lovers of Greek
food. Mon, Tues & Sat 5pm–1am, Wed–Fri
noon–3pm & 5pm–1am, Sun noon–late.
Inexpensive.

Poppy's 230 Lygon St, Carlton ☏9663 3366.
The decor is basic in this popular Thai
restaurant because they focus on serving
well-prepared spring rolls and satay, and
solid mains of curry and stir-fried dishes.
Daily 6pm–late. Cheap to inexpensive.

Retro Café 413 Brunswick St, Fitzroy
☏9419 9103. Inviting and casual eatery
with a plethora of 1970s kitsch. Whether
your preferences are for savoury pancakes,
pasta dishes or even kangaroo, you'll be
guaranteed to leave pleasantly stuffed. Also
serves good coffee, cheap muffins and
syrupy-sweet desserts. The window seats
are a great place to people-watch. Daily
7am–11.30pm. Inexpensive to moderate.

Rhumbarella's 342 Brunswick St, Fitzroy
☏9417 5652. The neon sign in the window
is one of the street's landmarks, and the
interior of this stylish café is just as vibrantly
coloured. *Rhumbarella's* hums to the sound
of jazz and conversation. Breakfast until
midday – eggs Benedict is a favourite –
then anything from focaccia to steak. Daily
9am–1am. Cheap to inexpensive.

Sala Thai 266 Brunswick St, Fitzroy
☏9417 4929. Dark interior with plenty of
cushions scattered around the place, *Sala*

Thai enjoys a deserved reputation for fine Thai food and cheery service. Daily 6pm–late. Cheap to inexpensive.

Shakahari 201–203 Faraday St, Carlton ☎9347 3848. Excellent, well-priced and superbly presented vegetarian favourites such as satays, curries and laksas. This has been Carlton's benchmark in dining for sophisticated lentil-lovers for years. Mon–Thurs noon–3pm & 6–9.30pm, Fri & Sat noon–3pm & 6–10pm, Sun 6–9.30pm. Inexpensive.

Shanti 285 Brunswick St ☎9416 2170. Serves tandoori dishes as well as Southern Indian specialities, cooked in coconut milk rather than cream and yoghurt. Lots of vegetarian options and seafood. The masala dosa is especially good value. Mon–Wed & Sat 5.30pm–late, Thurs, Fri & Sun noon–2.30pm & 5.30pm–late. Inexpensive.

Small Block 130 Lygon St, East Brunswick ☎9381 2244. Fantastic coffee, great breakfast and an ever-changing lunch list makes this daytime café a favourite for both locals in the know and those wanting to escape the Brunswick Street scene. Mon–Fri 7.30am–5pm, Sat & Sun 8.30am–4pm. Cheap.

Tiamo 303 Lygon St, Carlton ☎9347 5759. Family-run Carlton establishment with cheaper eating downstairs and a posher dining room upstairs (inexpensive). The food, including Italian favourites such as lasagne and carbonara, isn't flash but is cheap and hearty. Timber tables and walls adorned with 1950s posters, plus the strip's best coffee and tiramisu, make this little gem a favourite with students and locals alike. *Tiamo 2*, next door (also cheap to inexpensive), is more upmarket,

but still excellent value. Mon–Sat 7.30am–11pm, Sun 9.30am–10pm. Cheap to inexpensive.

Toofey's 162 Elgin St, Carlton ☎9347 9838. A magnet for local fishophiles, Toofey's extremely fresh seafood dishes are prepared in an adventurous Mediterranean or Middle Eastern style. There's steak and exquisite desserts too, and wines by the glass. Book ahead. Tues–Fri noon–3pm & 6–10.30pm, Sat 6–10.30pm. Moderate to expensive.

Toto's Pizza House 101 Lygon St ☎9347 1630. Melbourne's first pizzeria, dating from the 1950s – cheap, cheerful and impossibly noisy at weekends. Daily noon–11pm. Inexpensive.

Trotters 400 Lygon St, Carlton ☎9347 5657. Popular for breakfast, Trotters is a cosy and sometimes cramped spot where you can plough through big servings of bacon and eggs, home-made cakes and good coffee. Mon–Fri 7.30am–10.30pm, Sat 8am–10.30pm, Sun 9.30am–10.30pm. Cheap to inexpensive.

University Café 255 Lygon St, Carlton ☎9347 2142. The outdoor tables here are possibly the best spot on the street for reading the newspaper, drinking lattes and eyeballing the locals. Food from the bar/café is unpretentious but filling. Daily 7am–midnight. Cheap to inexpensive.

The Vegie Bar 380 Brunswick St, Fitzroy ☎9417 6935. Cavernous in appearance, *The Vegie Bar* is popular and hip rather than hippie. Simple, fresh food such as tofu burgers and salads cooked to order with a range of healthy nibbles for gym bunnies and whippet-thin regulars. Daily 11am–10pm. Cheap.

Richmond and Hawthorn

The following are marked on the map p.8, except where indicated.

Fenix 680–682 Victoria St, Richmond ☎9427 8500. Great views over the sluggish, brown Yarra, especially in summer on the deck. Take your pick from the pasta, steak, fish or steamed pudding, all of it decently priced and well presented. Mon–Fri noon–3pm & 6–10pm, Sat & Sun 8.30am–3pm & 6–10pm. Moderate to expensive.

The Imperial House 120 Victoria St, Richmond ☎9428 3264. Another much-frequented

establishment in this busy strip of Vietnamese places. Reliable, with good soups and fish dishes, plus set lunch menus for the uninitiated. Daily 11am–11pm. Cheap.

Pearl 631–633 Church St, Richmond. ☎9421 4599. See map p.77. Slickly designed establishment with loads of natural light and attentive service. Inventive, modern Australian food consistently impresses the loud, young crowd. The bar offers a cheaper, snack-like menu, but is just as interesting. If you come for breakfast, try the "famous" coddled-egg toastie, salmon caviar or white nectarines with organic yoghurt. Mon–Fri noon–3pm & 6–10.30pm, Sat & Sun 9am–3pm & 6–10.30pm. Inexpensive to expensive.

Penang Coffee House 359 Burwood Rd, Hawthorn ☎9819 2092. Some of Melbourne's best hawker food in a suburban hideaway – try the curry laksa, *mee goreng* or sublime, chilli-infused *kway teow*, all served with "sky juice" (water) or Chinese tea. Tues–Fri & Sun 11.30am–2.30pm & 5–9.30pm, Sat 5–9.30pm. Cheap to inexpensive.

Richmond Hill Café and Larder 48–50 Bridge Rd, Richmond ☎9421 2808. Exquisite though pricey food from Stephanie Alexander, celebrated local chef and food writer. As well as a casual dining area, there's a grocery, cheese shop, and a bar which is perfect for a coffee whilst poring over the morning papers. Mon 9am–5pm, Tues–Fri 9am–late, Sat & Sun 8.30am–late. Moderate to expensive.

Tho Tho 66 Victoria St, Richmond ☎9428 2036. This enormous, brasserie-style restaurant is much flashier than its neighbours. The Vietnamese food (great rice-paper rolls and crispy quail) is incredibly cheap, and the place is usually packed and noisy. Daily 11am–midnight. Cheap to inexpensive.

Thy Thy 1 142 Victoria St, Richmond ☎9429 1104. Climb the stairs to one of the most popular Vietnamese restaurants in Melbourne. The food, which includes crispy spring rolls, noodles and chicken dishes, is basic but great. Daily 8am–10pm. Cheap.

Tofu Shop International 78 Bridge Rd, Richmond ☎9429 6204. A great example of healthy food being really delicious, this tiny place has been going for years, serving consistently good vegetarian meals. Treat your body to salads, bean curd and veggie dishes, or splurge on spring rolls, pasta and hummus dips with pitta bread. Mon–Fri noon–9pm, Sat 10am–5pm. Cheap to inexpensive.

Vlado's 61 Bridge Rd, Richmond ☎9428 5833. Sausages, hamburger, liver, steak, you name it – if it has four legs it'll end up on the set-price four-course menu. Heaven for carnivores, the wine list here supports the simple fleshy cuisine. Vegetarians, however, will find it hellish. Mon–Fri noon–3pm & 6–11pm, Sat 6–11pm. Moderate to expensive.

South Yarra, Prahran and Toorak

Candy Bar 162 Greville St, Prahran ☎9529 6566. Funky joint, popular for eating, drinking and dancing into the early hours. Sample a range of food from noodles and curries to polenta whilst sitting on comfy sofas under a giant mirror ball. Mon–Fri noon–late, Sat & Sun 10am–late. Inexpensive.

Chinta Ria Jazz 176 Commercial Rd, Prahran ☎9510 6520. Consistently good hawker fare – the fat Hokkein noodles, roti bread and curry laksa, in particular, are to die for. Mon–Fri noon–3pm & 6–10.30pm, Sat & Sun 6–10.30pm. Cheap to moderate.

France-Soir 11 Toorak Rd, South Yarra ☎9866 8569. The food's modest but the wine list, sporting exceptional bottles of French plonk, must rank as one of Melbourne's finest. Tables are often filled with intimate couples and well-heeled tourists. Daily noon–3pm & 6pm–midnight. Moderate.

Globe Café 218 Chapel St, Prahran ☎9510 8693. Fabulous breads and vegetarian food, sinful cakes, a good wine list and prompt, attentive service. Excellent value. Mon–Thurs 8.30am–10pm, Fri 8.30am–late, Sat & Sun 9am–late. Cheap to inexpensive.

Greville Bar 143 Greville St, Prahran ☎9529 4800. Dim and sexy with a sophisticated international menu, and a bar that carries on long after the kitchen closes. Mon–Sat 5pm–late; during winter also Wed–Sun noon–5pm. Moderate.

Jacques Reymond 79 Williams Rd, Windsor ☎9525 2178. Jacques Reymond's shrine to fine food brings together eclectic ingredients from Europe, Australia, Asia and the Pacific to startling effect. The space is glamorous and striking, with two-, three- or four-course fixed-price menus on offer or a six-course *dégustation* menu for the adventurous. Tram #64 from Swanston Street. Tues, Wed & Sat 6.30–10pm, Thurs

& Fri noon–2pm & 6.30–10pm. Expensive to very expensive.

Lynch's 133 Domain Rd, South Yarra
℡9866 2425. Popular dining place for wealthy locals, who come for the first-class service, private rooms, old-fashioned food, racy nudes hanging on the walls and the child-free environment. Mon–Fri noon–2.30pm & 6.30–10.30pm, Sat 6.30–10.30pm. Expensive to very expensive.

Windsor Castle Hotel 89 Albert St, Windsor.
℡9525 0239. The revamped take on pub-grub classics, the chocolate velour seating and the open fire and beer garden make this a great place to stop for a while. Keep an eye out for the pink elephants on the lime green roof. Mon–Thurs 4–11pm, Fri & Sat noon–1am, Sun noon–11pm. Cheap to inexpensive.

St Kilda, Balaclava and Elwood

189 Espresso Bar 189 Acland St, St Kilda
℡9534 8884. Stainless-steel tables, timber floors, huge *pides*, pizza, pasta, salads, cakes and coffees. Outside tables make this a good place for crowd surveillance. Daily 7am–5pm. Cheap to inexpensive.

Bala's Café 1e Shakespeare Grove, St Kilda
℡9534 6116. Hugely popular café that's perfect for a quick fuel stop or takeaway. Although the seating at large wooden tables is cramped, the Southeast Asian food is fast and affordable, and includes Malaysian noodles, Thai curries, Indian samosas and cooling lassis. Mon–Sat noon–10pm, Sun noon–9.30pm. Cheap.

Barcelona Café 25 Fitzroy St, St Kilda
℡9525 4244. A decent selection of tapas and mains, in a lovely interior with high-ceilings and wood-panelled walls, which lend the place a warm atmosphere. Tues–Fri 5pm–late, Sat noon–late, Sun 9am–late. Inexpensive to moderate.

Big Mouth 168 Acland St, St Kilda ℡9534 4611.
Relaxed and unpretentious, this large, triangular restaurant and bar has mix 'n' match decor and eclectic food, and great views of the street. The downstairs café (daily 8am–3am; cheap) is livelier and serves a variety of café-style fare to a hip local crowd. Daily 5pm–3am. Cheap to moderate.

Birdcage 129 Fitzroy St, St Kilda ℡9534 0277.
In a corner of the *George Hotel* foyer, this tiny bar-cum-bistro does a great line in Japanese tapas-style dishes, or "Japanesque", as they like to call it. Choose from sashimi, noodle, rice and soup dishes, which can be scoffed in booths, or on stools at the bar. Mon–Fri noon–11pm, Sat & Sun 5pm–late. Moderate.

Café Di Stasio 31 Fitzroy St, St Kilda
℡9525 3999. Small and understated, with

occasionally temperamental waiters, *Café Di Stasio* serves up a masterful blend of traditional and modern Italian cooking. The two-course lunch menu with a glass of wine is good value at $25. Daily noon–3pm & 6–11pm. Expensive.

Café Racer 15 Marine Parade, St Kilda
℡9534 9988. Ocean-facing café providing an ideal rendezvous for lycra-clad cyclists in search of turbo-charged snacks and their next caffeine hit. Daily 6.30am–6pm. Inexpensive.

Chinta Blues 6 Acland St, St Kilda ℡9534 9233.
Malaysian restaurant with a blues music theme. Fortunately the authentic and reasonably priced dishes more than make up for the daft concept. Mon–Thurs noon–2.30pm & 6–10.30pm, Fri & Sat noon–2.30pm & 6–11pm, Sun noon–10pm. Inexpensive to moderate.

Cicciolina 130 Acland St, St Kilda ℡9525 3333.
A sociable atmosphere prevails at the tightly packed tables of this small and always crowded space; the Italian/modern Mediterranean food is of a high standard. You can't book, so be prepared to wait in the cosy bar out back. Mon–Sat noon–11pm, Sun noon–10pm; bar Mon–Sat 4.30pm–1am, Sun 3.30–11pm. Moderate.

Circa The Prince St Kilda, 2 Acland St, St Kilda ℡9536 1122. Part of the multimillion-dollar redevelopment that has transformed this once-grungy pub into an Art Deco treasure. Touted as one of Melbourne's best restaurants, *Circa* has a magnificently theatrical fit-out, excellent food and wine, and boasts superb service. Daily 7–11am, noon–3pm & 6.30pm–late. Expensive to very expensive.

Claypots Seafood Bar 213 Barkly St, St.Kilda.
℡9534 1282 You can't book, so arrive

△ Cake shop, Acland Street, St Kilda

early at this tiny and perpetually busy eatery, which offers fabulous blackboard specials and "claypots" that are used to casserole everything from seafood to lamb and tempting veggie combinations. Come summer escape the heat of the open kitchen and head out back to the courtyard. Daily 9am–3pm & 6–10.30pm. Cheap to moderate.

The Dog's Bar 54 Acland St, St Kilda T9525 3599. One of the first café-bars in St Kilda, and as popular as ever, even if its distressed paint finish and fake cracks are beginning to look more alarmingly genuine with every year. Italian-style food, simple and reasonably priced, and a good range of wines. Mon–Fri noon–1am, Sat & Sun 10am–1am. Inexpensive.

Donovans 40 Jacka Blvd, St Kilda ⊕9534 8221. Originally a 1920s bathing pavilion, *Donovans* is now a relaxed beach-house restaurant, complete with sofas and oceanfront views. The atmosphere's homely and the menu mainly seafood, and it's one of the best places for lounging around the fireplace in winter. Daily noon–late. Expensive.

The Espy Kitchen The Esplanade Hotel, 11 Upper Esplanade, St Kilda ⊕9534 0211. This restaurant at the back of the *Esplanade Hotel* (see p.128) is casual and slow, but has recently been spruced up, and the excellent comfort food is worth the wait. On Monday nights $10 will get you a beef/chicken/veggie burger with chips and a pot of beer. Daily noon–3pm & 6–8pm. Inexpensive.

Il Fornaio 2 Acland St, St Kilda ⊕9534 2922. Hip bakery serving excellent breads, pastries, pastas and coffee, and at night more expensive mains (in the evenings you may even get a loaf of unsold bread to take away with you). Popular at breakfast time, with seating both inside and out. Daily 7am–10pm. Cheap to inexpensive.

Jerry's Milk Bar 345 Barkly St, Elwood ⊕9531 3078. Cornershop milk bar-cum-café brimming with old-fashioned trappings (check out the lolly counter and collection of milk-shake makers), not to mention the locals who come for the coffee and delicious soups, pasta, risotto and waist-weakeners such as Portuguese custard tarts. Daily 8am–6pm (kitchen till 4pm). Cheap to inexpensive.

Melbourne Wine Room The George Hotel, 125 Fitzroy St, St Kilda ⊕9525 5599. Excellent Victorian wine list and an innovative menu from either the bar (inexpensive) or more upmarket dining area (expensive). Top service, top setting, top place. Restaurant Wed–Sat 6–11pm; bar Mon–Thurs 3–11pm, Fri–Sun noon–11pm. Inexpensive to expensive.

One Fitzroy Street 1 Fitzroy St, St Kilda ⊕9593 8800. Hard-to-beat location at the corner of Fitzroy Street and the Esplanade, with a café and bar downstairs (moderate), and an ultramodern restaurant upstairs, sporting a balcony that compensates for the higher prices with stupendous views over Port Phillip Bay. Restaurant: Mon–Fri noon–3pm & 6pm–midnight, Sat & Sun 10am–midnight; bar: Mon–Fri noon–midnight, Sat & Sun 10am–midnight. Expensive.

Pelican 16 Fitzroy St, St Kilda ⊕9525 5847. Groovy and always buzzing tapas bar that offers a menu with more than a few standouts. The outdoor deck is perfect for lazy summer breakfasts. Daily 7.30am–1am. Cheap to inexpensive.

Café Scheherazade 99 Acland St, St Kilda ⊕9534 2722. Hangout for elderly Eastern European émigrés, *Scheherezade* was opened by a Jewish couple in the 1950s and has grown in popularity to become an Acland Street institution. Famous for its chicken broth (some swear it has medicinal properties) and inexpensive mains, it's a great escape from modern-day, *haute cuisine*. Daily 9am–midnight. Inexpensive.

Soulmama Level 1, St Kilda Sea Baths, 10 Jacka Blvd, St Kilda ⊕9525 3338. Glam vegetarian café, serving wholesome food in three bowl sizes from the tempting *bains-marie*, including beetroot in tahini and zesty tofu curries. Great beach views and a formidable drinks list. Daily noon–late. Cheap.

The Stokehouse 30 Jacka Blvd, St Kilda ⊕9525 5555. Boasting a spectacular beachfront location and views, this converted teahouse is one of the most popular eating spots in Melbourne. Both the café-bar downstairs (Mon–Sat 11am–late, Sat & Sun 10am–late; inexpensive) serving snacks and nibbles and the stylish restaurant upstairs (expensive) are always busy – the former sometimes annoyingly so. Although the restaurant menu has a leaning towards seafood, there's always a wide variety of inventive dishes available. Daily noon–2.30pm & 6–10pm. Inexpensive to expensive.

Termini 60a Fitzroy St, St Kilda ☎9537 3465.
Termini, set in the old St Kilda railway station, has slightly patronizing staff serving simple and rustic but excellent main courses, from pasta to pork; desserts, such as the rich chocolate *sfomato* (soufflé), are sensational. There's also a great two-course set lunch ($17) which includes a glass of wine. Daily noon–11pm. Moderate.

Topolinos 87 Fitzroy St ☎9534 4856. A dimly lit, noisy and smoky St Kilda institution, which pumps out pizzas, generous pasta dishes and good cocktails until dawn. Mon–Thurs & Sun noon–3am, Fri & Sat noon–6am. Cheap to inexpensive.

Veludo 175 Acland St ☎9534 4456. Upstairs restaurant that mixes dark-stained floor-boards, red-brick walls and 1950s decor with interesting and stylishly presented European dishes. The groovy downstairs bar area also has simple but good food, such as pies, mash and salads. Mon–Fri 7am–10.30pm, Sat & Sun 7am–11pm. Cheap to expensive.

Wall Two 80 280 Carlisle St ☎9593 8280. Restored kosher butcher's shop that's one of the coolest cafés in the city, offering simple but delicious food (mostly toasted *pides*) and good coffee. Inside is a series of small alcoves and a larger space dominated by a wooden communal table, perfect for chit-chat. Check out the takeaway window and milk crates for seating outside. Daily 7.30am–6pm. Cheap.

Williamstown

Hobson's Choice Foods 213 Nelson Place ☎9397 1891. Expansive menu has everything from eggs, home-made shepherd's pie and laksa to croissants and pastries. With seafront views and a breezy atmosphere, this is a popular place for breakfasts and lazy Sunday lunches. Daily 7am–1am. Cheap.

Lever & Kowalyk 42 Ferguson St ☎9397 6798. One of the first places to combine a café with a high-quality foodstore, the best bet at *L&K* is the huge breakfasts, though the upmarket dinner menu is worth a splurge. Buy some high-quality snacks for portside picnicking. Mon 8am–5pm, Tues–Fri 8am–10pm, Sat 9am–10pm, Sun 9am–5pm. Breakfast and lunch cheap, dinner moderate.

Siam Orchid Restaurant 145 Nelson Place ☎9397 5303. Busy, comfortable place with friendly service and filling, but affordabe Thai food in the middle of a very competitive restaurant strip. Tues–Sun 5–10.30pm. Cheap to inexpensive.

Siren's Beach Dressing Pavilion, The Esplanade ☎9397 7811. Located in a former bathing pavilion, *Siren's* dishes up above-average seafood in its formal restaurant (moderate), while the cheaper bistro (inexpensive) serves a good spread of light meals. Great for grabbing a pot of beer and plate of chips, then heading to the deck for the fantastic beach views. Daily 10am–10pm. Inexpensive to moderate.

Stag's Head Inn Cnr Ann & Cecil streets ☎9397 5303. This backstreet treat is one of the few pubs in the area that retains its traditional pub character. The menu is hearty unpretentious pub grub including steaks, pastas and a truly intimidating club sandwich. Daily noon–late. Cheap.

Pubs, bars and clubs

Melburnians take their drinking very seriously and their love affair with all things alcoholic is reflected in the city's excellent **pubs and bars** – from places so obscure and cutting-edge you'll only know they exist by word of mouth to large establishments catering to broader and louder tastes. The push to revive Melbourne's once staid CBD has seen many older watering holes transformed into lively, youth-oriented venues, while cheap bar licences and increased competition have led to a new generation of bars popping up in hidden pockets of the city on a regular basis. The relaxing of Melbourne's once draconian **licensing laws** means that it's now possible to drink from noon until dawn, and to draw in the customers city pubs today offer better food, a classier selection of booze and plenty of live entertainment. The only downside is that **dress codes** are often rigidly enforced, and drinks can be expensive; some places also have a cover charge if there's live entertainment or a DJ.

For online information, visit ⓦwww.melbournepubs.com, which has a searchable guide to the city's drinking spots; otherwise, *The Age Bar Guide* is available from bookshops. If you're interested in finding out how beer is made, Aussie-style, the **Carlton and United Brewery Centre** on the corner of Nelson and Thompson streets in Abbotsford runs ninety-minute tours (Mon–Fri 10am & 2pm; $15; bookings essential ☎9420 6800) highlighting everything from the brewing process to final production, and with free samples at the end of the tour.

Melbourne's **club culture** is as vibrant as its bar scene and all but the most resolute party animals will find plenty to keep them entertained. Clubs focus on myriad dance styles, particularly house, techno and break-beat, while indie and retro heads are also well looked after. The hot spots are **Chapel Street** in South Yarra, the **CBD** and the **Docklands**, but clubs take root anywhere they can, from big commercial nights in the suburbs to obscure experimental sessions in inner-city nooks and crannies. Overseas DJs visit frequently, and local talent keeps the scene thriving.

The bigger the night, the more the **cover charge**, though it rarely tops $15 unless there's an international guest. Most clubs offer discounted or even free entry to punters with a pass available free from record shops such as Gaslight Music (see p.158), some bars and fashion outlets. These places also hand out copies of Melbourne's essential clubbing **guides**: *Beat* and *Inpress* magazines. Also look out for posters on billboard sites around town, announcing the next rave event.

City Centre

For locations of the following see the maps on p.34, p.46, p.56 and p.65.

Bars and clubs

Belgian Beer Café Bluestone 557 St Kilda Rd ☎9529 2899. Sprawl on the lawn with Belgian fries and mayonnaise or tuck into some mussels, veal or pork sausages inside this handsome nineteenth-century building. Large range of beers served by good-looking and super-efficient bar staff. Mon–Fri 8am–late, Sat 11am–1am, Sun 11am–11pm.

Bond 24 Bond St, off Flinders Lane ☎9629 9844. Sleek and roomy club, with a space-age feel and very high cool factor, where you can relax in the cigar lounge or pose in one of the darker corners. Wed & Thurs 4pm–1am, Fri 4pm–3am, Sat 9pm–5am

Bunker Lounge 407 Swanston St ☎9650 5099, ⓦwww.bunkerlounge.com.au. Eighties video games and cool staff set the tone of this downstairs den. Lounge on the generous sofas and listen to the local DJs. Mon–Wed 4pm–midnight, Thurs–Fri 4pm–3am, Sat 9pm–3am.

Chaise Lounge 105 Queen St ☎9670 6120, ⓦwww.chaiselounge.com.au. This underground bar filled with opulent antique furnishings has an extensive list of cocktails and beers, good snacks and DJs (Thurs–Sat) playing down-tempo numbers to keep the vibe suitably chilled. Mon–Wed 4pm–midnight, Thurs–Fri 4pm–3am, Sat 9pm–3am.

Club 383 Francis Hotel, 383 Lonsdale St ☎9670 6575. Dark, maze-like club with a clientele of hip young things who like to dance to alternative retro and indie pop. Cheap entry and drinks, just right for a student crowd clubbing on a budget. Entry $7 or $5 with pass. Fri & Sat 10pm–5am.

Cookie 252 Swanston St ☎9663 7660. Quirky but cool, *Cookie* successfully combines cocktail bar, beer hall and Thai restaurant in a large open space that still manages to feel dark and intimate. Mon–Fri 5pm–late, Sat 8pm–late.

The Croft Institute 21–25 Croft Alley, off Paynes place, off Little Bourke St ☎9671 4399. Tucked down a dark lane and boasting a large collection of laboratory apparatus, this bar is a must on Melbourne's bar scene. Spread over three levels (two of which pump out hard house until dawn), *Croft* could be straight out of the London underground club scene. Mon–Fri 5pm–late, Sat 8pm–late

Ding Dong Lounge 18 Market Lane ☎9662 1020. Sister bar to the rock 'n' roll hangout in New York but with a modern Australian touch and a varied line-up of local and touring international bands. Tues–Thurs 5pm–late, Fri & Sat 5pm–4am.

Double Happiness 21 Liverpool St ☎9650 4488. Tiny hole-in-the-wall bar with a Communist China aesthetic and nuclear-strength cocktails and nightcaps like "The Great Leap Forward". If you really like the place you can buy a "keep bottle" which is stored behind the bar for your next visit. Sun–Wed 5pm–1am, Thurs–Sat 5pm–3am.

Double O Sniders Lane, corner of Lonsdale and Swanston streets ☎9654 8000. Business people file into *Double O's* two smallish rooms – one filled with snug resting spots and bathed in moody lighting, the other with a token dance floor – for pre-dinner drinks. Fri & Sat 10pm–5am.

Ffour 2/322 Little Collins St ☎9650 4494 Constructivist-inspired decor, suave bar staff and a classy DJ roster make this a happening hideout. Wed–Fri 5pm–5am, Sat 10pm–5am.

Gin Palace 10 Russell Place, off Little Collins St ☎9654 0533. Glamorous subterranean joint with an upmarket drinks list specializing in cocktails (including nine different martinis) – not cheap, but generous. A favourite is the "Luis Buñuel's Surrealist Martini", in which all the ingredients are frozen for two days before use. Good food and chilled lounge music too. Daily 4pm–3am.

Hairy Canary 212 Little Collins St ☎9654 2471, ⓦwww.hairycanary.com.au. This modern, stylish bar is perfect for whiling away an afternoon or nursing a hangover, with an extensive menu available most of the day, plus cocktails and a wide range of local and imported beers and wines. Mon–Fri 7.30am–3am, Sat 9am–1am, Sun 9am–1am

Heat Level 3, Crown Casino, 8 Whiteman St ☎9699 2222. Officially known as the *Heat Discotheque and Cocktail Bar*, this swanky joint is extremely popular with Melbourne's early-twenties crowd, and has long opening hours, a state-of-the-art light show, hysterically funny karaoke sessions and mainstream dance music. Strict dress code applies. Cover from $5–12. Thurs–Mon 9pm–late, Sat 2pm–2am.

Honkytonks Duckboard Place, off Flinders Lane ☎9662 4555. Quirky, lush establishment up a staircase in a dark alley mixing the best of pared-down design with over-the-top flourishes like a hollowed-out grand piano that acts as DJ booth, and a tropical garden chillout zone. Plays host to more cutting edge DJs, both local and international, but you have to brave the door police first. Tues–Sun 5pm–3am.

Khokolat 43 Hardware Lane, off Bourke St ℡9642 1142. In the basement of a former Chinese restaurant, *Khokolat* attracts a laid-back crowd in search of cool retro style, sophisticated sounds and simple but tempting lunch food. Mon–Thurs noon–late, Fri & Sat noon–5am.

La La Land Corner of Hardware Lane & Little Lonsdale St ℡9670 5011. European alpine-inspired place with fondue and schnapps on offer in cosy, comfortable surroundings. DJs spin cool lounge-inspired sounds with a dancing crowd after 10pm. Mon–Fri 5pm–late, Sat & Sun 7pm–late.

Loop 23 Meyers Place ℡9654 0500. Super stylish venue that's a big hit with the local intelligentsia. Apart from screening experimental films, there's a regular line-up of DJs dropping everything from new wave cuts and 1980s UK electronic pop to disco, techno and funk. Mon–Fri 4pm–4am, Sat–Sun 6pm–4am.

Lounge 243 Swanston St ℡9663 2916. A veritable grandaddy of the inner-city scene. Like its newer competitors, the focus is on cool electronic tunes and a beatnik vibe. There are daytime drinks and snacks, but late at night the floor is cleared for clubbers with attitude. The balcony is a treat on hot summer nights and the large and friendly upstairs bar has pool tables and a pinball machine. Entry charge around $10 Wed–Sun after 10pm. Mon, Tues & Sun 10am–2am, Wed–Sat10am–7am.

Metro 20 Bourke St ℡9663 4288, ⊛www .metronightclub.com. A Melbourne clubbing institution, *Metro* is a large, stylish venue converted from a sumptuous old cinema. Popular with mainstream clubbers, its regular nights focus on accessible dance, pop and alternative sounds, and it's also a popular venue for big-name touring acts like Fat Boy Slim, the Beastie Boys and the Chemical Brothers. Expect to queue. Entry $6–10. Thurs–Sat 9pm–5am.

Meyers Place 20 Meyers Place, off Bourke St ℡9650 8609. Designed by rising Melbourne architectural firm Six Degrees, this swish, dimly lit hole in the wall has proved a

massive hit with Melbourne's trendy professionals. The grooviest place to fall down on a Friday night, bar none. Tues & Wed 4pm–late, Thurs & Fri 2pm–4am, Sat 4pm–4am.

Misty 3–5 Hosier Lane, off Flinders St ℡9663 9202. On Melbourne's coolometer, *Misty* can't be beat, although the choice of tipples is limited. Most nights it's filled with hairdressers, students and assorted poseurs; just pull up a stool, pretend you're an architect, and you'll fit right in. Mystifyingly hard to find, so look out for the gleaming light box at the entrance. Tues–Thurs 5pm–1am, Fri & Sat 5pm–3am, Sun 4–11pm.

Phoenix 82 Flinders St ℡9650 4976. Covering four levels, from subterranean dance floor to the "quieter" top-floor lounge area, there are plenty of places to lose yourself here, while better-than-average bar snacks make it a popular haunt for the post-work crowd. Mon–Wed 4pm–late, Thurs & Fri noon–4am, Sat 4pm–4am, Sun 4pm–late.

Pony 68 Little Collins St ℡9662 1026. Crowded, low-ceilinged, dimly lit favourite that brings in the diehards with its 7am weekend closing. Wed 4pm–2am, Thurs 4pm–4am, Fri 4pm–7am, Sat 6pm–7am, Sun 6pm–2am.

Purple Emerald 191 Flinders Lane ℡9650 7753. Funky space that often has live acts of a jazz-cum-soul nature (Wed–Sat, no cover charge). The open-plan seating means it never feels too crowded. Mon–Thurs 1pm–1am, Fri 1pm–3am, Sat 7pm–3am.

Rue Bebelons 267 Little Lonsdale St ℡9663 1700. So laid-back that the bar staff flip the vinyl in between serving drinks, this small European-style place has friendly service and a simple but reasonably priced selection of beers and snacks. Tues–Fri 8am–3am, Sat 11am–3am, Sun 2–8pm.

Scubar 228 Queen St ℡9670 2105. Sexy, 1970s-style underground hangout, populated in equal parts by seedy-looking "intellectuals" and moneyed professionals, with local and visiting DJs each night. Daily 4pm–late.

Spleen 41 Bourke St ℡9650 2400. A warren of a place, aimed at precocious party animals, *Spleen* fills up rapidly at weekends with those warming up for a big night or having a drink after the movies. Live music Wed and Thurs. Decent and inexpensive snacks available too. Mon–Fri 4pm–3am, Sat & Sun 5pm–late.

Three Degrees Bar Brewery Brasserie Queen Victoria Complex, Swanston St ☎9639 6766. Fusing pub, bar, café, restaurant and a two-storey microbrewery serving "three", their signature beer, *Three Degrees* seems to have popped its cork and overflowed. Fortunately, it's an appealing place, where thirtysomethings compete in the glamour stakes after trawling the shopping lanes below. Occasionally sloppy service though. Mon–Wed 11am–midnight, Thurs & Fri 11am–late, Sat–Sun 10am–late.

Transport Federation Square ☎9654 8808. Enormous pub complex with a staggering range of beers and good local wines on offer. Noisy and fun, it attracts a mixed crowd of suits and film school students – Monday nights they show cool new short films. Friday nights are especially busy, so be prepared to queue. Daily noon–late.

Troika 106 Little Lonsdale St ☎9663 0221. Inner-city crowd meets suburban trendies and creative types in a relaxed, casual atmosphere, with a selection of local and imported beers that will satisfy the most discerning punter. Tues–Fri 4pm–late, Sat 5pm–late.

Velour Bar 121 Flinders Lane ☎9663 5589. Large and popular (especially on Saturdays when it attracts a dancing crowd), this place incorporates a dance floor and bar into its split-level design, and offers a comprehensive range of bottled beers and spirits. Cover charge $5 Fri & Sat. Thurs 4.30pm–2am, Fri 4.30pm–4am, Sat 9pm–4am.

Pubs

Stork Hotel 504 Elizabeth St ☎9663 6237, Ⓦwww.storkhotel.com. This historic watering

Irish and English Pubs

The list below recognizes just some of the growing band of Irish and English theme pubs sprouting across Melbourne – each offering atmosphere and entertainment, as well as cheap pub tucker that's a long way from fish fingers and baked beans on toast.

Bridie O'Reilly's 62 Little Collins St, City ☎9650 0840. Above-average theme pub sporting lots of Emerald Isle gewgaws, and attracting hordes of customers with hearty, humungous dishes such as stew, steak, bangers and mash, and beef and Guinness pie. Also at Chapel St, South Yarra and Sydney Rd, Brunswick. Daily 11am–late.

Charles Dickens Tavern 290 Collins St, City ☎9654 1821. Cosy place for homesick Brits, with bitter and Guinness on tap, pint glasses, and live soccer and rugby on a big-screen TV. Also rustles up excellent grub at non-rip-off prices. Mon–Wed noon–11pm, Fri–Sun noon–late.

The Irish Times 427 Little Collins St, City ☎9642 1699. Striving to provide a real taste of Dublin, *The Irish Times* has simple, comfy decor, contemporary Irish cuisine and regular live entertainment. Mon–Thurs noon–midnight, Fri noon–3am, Sat 5.30pm–late.

Pugg Mahones 106–112 Hardware Lane, City ☎9670 6155. Irish theme pub with a great weekend party atmosphere fuelled by bands playing a mix of folk and R&B. Despite having a 24hr licence, it does shut its doors sometimes, although closing time usually depends on the crowd. Also on Elgin St, Carlton. Mon, Fri & Sun noon–3am, Tues–Thurs noon–1am, Sat 4pm–3am.

The Elephant and Wheelbarrow 94–96 Bourke St, City ☎9639 8444. English theme pub kitted out in timber booths, with a log fire in winter, and photographs of the Beatles and Big Ben on the wall. The food is simple, wholesome and inexpensive. Its St Kilda sister pub (169 Fitzroy St ☎9534 7888) has a Monday night "Meet the Neighbours", when stars of the Australian soap play trivia games, hand out prizes and generally rub shoulders with the punters. Mon–Thurs & Sun 11am–1am, Fri & Sat 11am–3am.

Molly Blooms 39 Bay St, Port Melbourne, ☎9646 2681. One of Melbourne's oldest Irish pubs, *Molly's* still proudly maintains its original character, and with a good Irish menu (lunch & dinner daily) and lively, knockabout music, it's the place of choice for local expatriates. Mon–Wed & Sun noon–midnight, Thurs noon–1am, Fri & Sat noon–3am.

hole, located in a hotel from the goldrush era, features lovely Art Deco fittings and superb artwork from some of Australia's finest cartoonists. There's live music Tues–Sat and regular theatre/comedy events. Mon–Sat 10am–12.30am, Sun noon–12.30am.
Young & Jackson's Corner of Swanston & Flinders streets ☎9650 3884. Victoria's oldest

and most famous boozer (see p.35) has been given a major make-over, and now contains a café/bar area, plus two central bars. Despite the facelift, it's still as good a place as anywhere to start drinking your way around town. In winter, a boisterous footy crowd usually descends after matches. Daily 10am–late.

Fitzroy and Carlton

For locations of the following see the maps on p.69, p.70 and p.74.

Bars and clubs

Bar Open 317 Brunswick St ☎9415 9601, ⓦwww .baropen.com.au. Funky little bar attracting an arty crowd, popular at weekends, when free live jazz spills out into the rear courtyard. Get in early to secure a window seat. Mon–Sat 1pm–3am, Sun 1pm–2am.
Carlton Yacht Club Bar 298 Lygon St ☎9347 7080. Decidedly landlocked, but seafaring kitsch, well-priced cocktails, a good beer list and tapas have this bar firmly moored as a favourite in local hearts. Mon–Wed & Sun 5pm–1am, Thurs–Sat 5pm–3am.
Night Cat 141 Johnston St ☎9417 0090. Ten years on since it opened, this retro-opulent venue still maintains its cool charm. Plenty of dimly lit tables and lounges for slouching, plus a large dance floor if you're taken by the live music, ranging from swinging jazz to up-tempo Latin. Door charge Fri & Sat $5. Thurs–Sun 9pm-late
Polly 401 Brunswick St ☎9417 0880. Bespectacled student types descend on this opulent velvet and rococo joint to colonize the large central bar, and finger through the comprehensive but pricey cocktail list. Mon–Thurs & Sun 5pm–1am, Fri & Sat 5pm–3am.
Yelza 245 Gertrude St ☎9416 2689. Having maintained its role as a neighbourhood meeting place while becoming a great destination for those seeking Melbourne's finest daiquiri, this place is well worth making the effort. Wed–Sun 6pm–1am.

Pubs

The Builders Arms 211 Gertrude St ☎9419 0818. Hip without being exclusive, *The Builders Arms* has guest DJs at weekends,

when it's easily identifiable by the punters queueing to get in. Meals and snacks are available too and the "No Pokies" sign above the door has become a Melbourne landmark. Mon–Wed 5pm–11pm, Thurs 5pm–1am, Fri noon–1am, Sat & Sun 1pm–1am.
The Napier Hotel 210 Napier St ☎9419 4240. Small, eclectic pub with friendly service and seven beers on tap. The outside tables are ideal in the summer, and the cosy lounge with pool table is perfect for a winter's day. There's also down-to-earth grub at reasonable prices and the kitchen keeps long hours. Mon–Wed 3–11pm, Thurs 3pm–midnight, Fri 3pm–1am, Sat 1pm–1am, Sun 1–11pm.
The Rainbow Hotel 27 St David St ☎9419 4193, Cosy little boozer featuring free live music (jazz, blues, funk or country) nightly and on weekend afternoons. Although crowded at weekends, the front bar is comfortable and relaxing, and the bands aren't so loud as to spoil conversation. Daily 3pm–1am.
The Rose Hotel 406 Napier St ☎9417 3626. A good example of what inner-city pubs were like before pokies (slot machines) and architects axed much of their character. Although busy at weekends and evenings, it's retained the feel of a family-run pub, with a basic range of alcohol and hearty meals like T-bone steak. Mon 11am–11pm Tues–Thurs 11am–midnight, Fri & Sat 11am–1am, Sun noon–midnight.
The Standard Hotel 293 Fitzroy St, Fitzroy. ☎9419 4793. Fitzroy's quintessential local, with a landscaped beer garden and a decent pub menu to boot. Students and locals alike come here to soak up the authentic pub feel. Mon–Sat noon–11pm, Sun noon–9pm.

South Yarra, Prahran and South Melbourne

For locations of the following see map, p.77.

Bars and clubs

Blue Bar 330 Chapel St, Prahran ☎9529 6499.
Intimate, Japanese-influenced bar that
spills out onto the street at weekends, with
groovers checking each other out while
sipping mineral water. Good range of local
and imported beers, as well as a bar snacks
menu. There's no sign, so look for the blue
neon bar above the door. Mon–Wed & Sun
noon–1am, Thurs–Sat noon–3am.

The Butterfly Club 204 Bank St, South Melbourne
☎9690 2000, ⓦwww.thebutterflyclub.com.
A dash of artsy cocktail bar mixed with a
cabaret salon, The Butterfly Club is one of
Melbourne's more camp environments. Keep
an eye out for exotic Madame Sin and her
merry band of mistresses. Dinner and show
packages available. Wed–Sun 7.30pm–late.

Candy Bar 162 Greville St, Prahran ☎9529 6566.
Attracting a twentysomething, party-going
crowd, this is a good place to head for
some solid drinking and dancing. Dress up,
however, or you may have trouble getting
past the fashion police at the door. Meals
available, with breakfast offered at weekends.
Mon–Fri noon–late, Sat & Sun 10am–late.

161 161 High St, Prahran ☎9533 8433. One
of the coolest bars south of the river and a
veritable 1970s den – all shagpile carpet,
volumes of vinyl and gold walls as far as the
eye can see. Wed 8.30pm–3am, Thurs–Sat
8.30pm–late.

Revolver 229 Chapel St, Prahran ☎9521 5985,
ⓦwww.revolverupstairs.com.au. Revolver has
established itself as a popular venue with
Melbourne's drinking and partying crowd.
Cult-like electronic beat DJs and artists
create a cool vibe every night, bands play
most weekends (a modest cover charge
applies), and it's the perfect place for a
chilled-out Saturday afternoon. You can
grab a snack in the Thai restaurant, lounge
around with a drink in the spacious main
area, or boogie in the back room. Entry
from $5 to $10 depending on the guest DJ.
Mon–Thurs noon–3am, Fri noon through to
Sun 3am, non-stop DJs.

So Bar 630 Chapel St, South Yarra ☎9824 0400,
ⓦwww.hotelcomo.com.au. Trendy bar attached
to *The Como*, where jazz is performed every
Friday night and Wednesday 6–8pm is happy
hour. Daily 4pm–late.

The Viper Room 373 Chapel St, South Yarra
☎9827 1771. If it's a young, body-conscious
crowd and progressive trance, big beats
and hard techno you're looking for, this is
the place for you. Fri–Sun 11pm–7am.

Cigar and supper clubs

Melbourne's smart society is currently flourishing, as witnessed by the city's
increasing number of **cigar and supper clubs**. Popular with an older crowd, these
nightspots are guilt-free havens for cigar smokers; their dark and leathery confines
offer plenty of cheap food and live or recorded music. All are open late, and usually
charge no admission.

Fidel's Cigar Room Lower Ground Floor, Crown Casino, 8 Whiteman St, Southbank,
City ☎9292 6885. A must for aficionados of fine liquor and cigars, the latter ranging
in price from $10 to over $100. The interior is filled with antiques, leather armchairs,
humidors, rare books and stylish modern furnishings. Although expensive, drinks
are generous.

Melbourne Supper Club Level 1, 161 Spring St, City ☎9654 6300. This convivial
upstairs lounge opposite Parliament House exudes an air of decadence and attracts
a lively mixed crowd. As well as an excellent drinks list, the club offers cigars,
inexpensive food, and deep leather sofas to flop onto.

Tony Starr's Kitten Club Level 1, 267 Little Collins St, City ☎9650 2448. Sleek and
stylish 50s/60s-inspired interior mixed with slightly Oriental furnishings make this a
great place for lolling around cradling a cocktail and nibbling on Asian-inspired food.
Has live music and cabaret nights worth looking out for too.

Richmond and Collingwood

For locations of the following see map p.80.

Bars and clubs

A Bar Called Barry 64 Smith St ☎8415 1464. Silly name but seriously cool in every other way, *Barry* (to his mates) has become a Collingwood institution thanks to a slick interior, ever-changing roster of DJs and fashionable young crowd. Fri–Sat 9pm–5am.

Good Morning Captain 20 Johnston St ☎9419 6049. This grungy converted house rambles through three rooms with the backroom hosting up-and-coming bands or poetry gigs. Nights are packed with a cool arty crowd who often stay for the big weekend breakfasts. Wed 4pm–10pm, Thurs–Fri 4pm–1am, Sat 10am–1am, Sun 10am–10pm.

Ilk 187 Johnston St ☎9417 1687. Stepping into *Ilk* is like accidentally stumbling into someone's house party. A good place to chat in nicely idiosyncratic surroundings, popular with thirtysomethings. Thurs, Fri & Sat 6pm-1am

Pubs

All Nations Hotel 64 Lennox St ☎9428 5612. Traditional and largely unchanged Melbourne pub, complete with horseshoe bar, a "snug" bar, hugely popular dining room out back serving great food and a courtyard. Mon & Tues 11am–10pm, Wed–Sat 11am–11pm, Sun noon–9pm (lunch daily, dinner Thurs–Sat).

Curry Family Hotel Corner of Hotham & Wellington streets ☎9419 4458. Seek out this backstreet boozer for a local pub that has frequent quiz nights (so popular they require reservations), free pool on Mondays, occasional DJs and always cheerful staff. Daily 11am–10pm

The Public House 433 Church St ☎9421 0187. Ultra chic but with a remarkably relaxed vibe, The Public also has a tempting tapas-style menu if you fancy some food with your drinks. On warm nights head upstairs to the terrace. Mon–Sat noon–midnight.

St Kilda

For locations of the following see map p.87.

Bars and clubs

Dog's Bar 54 Acland St ☎9525 3599. Terrific wine list, surprisingly poor beer selection and great tucker in this very chic bar. The outdoor area at the front is a perfect place for eyeballing passers-by, especially on a sunny afternoon. Mon–Fri noon–1am, Sat & Sun 10am–1am.

Doulton Bar 202 Barkly St ☎9534 2200. Part of the *Village Belle Hotel*, but ignore the front bar and head for the old-fashioned *Doulton Bar* – via a discreet door next to the bottle shop – for a relaxing oasis from the St Kilda crowds, with a one-way window overlooking the street. Sun–Wed 1pm–1am, Thurs–Sat 1pm–3am.

The George Public Bar 127 Fitzroy St ☎9534 8822. Cool underground bar with an upbeat design. Favoured by locals, travellers and artists, it has a large range of beers on tap plus a pool table and free live music on Saturday afternoons. The service is friendly and the kitchen is open until around 10pm, serving a wide range of snacks and good-value meals. Mon–Wed & Sun noon–1am, Thurs noon–2am, Fri & Sat noon–3am.

Mink Bar The Prince St Kilda, 2b Acland St ☎9536 1199. Carved out of the remade part of *The Prince St Kilda*, this subterranean space has back-lit refrigerated shelves stacked high with an astonishing array of vodkas, including Japanese. There are also private booths for intimate chats and regular movie nights. If you're hungry, try the antipasto platters, or head straight for the caviar and Cuban cigars. A great place for convivial quaffing and mellowing. Daily 6pm–late.

Pause 268 Carlisle St ☎9537 0511. Moorish-themed decor, great bar menu (lunch and dinner) and friendly local feel. Keep an eye out for "barket", a bar and market rolled into one and held on the first Sunday of the month. Daily noon–1am.

Sunset Bar 16 Grey St ☎9534 9205. Cross between a strip joint and a cabaret lounge on a cruise ship. With a deafening sound system, cheap drinks and a late close, it's a popular place with backpackers from the nearby hostels. Moderate cover charge applies after midnight on Friday and Saturday. Daily 9pm–5am.

Veludo 175 Acland St ☎9534 4456, ⓦwww .veludo.com. A magnet for St Kilda's fashionable crowd, Veludo sports a bar downstairs with interesting and cheap food, and a smart restaurant upstairs (see p.120). Spacious and stylish, with live music some nights,it really gathers steam at the weekends. Bar/club hours: Mon–Fri 5pm–2am, Sat & Sun 3pm–3am.

Pubs

The Esplanade Hotel 11 Upper Esplanade ☎9534 0211, ⓦwww.espy.com.au. Famous for its beachside views, this hotel is the epicentre of St Kilda's drinking scene and shouldn't be missed. Bands play every night and there are inexpensive meals from *The Espy Kitchen* at the rear, plus pool tables and pinball machines. Mon–Thurs & Sun noon–1am, Fri & Sat noon–3am.

The Prince St Kilda 29 Fitzroy St ☎9536 1177. Defiantly local and no-frills, the downstairs public bar at *The Prince St Kilda* has an air of stubborn resistance in the face of St Kilda's freewheeling gentrification. Frequented in equal parts by colourful local personalities and desperadoes, this hotel is not for the faint-hearted. Mon–Wed 11am– 2am, Thurs–Sun 11am–3am.

Live music

M elbourne has arguably the best live **music scene** in Australia – on any given night you'll find scores of bands playing at venues around the city, covering everything from grunge rock and retro to blues, jazz, folk and avante-garde. Despite an inner-city culture of gentrification, which has seen some of the city's best rock venues replace PA systems with pokies (slot machines), a booming DJ-driven rave scene and an increase in residential noise complaints that has forced many places to cancel loud bands, Melbourne's music scene has remained healthy and remarkably resilient. The city boasts the largest concentration of live music venues in Australia, and there are still several long-time, reliable pubs and bars such as *The Corner Hotel* (see p.130) that keep their doors open.

The city's rock and pop heritage is a rich one. During the 1970s and 1980s, Melbourne spewed forth numerous high-calibre bands like the Skyhooks, Daddy Cool, the Sports, incendiary punk-blues outfit The Birthday Party and sweaty pub-rock stalwarts Hunters and Collectors, while Powderfinger, The Cat Empire and the AC/DC-inspired Jet all got their start on the local live music scene before breaking into the charts. With a little inside knowledge, you could also catch one of the bigger and more expensive touring acts for next to nothing at one of the "secret shows" that abound at the city's smaller venues. Label-wise, the seminal Melbourne-based Mushroom Records (see box on p.131) was responsible for launching the vocal talents of both indie and mainstream singers such as Kylie Minogue and Peter Andre onto an unsuspecting world.

Comprehensive listings of bands and venues can be found in the free *Beat* and *Inpress* magazines, available from cafés, record shops and fashion boutiques in the inner city, or the "EG" insert in the Friday edition of *The Age*. Probably the best listings, however, are found in the *Herald Sun*, Melbourne's other daily, which has an excellent liftout called "Hit" every Thursday. You can also tune into one of Melbourne's community radio stations, such as 3RRR (102.7 FM) or 3PBS (106.7 FM), and there's a good gig guide available on Triple J radio's website (ⓦtriplej.yourevents.com.au).

For larger events you may need to **book in advance** through Ticketmaster (ⓣ13 61 66, ⓦwww.ticketmaster.com.au) or Ticketek (ⓣ13 28 49, ⓦpremier .ticketek.com.au), or at music stores like Gaslight Music (see p.158). At pubs and smaller venues you can pay at the door; entry to gigs ranges from about $10 to $35 depending on the calibre of the band.

In summer, Melbourne hosts a number of outdoor **music festivals**, including the groovy Good Vibrations (see p.140), the national and international line-up of Big Day Out (see p.139), and the laid-back Melbourne International Music and Blues Festival (see p.140).

The city is also blessed with a fine **classical music** scene. The Melbourne Symphony Orchestra gives regular performances at the Melbourne Concert Hall in the Victorian Arts Centre (see p.58) and at Melbourne Town Hall (see p.35). Opera Australia has productions during the season (March–May & Nov–Dec) at the State Theatre in the Arts Centre and the newly renovated Opera Centre at 35 City Rd, Southbank, while chamber music can be heard at the Melbourne Concert Hall and Melbourne Town Hall. Expect to pay $40–80 for classical music performances, $60–130 for opera; tickets can be obtained from Ticketmaster.

Indie and mainstream rock

City Centre

Ding Dong Lounge 18 Market Lane ☎9662 1020. The kind of bar The Strokes would feel right at home in – full of cool rock 'n' roll types, with padded booths lining the walls and beer taps shaped like guitar necks. Expect a soundtrack of loud, classy rock favourites or regular DJs playing more dancy tunes.

Green Room Cnr Elizabeth & Flinders streets ☎9614 2777. Tiny downstairs bar with bands every night, and plenty of smoke, beer and body odour.

The Hi Fi Bar and Ballroom 125 Swanston St ☎9654 7617. Reasonably spacious underground space with two bars on different levels where you can view acts in relative comfort or head for the overheated mosh-pit below. A mainstay venue for high-profile local and international indie-rock bands.

Carlton and Fitzroy

The Arthouse Cnr Elizabeth & Queensberry streets, Carlton ☎9347 3917. Something of a dive, with punk and metal bands most nights of the week aimed squarely at those who like their music at ear-bleeding volumes. Despite its hardcore credentials, occasional poetry readings and film screenings are also held here.

The Empress Hotel 714 Nicholson St, North Fitzroy ☎9489 8605, ⊛www.aian.com.au/ empress. A mecca for Melbourne's quirkier bands, with a friendly, low-key atmosphere, cheap meals and occasional screenings of cult films. To reach North Fitzroy, take tram #11.

Evelyn Hotel 351 Brunswick St, Fitzroy ☎9419 5500. Stalwart of the Fitzroy scene, the cave-like *Evelyn* is a good introduction

to Melbourne's alt-rock bands, who play here nightly. Good beer garden.

The Rob Roy Hotel 51 Brunswick Street, Fitzroy. The dress code at the *Rob Roy* is strictly flea-market chic, which suits the mainly student crowd who flock here for an eclectic array of local and touring national underground bands.

Rochester Castle 202 Johnston Street, Fitzroy. Indie and UK-flavoured pop music over two nights of the week. Apart from the music, come for the friendly, blissed-out atmosphere and frequent giveaways.

Collingwood and Richmond

The Club 132 Smith St, Collingwood ☎9417 4039. Small and claustrophobic, featuring mainly unknown acts performing at weekends only, until late into the night. There's also an upstairs bar, where you can drink until 7am and play pool. Minimal cover charge ($3–5).

The Corner Hotel 57 Swan St, Richmond ☎9427 7300. Dark, grungy, but reasonably spacious hotel with two bars showcasing local and international bands, mostly of a geetar-toting indie-rock persuasion.

The Tote 71 Johnston St, Collingwood ☎9419 5320, ⊛www.aian.com.au/thetotehotel. Classic Melbourne rock 'n' roll venue, with sharp-tongued staff, stained carpet and plastic beer glasses. Home to Melbourne's punk and hardcore scene, with nightly bands that will blow your socks off. If you've ever owned a Ramones record, this is the place for you.

Prahran

Revolver 229 Chapel St, Prahran ☎9521 5985, ⊛www.revolverupstairs.com.au. Catering mainly to a techno crowd, Revolver has bands at weekends, and also doubles as a nightclub (see p.126). Always something going on and plenty of room to dance.

St Kilda

The Esplanade Hotel 11 Upper Esplanade, St Kilda ☎9534 0211, 🖤www.espy.com.au. Long-established fixture in Melbourne's pub-rock and drinking scene (see p.128), attracting both established and fledgling acts. Bands nightly, either free in the front bar, or with a nominal cover charge in the *Gershwin Room* at the rear. No frills, but hugely enjoyable.

The Greyhound Hotel 1 Brighton Rd, St Kilda ☎9534 4189. A bit seedy, but still a good place to see established local artists as well as younger bands strutting their stuff. Bands nightly, with an emphasis on stripped-down rock 'n' roll, competing with great drag shows on Saturday nights and

karaoke on Sunday night. There's usually a small cover charge ($3–5).

The Palace Lower Esplanade, St Kilda ☎9534 7558, 🖤www.palace.com.au. One of Melbourne's larger indie venues, *The Palace* also doubles as a nightclub. It can get suffocating when packed, but it's still one of the few places where mid-range local and international acts play to large audiences without resorting to stadiums such as Melbourne Park or the MCG.

The Prince St Kilda 2 Acland St ☎9536 1111, 🖤www.theprince.com.au. Although renovated, this historic live music venue has been part of the Melbourne music scene for over twenty years. Generally haunted by Melbourne and overseas band rats, as well as people who think peroxide spikes are still sexy, it also attracts international DJs and hip-hop acts. Touring artists such as Pink often use the venue for "secret shows".

Blues and folk

Carlton and Fitzroy

The Dan O'Connell Hotel 225 Canning St, Carlton ☎9347 1502. Friendly hotel with a large back room where there's often an expatriate Irish crowd in full swing. Bands most nights of the week, usually Irish folk or

excellent acoustic blues, either free or with a minimal door charge.

The Rainbow Hotel 27 St David St, Fitzroy ☎9419 4193. Comfy, intimate venue (see p.125) with a mellow atmosphere and interesting crowd, not to mention a good selection of live blues. No cover charge.

Mushroom Records

Until its sale in 1998, **Mushroom Records** was the largest independent record label in Australia, handling over four hundred local artists, with over eight thousand releases and sales of more than eight million. The label was founded in 1972 by Michael Gudinski, an ambitious 19-year-old who quickly rose to become the most successful entrepreneur in the Australian music industry. His encouragement of domestic talent spawned a whole swag of memorable pop songs, including Split Enz's "I Got You" (their album *True Colours* was the label's first international hit), Skyhooks' "Living in the '70s", Paul Kelly's "Before Too Long" and Kylie Minogue's "I Should Be So Lucky". Gudinski's patronage of Australian music gave exposure to Melbourne-based acts the Sports, Black Sorrows and Hunters and Collectors, while others such as Nick Cave and Peter Andre also graced the Mushroom roster, delivering several no.1 UK hits and contributing substantial revenue to the label's coffers.

Twenty-six years of Mushroom Records ended when Gudinski flogged his remaining stake to News Limited for $40 million. As a last hurrah, Gudinski staged a mammoth "Concert of the Century" at the MCG, where groups ground their way through past Mushroom songs to over 70,000 dewy-eyed fans.

Jazz

City Centre

Bar Deco Grand Hyatt, 123 Collins St
☎9657 1234. Located just off the hotel's lobby, *Bar Deco* has an exclusive lounge-like ambience, where you can settle back with a martini and a good cigar and watch live jazz from Wednesday to Saturday (10.30pm–1am; free).

Bennett's Lane Jazz 25 Bennett's Lane, off Little Lonsdale St ☎9663 2856, ⓦwww .bennettslane.com. One of Melbourne's more interesting jazz venues, *Bennett's Lane* has recently been expanded to include a larger back room to complement the original cramped, archetypal 1950s-style cellar. Most nights feature high-quality local and touring acts, which play to knowledgeable and appreciative audiences. Entry is around $10.

Manchester Lane 234 Flinders Lane
☎9663 0630. Popular purpose-built, split-level, amphitheatre-style jazz venue that has a small dance floor, comfy tables and booths, plus a good range of predominantly local acts.

Richmond

Dizzy's 90 Swan St, Richmond ☎9428 1233. Housed in the original heritage-listed Richmond post office, *Dizzy's* blasts out contemporary jazz courtesy of local, national and international acts. The main bar is smoke-free, although a covered courtyard caters to those needing a nicotine hit. Shows are free from 5.30pm to 8pm, after which a cover charge of $9 applies.

Gay Melbourne

ttitudes to gays, lesbians and transgendered people in Australia are among the most relaxed in the world. With one of the highest official populations of same-sex couples in the world (bigger, even, than Sydney), it's hardly surprising that Melbourne is so gay-friendly. Pockets of gay and lesbian life exist all over inner-city Melbourne, especially along **Commercial Road**, which bisects the suburbs of Prahran and South Yarra and houses popular nightclubs, bookstores, boutiques, cafés and gymnasiums. Saturday morning at **Prahran Market** is the time to people-watch, while Brunswick Street in Fitzroy and nearby **Smith Street** in Collingwood also offer a large and eclectic range of gay-oriented eateries, retail outlets and nightspots. The final must-go area is **St Kilda**, especially Acland and Fitzroy streets, which have one of the highest concentrations of lesbian and gay residents in Australia. There's an official **gay beach** at Port Melbourne, near the sand dunes (known as "Screech Beach"), while the beaches at Elwood, St Kilda and the stretch between Middle Park and Port Melbourne are also popular.

Festivals to watch out for are the fabulous **Midsumma Festival** (early Feb see p.139), which has a wide range of sporting, artistic and theatrical events in multiple venues throughout the city; and the **Melbourne Queer Film and Video Festival** (mid-March; ☎9510 5576).

Free weekly **gay and lesbian newspaper** *Melbourne Community Voice* (MCV) and fortnighly newspapers – *Bnews* and *Melbourne Star* – are available locally at gay and lesbian venues, bookshops and gay-friendly businesses, where you will also find free interstate newspapers and guides to sights and activities. *Identity*, a monthly magazine for gay men with clubbing and entertainment news, is widely available, as is another monthly magazine, *Lesbiana*, which comes with a moderate cover price. Other good sources of **information** are Tourism Victoria (Ⓦwww .visitvictoria.com), which publishes the *Melbourne Gay & Lesbian Visitors' Guide*; Ⓦwww.out.com.au, an online portal for shopping, entertainment and travel; the *Rough Guide to Gay and Lesbian Australia* (ed. Neil Drinnan, Rough Guides Ltd. UK & Australia); the *Gay Australia Guide*, focusing on gay and lesbian travel in Australia (available at gay venues in Melbourne); *Over the Rainbow*, a guide to the law for lesbians and gay men in Victoria (available from Victoria Legal Aid, ☎9269 0223); or you can tune into Joy Melbourne 90.7 FM, Australia's only full-time queer radio station. Alternatively, check out the organizations and groups listed overleaf. Entry to pubs and clubs in the following listings is free most nights of the week, although a door charge (no more than $15) occasionally applies at the weekend. Melbourne's best gay bookshop, Hares and Hyenas (☎9824 0110), is at 135 Commercial Rd; it also has a virtual bookshop and a book review magazine covering lesbian, bisexual, transgender, gay, feminist and homosexual literature at Ⓦwww.hares-hyenas.com.au.

Melbourne is blessed with a dazzling variety of gay and lesbian organizations, support services and businesses, the most important of which are listed below. Everything else, from gay vets to lesbian psychologists, can be found in the *ALSO Directory* (see below).

AIDS organizations and medical care AIDS Line (℡9347 6099 or ℡1800 133 392; Mon–Fri 9am–10pm, Sat & Sun 11am–2pm & 7–10pm) for phone counselling, referral and information; Gay Men's Health Centre and the Victorian AIDS Council (℡9865 6700 or ℡1800 134 840), 6 Claremont St, South Yarra; People Living With Aids at the Positive Living Centre, 46 Acland St, St Kilda (℡9525 4455); Positive Women (℡9276 6918 or ℡1800 032 017), run by and for women with HIV, through the Melbourne Sexual Health Centre.

ALSO Foundation 1st floor, 35 Cato St, Prahran (℡9510 5569, ⓦwww.also.org.au). Organizes events and publishes the *ALSO Directory*, free from community outlets.

Gay and Lesbian Switchboard Information Service (℡0055 12504). Recorded 24hr information service covering entertainment, as well as social and support groups.

Gay and Lesbian Switchboard (Mon, Tues & Thurs–Sun 6–10pm, Wed 2–10pm; ℡9510 5488) for counselling, referral and information.

Women's Information and Referral Exchange (WIRE; Mon–Fri 9.30am–5.30pm; ℡1300 134 130). Information about lesbian groups, referral to female doctors, solicitors, and the like.

Accommodation

For further accommodation possibilities, other than those listed below, ring **Gay Share** (℡9691 2290), which arranges house shares for gays and lesbians, or visit the Gay and Lesbian Accommodation website at ⓦwww.galavic.com.

169 Drummond 169 Drummond St, Carlton ℡9663 3081, ⓦwww.169drummond.com.au. Non smoking B&B in two adjacent, two-storey refurbished Victorian mansions. Eleven rooms with en-suite or shared facilities. ❹

California Motel 138 Barkers Rd, Hawthorn ℡9818 0281, ℡1800 331 166, ⓦwww.californiamotel .com.au. Gay-friendly motel accommodation close to the city, with parking available. ❻

Fitzroy Stables 124 Victoria St, off Brunswick St, Fitzroy ℡ & Ⓕ9415 1507. Lovely self-contained unit with a cathedral ceiling, mezzanine bedroom and small kitchen, facing a courtyard with a cottage garden. ❻

The Laird 149 Gipps St, Abbotsford ℡9417 2832, ⓦwww.lairdhotel.com. One of Melbourne's oldest hotels, *The Laird* has large, comfortable rooms on offer for gay men only. The service is especially helpful with tips on nightspots and local eateries. ❺

Palm Court B&B 22 Grattan Place, Richmond ℡9427 7365 or ℡0419 777 850. Spacious rooms at a moderate rate, and open fireplaces set in restored Victorian grandeur. It's one block directly east of the Richmond Cricket Ground in Yarra Park, across Punt Road. Nonsmoking. ❸

Cafés

Jackie O 204 Barkly St, St Kilda ℡9537 0377. St Kilda's first recognized gay café, Jackie O has quickly risen to become the most popular place to be gay (and be seen) in Melbourne. The food is standard, but portions are large and incredibly cheap, the

atmosphere relaxed and the music house-infused, while the view along Acland Street is well worth the price of a drink from the bar. Daily 7.30am–late.

Red Orange 194 Commercial Rd, Prahran ℡9510 3654. Formerly the Blue Elephant, this cosy, inexpensive café in the heart of Prahran is one of the sceniest gay spots in Melbourne. While the body beautiful is still on display, the last couple of years have seen a more mixed crowd enjoying the café's cheap eats and party atmosphere. Daily 7am–late.

Pubs, bars and clubs

Many venues in Melbourne are not exclusively gay or straight but are home to an easy-going mixed crowd. The *Night Cat* (see p.125) is a good example.

The Glasshouse Hotel 51 Gipps St, Collingwood ℡9419 4748. Relaxed and friendly hotel popular with Melbourne's pool-playing lesbians and their admirers. Good, inexpensive meals, and bands often play on Sunday evenings. Wed–Sun 11am–1am.

The Laird 149 Gipps St, Abbotsford ℡9417 2832. Operating for over twenty years, Melbourne's sole men-only pub attracts a mainly leather crowd, and has two bars, DJs, a beer garden and games room. The atmosphere is relaxed and welcoming, and accommodation for gays is also provided by the hotel (see opposite page). Mon–Thurs 5pm–1am, Fri & Sat 5pm–3am, Sun 5pm–midnight.

The Peel Dance Bar Cnr Peel & Wellington streets, Collingwood ℡9419 4762. Busy dance floor, pumping grooves, music videos and shows. A longstanding favourite with a mainly male crowd. Wed–Sun 10pm–dawn.

Xchange Hotel 119 Commercial Rd, South Yarra ℡9867 5144. Mainly men-only drinking and dancing spot. On Friday and Saturday nights the front bar turns into a disco. Daily 2pm–late.

Theatre, comedy and cinema

Melbourne's standing as the centre of Australian **theatre** has been recognized since 1871, when visiting English novelist Anthony Trollope remarked on the city's excellent venues and variety of performances. Nowadays, you can see a host of quality productions most nights of the week, from big musicals to experimental drama. And, judging by box-office returns, they're generally well supported. **Tickets** can be booked through Ticketmaster (☎13 61 66, ⊛www.ticketmaster.com.au) and Ticketek Victoria (☎13 28 49, ⊛premier.ticketek.com.au), while Half Tix (☎9650 9420; Mon & Sat 10am–2pm, Tues–Thurs 11am–6pm, Fri 11am–6.30pm), in the middle of Bourke Street Mall, has discounted tickets (cash only) on the day of performance. A highlight of the city's theatrical year is the **Melbourne Festival** (see p.142), which runs for a couple of weeks in late October.

After a few wobbly years, Melbourne is still the heart of Australian **comedy**, with regular performances by home-grown and overseas comedians in pubs and clubs. Don't miss the **Melbourne International Comedy Festival** in late April, when more than a thousand comics converge on the city.

There are plenty of mainstream **cinemas** in Melbourne, mostly in and around Bourke Street, plus a growing number of plush arthouses. Tickets are usually cheaper on Tuesdays and, in some places, Mondays too. The centrepiece of Melbourne movie life is the annual **Melbourne International Film Festival** (see p.140), which runs for two weeks during late July in venues like the Village Centre and the Forum, showcasing hundreds of local and international releases.

For theatre, comedy and cinema **listings**, check *The Age* (especially Friday's comprehensive arts and entertainment guide, "EG") and "Hit", the Thursday supplement of the *Herald Sun*. Another good source is *Melbourne Events*, a free monthly calendar to citywide events, available from the Melbourne Visitor Information Centre, leading newsagents and information booths.

Theatre

Athenaeum Theatre 188 Collins St, City ☎9650 **1500.** Built in 1842, the Athenaeum Theatre stages everything from Shakespearean drama to comedy and fringe performances.

CUB Malthouse 113 Sturt St, South Melbourne ☎9685 5111. Former brewery now transformed into state-of-the-art performance-and-gallery complex. Contains the small 200-seater Beckett Theatre, the larger Merlyn Theatre and the newish Tower Room. The resident company – the Playbox Theatre Centre – produce contemporary Australian plays. To get there, take tram #1 from Swanston Street or St Kilda Road.

The Forum Theatre 154 Flinders St, City ⊤9299 9700. Opposite Federation Square, this grand old theatre with its distinctive copper domed clock and grandiose interior opened in 1929 and is the place for popular musicals, comedies and touring acts.

Her Majesty's Theatre 219 Exhibition St, City ⊤9663 3211. Fabulously ornate theatre built in 1886 – now features popular retro throwbacks like *Chicago* and *Grease*.

La Mama 205 Faraday St, Carlton ⊤9347 6948. A Carlton institution for over thirty years, La Mama hosts low-budget, innovative works by local playwrights. Ticket prices are probably the cheapest in town.

Playhouse Theatre Victorian Arts Centre, 100 St Kilda Rd, City ⊤9281 8000. Wide-ranging choice of programmes, usually performed by the renowned and very popular Melbourne Theatre Company, who also perform at the Fairfax in the Victorian Arts Centre.

Princess Theatre 163 Spring St, City ⊤9299 9800. Established at the height of the goldrush, this small, exquisitely restored theatre is one of the city's best-loved venues, and stages musicals and mainstream theatrical productions.

Red Stitch Actors Theatre Rear 2, Chapel Street, St Kilda ⊤9533 8082. Set up by a group of local actors, this theatre specializes in performing works by Melbourne playwrights though they occasionally diversify.

Regent Theatre 191 Collins St, City ⊤9299 9500. Opened in 1929, this mammoth, lavishly restored theatre presents razzle-dazzle West End/Broadway productions like Sunset Boulevard and Showboat.

Theatreworks 14 Acland St, St Kilda ⊤9534 4879. Cutting-edge Australian plays in a reasonably large, wooden-floored space that was formerly a church hall.

Universal Theatre 19 Victoria St, Fitzroy ⊤9419 3777. Venue for productions by smaller local theatre companies and fringe plays by overseas guests.

Comedy

The Comic's Lounge 26 Errol St, North Melbourne ⊤9348 9488, ⊛www .thecomicslounge.com.au. This out-of-the-way club has big laughs six nights a week with local funny men matching wits with the odd touring comic.

The Comedy Club The Athenaeum Theatre, 188 Collins St, City ⊤9650 1977. Rattling the

No laughing matter

Melbourne has long been regarded as the home of Australian **comedy**. During the 1970s, a comedy cabaret scene developed around small theatre-restaurants such as *The Flying Trapeze* and *The Comedy Café*, later evolving into a healthy stand-up circuit in the 1980s at venues such as *The Last Laugh* and the *Prince Patrick Hotel*, which drew passionate and loyal followers and launched myriad careers. Founded in 1987, the **Melbourne International Comedy Festival** (see p.140), which has grown to become one of the world's top three comedy events alongside those in Toronto and Edinburgh, usually attracts around a thousand national and international comics. Some of Melbourne's **comedy stalwarts** include Greg Fleet, a wonderfully surreal stand-up comic who gained enormous exposure in the long-running TV show *Neighbours*; Anthony Morgan, whose tear-streaming comic timing and deadpan delivery have made him one of Australia's most adored performers; and fully fledged "national treasure" Rod Quantock. In recent years, however, Melbourne's live comedy scene has taken something of a battering with both St Kilda's *Esplanade Hotel* and the *Prince Patrick Hotel* ending their long association with local comedy.

Cinema

rafters in this historic theatre, The Comedy Club offers a decent dinner and show deal (from $35) with local stars making regular appearances.

Astor Theatre Cnr Chapel St and Dandenong Rd, St Kilda ☎9510 1414. Built in 1936, the Astor's fabulous Art Deco architecture, popular front steps and divine banana choc-tops have made it a favoured meeting place for film buffs. It shows a mix of classics, recent releases and cheesy double bills. On Saturday night there's a pianist and singer between films.

Australian Centre for the Moving Image (ACMI) Federation Square, Cnr Flinders & Swanston streets, City ☎8663 2583, ⓦwww.acmi.net.au. Swish new venue with one large screen and a smaller site showing a varied schedule of screenings and events.

Cinema Como Cnr Toorak Road and Chapel Street, South Yarra ☎9827 7533. Boutique, three-cinema complex within the giant Como Complex. Screens international and new releases.

Cinema Nova Lygon Court Plaza, 380 Lygon St, Carlton ☎9347 5331. Labyrinthine theatre noted for its lurid crimson-and-purple decor. Specializes in arthouse and European films.

Cinemedia at Treasury Theatre 1 MacArthur Place, East Melbourne ☎9651 1515. Cinemedia is dedicated to promoting cinema culture through independent films and festivals, ranging from screenings of domestic and international films to animation and documentaries.

George Cinema 133–137 Fitzroy St, St Kilda ☎9534 6922. New independent releases, mostly from the USA, and excellent choc-top ice creams. *Lip* restaurant in the same complex is ideal for supper or an after-movie coffee.

IMAX Theatre Rathdowne St, Carlton ☎9663 5454. Part of the Melbourne Museum complex (see p.71), IMAX has kitsch interiors and awesome technology, including a gigantic screen and film reels

so big they require a fork-lift to move them. Shows both 2-D and 3-D films, usually lasting between 45min and 1hr, mostly documentaries on inaccessible places or anything involving a tyrannosaurus rex. The complex also includes two candy bars, a licensed bar and a restaurant.

Kino 45 Collins St, City ☎9650 2100. Sophisticated, civilized and recently refurbished complex beneath the Collins Place atrium showing new – predominantly arthouse – releases for the city's cinephiles.

Lumiere 108 Lonsdale St, City ☎9639 1055. A beacon for moviegoers seeking quality avant-garde movies, classic re-releases and alternative films from around the world.

Moonlight Cinema Royal Botanic Gardens ☎9663 9555, ⓦwww.moonlight.com.au. Cinema buffs can swap popcorn for picnic baskets each year from late December to early March when arthouse, cult and classic films are projected, weather permitting, onto a big outdoor screen on the central lawn of the Royal Botanic Gardens. Don't forget to take a cardigan, a rug and, most importantly, insect repellent. Movies begin when the sun goes down, but gates open at 7.30pm. Tickets can be bought at Gate D, Birdwood Avenue, or through Ticketmaster (☎13 61 66).

Trak Cinema 445 Toorak Rd, Toorak ☎9827 9333. Arthouse and quality mainstream films, often with a focus on European work.

Village Jam Factory, 500 Chapel St, South Yarra ☎9827 2424. Sprawling multiplex containing two movie houses: an eleven-screen cine-city showing a steady stream of blockbusters, and, opposite but on the same level, the opulent Cinema Europa (☎9827 2440), which has three small arthouse cinemas in which Australian short films precede the main event. Big, roomy seats at both cinemas, although the food and drink from the "Lollywood" candy bars is hideously expensive.

Festivals and events

Melbourne is renowned for its multitude of **festivals and events**, which bring together an array of Australian and international talent to collaborate on major exhibitions, performing arts productions and sporting spectaculars – from the high-octane excitement of Formula One motor racing to peddling to breakfast with a well-known chef as part of the Melbourne Food and Wine Festival. Melbourne also boasts an enviable range of venues and arenas to host these events – all within walking distance or a short tram ride from the city.

The following are the major festivals only; for one-offs or smaller goings-on, pick up a copy of *Melbourne Events* – available from hotels, newsagents or the Melbourne Visitor Information Centre – which lists monthly happenings throughout the city, or visit the City of Melbourne and Tourism Victoria websites at Ⓦwww.thatsmelbourne.com.au and Ⓦwww.visitvictoria.com, respectively. For most festivals, **tickets** can be obtained through the booking offices of Ticketmaster (Ⓣ13 61 66, Ⓦwww.ticketmaster.com.au), Ticketek (Ⓣ13 28 49, Ⓦpremier.ticketek.com.au), Half Tix (Mon & Sat 10am–2pm, Tues–Thurs 11am–6pm, Fri 11am–6.30pm; Ⓣ9650 9420), or at the venue concerned.

January

Australian Open Tennis Championship January 17–30 The year's first Grand Slam attracts hordes of zinc-creamed tennis fans to see the best players in international tennis compete at Melbourne Park. Ⓦwww.australianopen.com.

Big Day Out Late January Held at the Melbourne RAS Showgrounds, this event lines up an astonishing array of bands and DJs – annual visitors include the likes of the Dandy Warhols, Metallica, The Strokes and Aphex Twin. Apart from music, there are also skating shows, carnival rides and an enormous techno room. Bring a hat and sunscreen. Ⓦwww.bigdayout.com.

Chinese New Year January 29–30 Melbourne's Chinatown hosts a packed arts and cultural programme, featuring music, dance, food, and an appearance by Dai Loong, the world's longest ceremonial dragon. Ⓣ9650 6468.

Midsumma Mid-January to early February Politically supported month-long gay and lesbian festival celebrating local, national and international queer talent and transgender art in all its finery. Some of the bigger events include the opening night Street Party, Red Raw Dance Party, Pride March and Carnival Day, but there are also myriad smaller events in venues around the city. Ⓣ9415 9819, Ⓦwww.midsumma.org.au.

February

Good Vibrations February 1 This outdoor music event at the Sidney Myer Music Bowl incorporates live stages and DJ areas, complemented by a chillout area. Recent line-ups have included Moloko and Blackalicious playing live, as well as DJ sets from Gilles Peterson. A wide variety of food and drink options only add to the experience. Ⓦwww.jammusic.com.au/goodvibrationsfestival.

St Kilda Festival February 4–8 Grown from a Sunday-only event to a five-day music, arts and culture extravaganza, climaxing with a Sunday street party of tinnitis-inducing live bands along St Kilda's foreshore, the Esplanade and Acland Street. The festival's longer programme and "something-for-everyone" approach has seen the introduction of dusk cinema screenings, street performances, art exhibitions and carnival rides, not to mention huge crowds. Ⓣ9209 6139, Ⓦwww.stkildafestival.com.au.

Melbourne Informational Music and Blues Festival February 7–9 Weekend blues binge at the Melbourne Exhibition Centre has dozens of overseas and home-grown acts performing over three stages. Ⓣ9596 8744, Ⓦwww.melbournebluesfestival.com/main.htm).

March/April

Australian Grand Prix Early March Rev-head mania takes over Melbourne for four noisy days, with Formula One action centred on the purpose-built Albert Park race track in South Melbourne. Ⓣ9258 7100, Ⓦwww.grandprix.com.au.

Melbourne Moomba Festival Early March One of Australia's largest outdoor festivals, focusing on the Yarra, the adjacent Alexandra Gardens and city centre, with a mixture of cultural and sporting events like water-skiing, dragon-boat racing and night parades. Don't miss the "Birdman Rally" in which various flying contraptions assemble at Princes Bridge and attempt to defy gravity. Ⓣ9650 9744, Ⓦwww.melbournemoombafestival.com.au).

Antipodes Festival March 10–April 25 Established in 1987, this award-winning festival is a celebration of Greek culture, with film, arts and crafts, sport and commerce events held in venues throughout the city Ⓣ9662 3307, Ⓦwww.antipodesfestival.com.au

Melbourne Queer Film and Video Festival March 11–21 A big highlight of queer Melbourne's arts and culture calendar, with Australian and international features, documentaries, shorts, and experimental works. Ⓦwww.melbournequeerfilm.com.au.

Brunswick Music Festival March 14–21 Music and community events in and around Brunswick, with a pumping street party the main act. Ⓦwww.brunswickmusicfestival.com.au.

Melbourne Fashion Festival March 14–21 Sponsored by L'Oréal, this week-long fashion festival pushes mainstream and emerging Australian design. Catwalk shows, intimate salon presentations, business seminars, installations and exhibitions and, of course, heaps of absolutely fabulous parties, darling. Ⓣ9510 8870, Ⓦwww.mff.com.au.

Melbourne Food and Wine Festival March–April Australia's premier food-and-wine event, at various venues in Melbourne and regional Victoria, showcasing specially prepared dishes by some of the city's finest chefs and excellent wines from around the state. Highlights include the "World's Longest Lunch" and guided tours of Melbourne's best-known eating streets. Ⓣ9412 4220, Ⓦwww.melbournefoodandwine.com.au.

Melbourne International Flower and Garden Show Late March to early April Held in Carlton Gardens, this is Australia's largest and most prestigious horticultural event, with hundreds of floral and landscape displays against the backdrop of the Royal Exhibition Building and the Melbourne Museum. Ⓣ9639 2333, Ⓦwww.melbflowershow.com.au.

Melbourne International Comedy Festival Late March to early April Leading laughathon that attracts more than a thousand home-grown and overseas comics. Based in the Melbourne Town Hall, but with programmes in over fifty other city venues, spanning stand-up comedy, plays, film, TV and street theatre Ⓣ9417 7711, Ⓦwww.comedyfestival.com.au.

May

Next Wave Festival May 18–30 Biennial festival featuring cutting-edge multimedia, visual arts and writing, created and performed by emerging Australian artists, mainly in inner-city pubs and other locations in Fitzroy, but also as far afield as Geelong. ☎9417 7544, ⓦwww .nextwave.org.au.

St Kilda Film Festival Late May St Kilda's Palais Theatre and George Cinema stage this small but good survey of contemporary Australian short films and videos, with a spotlight on emerging film-makers and new media. Includes an industry market day for film boffins ☎9209 6217, ⓦwww .stkildafilmfestival.com.au.

July

Melbourne International Film Festival July–August Hugely popular fortnight with a big focus on Australian, cult and arty films, plus a multimedia component highlighting the latest in film technology. Hundreds of films from a variety of countries are shown, while a who's who of local and overseas film-makers attend to talk about their work. Venues city-wide include the Forum Theatre, Arts Centre, Greater Union and Village Centre cinemas and the Australian Centre for the Moving Image (ACMI). ☎9417 2011, ⓦwww .melbournefilmfestival.com.au.

August

Melbourne Writers' Festival August 21–31 Hundreds of Australian and overseas writers converge on Melbourne, where they get completely plastered, forget their hotel keys, wangle deals with publishers and, when sober, give talks and lectures to members of the book-loving public. Activities centre on the CUB Malthouse in South Melbourne – setting the tone for the festival (and always good for a writers' punch-up) – except for the keynote address which takes place at the Melbourne Town Hall. ☎9685 9244, ⓦwww.mwf.com.au.

Asian Food Festival August–September Various venues around town celebrate and promote Melbourne's Asian culture and cuisine. The month-long event also includes food tours, cooking classes using a huge golden wok, celebrity dinners, travel competitions, banquets and more. ☎9690 2555.

September

Royal Melbourne Show Late September Eleven-day agricultural bonanza at the Royal Melbourne Showgrounds, preceded by a parade of animals and farm machinery down Swanston Street. Rides, baked potatoes and candyfloss compete with contests featuring everything from Jersey-Holstein cows to wood-choppers. ☎9281 7444, ⓦwww.royalshow.com.au.

AFL Grand Final Last weekend in September Close to 90,000 people pack the MCG to watch the final between the two best teams in the AFL, while untold millions catch the game via cable TV worldwide. ☎9643 1999, ⓦwww.afl.com.au.

Melbourne Fringe Festival Late September Kicks off the day after the AFL Grand Final with the outrageous Brunswick Street parade and all-day party, and ends in a raucous gathering of feral types in an inner-city venue. Other debauched events typically include street raves, saucy plays, slam poetry, spoken word performances and watching people having their bodies pierced. ☎9481 5111, ⓦwww .melbournefringe.com.au.

October

Spring Racing Carnival Early October to mid-November Six weeks of metropolitan racing and country meets, parties, balls and the most extraordinary displays of hats – from oversized ensembles with lots of everything to chic and beautifully crafted millinery creations – that culminate in the running of the famous Melbourne Cup. ☎9258 4258, ⊛www.racingvictoria.net.au.

Melbourne Oktoberfest Late October Not as grand an event as its notorious Bavarian equivalent, this three-day beer- and foodfest at the Royal Melbourne Showgrounds is still a lot of fun, with revellers sculling a range of local and imported beers, before tucking into pork shanks and schnitzels. If you're still standing, you can watch folk bands or large men bundled into lederhosen dancing up a storm. ☎9529 5211.

Lygon Street Festa Late October Founded in 1978, Australia's oldest street festival was masterminded by the traders and restaurateurs of Carlton's cappuccino belt. Crowd favourites include the waiters' race, the pizza-throwing competition, *bocce* (bowls), fencing and ballroom dancing Italian-style. ☎9663 0886.

Melbourne Festival Late October One of Australia's pre-eminent annual arts events, the festival has a cast of thousands drawn from the fields of music, opera, dance and theatre. Ticketed and free performances are held both indoors and on Melbourne's streets. ☎9662 4242, ⊛www .melbournefestival.com.au.

November

Chapel Street Food and Fashion Festival Early November Sections of South Yarra's Chapel Street are closed off to traffic over this weekend of music, food and fashionistas.

December

Boxing Day Cricket Test December 26–30 One of the most keenly awaited matches on the cricket calendar, the Boxing Day Test pits Australia against whichever cricketing nation is touring the country at the time. ☎9653 1100.

Sport and activities

The acknowledged **sporting capital** of Australia, Melbourne was the birthplace of Test cricket and Australian Rules football, and is today home to a string of major events including the AFL Grand Final, the Australian Grand Prix, the Australian Tennis Open, the Melbourne Cup and a number of important golf tournaments. Its leading position has been enhanced by the opening of major sporting facilities such as Telstra Dome and the Vodafone Arena, while the famous and much-loved Melbourne Cricket Ground (MCG), currently undergoing major redevelopment in time for the 2006 Commonwealth Games, continues to draw mammoth crowds. Visitors can watch a range of spectator sports, including Aussie Rules, basketball, cricket, rugby union and soccer. In addition to its regular calendar of sporting events, Melbourne offers a number of **recreational sports**, with cycling, rollerblading, swimming, surfing and sailing all widely enjoyed.

You can catch live big-screen sport at a number of CBD and inner-city drinking spots, including the Crown Casino (see p.60) and the *Charles Dickens Tavern* (see p.124). For **tickets** to most sporting events, book through Ticketek Victoria (☎13 28 49, Ⓦpremier.ticketek.com.au).

Australian Football League (AFL)

The **Australian Football League** ("Aussie Rules", or simply "the footy") is a Melbourne institution. Originally contested by the city's suburban teams, the AFL has now grown into a national league, with teams from Melbourne, Adelaide, Perth, Sydney and Brisbane playing games each weekend from March to September, culminating in the AFL Grand Final at the MCG on the last Saturday in September. Melbourne has ten of the sixteen AFL teams – Carlton, Essendon, North Melbourne and Hawthorn are some of the most successful – and consequently hosts the majority of games.

The most accessible **stadiums** are Telstra Dome (any train to Spencer Street Station, or tram #96 along Spencer Street or down Bourke Street), the MCG (tram #75 along Wellington Parade, or the Epping line train from Flinders Street Station to Jolimont Station) and the Optus Oval in Carlton (tram #19 from Elizabeth Street). **Tickets** can be bought from the grounds or through Ticketmaster (☎13 61 66, Ⓦwww.ticketmaster.com.au). Availability is generally good, even on match days, but for Telstra Dome, it pays to book tickets as early as possible.

To those unfamiliar with the game, **Australian Football** may seem bizarre, but once you've experienced it live and understand a few basic rules, you'll be richly rewarded. The game was originally conceived as a winter fitness routine for Melbourne's cricketers, which is why it's played on a cricket oval. At each end of the oval are two upright posts, with another two (shorter) posts on either side of these. Each team is made up of eighteen players (plus four reserves or interchange players) who run around in incredibly tight shorts attempting to kick the football – in size and shape somewhere between a rugby ball and an American football – between the posts. A goal (worth six points) is when the ball is kicked through the two inner posts; a "behind" (worth one point) is when the ball passes between the two outer posts.

The game has four quarters of twenty minutes each. There are no offside rules, and players can run with the ball, although they must bounce it every 15m. A tackle can only be made below the shoulders and above the hips, but there's plenty of scope in the rules for a legal "bump" with the hip or shoulder which, when done correctly, produces an intensely violent level of body contact. If a player catches a ball which has travelled over 10m before it bounces, he's awarded a free kick. This produces the game's trademark signature: a player leaping for a mark or "speccie", often high enough to rest his knees or feet on an opponent's shoulders. An incredible seven umpires (don't call them "refs") officiate – two goal umpires, two boundary umpires and three main umpires on the field. Umpires are traditionally booed whenever they run onto the ground and throughout the game, but the animosity from the one-eyed, scarf-waving fans is mostly good-natured.

Basketball

There are over 600,000 registered **basketball** players in Australia, and games involving Melbourne's two teams – the Melbourne Tigers and the Victorian Titans – enjoy considerable support. The city's main basketball venue is Melbourne Park (T9286 1600), Australia's largest indoor entertainment arena, in Yarra Park near the MCG; it's easily accessible by tram #75 along Wellington Parade (which runs along the southeastern corner of Fitzroy Gardens), or the Epping line train from Flinders Street Station to Jolimont Station. Tickets can be obtained through Ticketek Victoria (see p.143), and the season runs from October to March.

Cricket

When the footy season is over, the **cricket** begins. The MCG and Telstra Dome host all the major games, such as the Boxing Day Test match and four-day Sheffield Shield matches involving the Victorian state team, plus limited-overs day-and-night matches involving state and national teams (usually held between December and February), which regularly attract huge crowds. There are also eighteen club and district teams such as Carlton and St Kilda, which compete in the Light Ice Cup one- and two-day cricket competition between October and April at various suburban grounds (contact the Victorian Cricket Association on T9653 1100 for fixtures and locations).

Cycling

Melbourne is thronged with an extensive network of quality **cycling tracks**. Popular routes include the Yarra riverside track from Southgate to Eltham (see p.82), the bayside trail from Port Melbourne to Brighton, the Docklands network, the Maribyrnong river trail from Footscray Road to Brimbank Park, and a two-kilometre trail on the Yarra (600m of which is on pontoons to avoid flooding), which runs alongside the Monash Freeway on the river's north bank from Burnley to Morell Bridge, near the Rod Laver Arena.

A refreshing alternative to cycling in amid Melbourne's urban sprawl is rural and suburban **railtrails**, abandoned railway tracks converted into paths for cycling, rollerblading, horse riding or walking. Over 500km of rail lines have now been reclaimed across Victoria, with public access trails in Melbourne, the Yarra Valley, the Dandenong Ranges, and Mornington Peninsula and Phillip Island, among other regions. For more information, visit ⓦwww.railtrails.org.au.

One of the best ways to see the city is to participate in the **Great Melbourne Bike Ride**. Run each year in March, it's a leisurely 45km ride in and around the city, with plenty of rest and refreshment stops en route. For more information, or to pick up entry forms, visit Bicycle Victoria at 19 O'Connell St in North Melbourne (Mon–Fri 8.45am–5.15pm; ⓣ8638 8888, ⓦwww.bv.com.au). They can arrange other rides from 10km to 100km ($20–65), and they hand out "The Great Rides Wall Planner" listing their organized bike rides in Victoria and interstate; cycle enthusiasts might also want to buy a copy of the **booklet** *Discovering Victoria's Bike Paths* ($18.95) or *Bike Rides Around Melbourne* ($32), available here or at newsagents. Another free publication is *Fun on Trails*, a fold-out map available from the Melbourne Visitor Information Centre. For details of **bike rental**, see p.163. Alternatively, many Melbourne hostels rent out bikes. Wearing a **helmet** is compulsory in Victoria, and you must have front and rear **lights** on your bike for night riding. During off-peak periods bikes can be carried free on **trains**, which helps if you run out of steam along the way.

Diving

Diving in Victoria, with its wrecks, reefs and drifts, is every bit as good as diving in Australia's more illustrious northern states. A particularly good spot is Port Phillip Heads, which forms the narrow entrance to Port Phillip Bay. Here, you can dive the "Yellow Submarine", a J-class submarine, scuttled outside the heads in the 1920s. Port Phillip Bay itself also has some great dives – Popes Eye and Portsea Hole, the most popular dives in Victoria, are both renowned for their vast array of marine life. Other popular diving sites are found along the Great Ocean Road, where there are dozens of turn-of-the-twentieth-century wrecks waiting to be explored. **Dive centres** providing boat and shore dives along Victoria's coastline are scattered in and around Melbourne, Dive Victoria (ⓦwww.divevictoria.com.au) is one. For the best dive access, base yourself in the beachfront towns of Portsea, Sorrento or Queenscliff. Courses are conducted at numerous dive centres if you want to learn or become more advanced.

Golf

Melbourne is one of the great meccas of golf in the world, with excellent sandbelt courses in the city's southeastern suburbs, a favourable climate and a strong golfing heritage. There are no fewer than eighty **golf courses** around the city, four of them ranked in the world's top one hundred courses. Although some are members-only with waiting lists several years long, there are also dozens of public courses. Typical green fees are around $25 for an eighteen-hole round, but check in advance. One of the best and most accessible courses is the Albert Park Public Golf Course on Queens Road (daily 6.30am–sunset; ☎9510 3588; tram #72 from St Kilda Road), which has 65 tee-off bays, four target greens, an eighteen-hole course and experts on hand to fix your technique. Albert Park also has an excellent driving range at Aughtie Drive, Albert Park (☎9696 4653). Other good courses include the nine-hole Royal Park Public Golf Course, Popular Road, Parkville (☎9387 3585), the eighteen-hole Yarra Bend Golf Course, (☎9481 3729), the eighteen-hole Brighton Golf Course (☎9592 1388), and the eighteen-hole Sandringham Golf Links, Cheltenham Road, Cheltenham (☎9598 3590). Most have pro shops where you can rent clubs and buggies, or book lessons. Beyond the city, you can try some of the newer pay-as-you-play courses on the Mornington and Bellarine peninsulas.

Gyms and fitness centres

Melbourne has plenty of **gyms and fitness centres**. Gym fees are around $15 per session for aerobics, weights or circuits. The Melbourne City Baths, at 420 Swanston St (Mon–Fri 6am–10pm, Sat & Sun 8am–6pm; ☎9663 5888) have excellent facilities, including a large gym, massage room, pools (including a thirty-metre heated indoor pool), floor and water aerobics classes, and saunas and spas. Other good centres include the Melbourne Fitness Club, Level 1, 385 Bourke St (Mon–Fri 6am–8.30pm, Sat 9am–3pm; ☎9642 0288), and the St Kilda Sports and Fitness Centre, 97 Alma Rd, St Kilda (Mon–Thurs 6am–10pm, Fri 6am–8pm, Sat & Sun 9am–6pm; ☎9510 9409).

Horse and greyhound racing

Horse racing is a popular spectator sport, especially during the Spring Racing Carnival, which runs from mid-October to mid-November. The centrepiece is the 3.2-kilometre **Melbourne Cup**, arguably the top event in the country's entire sporting calendar (see box opposite). Melbourne's other metropolitan racecourses are the Caulfield Racecourse, Station Street, Caulfield (☎9257 7200); the Sandown Racecourse, Princess Highway, Springvale (☎9518 1300); and the Moonee Valley Racing Club, McPherson Street, Moonee Ponds (☎1800 062 644), which also has night racing on weekdays.

If you fancy a flutter on the dogs, there's **greyhound racing** at the Sandown Greyhound Racing Club on Lightwood Road, Springvale (☎9546 9511; Dandenong line from Spencer Street Station to Sandown Station). For information on race meets at other city locations or throughout the state, contact the Melbourne Greyhound Racing Association (☎9428 2145). When betting at the tote at trackside, "call out" your picks to the operator at the counter (who then gives you a ticket), rather than filling out a betting slip.

Melbourne Cup

On the first Tuesday in November, the nation stops for one of the world's most famous horse races – the **Melbourne Cup**. The celebrated highlight of the Spring Racing Carnival, "Cup Day" (a Victorian public holiday) is a festive occasion, with racegoers enjoying champagne and canapés and flaunting their finest outfits, particularly their **hats**. If they're not actually at the event, Australians gather around television sets or radios to watch or listen to the calling of the race. Indeed, visiting American writer Mark Twain was so transfixed he wrote: "Cup Day is supreme it has no rival. I can call to mind no specialised annual day, in any country, whose approach fires the whole land with a conflagration of conversation and preparation and anticipation and jubilation."

The home of the event is the **Flemington Racecourse**, Epsom Road, Flemington (☎1300 727 575; tram #57 from Elizabeth Street), where up to 100,000 people gather to watch the race. Owners, trainers and jockeys from as far afield as Ireland, Hong Kong, Dubai and the USA come to compete in the event, which began in 1861 and has been run every year since.

Hot-air ballooning

One of the more unique ways of seeing Melbourne is to take a flight in a **hot-air balloon**. Balloon Sunrise, 41 Dover St, Richmond (approximately $310 per person; ☎9427 7596; ⒲www.balloonsunrise.com.au) operates one-hour balloon flights over the city, taking in sights such as the Royal Botanic Gardens and the MCG, with a champagne breakfast thrown in. Flights are subject to weather conditions, and bookings are essential.

Motor sports

The **Australian Grand Prix**, the opening race of the Formula One World Championship season, is held over four days each year in March at Albert Park (tram #96 from Bourke Street or #12 from Collins Street). Over 300,000 fans and feted guests attend Australia's largest corporate event, which, apart from the main race, includes celebrity challenges, motor shows, motocross, air displays, live bands and hospitality on tap in the many marquee tents. Attempts to make the Grand Prix less male-dominated have seen the introduction of make-up salons and merchandise superstores, while the addition of "track boys", complementing the traditional line-up of "grid girls", is another new ploy to lure potential female fans.

Tickets can be bought through Ticketmaster (☎13 61 66, ⒲www .ticketmaster.com.au), or at ⒲www.grandprix.com.au. For general admission, expect to pay around $55–95 (depending on the day) for a one-day ticket, $150 for a four-day ticket, or between $350 and $550 for a grandstand seat. Trams to Albert Park are free from Spencer and Swanston streets. Away from the track, you can catch the action on the big screen at Federation Square, where car displays, grid girls, interactive activities, giveaways, bands and video DJs add to the mix.

Melbourne's other major motor-sports event, the **Qantas Australian Motorcycle Grand Prix**, is held at the Phillip Island Racing Circuit over three days in early October.

Rollerblading

Rollerblading is all the rage in summer, especially along St Kilda's bayside bike tracks. Skates and equipment can be rented from Bob's Boards and Blades, 17 Fitzroy St, St Kilda (Mon–Fri 11am–6pm, Sat & Sun 10am–7pm; ☎9537 2118), and Apache Junction Skate Hire, 21 Carlisle St, St Kilda (daily 10am–5pm; ☎9534 4006). Around $7 will get you a pair of skates for an hour; $20 for a day.

Rugby

Rugby union has experienced slow growth in Melbourne, which now has twenty club sides (involving around 3000 players), eight of them in the first division, including championship-winning teams Melbourne Rugby Club and Harlequins. Like union, **rugby league** traditionally received little support in Melbourne, at least until the creation in 1998 of a new city team, the Melbourne Storm. Formed the previous year as part of the National Rugby League's push to nationalize the code, the Storm enjoyed remarkable success, beating more highly fancied Sydney- and Brisbane-based clubs to reach the finals, then winning the Australian Rugby League (ARL) Grand Final in 1999. In doing so, they captured Melbourne's imagination, and have since drawn healthy crowds to their home ground at Olympic Park, dubbed "The Graveyard" by fans because of its cauldron-like atmosphere and a propensity for visiting teams to lose matches.

Both union and league are played from April to September. International matches involving both codes are held at Telstra Dome.

Sailing

There are a number of **sailing** schools dotted around the bayside suburbs. The Jolly Roger Sailing Centre (☎9690 5862, ⓦwww.jollyrogersailing.com.au) on Aquatic Drive, Albert Park, holds sailing lessons ($55 per hour) on the Albert Park Lake, and you can hire aqua bikes for two ($22 for 30min); while Yachtpro at the Royal Melbourne Yacht Squadron, Pier Road, St Kilda (☎9525 5221) has basic courses in sailing and navigation ($205 for 8hr tuition). One of Melbourne's more scenic sailing spots is on the Yarra at Boathouse Road, Kew, where Studley Park Boathouse (☎9853 1972) rents out boats for $11 per half-hour, $20 per hour. **Sailboarding** is also popular: Repeat Performance Sailboards, at 87 Ormond Rd in Elwood (☎9525 6475), rents sailboards and offers individual windsurfing lessons by appointment ($45 per hr, or $33 per person for groups of three or more).

Soccer

Soccer is well supported in Melbourne, especially by the city's Italian, Greek and Croatian communities. There are currently four clubs in the city – South Melbourne, Carlton, Melbourne Knights and the Gippsland Falcons – which compete in the Ericsson Cup national league (call the Victorian Soccer Federation on ☎9682 9666 for details). The season runs from October to May; venues include the Bob James Stadium in South

Melbourne (tram #12 from Collins Street to the end of the line) and the Optus Oval on Royal Parade, Carlton (tram #19 from Elizabeth Street). Admission is around $18.

Surfing

Some of Victoria's more popular **surfing** spots include Phillip Island, Mornington Peninsula, Torquay and nearby Bells Beach, which hosts the eleven-day international Rip Curl Pro each Easter for professional surfers (expect to pay around $10 to enter the Bells Beach Surfing Recreation Reserve to catch a glimpse of the action in the water). For daily surf reports, call the Triple J Surfline (☎1900 922 996), or for the Mornington Peninsula call ☎1900 983 268, or log on to the Surf Shop Victoria website (ⓦwww .surfshop.com.au), which has comprehensive information on Victoria's beaches, surf events and where to buy equipment. Surfing schools are also plentiful along the Great Ocean Road and on the Mornington Peninsula. In most cases, equipment is provided.

Swimming

Swimming is popular over the hot summer months, when Melburnians pack the metropolitan **beaches** at Port Melbourne, Middle Park, St Kilda and Elwood, and the beaches further afield at Brighton, Sandringham and Mentone (all accessible by public transport). There's also a **nudist beach**, popular with both gawpers and the trendy set, south of Melbourne at Half Moon Bay, twenty minutes from the city, off Beach Road in Black Rock. Surf lifesavers patrol Victoria's most popular beaches at weekends and public holidays during the summer months from November to March (always swim between the red and yellow striped flags). **Pools** include the cavernous Melbourne Sports and Aquatic Centre (see also p.160), currently being redeveloped in time for the 2006 Commonwealth Games, on Aughtie Drive, Albert Park (Mon–Fri 6am–10pm; fifty-metre pool Mon–Fri 5.30am–8pm, Sat & Sun 7am–8pm; admission $4.90; ☎9926 1555; tram #96 from Bourke Street); the Fitzroy Pool, corner of Alexander Parade and Young Street, Fitzroy (Mon–Fri 6am–8pm, Sat & Sun 8am–6pm; $3.40; ☎9417 6493; tram #11 from Collins Street); the Prahran Aquatic Centre, 41 Essex St, Prahran (Mon–Fri 6am–7.30pm, Sat & Sun 8am–6pm; $3; ☎9522 3248; tram #6 from Swanston Street); and the St Kilda Baths (see p.90), a seawater alternative to the chlorine pools and recreation centres.

Tennis

The highlight of Melbourne's **tennis** season is the annual Ford Australian Open, one of the world's four grand slam tennis events, which takes place over two weeks from January to February at the Rod Laver Arena in Melbourne Park, next to the MCG. Tickets range from $28 to $99 (bookings through Ticketek Victoria, see p.143 ; a T icketmaster office operates in the foyer Mon–Fri 9am–5pm; tram #75 along Wellington Parade, or the Epping line train from Flinders Street Station to Jolimont Station). If you want a knock about, the Rod Laver Arena has 21 outdoor and five indoor public courts

In recent years, Melbourne's hotels have invested enormous sums of money into **spas** and **well-being centres**. Many of them have expanded their repertoire to include walk-in treatments promoting both physical and mental health, unisex packages, juice bars, even restaurant facilities offering food designed to keep patrons lean and healthy. The list below offers a selection of some of Melbourne's best places for pampering, healing and well-being. If you're looking to rejuvenate outside Melbourne, visit the sublime Hepburn Spa Resort in Hepburn Springs (see p.191), Queenscliff Day Spa (p.204) or Werribee Park Mansion (see p.199).

Aurora *The Prince St Kilda*, 2 Acland St, St Kilda ☎9536 1130, ⓦwww .aurorasparetreat.com. Housed in The Prince St Kilda complex, the hip Aurora, reputedly Australia's largest spa retreat, offers 17 purpose-built treatment rooms and, due to recent expansion, a courtyard so you can work on your tan. Specialized treatments include the "kitya karnu" signature treatment (desert salts and oils are rubbed all over your body in a steam room), body care, water therapies (rain shower room, steam room, geisha tub), skincare, exfoliation, nutrition and well-being activities, and range in duration from just over two hours to up to five days. Between treatments you can sip herbal tea or graze on vegetarian morsels prepared by staff at *Circa* (see p.117). Come prepared to relax. Mon–Fri 7am–10pm, Sat & Sun 10am–7pm.

Crown Spa Crown Towers, Level 3, 8 Whiteman St ☎9292 6666. Huge, opulent spa that has everything from massages and saunas to body wraps, facials, hair and beauty make-overs, and private lift access. There's also a 25-metre multi-level indoor pool, complete with gold-rimmed skylights and a glass wall that folds back to reveal a timber sun terrace, available to day spa users if their spa treatment is over one hour long. Daily 10am–8pm.

Geisha Level 1, 285 Collins St ☎9663 5544. Intriguing Japanese-styled hair salon that doubles as a shiatsu massage parlour. Prior to being pampered by a team of experience practitioners, don a comfortable robe and sip tea in a tradtional tatami room.

Ofuroya 59 Cromwell St, Collingwood ☎9419 0268. If you've been partying or working hard, this traditional Japanese bath house is the solution. Guests can indulge in a hot tub, sauna and cooling shower, then wrap up in plush cotton robes and lounge around drinking green tea, Japanese beer or sake. Tues–Fri 3–11pm, Sat & Sun noon–8pm; last booking accepted two hours prior to closing.

Retreat on Spring 49 Spring St ☎9654 0909, ⓦwww.retreatspas.com.au. Housed in a Nonda Katsilidis-designed building, Retreat spans three levels of hedonistic delight. With holistic spa, Aveda treatments and Philippe Starck bath fittings, not to mention a cocktail-style juice bar menu and nail salon, you're bound to come out glowing with satisfaction and feeling suitably refreshed. Recommended is the "recharge" – a masseur pumps life back into your body with a back massage, scalp massage, facial and eye-zone wrap. Like Aurora, Retreat on Spring has expanded to include walk-in treatments for everything from weight reduction to giving up smoking, plus there are chiropractic, osteopathy and hypnotherapy ($95 for 1hr) rooms. Mon, Tues & Sat 10am–6pm, Wed 10am–7pm, Thurs & Fri 10am–9pm, Sun noon–5pm.

Surfcoast Spa Retreat 403 Bay St, Port Melbourne ☎9646 3422. Offers the usual pampering and therapeutic treatments with a touch of the unusual such as Egyptian ear candling and Geisha soaks. Employs some of Melbourne's best personal trainers.

(Mon–Fri 7am–11pm, Sat & Sun 9am–6pm; bookings ☎9286 1244). Rates are around $24 per hour for an outdoor court, $28 per hour for an indoor court. Other public courts include the Collingwood Indoor Tennis Centre at

100 Wellington St, Collingwood (☎9419 8911), the Albert Reserve Tennis Centre, on the corner of St Kilda Road and Hanna Street, South Melbourne (☎9510 3311), the East Melbourne Tennis Centre at 61–63 Albert Street, East Melbourne (☎9417 6511), and the Fawkner Park Tennis Centre in Fawkner Park on Toorak Road West, South Yarra (☎9820 0611).

Tenpin bowling

During the week, you'll find young and old rolling in style at **bowling alleys** around town. Open late, alleys have become cool again, attracting a hip clientele keen to slip on retro footwear, slurp cocktails, watch music clips on a giant video screen and, er, bowl. You can even get in a bit of pre-clubbing action with regular DJ nights, or party on at one of the private rooms. One of Melbourne's most popular places is King Pin at the Crown Casino, 8 Whiteman St, Southbank (☎9292 7009). Alley cats can strike all night long at this 24hr bowling lounge, which also offers a fully licensed bar, DJ music, disco lighting, pool tables and sports telecasts. Another good bowling venue is Strike on Chapel, 325 Chapel St (☎9753 9573, ⓦwww.strikeentertainment.com), an architect-designed space, with luxe banquets and modern artwork adorning the walls, loud music and low lighting. When your arm is no longer willing, check out the bar, which has an extensive drinks list and an assortment of smart eats. There's also a pool hall, karaoke and interactive games. For both venues, expect to pay around $20 for a few games plus shoe hire.

Shopping

Melbourne's eclectic **shopping** scene accurately reflects the preoccupations of its lifestyle-conscious citizens, from the chic boutiques of Collins Street and South Yarra to the ethnic foodstalls of the Queen Victoria Market.

Shopping hours are generally Monday to Wednesday 9am–5.30pm, with late-night shopping until 7pm or 9pm on Thursday and Friday evenings; many places are also open at weekends from around noon to 5pm. Shops in some suburban areas such as Carlton, Fitzroy, South Yarra and St Kilda open seven days a week and keep varying hours, as noted in the following listings. Shopping hours are also extended by up to two hours during daylight-saving months (Nov–March).

Bargain hunters should make a beeline for the suburb of Richmond (especially Bridge Road and Church Street; trams #48 or #75 from Flinders Street), a clearance centre for some of Australia's most popular designers, or look out for stocktake sales during January and July. Otherwise, copies of *The Bargain Shopper's Guide to Melbourne* and *Pam's Guide to Discount Melbourne* are available from newsagents and bookshops.

Tours to Melbourne factories and warehouses, often with lunch thrown in, can be arranged through Shopping Spree Tours (departing daily except Sunday, ☎9596 6600), Go Get Around Shopping Tours (☎9387 7733) and Melbourne Shopping Tours (☎9826 3722).

For retail outlets specializing in the more unusual or exotic, pick up a copy of *Shopping Secrets Melbourne*, available at most bookshops.

Books and maps

City Centre

Foreign Language Bookshop 259 Collins St ☎9654 2883, Ⓦwww.languages.com.au. One of Australia's largest selections of travel guides and maps, plus foreign-language novels, magazines, dictionaries, videos and learning kits for over seventy languages. Mon–Thurs 9am–6pm, Fri 9am–7pm, Sat 10am–5pm.

Haunted Bookshop 15 McKillop St, off Bourke St ☎9670 2585, Ⓦwww.haunted.com.au. Decked out with dim lighting, red velour curtains and a resident black cat, this is Australia's leading occult, paranormal and mystical bookshop – titles range from lycanthropy and vampirism to spellcraft and demonology. The shop also holds regular tarot readings and seances, and organizes the "Haunted Melbourne Ghost Tour" (Sat 8.30pm; $20), which takes you to some of Melbourne's spookier haunts. Mon–Fri 11am–5.30pm, Sat noon–4pm.

Mapland 372 Little Bourke St ☎9670 4383, Ⓦwww.mapland.com.au. Travel guide and map specialist, plus globes, compasses, GPS products, marine charts and travel accessories like money-belts. Mon–Thurs 9am–5.30pm, Fri 9am–6pm, Sat 10am–5pm.

Carlton and Fitzroy

Brunswick St Bookstore 305 Brunswick St Fitzroy ☎9416 1030. Renowned for its huge range of art and design titles, you can also dip into all the latest fiction at this well-stocked store right in the heart of Brunswick Street. In the light-filled room upstairs it's easy to spend hours browsing through magnificent books on subjects ranging from Le Corbusier to Japanese Manga. Daily 10am–11pm

Polyester Books 330 Brunswick St, Fitzroy ☎9419 5223, ⓦwww.polyester.com.au. Controversial store that's been denounced for its racy and offbeat titles. Among the popular culture, drug titles, adult comics and magazines are works by literary outlaws William Burroughs, Lenny Bruce, Jean Genet, the Marquis de Sade and Adolf Hitler. Mon–Thurs 10am–9pm, Fri & Sat 10am–11pm, Sun 11am–9pm.

Readings 309 Lygon St, Carlton ☎9347 6633, ⓦwww.readings.com.au. Shelves of books on history, food and wine, and literary and children's titles dominate this Carlton institution, while there's enough cultural theory detritus to stone a dozen academics, and a music section bulging with jazz, classical and world music CDs. Other branches in Hawthorn, Malvern and Port Melbourne. Mon–Sat 9am–11pm, Sun 10am–11pm.

Travellers Bookstore 294 Smith St, Collingwood ☎9417 4179, ⓦwww.travellersbookstore .com.au. The store owner here knows her stuff, having worked in the industry for years and traipsed her way around the globe many times over. A vast collection of guides, phrasebooks, maps and travel accessories. Also operates as a travel agency. Mon–Fri 10am–6pm, Sat 10am–5pm, Sun noon–5pm

South Yarra and Prahran

Borders The Jam Factory, Shop 1, 500 Chapel St, South Yarra ☎9824 2299, ⓦwww.borders .com.au. Melbourne's first mega-bookstore crams over 200,000 books, CDs, videos, magazines and daily newspapers onto its shelves. Also has loads of discounts, a licensed café, children's playing area and regular in-store events like cooking demonstrations, live music and author signings. Also stores in Lygon St, Carlton and Chadstone. Daily 9am–11pm.

Kill City 226 Chapel St, Prahran ☎9510 6661, ⓕ9521 4046. The store for all those with a fixation on hard-boiled characters and true crime. Titles by Elmore Leonard, James Ellroy, Carl Hiaasen, Robert Cray and Patricia Highsmith, plus cards, posters and excellent "Kill City" T-shirts. Mon–Sat 10.30am–5.30pm, Sun noon–5pm.

St Kilda and Albert Park

The Avenue Bookstore 127 Dundas Place, Albert Park ☎9690 2227. The stock in this shop is almost overwhelming – both in subject range and sheer quantity – and the staff really know their stuff. In particular, the store boasts a very comprehensive travel guidebook section. Daily 9am–7pm.

Cosmos 112 Acland St, St Kilda ☎9525 3852. Everything from the latest bodice-ripper to the most obscure items of esoterica, plus a comprehensive music catalogue. Daily 10am–10pm.

Williamstown

Seagulls Bookshop 141 Nelson Place, Williamstown ☎9397 1728. This very browsable independent bookstore stocks a good range of books about Australia, particularly guidebooks. They also specialize in maritime books to attract the passing sailing crowd. Sat–Thurs 10am–6pm, Fri 10am–8pm.

Clothes, shoes and jewellery

City Centre

Alice Euphemia 241 Flinders Lane ☎9650 4300. Edgy mix of up-and-coming, unconventional local designs and established Australian labels for women, plus hand-finished one-off scarves, stylish accessories such as precious jewellery and leather, and screen-printed tote bags. Mon–Thurs & Sat 10am–6pm, Fri 10am–8pm, Sun noon–5pm.

Calibre 3/182 Little Collins St ☎9654 8826. Small shop in the groovy "menswear alley" of Little Collins Street, with a great range of tailored trousers, shirts and jackets for the calorie-challenged male, and an impressive selection of imports, ranging from Helmut Lang and Vivienne Westwood to Patrick Cox. Also branches at Collins Place, Chapel Street, South Yarra and Greville Street, Prahran. Mon–Thurs 9.30am–6pm, Fri 9.30am–9pm, Sat 9.30am–5pm, Sun noon–5pm.

Chiodo 175 Little Collins St ☎9663 0044. Clean lines and an elegant interior design are echoed in Chiodo's stylish, bright garments, mostly for men. You'll also find Comme des Garçons fragrances and other assorted treats such as sunglasses and locally crafted jewellery. Mon–Thurs 10am–6pm, Fri 10am–8pm, Sat 10am–5pm, Sun noon–5pm.

Christine Accessories 181 Flinders Lane, ☎9654 2011. Accessories abound here, from fabulous bags and scarves to shoes, jewellery, trinkets and perfume.

Cose Ipanema 113 Collins St ☎9650 3457. Fashion frontliner harbouring super-chic labels like Issey Miyake, Yohji Yamamoto, Armani Collezione, Jean-Paul Gaultier, Dries Van Noten and Dolce & Gabbana. Their sales often provoke a buying frenzy as the usually expensive labels are snaffled up at bargain prices. Mon–Thurs 9.30am–6pm, Fri 9.30am–8pm, Sat 10am–5pm.

Cyberia 285 Carsons Place, 285 Little Collins St ☎9639 7663. Girls' and guys' store sunk below street level and offering an array of Italian imports spiced with the pick of new millennium must-haves from French labels barbara bui and love sex money, and Buddhist Punk, Diesel and Vivienne Westwood. Also at 579 Chapel St, South Yarra. Mon–Thurs 10am–6pm, Fri 10am–7pm, Sat 11am–5pm.

e.g.etal 185 Little Collins St ☎9663 4334. Designer gold- and silversmiths showcase their art – both functional and decorative – in this little shop in the heart of boutique land. Spend money here on something small but beautiful. Mon–Thurs 10am–6pm, Fri 10am–8pm, Sat 10am–5pm.

Gallery Funaki 4 Crossley St, ☎9662 9446. Contemporary jewellery by renowned international and local artists with regular exhibitions. Commission works available. Mon–Thurs 10am–5pm, Fri 10am–8pm, Sat 11am–4pm.

Genki Shop 5, Cathedral Arcade, 37 Swanston St ☎9650 6366. Japanese for "happy, healthy and feeling fine", Genki is a store for quirky Melburnians, stocking hard-to-find Japanese, European and US streetwear, especially home-brand T-shirts for "It girls". There's also lots of inspired frippery like sequinned purses, pocket polaroid cameras, Japanese pretzels dipped in chocolate, and other assorted nick-nacks and food items from around the world. Mon–Thurs 10am–6pm, Fri 10am–8pm, Sat 11am–6pm.

Ivy Hopes Shop 6/37 Swanston St, cnr Flinders Lane. ☎9662 1153. At Ivy Hopes you'll find the best of Australian and New Zealand design talent for men and women, plus an eclectic mix of accessories and artworks. Mon–Thurs & Sat 10am–6pm, Fri 10am–8pm, Sun noon–5pm.

Kozminsky 421 Bourke St ☎9670 1277, ⦿www.kozminsky.com.au. Esteemed antique and twentieth-century jewellery firm housed in an elegant former stock and station agent's premises. Upstairs, an art gallery boasts works by Brett Whitely and Arthur Streeton, among others. Mon–Fri 10am–5.30pm, Sat 11am–4pm.

Le Louvre 74 Collins St ☎9650 1300. Melbourne's A-list celebs come here for eat-your-heart-out Gallianos, Givenchys and Richard Tylers, all hidden away behind closet doors. If the atmosphere doesn't intimidate you, the prices will. Mon–Fri 9am–5pm; appointments taken outside these times.

Makers Mark 101 Collins St ☎9654 8488, ⦿www.makersmark.com.au. Makers Mark's bracelets, necklaces and chokers are some of the finest examples around. Showcases the crop of the country's top designers, with monthly exhibitions featuring everything from fancy opera rings to handcrafted pens. Mon–Thurs 10am–6pm, Fri 10am–7pm, Sat 10am–5pm, Sun noon–4pm.

Nike Superstore Cnr Bourke & Swanston streets ☎8660 3333. Nike's first superstore in the Southern Hemisphere is a two-storey affair of immense video screens, footwear, apparel, accessories and equipment. Mon–Thurs & Sat 10am–6pm, Fri 10am–9pm, Sun 11am–6pm.

Scanlan & Theodore 285 Little Collins St ☎9650 6195. Women's clothing from Melbourne duo Fiona Scanlan and Gary Theodore, who specialize in contemporary classics in simple shades cut from couture-grade fabrics. A second branch is on

SHOPPING | Clothes, shoes and jewellery

Chapel Street, South Yarra. Mon–Thurs 10am–6pm, Fri 10am–8pm, Sat 10am–5.30pm, Sun 11am–5pm.

Zambesi 167 Flinders Lane ☎9654 4299. Prestigious and stylish store showcasing cutting-edge designs of New Zealand labels Zambesi and Nom.D, with a solid range of other imports on board, including Belgian label Martin Margiela. Mon–Thurs 10am–6pm, Fri 10am–8pm, Sat 10am–5pm, Sun noon–4pm.

Fitzroy & Clifton Hill

Blondies 336 Queens Parade, Clifton Hill ☎9481 6978. Generously stocked boutique with interesting and colourful fabrics. Expensive, but the kind of gear you buy, then wear for ages. Mon–Thurs 9.30am–6pm, Fri 9.30am–7pm, Sat 9.30am–5pm, Sun 11am–5pm.

Clear It 188 Brunswick St, Fitzroy ☎9415 1339. A clothing clearance outlet for Aussie labels Allanah Hill, Dangerfield and Revival, Clear It also sells accessories and 1960s and 1970s furnishings. Head upstairs for super-cheap clothes from a few seasons ago. Mon–Thurs & Sat 10am–6pm, Fri 10am–7pm, Sun 11am–6pm.

Dangerfield 289 Brunswick St, Fitzroy ☎9416 2032. Reasonably priced club- and streetwear with just a touch of glamour, including crotch-clutching cords, US workwear and jewellery for guys and girls. Has another five city locations and stores in Greville Street, Prahran and Chapel Street, South Yarra. Mon–Thurs & Sat 10am–6pm, Fri 10am–8pm, Sun 11am–6pm.

Douglas & Hope 181 Brunswick St, Fitzroy ☎9417 0662. Using antique silk kimonos, as well as modern cotton reproductions of old design patterns, Douglas & Hope produce exquisite quilted bedding, soft furnishings and cushions, every item an unrepeatable original. A few fashion labels and accessories are also stocked, alongside their own natural skincare range. Stores in Block Arcade in the City and Barkly Street, St Kilda. Mon–Sat 11am–6pm, Sun noon–5pm.

Fat 52 52 Johnston St, Fitzroy ☎9486 0391. Flogs the work of Melbourne's up-and-coming designers, with a well-edited mix of posh trousers, T-shirts, tops, skirts and dresses. There's also skincare products, eccentric lines of jewellery and quirky furniture items. Their Prahran store (Fat 272, 272 Chapel St) has a slightly wider range and some exclusive clothing lines. Mon–Thurs noon–6.30pm, Fri 10.30am–7pm, Sat 10.30am–6pm, Sun noon–5pm.

South Yarra, Prahran and St Kilda

Collette Dinnigan 553 Chapel St ☎9827 2111, ⓦwww.collettedinnigan.com.au. Intricate, opulent and expensive fare from the New Zealand-born, Sydney-based, Paris-feted designer extraordinaire. Mon–Fri 10am–6pm, Sat 10am–5pm, Sun noon–6pm.

Country Road Cnr Chapel St & Toorak Rd ☎9824 0133, ⓦwww.countryroad.com.au. Flagship store offering a small but considered selection of home wares, plus good basic clothing, shoes and accessories for men and women and a childrens' clothing line.

Dinosaur Designs 562 Chapel St ☎9827 2600, ⓦwww.dinosaurdesigns.com.au. Chunky Flintstone-like resin and sterling silver jewellery, crockery and cult-in-the-making glassware, all designed and handmade in Australia. Affordable. Mon–Sat 10am–6pm, Sun noon–5pm.

Hudson 229 Carlisle St, Balaclava ☎9525 8066. Coolest kid on the block, Hudson is leading the retail revival of Balaclava's bagel belt. Arty types stock up on Japanese talking watches, kooky handmade knitted toys, exclusive US and UK street labels and fresh local talent. Keep an eye out for regular kick-arse art exhibitions. Daily 11am-6pm

Kinki Gerlinki 122 Greville St, Prahran ☎9529 4599. Good for medium-priced, off-the-wall women's fashion and accessories, whipped up by some of Asia's best young designers. Cardigans in riotous colours and handbags fashioned from goat hair are among the treats. Also has an outlet at 360 Brunswick Street, Fitzroy. Mon–Thurs & Sat 10am–6pm, Fri 10am–8pm, Sun 11am–5pm.

Marcs 459 Chapel St ☎9827 5290. Huge range of men's and women's wear, including T-shirts, button-downs, jeans, suits, knits and shoes. Does a good line in the maverick fashion house Diesel. Mon–Thurs 10am–6pm, Fri 10am–8pm, Sat 10am–6pm, Sun 11am–5pm.

Mooks 491 Chapel St ☎9827 9966, ⓦwww.mooks.com. Covetable streetwear and accessories, including beanies, trucker caps, backpacks, quirky T-shirts and ziphood sweats. Mon–Thurs 9.30am–6pm, Fri 9.30am–8pm, Sun 10am–6pm, Sun 11am–5.30pm.

Crafts, souvenirs and gifts

Craft Victoria 31 Flinders Lane ☏9650 7775, ⓦwww.craftvic.asn.au. Contemporary jewellery, craft and other objects by Australian designers, plus a programme of regular exhibitions. Tues–Sat 11am–5.30pm.

Kleins Perfumery 313 Brunswick St, Fitzroy ☏9416 1221. Luscious-smelling boutique with over sixty product lines including Aesop, L'Occitane, Acca Kappa, Jurliue and Crabtree and Evelyn. From perfumes to scented candles, soaps, oils and body products, it's a veritable lolly shop for the adult scent enthusiast. Mon–Thurs, Sat & Sun 9.30am–6pm, Fri 9.30am–9pm.

R.G. Madden 269 Coventry St, South Melbourne ☏9696 4933. The jewel in the Coventry Street home wares hub, R.G. Madden offers up a superb assortment of design classics – from Alessi kettles and Starck toilet brushes to chunky doorstops and spiky Dish Doctors by Australian style guru Marc Newson. Other branches are in Church Street, Richmond and Little Collins Street in the City. Mon–Fri 9.30am–5.30pm, Sat 10am–5pm, Sun 11am–4pm.

Department stores and shopping malls

Chadstone Shopping Centre 1341 Dandenong Rd, Chadstone ☏9530 9864. One of Australia's first shopping malls, the huge American-style Chadstone Shopping Centre is filled with major brand retailers, Australian designers and specialty shops. You'll also find cafés, cinemas, plenty of diversions for the kids, plus interactive Australian sculptures. Mon–Sat 10am–6pm, Sun noon–6pm.

David Jones Bourke St Mall ☏9643 2222, ⓦwww.davidjones.com.au. Upmarket retailer with stores either side of Bourke Street Mall. Renowned for its domestic and international designer range, beauty section and newly renovated food hall. Mon–Wed, Sat & Sun 10am–6pm, Thurs 10am–7pm, Fri 10am–9pm.

GPO Cnr Bourke & Elizabeth Sts. The grand old general post office site has been refurbished and now offers dozens of retail outlets, many exclusive to the centre, including Mandarina Duck, Georg Jensen, Ben Sherman, Mimco, Belinda Seper and Kerna Millen.

Melbourne Central Cnr Latrobe & Swanston Sts. Re-launching itself as a one-stop sartorial shop, the new "Central" is a shadow of the former centre that once housed Diamaru, but it still has myriad shops including the country's largest Kookai and De Cjuba concept stores, the Marcs flagship store, G-Star, General Pants Co and plenty of others.

Myer Bourke St Mall ☏9661 1111, ⓦwww.myer.com.au. Six floors spread across almost two blocks with perfumes, lipsticks, jewellery, home wares, electrical goods, local and imported fashion, books, records, and a giant sporting emporium. Mon–Wed & Sat 9am–6pm, Thurs 10am–7pm, Fri 10am–9pm, Sun 10am–6pm.

QV Centre Cnr Swanston & Lonsdale Sts. The old Queen Victoria Hospital once occupied this site, which is now a huge complex of laneways and shops, cafés, pubs and restaurants. Pitched as a gritty urban precinct, the centre's focus is dynamic retail and fashion, with a grand, European-style piazza providing a welcome outdoor public space at this end of the city. Stores include Cactus Jam, Loreak Mendian, Nicola Finetti and Christensen Copenhagen.

Food and drink

Becco 11–25 Crossley St, off Bourke St ☏9663 3000, ⓦwww.becco.com.au. Food shop tacked on to the popular restaurant of the same name. Stocks chic food such as pinot sourdough bread, plus fresh fruit and veg, fish, meats, wines and cheeses. Mon–Sat 8.30am–4.30pm (accessible via restaurant until about 10pm).

Make no mistake, Melburnians love their shopping. They also love their food, so what better way to combine the two than to create a retail experience in which to graze while you shop.

Hermon & Hermon Plus 556 Swan St, Richmond ☎9427 0599. Speciality furniture and home wares store with an excellent café attracting a mixed crowd of shoppers, workers and locals. Mon–Fri 8am–5pm, Sat 9am–5pm, Sun noon–5pm.

Husk 557 Malvern Rd, Toorak ☎9827 2700. Beautiful, restful space which combines elegant items such as Moroccan glassware and designer clothes for men and women including Akira, Easton Pearson, Kate Sylvester, Vixen and more, with a sensible courtyard café serving home-made herbal teas, authentic Bedouin coffee, hearty soups and cakes. Mon–Thurs 9am–5.30pm, Fri 9am–6.30pm, Sun 9am–5.30pm. Also at Dundas Place, Albert Park and 176 Collins St in the City.

Mary Martin Bookshop Melbourne Paramount Centre, Shop 8, 108 Bourke St, City ☎9663 9633. Good spot for breakfast or lunch with lots of specials on offer, such as pasta, risotto or soup, and a relaxing way to pore over the merchandise. Mon–Wed 7am–7.30pm, Thurs & Fri 7am–8pm, Sat 9am–8.30pm, Sun 9am–3pm.

Verve 177 Little Collins St, City ☎9639 5886. Amidst the designer clothing (chic labels such as Princess Highway) and accessories are tables and stools where you can drink excellent coffee and eat mouthwatering foccacias, soups and sticky cakes. After stuffing your face simply begin your spree. Mon–Fri 7.30am–5pm, Sat 8.30am–5pm.

17

SHOPPING | Food and drink

Haigh's 7 & 8 Block Arcade, 282 Collins St ☎9654 7673, ⓦwww.haighs.com .au. The oldest family-owned chocolate manufacturer in the country sells award-winning premium chocolates. Also stores at Swanston Walk and 26 Collins St. Mon–Thurs 8.30am–6pm, Fri 8.30am–7.30pm, Sat 9am–5pm, Sun 11am–4pm.

Jock's Ice Cream & Sorbets 83 Victoria Ave, Albert Park ☎9686 3838. Jock Main's ice-creams are worth crossing town for, with a great spread of flavours; try the seasonal cinnamon with a fig ripple. Mon–Thurs & Sun noon–8pm, Fri & Sat noon–9pm.

King and Godfrey 293 Lygon St, Carlton ☎9347 1619. Established in 1870, this Carlton landmark boasts a great deli with Italian pasta, cheeses, breads, salamis and other small meats, sweets, biscuits and crackers, plus a superb stock of wine, beer and spirits. Mon–Sat 9am–9pm, Sun 11am–6pm.

Prahran Market Commercial Rd, Prahran ☎9522 3301. Excellent, upmarket food emporium selling fish, meat, fruit, vegetables, and with a delicatessen for the gourmand. Also houses The Essential Ingredient, stocking local and imported spices, oils, pastas, pastes, dry goods, cookbooks and kitchenware. Tues dawn–5pm, Thurs & Fri dawn–6pm, Sat dawn–5pm, Sun 10am–3pm.

Richmond Hill Café and Larder 48 Bridge Rd, Richmond ☎9421 2808. Owned by well-known Australian chef and food writer Stephanie Alexander, with a good though pricey selection of groceries including bread, preserves, savouries, sweets and magnificent cheeses. Mon–Fri 10am–5pm, Sat 8am–5pm, Sun 9am–5pm.

Simon Johnson 12–14 St David St, Fitzroy ☎9486 9456, ⓦwww.simonjohnson.com.au. Food merchant with top-quality produce, including oils, vinegars, chocolates and a great cheese room. Store at 471 Toorak Rd in Toorak keeps slightly longer hours (☎9826 2588). Mon–Fri & Sun 10am–5pm, Sat 10am–5pm.

South Melbourne Market Cnr Cecil & York streets, Sth Melbourne ☎9209 6295. Established over 120 years ago, Melbourne's second-oldest market sells a huge range of fresh fruit and vegetables, delicatessen goods and household items. Wed 8am–2pm, Fri 8am–6pm, Sat & Sun 8am–4pm.

Markets

Camberwell Market Station Street car park, Camberwell ☎1300 367 712. A Melbourne institution for over twenty years, this early-morning market is set in a car park that metamorphoses into a sea of trestle tables and racks buried under secondhand clothing, furniture, watches, records, cards, stuffed toys, curios – you name it. There are over 200 regular stalls, and spaces can be hired for around $40. To get there, take tram #75 from Flinders Street. Sun 7am–12.30pm.

Chapel St Bazaar 217–223 Chapel St, Prahran ☎9510 9841. An Aladdin's cave of over sixty dealers' stalls displaying everything from Coca-Cola memorabilia to Royal Doulton china. Eclectic, to say the least. Daily 10am–6pm.

Queen Victoria Market Cnr Victoria & Elizabeth streets ☎9320 5822. The place to go for fresh fruit and vegetables, meat, poultry, fish, deli goods and other fine things to eat. It's also an arts and crafts market that's been a major draw for locals and tourists for years, though you'll have to do a little rummaging before you find a bargain. Paintings, jewellery, leatherwork and didgeridoos are just some of the goods on offer. Tues & Thurs 6am–2pm, Fri 6am–6pm, Sat 6am–3pm, Sun 9am–4pm; also night market Wed 5.30–10.30pm mid-Nov to Feb.

St Kilda Arts and Craft Market Upper Esplanade, St Kilda ☎9209 6706. Combines the heady aromas of fresh produce with the musty whiff of secondhand clothing and century-old fittings. Sun 10am–6pm.

Music

Basement Discs 24 Block Place, off Little Collins St, City ☎9654 1110. Discreet underground space with an exhilarating range of jazz and blues displayed amid inviting sofas, flower displays and excellent listening stations stocked with lollies. Mon–Wed 10am–6pm, Thurs 10am–7pm, Fri 10am–9pm, Sat 9am–6pm, Sun 11am–6pm.

Discurio 113 Hardward St ☎9600 1488, ⑩www.discurio.com.au. Having relocated from Elizabeth Street to Hardware Street (its fourth move in recent years), Discurio has finally settled down, continuing with its broad range of jazz, R&B, soul, country, classical, world music and movie sound-tracks in another sleek environment. You can also grab the latest issue of *Jazz Times* to go with your Coltrane. Mon–Fri 10am–6pm, Sat 10am–5pm.

Gaslight Music 85 Bourke St ☎9650 9009. Renowned for its huge music, DVD, videos and games collection, Gaslight gained infamy for its annual "Nude Day" celebrations (now sadly scrapped), when in-the-buff music buffs browsed the racks. Mon–Sun 10am–late.

Northside Records 236 Gertrude St, Fitzroy ☎9417 7557. Choice inner-city music store specializing in cool funk, the latest hip-hop and world music on CD and vinyl. Mon–Fri 10am–6pm, Sat 10am–5pm.

Record Collector's Corner 240 Swanston Street ☎9663 3442. Mecca for DJs hunting vintage vinyl as well as collectors seeking out rare Japanese import CDs. This is a specialist store with a good range of old and new CDs and records. Mon–Sat 10am–6pm.

Rhythm and Soul Records 128 Greville St, Prahran ☎9510 8244, ⑩www.rhythmandsoul .com.au. Aimed at boys and girls who love their beats phat and furious, this store is also where Melbourne and Australia's foremost DJs come to shop. Hours are flaky at best, so ring in advance. Also at Shop 6 and 7 at 306 Little Collins Street in the City. Mon–Tues 11am–6pm, Wed 11am–7pm, Thurs 11am–8pm, Fri 10am–8pm, Sat 10am–6pm, Sun noon–5pm.

Sister Ray 260 Brunswick Street, Fitzroy ☎9417 3576. A long-established independent record store that has a big selection of used CDs and records upstairs, and new stuff downstairs, including their famous big bargain tables. Daily 10.30am–6pm.

Synaesthesia Level 1, 28 Block Place ☎9663 3551, ⑩www.synrecords.com. Dance music, white hip-hop, quirky jazz and enough esoteric samplings to keep Moby in music for years. Mon–Thurs & Sat 11am–6pm, Fri 11am–8pm.

18

Kids' Melbourne

elbourne has a wide range of **activities for children**, whether splashing about at the Melbourne Sports and Aquatic Centre, feeding the animals at the Collingwood Children's Farm, or checking out the exhibits at the Melbourne Aquarium and the Melbourne and Scienceworks museums. Other childproof diversions include amusement parlours, indoor play centres and recreational areas such as St Kilda beach and foreshore, as well as stopping off in the major parks, most of which have playgrounds.

If you are hankering for a latte, someone else's cooking, and a glimpse of your old life, children are generally welcome in Melbourne's cafés and restaurants, especially the city's ethnic varieties. Most also provide child-sized portions and free "babycinos", a local interpretation of a child's cappuccino – milk froth sprinkled with chocolate. A couple of good places for babycinos are *Mario's* (see p.114) and *Tiamo* (see p.115), in Fitzroy and Carlton respectively; they also have highchairs and do small servings.

Action plans can be plotted by scouring *The Age*'s Friday entertainment supplement, "EG", which lists a range of family activities, and the "Seven Days" section in *The Sunday Age*. Other good resources include *Melbourne Events*, a free monthly calendar available from the Melbourne Visitor Information Centre, hotels and newsagents; and "the bub hub", an online directory of baby and toddler activities, play centres, cinemas, parks and restaurants around Melboure – find it at Ⓦwww.vic.bubhub.com.au.

Children can also rent bikes and rollerblades (see the "Sport and activities" chapter), and there's much to amuse tots at the numerous festivals (see the "Festivals and events" chapter); highlights include the carnival rides at the St Kilda Festival and watching parading animals at the Royal Melbourne Show.

Victoria's school holidays

Summer Five to six weeks, beginning roughly five days before Christmas to the last week in January.

Autumn Two weeks, from early April to mid-April (incorporating Easter).

Winter Two weeks, normally from the end of June to the second week in July.

Spring Two weeks, beginning late September.

In general, private schools break up earlier and come back later than state schools. Information on school holiday programmes such as *My School Holiday Guide*, a quarterly publication on kids' activities and events, is available for free from schools and local councils. Also check out the Victoria Department of Education and Training website (Ⓦwww.sofweb.vic.edu.au), which has information on school holiday programmes and major sights around the city with free entry for children.

Indoor

Australian Centre for the Moving Image (ACMI)
Federation Square, Cnr Flinders & Swanston
streets, City ☎8663 2583, ⓦwww.acmi.net.au.
ACMI has loads of special screenings for
kids, regular cartoon festivals and Japanese
animation.

Bernard's Magic Shop 211 Elizabeth St
☎9670 9270. Chock-a-block with puzzles
and games, plus silly glasses, exploding
dog turds, jumbo tongues and plenty of
copies of that perennial children's favourite,
Teach Yourself Rope Magic.

Classic Cinema 9 Gordon St, Elsternwick
☎9523 9739. The oldest continually running
cinema in Melbourne and the perfect place
for junior film buffs. Weekend "Kids Pics"
sessions screen a mix of new releases and
old favourites; new releases are also shown
each day of the school holidays. Sat &
Sun, daily during school holidays; $7.50.
Sandringham line from Flinders Street
Station to Elsternwick Station.

Hop, Step and Jump 300 Bridge Rd, Richmond
☎9428 2820. Educational toy store with
good playground and café at the back
serving foccacias, milk shakes, muffins,
pies and pasties. A birthday menu is
available, and there are nappy-changing
facilities. Daily 9.30am–5.30pm.

IMAX Theatre Rathdowne St, Carlton
☎9663 5454. Adjoining the Melbourne
Museum (see p.71), IMAX has big comfy
seats in which to enjoy 2-D and 3-D films
(lasting 45–60min) on a giant eight-storey-
high screen. The complex also has two
candy bars, a licensed bar and restaurant.
Films screened every hour daily 10am–
11pm; $16.20, under-15s $10 (extra $1.10
for 3-D films).

Melbourne Aquarium Cnr Queenwharf Rd & King
St ☎9620 0999, ⓦwww.melbourneaquarium
.com.au. Harbouring thousands of creatures
from the Southern Ocean, the Melbourne
Aquarium also comprises a hands-on
learning centre where children gain a glimpse
of life underwater, "Ride the Dive" platforms
that simulate an underwater roller-coaster,
cafés, shop and a restaurant. Jan daily
9am–9pm, Feb–Dec daily 9am–6pm; $19,
under-16s $9.90.

Melbourne Museum Carlton Gardens, Carlton
☎8341 7777, ⓦwww.melbourne.museum
.vic.gov.au. Tram #96. State-of-the-art
museum over many levels housing several
superb galleries and spaces, including the
Children's Museum, where the exhibition
gallery, "Big Box", is built in the shape
of a giant, tilted cube painted in brightly
coloured squares. Also check out the
Forest Gallery, a living, breathing indoor
rainforest containing over 8000 plants, as
well as birds, insects, snakes, lizards and
fish. Daily 10am–6pm; $15; under 16s $8.

Melbourne Observation Deck Rialto Towers
☎9629 8222, ⓦwww.melbournedeck.com.au.
View Melbourne through high-powered
lenses at the tallest office building in
the Southern Hemisphere. Included
with admission is the twenty-minute film
"Melbourne the Living City", which tests
the patience of all ages. Daily 10am–late;
$11.80; under 15s $6.80.

Melbourne Sports and Aquatic Centre Aughtie
Drive, Albert Park ☎9926 1555. Tram #96.
Part sporting facility, part fun park and
host to a number of major sporting
events, the centre has a pool for every
occasion: a wave and toddlers' pool, a
fifty-metre pool, a 25-metre lap pool, a
twenty-metre multipurpose pool, a dive
pool and a pool garden. Childcare is
available (Mon–Fri 9am–noon; ☎9926
1555; $4.40/90min), and the centre also
runs an excellent day-long school-holiday
programme, "Planet Sport", for 5- to 12-
year-olds ($28.60/day), and a Saturday-
morning kids' session (9–10am; $10)
with games, sports and arts and crafts
activities. Mon–Fri 6am–10pm, Sat & Sun
7am–8pm; $4.90, under-14s $3.90.

Pipsqueak 811 High St, Armadale ☎9500 9181.
This shop's wardrobe resembles a Lilliputian
collection fresh from the catwalks of Paris
and Milan, with the extravagant partywear
upstairs being the ultimate attraction
for little lords and ladies. Mon–Thurs
9.30am–5.30pm, Fri 9.30am–6pm, Sat
9.30am–3pm. Tram #6 or the Frankston
line from Flinders Street Station.

Scienceworks 2 Booker St, Spotswood
☎9392 4800. Learn about science and
technology through a series of interactive
exhibitions on sport, insects and, erm,
contraception. There's also a digital
planetarium and plenty of hands-on
activities, as well as school-holiday

Melbourne's CBD is relatively family-friendly, with child care and other elements of community infrastructure in place. A new child-care "arthouse" has opened next to Federation Square and there is also a child-care centre currently proposed for the QV complex (see p.39).

East Melbourne Child Care Co-operative Cnr Grey & Simpson streets, East Melbourne ☎9419 4301. Children up to 5 years. Book early as there may be a waiting list. Mon–Fri 7.30am–6pm; $50 full day, $25 half-day or $225 weekly.

Kids on Collins Level 3, 600 Collins St ☎9629 4099. Children up to 6 years. Mon–Fri 7am–7.30pm; $81.90 full day or $339.50 weekly.

Young Melbourne Child Care 77 Parks St, South Melbourne ☎9686 6366. Children 3 months to 5 years. Mon–Fri 7.30am–6.30pm; $68-71 full day (cost varies depending on child's age).

programmes on the human mind and body, and touring exhibitions. Daily 10am–4.30pm; Scienceworks only adults $6, under-16s free, combined Scienceworks and Planetarium adults $12.30, child $4.10. Williamstown and Werribee lines from Flinders Street Station to Spotswood Station.

World Wide Wear Shop B10–B112, 1341 Dandenong Rd, Chadstone ☎9530 9864. Located in the mammoth Chadstone shopping complex, World Wide Wear has great clothing and accessories (think foam backpacks and holographic T-shirts) for street-savvy girls and boys twelve years and under. Mon–Sat 10am–6pm, Sun noon–6pm.

Outdoor

CERES Cafe 8 Lee St, East Brunswick ☎9380 8861. An environmentally sustainable farm where local parents gather to let their broods free range. Organic, vegetarian snacks include spinach and cheese pides, samosas, muffins and cakes; babycinos are also available. Mon–Fri 10am–4pm, Sat 9am–4pm, Sun 10am–4pm (lunch from 11am, kitchen closes 3pm).

Collingwood Children's Farm St Heliers St, Abbotsford ☎9417 5806. At the bottom of a dead-end street and on the banks of the Yarra, this small working farm allows kids to feed animals such as "Lazy Charlie", a Wessex saddleback, other porkers and piglets, or goats (daily 9–10am). Nippers can also help with farm chores, have a go at milking a cow or do a farm tour and learn about plants and animals. Family days (first day of the month) include horse treks, and have a delicious farm lunch thrown in as well. Every second Saturday of the month, there's a farmers' market (8am–1pm), offering a selection of local produce. Daily 9am–5pm; $8, under-14s $4. Epping line

from Flinders Street Station to Victoria Park Station.

Luna Park 18 Lower Esplanade, St Kilda ☎9525 5033. Old-fashioned roller-coaster, ferris wheel and ghost-train rides, plus newer harum-scarum attractions like the "Gravitron", which will have you and your child hanging on for dear life. Wandering around is free, but you pay $4.35 for individual rides. Fri 7–11pm, Sat 11am–11pm, Sun 11am to dusk.

Melbourne Zoo Elliot Ave, Parkville ☎9285 9300. Apart from watching monkeys scratching their privates, children can line up for daily meet-the-keeper sessions (wombats 11.15am, seals 2pm, pelicans 2.30pm, penguins 3.30pm; free) or go on twilight tours (Jan Thurs–Sun, Feb Fri–Sun; free) for better views of the nocturnal animals, nightly discussions with zookeepers and live concerts. Other highlights include a discovery trail, where children can collect animal stamps for a zoo calendar, National Zoo Month (Oct) and the Freddo Frog Festival (Nov), as well as

In addition to its many family-friendly attractions, the city of Melbourne recently created ArtPlay, an enterprising programme of events for children aged five to twelve years, aimed to increase families' engagement in city life by fostering creativity and imagination within the confines of **Birrarung Marr**, Melbourne's newest park. As the name suggests, ArtPlay offers a range of weekend and holiday workshops, where children are encouraged to take part in arts activities, both individually and collaboratively, and to romp around in a variety of indoor and outdoor play, exhibition and performance spaces, all located in Birraraung Marr on the northern banks of the Yarra River, adjacent to Federation Square. For programme information and weekend and holiday workshops, ℡9664 7900 or visit ⓦwww.artplay.com.au.

various school-holiday children's activities (see also p.73). Daily 9am–5pm; $16.40, under-15s $7.40, under-4s free. Tram #55, #56 or #68.

Polly Woodside Maritime Museum Map 4, C7. Lorimer St East, Southbank ℡9699 9760. Clamber over the tall ship *Polly Woodside* (see p.60) and beneath the skull-and-cross-bones, walk the plank, wander through nautical displays and relics, then venture to the playground with its wooden pirate ship. From the museum, cruises go to Port Melbourne and Williamstown, and there's a water taxi to Southbank. Daily 10am–4pm; $9.90, under-16s $6.60, under-5s free.

Pony rides Beaconsfield Parade, St Kilda ℡0412 581 350. Weather permitting, the little 'uns can have a ride atop a Shetland pony along a small circuit on St Kilda's scenic foreshore. Sat & Sun 10am–5pm; $4 per ride. Tram #96.

Royal Botanic Gardens Birdwood Ave, South Yarra. Young ones can feed the swans or wander along winding leafy paths. School-holiday programmes are especially fun, as they allow children to dig for worms, hunt for slugs and spiders, or do a spot of face painting (under-15s $12, accompanying adults free). Mon–Fri 9am–5pm, Sat & Sun 9.30am–5pm.

St Kilda Adventure Playground Newton Court, off Eildon Rd, St Kilda ℡9209 6348. Hidden away, this huge playground has a flying fox, skate ramp, two trampolines, wooden maze, home-made billy carts and a giant plane, as well as cubbyhouses, a dance studio and a kitchen and eating area for adults. What more could the kids want? Tram #96.

Werribee Open Range Zoo K Rd, Werribee ℡9731 9600, ⓦwww.zoo.org.au. Great place for watching a bunch of African wildlife (rhinos, hippos, zebras and giraffes) cavorting in a natural environment. Highlights include a bus safari (first at 10.30am, last at 3.40pm), the thirty-minute Volcanic Plains Walking Trail, a "Behind the Scenes" tour in which you can visit the kitchens where staff prepare food to feed the animals and the Savannah Discovery Centre. See also p.199. Daily 9am–5pm; $16.40, under-15s $7.40, under-3s free. Werribee line from Flinders Street Station to Werribee Station.

Directory

Airlines Air Canada ☎1300 655 767, ⍟www.aircanada.ca; Air New Zealand (domestic) ☎13 24 76, ⍟www.airnz.co.nz; Alitalia ☎1300 653 747, ⍟www.alitalia .it; British Airways ☎9603 1133, ⍟www .british-airways.com; Garuda Indonesia ☎1300 365 330, ⍟www.garuda-indonesia .com; Japan Airlines ☎9654 2733, ⍟www .jal.co.jp; Jetstar (domestic) ☎13 15 38, ⍟www.jetstar.com.au; KLM ☎9654 5222, ⍟www.klm.com; Lauda Air ☎1800 642 438, ⍟www.laudaair.com; Malaysia Airlines ☎13 26 27, ⍟www.malaysiaair.com; Olympic ☎9629 5022, ⍟www.olympic -airways.gr; Qantas ☎13 13 13, ⍟www .qantas.com.au; Singapore Airlines ☎13 10 11, ⍟www.singaporeair.com; Thai International ☎1300 651 960, ⍟www .thaiair.com; United ☎13 17 77, ⍟www .united.com; Virgin Blue (domestic & Pacific) ☎13 67 89, ⍟www.virginblue.com.au.

Airport enquiries ☎9297 1600.

Airport tax International departure tax from Melbourne's Tullamarine Airport is automatically included in your airline ticket.

American Express 233–239 Collins St (Mon–Fri 8.30am–5.30pm, Sat 9am–noon; ☎9633 6333).

Banks and exchange All major banks can be found on Collins St. Standard banking hours are generally Mon–Fri 9.30am–4pm (Fri until 5pm), although some branches of the Bank of Melbourne, including the one at 142 Elizabeth St, are open Sat 9am–noon. Most banks have 24-hour ATMs, which accept a variety of cash, credit and debit cards. Thomas Cook is at 257 Collins St (Mon–Fri 8.45am–5.15pm, Sat 9am–5pm); other branches are at 330 Collins St and 261 Bourke St. The Thomas Cook desks at

the international and domestic terminal of Tullamarine Airport are open 24hr.

Bicycles Bikes and cycling equipment can be rented from Bicycle Victoria, 19 O'Connell St, North Melbourne (☎9328 3000); Borsari Cycles, 193 Lygon St, Carlton (☎9347 4100); Fitzroy Cycles Bike Hire, 224 Swanston St (☎9419 4397); Freedom Machine, 401 Chapel St, South Yarra (☎9827 5014); Hire a Bicycle, beneath Princes Bridge (☎0412 616 633); St Kilda Cycles, 11 Carlisle St, St Kilda (☎9534 3074).

Buses Buy last-minute tickets at the bus company offices in the Spencer Street and Franklin Street terminals (V/Line ☎13 61 96, ⍟www.vlinepassenger.com.au). Operators include Greyhound Pioneer (☎13 20 30, ⍟www.greyhound.com.au); McCafferty's, Spencer Street Coach Terminal (☎13 14 99, ⍟www.mccaffertys.com.au); Firefly, Spencer Street Coach Terminal (☎9670 7500). For advance bookings, it's easier to go to the Bus Booking Centre (BBC), 24 Grey St, St Kilda (Mon–Sat 10am–6pm; ☎9534 2003), or Backpackers Travel Centre, Shop 1, 250 Flinders St (Mon–Fri 9am–6pm, Sat 10am–4pm; ☎9654 8477). They will shop around for you to find the cheapest deals, and they also sell bus passes, and make bookings for tours around Melbourne and one-way to Sydney or Adelaide. City bus information is available from the Met Transport Information Centre (☎13 16 38).

Car rental The main rental companies are Avis ☎9663 6366; Budget ☎13 27 27; Delta ☎9600 9025; Hertz ☎9663 6244; National ☎9329 5000; and Thrifty ☎9663 5200. Used-car companies with cheaper rates include Rent-A-Bomb

☎9428 0088 and Ugly Duckling ☎9525 4010. Campervans are available from Britz Australia ☎9483 1888; Koala Campervan Rentals ☎9415 8140; and NQ Australia Campervan Rentals ☎1800/079 529.
Dental Dental Hospital – emergencies only (☎9341 1040; Mon–Fri 7am–3.30pm).
Disabled travellers The Travellers Aid Society of Victoria, 2nd Floor, 169 Swanston St (Mon–Fri 9am–5pm, Sat & Sun 11am–4pm; ☎9654 2600), provides information and assistance for the disabled. It has another branch at Spencer Street Station (Mon–Fri 7.30am–7.30pm, Sat & Sun 7.30–11.30am; ☎9670 2873). Other resources include Disability Information Victoria, 454 Glenferrie Rd, Kooyong (☎1300 650 865); Paraquad Victoria, 208 Wellington St, Collingwood (☎9415 1200, ⊛www.paraquad.asn.au). Assistance is available at metropolitan, suburban, country and interstate stations, while relevant information for people with disabilities can be obtained by calling the Met Transport Information Centre (☎13 16 38). Buses are progressively being replaced with low-floor wheelchair accessible models; however passengers in wheelchairs still need to contact local bus operators for information. The Melbourne City Council produces a free mobility map of the CBD showing accessible routes, transport and toilets in the city centre, available from the front desk of the Melbourne Town Hall. Also look out for the Vic Venue Guide, which provides details on a range of disability access provisions at arts and entertainment venues – for more information, contact Arts Access (☎9699 8299). For wheelchair-accessible taxis, call Central Booking Service (☎1300 364 050).
Electricity 240 volts, AC 50 cycles, with three-pronged plugs the norm. Most hotels have provision for AC 110 volts. British and North American devices will require a transformer and adapter, available at most leading large hotels or hardware and electrical stores.
Email and Internet access Some backpacker hostels have Internet access for reading email, and some even have an Internet café for surfing, such as Backpackers World at *Hotel Bakpak* (see p.102; daily 8am–9pm; about $3 for 30min, $5 per hour). Traveller's Contact Point on the ground floor of 29–31 Somerset Place, a lane off Little Bourke Street between Elizabeth and Queen streets

in the city (Mon–Fri 8.30am–5.15pm, Sat 10am–4pm), provides Internet access among many other services including mail forwarding, voicemail, luggage storage and travel bookings. There are plenty of cybercafés throughout Melbourne. Most charge around $6–10 per hour online and there's usually an extra charge for printing out emails (around $0.25 for a laser printout). Cafe Wired, 363 Clarendon St, South Melbourne (Mon–Fri 9am–9pm, Sat noon–6pm), has Internet and computer-related services; Outlook Internet Café & Cyber Lounge, 196 Commercial Rd, Prahran (Mon–Fri 10am–9pm, Sat & Sun 10–6pm), is a good café opposite Prahran Market that also offers services such as scanning and photocopying.
Embassies Canada, 1st Floor, 123 Camberwell Rd, Hawthorn East (☎9811 9999); France, 492 St Kilda Rd (☎9820 0921); Germany, 480 Punt Rd, South Yarra (☎9828 6888); Italy, 509 St Kilda Rd (☎9867 5744); Norway, Suite 2, 416 High St, Kew (☎9853 3122); Sweden, 61 Riggall St, Broadmeadows (☎9301 1888); Switzerland, 420 St Kilda Rd (☎9867 2266); Thailand, 277 Flinders Lane (☎9650 1714); UK, 17th Floor, 90 Collins St (☎9650 4155); USA, 553 St Kilda Rd (☎9526 5900).
Emergencies Ring ☎000 for fire, police or ambulance.
GST (Goods and Services Tax) The GST is a broad-based tax of 10 percent on most goods and services such as accommodation, day tours, guides, translators, food, transport (including coach, rail and cruise) and other tourism services within Australia. International air fares do not attract GST.
Hospitals and clinics Major hospitals include the Alfred Hospital, Commercial Road, Prahran (☎9276 2000); Royal Children's Hospital, Flemington Road, Parkville (☎9345 5522); Royal Melbourne Hospital, Grattan Street, Parkville (☎9342 7000); and St Vincent's Hospital, Victoria Parade, Fitzroy (☎9807 2211). For vaccinations, anti-malaria tablets and first-aid kits contact the Travellers Medical and Vaccination Centre (TMVC), 2nd Floor, 393 Little Bourke St (☎9602 5788).
Immigration office Visas can be extended at the Department of Immigration and Multicultural Affairs at 2 Lonsdale St (Mon,

Tues, Thurs & Fri 9am–4pm, Wed 9am–3am; ☎13 18 81). You'll need to fill in Form 601; make sure you apply at least a month before your visa expires, as the process can take some time.

Laundries Most hostels and hotels have their own laundry. Commercial laundries include City Edge Laundrette, 39 Errol St, North Melbourne (daily 6am–11pm); The Soap Opera Laundry & Cafe, 128 Bridport St, Albert Park (Mon–Fri 7.30am–9.30pm, Sat & Sun 8am–9pm); and Blessington Street Launderette, 22 Blessington St, St Kilda (daily 7.30am–9pm).

Left luggage There are lockers at Spencer Street Station (daily 6am–10pm; $2; emptied nightly); luggage can be left overnight at the cloakroom ($3.50 per item). Flinders Street Station also has lockers (8am–8pm; $2), as do the Melbourne Transit Centre on Franklin St (accessible 24hr; $6–10) and the Travellers Contact (see "Email and Internet access" above). There are also lockers at the airport in the international terminal (24hr; $5–10).

Lost property Trains: Bayside Trains ☎1800 800 120; Connex Melbourne ☎1800 800 705. Trams: Swanston Trams ☎9610 3383; Yarra Trams ☎9610 3382. For buses and taxis, call the respective companies in the White or Yellow Pages.

Newspapers and magazines Melbourne's two daily newspapers are *The Age* (its Sunday edition is called *The Sunday Age*) and the tabloid *Herald-Sun*. Two national newspapers are also available – the *Australian Financial Review* (Mon–Sat) and the Rupert Murdoch-owned *Australian* (Mon–Sat). Magazines to look out for include *Melbourne Events*, a free monthly listings publication; *The Big Issue*, which supports Melbourne's homeless; and *Beat* and *Inpress*, two free and informative indie music magazines. Domestic and international publications can also be perused at the State Library (see p.41) or bought from major newsagents such as McGills, 187 Elizabeth St.

Parking Parking is often hard to find in the city centre, even though there are over 10,000 metered spaces and 42,500 off-street car spaces. Meters are mostly coin-operated; for car-park spaces, expect to pay around $5 an hour, or $10–15 daily.

Pharmacies Henry Francis Chemists, 286 Little Bourke St, City (Mon–Wed 9am–

5.45pm, Thurs 9am–6.30pm, Fri 9am–9pm, Sat 9.30am–5pm, Sun 10am–5pm); Leonard Long, cnr of Williams Road and High Street, Prahran (daily 9am–midnight); Mulqueeny's Pharmacy, corner of Swanston and Collins streets opposite the Town Hall (Mon–Fri 8am–8pm, Sat 9am–6pm, Sun 11am–6pm).

Police Melbourne City Police Station, 637 Flinders St, City (☎9247 5347); emergency ☎000.

Post offices Melbourne's General Post Office (☎9203 3044), 250 Elizabeth St, City, is open Mon–Fri 8.15am–5.30pm, & Sat 10am–3pm. Suburban post offices are generally open Mon–Fri 9am–5pm. For voicemail and mail forwarding, contact Travellers Contact Point (see "Email and Internet access" opposite). Stamps can also be purchased from Australia Post shops, newsagents, and some pharmacies and milk bars, as well as from the National Philatelic Centre, Ground Floor, 321 Exhibition St (☎9204 7736). Stamps cost $0.45 for a letter within Australia; $1 for a letter to New Zealand and Southeast Asia; $1.50 to the USA, Canada, UK and Europe. Postcards within Australia and to New Zealand and Asia are $0.05 cheaper than standard letters; $1 to the USA, Canada, UK and Europe.

Public holidays New Year's Day (Jan 1); Australia Day (Jan 26); Labour Day (first or second Mon in March); Easter (Good Friday, Easter Saturday and Monday, usually late March or early April); Anzac Day (April 25); Queen's Birthday (second Mon in June); Melbourne Cup Day (first Tues in Nov); Christmas Day (Dec 25); Boxing Day (Dec 26).

Taxis Major firms include Arrow Taxi Services (☎13 22 11); Black Cabs Combined (☎13 22 27); Embassy Taxis (☎13 17 55); Melbourne Combined Taxis (☎13 13 23); Silvertop Taxi Services (☎13 10 08; ⊛www.silvertop.com.au); and Yellow Cabs (☎13 19 24).

Telephones Melbourne is well stocked with public telephones. Local calls from a payphone cost a minimum of $0.40. Some backpacker hostels and shops in the city sell discount phonecards (such as Phoneaway, Unidial, EZI Great Rate Card, One Card and AAPT) which can be used in any payphone for cheap international calls, and which can be purchased from

Telstra shops, post offices, duty-free stores and newsagents. The official Telstra rate for a call from a public phone to the UK is $2 per minute Mon–Fri, $1.20 Sat & Sun. With one of the phonecards mentioned above, expect to pay about $0.39–55 per minute, plus a small connection fee (less than $1). Melbourne's General Post Office has several payphones plus a range of directories, including White and Yellow Pages. Overseas calls can be made by dialling ☎0011 (the overseas access code), followed by the country code, area code and required number. The cheapest time to make international calls is at off-peak periods (Mon–Fri 6pm–midnight, all day Sat & Sun). For emergencies phone ☎000; for operator services, call ☎12455 (local, national and international); for street addresses, phone numbers, email addresses, postcodes, national and international country codes, and time zones, call ☎12452; for reverse-charge calls, call ☎12550. If you want to know how much an interstate or international call will cost, ring ☎1234. The prefixes ☎13, 1300 or 1800 indicate a toll-free number. The area code for domestic calls to Melbourne from outside the city is ☎03. If ringing from overseas, dial the international access code followed by ☎613, then the number as listed in the guide.

TV and radio The government-funded Australian Broadcasting Corporation (ABC), the national broadcaster, provides Channel 2. Another government-sponsored station is the excellent multicultural Special Broadcasting Service (SBS) on Channel 28. Australia's major commercial stations are Channel 7, Channel 9 and Channel 10. The ABC provides a range of national radio channels (both AM and FM), including Radio National (621AM), 3LO (774AM), and Triple J (107.5FM), an alternative station geared for younger listeners. Melbourne also has a host of commercial radio stations, and more community stations per head than any other city in the world – try 3RRR (102.7FM) and 3PBS (106.7FM), both of which showcase new independent music.

Ticket agencies Tickets for festivals, concerts, sporting events, and film and theatre performances can be obtained through Ticketmaster (☎13 61 66, ⓦwww .ticketmaster.com.au), Ticketek Victoria (☎13 28 49, wpremier.ticketek.com.au), and Half Tix (☎9650 9420; Mon & Sat 10am–2pm, Tues–Thurs 11am–6pm, Fri 11am–6.30pm), in the middle of Bourke Street Mall.

Time Melbourne follows Australian Eastern Standard Time (AEST), half an hour ahead of South Australia and the Northern Territory, two hours ahead of Western Australia, ten hours ahead of Greenwich Mean Time and fifteen hours ahead of US Eastern Standard Time. Clocks are put forward one hour in November and back again in March for daylight savings. For international time, call ☎1900 912 073.

Tour operators With Melbourne as a base, a wide variety of tours can be made to the interior of Victoria or both east and west along the coast. Popular destinations – both as day-trips and one-way tours – are to the Grampians, Phillip Island and the Mornington Peninsula, and along the Great Ocean Road. For longer trips, you could consider several two- to four-day bushwalking excursions offered by several operators. Tour operators include Autopia Tours (☎9326 5536); Echidna Walkabout (☎9646 8249, ⓔekidna@netcore.com.au); Let's Go Bush (☎9662 3969); Oz Experience (☎1300 300 028); Wayward Bus (☎1800/882 823, ⓦwww.waywardbus .com.au); and Wild-Life Tours (☎9747 1882, ⓔwildlife@eisa.net.au).

Travel agents Backpackers Travel Centre, Shop 19, Centre Place, 258 Flinders Lane (☎9654 8477, ⓔinfo@backpackerstravel .net.au); Flight Centre, 19 Bourke St, 53 Elizabeth St and many other branches (☎13 16 00, ⓦwww.flightcentre.com); STA Travel, 273 Little Collins St, 142 Acland St, St Kilda, and other branches (book and pay over the phone ☎1300 360 960; or for nearest branch ☎13 17 76, ⓦwww .statravel.com.au); Student Uni Travel, Shop 4, 440 Elizabeth St (☎9662 4666); YHA Travel, 83 Hardware Lane (☎9670 9611, ⓦwww.yha.com.au).

Beyond
the City

Beyond the City

Mornington Peninsula to Wilsons Promontory

Just south of Melbourne, the **Mornington Peninsula** is a favourite seaside holiday destination boasting elegant beachfront towns like **Sorrento** and **Portsea**, prolific bush and native wildlife in the **Mornington Peninsula National Park**, excellent surfing and swimming spots (many of them patrolled), lookouts, walking trails and wineries. Southeast of here is scenic **Phillip Island**, whose main tourist drawcard is the **Penguin Parade**, where hordes of penguins waddle ashore each evening at sunset, while little-known **French Island** in Westernport Bay is a blissfully under-exploited gem – formerly the setting for a prison farm, it's now virtually undeveloped wilderness. Further southeast along the mainland, **Wilsons Promontory** is a nature-lovers' paradise. Known locally as "The Prom", it's one of Australia's best-loved national parks, renowned for bushland, wetlands and mountain walks, and excellent surfing and swimming beaches.

Mornington Peninsula

Curving around Port Phillip Bay from Frankston to Point Nepean, the **Mornington Peninsula** has traditionally been popular with Victoria's less affluent holidaymakers, whose caravans and tents – at last count, there were over thirty caravan parks on the peninsula – dot the peninsula's ti tree-studded foreshore, although the towns of Sorrento and Portsea at the tip of the peninsula remain the preserve of Melbourne's wealthy, many of whom decamp here for extended periods during the summer months. Water-based activities like surfing and swimming with dolphins are the main attractions, but when you tire of salty water and sandcastles, the peninsula hinterland hosts some excellent wineries, weekend markets, walking trails, sweeping views and historical sites. For information on attractions, activities, accommodation, touring and events, visit the official Mornington Peninsula website (@www .visitmorningtonpeninsula.org).

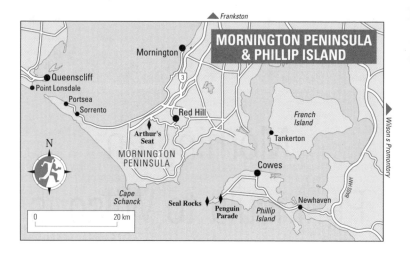

Regular **bus** services to all major towns on the Mornington Peninsula operate from Frankston, which is on the Frankston line from Flinders Street Station. In Frankston, connect with a Portsea Passenger Services **bus** (☎5986 5666) to Sorrento ($7.90) and Portsea ($8.20) from departure bays immediately outside Frankston Station; for timetable information, free call ☎1800 115 666. From Sorrento there's a community bus to Dromana via Blairgowrie, Rye and Rosebud (four daily Mon–Fri) but no transport to Arthur's Seat. If you're travelling **by car**, the most direct route is via the Mornington Peninsula Freeway, but an alternative is taking the Nepean Highway from Melbourne and then the Mornington turn-off.

Frankston to Cape Shanck

The peninsula starts at **Frankston**, 40km south of Melbourne, beyond which the peninsula's western coast is a succession of clean, safe and beautiful beaches, although they all become crowded and traffic-snarled in summer. Twelve kilometres further on, the old fishing port of **Mornington** has few attractions, although the lookout at the Matthew Flinders obelisk at Schnapper Point, where you can buy fresh fish straight off the boat, has great views. Beyond here, the coast road leads to **Dromana**, where seaside development begins in earnest. Inland from Dromana, the granite outcrop of **Arthur's Seat** rises to a height of 305m, providing breathtaking views of Port Phillip Bay. A chairlift makes the trip to the top, leaving from the picnic area on Arthur's Seat Road, just off the Mornington Peninsula Freeway (Sept to 2nd Mon in June daily 11am–5pm; rest of year Sat 11am–5pm, Sun 11am–5.30pm; $8.50 return). Attracting 100,000 visitors each year, the chairlift has recently been involved in several serious accidents, and talks are continuing over its long-term future. Only 500m from the summit is **Arthur's Seat Maze** (daily 10am–6pm; $10), which combines traditional hedge mazes with theme gardens and giant tree sculptures.

Nearby, at Merricks North, is **Muranna** (ⓦwww.muranna.com.au). This beguiling retreat is home to an extraordinary garden, whose centrepiece is an exotic herb garden ($5 entry) arranged into various medicinal and bush tucker uses. Excellent explanatory notes give the history and uses of herbs such as agrimony, once used to ward off snakes, and pennyroyal, used to restore failing memory in the aged. Beyond the herb gardens are a pretty walled garden and pond, and various gentle walks. If you want **to stay** overnight, two guest cottages with self-contained facilities provide child-friendly accommodation ($65 adults, $35 children per night).

Interspersed among the peninsula's bushland, orchards, craft outlets, berry farms and enormous French provincial-style houses are over thirty **wineries,** which produce superb, if pricey, Pinot Noir and Shiraz. The most notable wine-growing area is **Red Hill**, southeast of Arthur's Seat. Overlooking the calm waters of Western Port Bay at 52 Red Hill-Shoreham Road, Red Hill Estate (daily 11am–5pm; ☎5989 2838) has tastings, sales and light lunches, with restaurant dining on Friday and Saturday evenings. Nearby, at 33 Shoreham Road, the Montalto Vineyard and Olive Grove (☎5989 8412) offers both wine and an area of **wetlands**, which is home to over fifty species of birds. Another cracking winery is Mooruduc Estate, at 501 Derril Road, Mooruduc (Sat & Sun 11am–5pm; ☎5971 8506) at the northern end of the peninsula. Out back, the rough-and-tumble cellar door dispenses good Pinot and Chardonnay, while *Jill's*, the upmarket winery restaurant (Sat & Sun 6–11pm), serves a fabulous range of quality local produce – from roast free-range chicken to fresh fruits, vegetables and cheeses. Also in Red Hill, Ashcombe Maze on Red Hill-Shoreham Road (daily 10am–5pm; ☎5989 8387) is Australia's oldest and most famous **hedge maze**, with over 25 acres of gardens, woodlands and waterways.

As well as wineries, the peninsula's **community markets** selling local produce and crafts attract many city-dwellers; most are monthly affairs, so there's usually one every weekend. One of the biggest and best is Red Hill Community Market, Australia's oldest community market, held on the first Saturday of every month (Sept–May 7am–1pm), at Red Hill Recreation Reserve, Red Hill Road, 10km east of Dromana.

Further south, on the ocean side of the peninsula, **Cape Shanck** is the site of a 21-metre-high, red-topped lighthouse, which has protected sailors since 1849. From here, a timber staircase and boardwalk lead from the dramatic basalt cliffs down to the sea along a narrow neck of land, providing magnificent coastal views to swoon over.

Sorrento

Near the tip of the peninsula, **Sorrento** is the area's oldest and most affluent town (attempts by wealthier residents to fence off sections of the beach for their private use have not made the hoi polloi feel any more welcome). This is where Melbourne's big money relaxes – in the wide, tree-lined residential streets, the spectacular cliff-top properties hidden behind high fences, and in the town centre's abundant antique shops, galleries, cafés and restaurants.

After checking out the galleries on Ocean Beach Road, visit the **Collins Settlement Historic Site** (open access 24hr), 3km southeast in Sullivan Bay. This is where, in 1803, Captain David Collins attempted the first permanent European settlement of the Melbourne area, only to abandon the site less than a year later because of its chronic lack of water. A display centre on the site (Sun & holidays 1–4.30pm; free) fleshes out the story of the settlement, and the life of the local Aborigines who lived in the area previously.

From Sorrento, **ferries** run across the mouth of the bay to Queenscliff on the Bellarine Peninsula (see p.203), departing every hour from 7am to 6pm, returning from Queenscliff at the same hours. Tickets for passengers only are $8 one-way and $16 return. For one passenger with a car, tickets are $42, double that to return. Tickets can be purchased from the passenger lounges at Sorrento and Queenscliff; for group and coach bookings call ☎5258 3244, or visit ☻www.searoad.com.au.

Swimming with **dolphins** and **seals** has become one of the area's prime attractions, so much so that tour operators are obliged to follow a code of practice to ensure they don't adversely affect the animals. Two long-established operators are the environmentally conscious Polperro Dolphin Swims (☎5988 8437 or mobile ☎0428 174 160), who take the smallest maximum number of people, and Moonraker (☎5984 4211, mobile ☎0418 591 033). Both depart twice daily during the season (Sept/Oct–May), weather permitting, for a four-hour trip ($80 per swimmer, including wetsuit and snorkelling equipment; $42 for sightseers).

Portsea and the Mornington Peninsula National Park

A few kilometres further on, **Portsea** is quieter and more private than Sorrento, with the houses of its wealthy inhabitants contentedly secluded in the coastal scrub. In summer, Front Beach and Shelley Beach are for sunbathers, while on the other shore surfers and boardriders make for the swell of Portsea Ocean Beach, which also attracts a good number of hang-gliders. Like Sorrento, there are a number of good **galleries** to explore, including Libby Edwards, at 3745 Point Nepean Road (Tues–Sun 11am–6pm, ☎5984 2299), which has a good collection of local and national fine art. Each year around January 20, Portsea hosts the **Portsea Swim Classic**, an open-water race that attracts both young and old to the 1.2km course; for more information, visit ⊛www.portseasurf .com.au. For information on the larger and more famous Lorne Pier to Pub open-water swimming event, see p.208.

There are several stunning **walking trails** nearby – one leads to Cheviot Hill, from where you can see Cheviot Beach, the spot where Australian Prime Minister Harold Holt disappeared, presumed drowned in 1967.

Beyond Portsea at the tip of the peninsula, **Point Nepean** is where the **Mornington Peninsula National Park** begins, extending along 40km of the peninsula's ocean-facing coastline. The park is covered with original bushland, and is home to kangaroos, bandicoots and echidnas, as well as many species of forest and ocean birds. At the point of the peninsula, historic **Fort Nepean** has tunnels, bomb-proof rooms, gun emplacements, fortifications, glorious views of the Port Phillip Heads and spectacular cliff-top walking tracks leading off into secluded bushland. It is where the first Allied shots were fired during both World Wars – in 1914, a warning shot was fired across the bow of a German freighter and, in 1939, there was a similar response to an unidentified ship (later discovered to be the *Tasmanian Woniora*).

Phillip Island

Just under two hours' drive from Melbourne, and connected to the mainland by a bridge, **Phillip Island** is one of Victoria's most popular destinations, largely on account of the **Penguin Parade**, although the island also has large colonies of seals and koalas, fine coastal scenery, good swimming beaches, and enough nooks and crannies to create surfable waves all year round.

The first European to set foot on its shores was the English explorer George Bass in 1798. Since his visit, the island has undergone a number of name changes: originally called Westernport by Bass, it became Snapper Island, then Grant Island after Lieutenant James Grant visited in 1801, before finally being christened Phillip Island in honour of the First Fleet's Captain Arthur Phillip. A favoured hunting ground for whalers and sealers, the island later became a sheep and cattle run, and a farming region for chicory, a coffee additive that was grown and roasted in kilns for the first time in 1870 – you can still see the peculiar square-shaped chicory kilns dotted around the island.

Massive investment has boosted Phillip Island's infrastructure in recent years, but even now getting around still poses problems. From Spencer Street Station, there is a daily V/Line **bus** direct to Cowes (Mon–Fri 3.50pm; train and connecting coach run on Sat at 9.40am & 5.30pm and Sun 9.06am & 5.20pm; 3hr 20min; $16.50), the main settlement on the island, but little public transport once you get there. If you're short of time, a **bus tour** from Melbourne is a good way to see the penguins, and most tours also take in other island attractions as well. One of the best operators is the long-established Autopia Tours (☎9326 5536), who pick you up from central Melbourne or St Kilda. Their daily one-day tour (noon–midnight; $70 including entrance fees and morning tea) takes in the Wildlife Park, Koala Conservation Centre and Penguin Parade, as well as Seal Rocks and the Nobbies. Access **by car** is via the Monash Freeway, which joins the South Gippsland Highway beyond Dandenong.

On the way to Phillip Island, you can bring yourself up to speed on the world's longest earthworm (megascolides australis), the twelve-foot-long Gippsland earthworm, an endangered species that has transformed Korumburra from a near ghost town to a bustling tourist destination. Making a sucking and gurgling noise when it burrows, the giant worm is celebrated by the townsfolk in their annual worm festival held in March. It has also been immortalized at the **Wildlife Wonderland and Giant Worm Museum** in the nearby town of Bass (daily 9.30am–5.30pm; $11.90; ☎5678 2222). Visitors enter a 300-metre-long building, shaped like an earthworm, and can walk through a section that simulates the internal view of a worm's stomach – vile sounds and all. You can also get a worm's eye view of life below ground. When you're all wormed out, brace yourself for a rather uninspiring shark display and a wildlife park harbouring all the usual suspects: dingoes, koalas, kangaroos, wombats and the like.

Each year, Phillip Island switches gear for the 500cc **Australian Motorcycle Grand Prix**, held in October over three days. Accommodation on the island is scarce during the event, although there are plenty of campgrounds near the circuit to pitch your tent. The circuit (daily from 9am), often touted as the best course in the world, maintains its original 1950s layout.

Churchill Island

Just northwest of Newhaven, at the end of Swan Bay, **Churchill Island** is a tiny historic island only two kilometres long. First used by the Bunurong Aboriginals for hunting shark and oysters, the island was visited in 1801 by Lieutenant James Grant, who cleared and planted Victoria's first crops, and then purchased by Samuel Amess, a building contractor and former mayor of Melbourne, in 1872. Amess built a home on the island, which still stands today – you can wander through the heritage-listed weatherboard home-stead, which has been painstakingly restored in recent years. Surrounding the homestead are outbuildings, an orchard and fragrant gardens ideal for a picnic. Also here, a cannon taken from the US ship *Shenandoah* and given to Amess in appreciation of his hospitality when the ship visited Melbourne in 1865.

A working farm with Highland cattle, sheep, horses and free-roaming hens and ducks, Churchill Island is only accessible daily from 10am–4.30pm ($6; for more information, contact the Phillip Island Information Centre

®5951 2800). Churchill Island is 120km southeast of Melbourne; to get there, take the signposted turn-off which heads north off Phillip Island Road just 1km west of the Newhaven bridge.

The Penguin Parade

Despite the abundance of wildlife – fur seals, koalas, wallabies, emus, lyrebirds, even giant earthworms – that inhabits this sweep of land in southeast Victoria, none draws such a crowd as the Little penguins (sometimes known as "fairy penguins"). The enormously popular **Penguin Parade** (daily at sunset, $16, credit card bookings ®5956 8300, ⓦwww.penguins.org.au) takes place at Summerland Beach, near the western end of the island. Each evening at sunset, people rush to get see several thousand cute little penguins emerging from the surf and waddling to their nesting areas on the foreshore. It's an impressive spectacle, although the penguins are almost outnumbered by the hordes of tourists who look down from concrete stands onto the floodlit beach. The parade takes about fifty minutes, after which you can move onto the extensive boardwalks over the burrows and continue watching the penguins' antics for several more hours. The crowds are smaller in winter, when you should bring rugs, as winds blowing in from Bass Strait can make the experience unbearably chilly, plus something to sit on (there's only concrete tiers). If you hang around long enough, you get a much closer view of the penguins – some of their burrows are close to the road, meaning the birds have to take the longer route along the sides of the boardwalks.

Information, maps and tickets for the Penguin Parade are available from the tourist office in Newhaven, the first town on the island as you cross over the bridge from the mainland (daily 9am–5pm, longer in summer; ®5956 7447). Just above Summerland Beach, the excellent **Penguin Parade Visitor Centre** (daily 10am–7.30pm; admission included in the parade ticket) offers a simulated underwater scene of the hazards of a penguin's life, interactive displays, videos and even nesting boxes to which penguins have access from the outside, plus meals and souvenirs.

Around the island

A few kilometres beyond the Penguin Parade, at the western end of the island, the **Seal Rocks Sea Life Centre** at Point Grant no longer operates, after fierce winds ripped off the roof and the state government took control of the operation. While the cafés have closed down, you can still grab an ice cream and see the seals through the telescopes on the cliff edge ($1 for 3min). Below here, **the Nobbies** are two huge rock stacks with stunning views across to Cape Shanck on the Mornington Peninsula, while Seal Rocks are known for their thriving colony of Australian fur seals. On the boardwalk down to the blowhole, check out the little penguins' nesting burrows in the side of the cliffs – you might even see one of the birds lying asleep already or preparing for slumber.

Other highlights of the island include the **Koala Conservation Centre** on the Phillip Island Tourist Road between Newhaven and Cowes (daily 10am–5pm; $8.50), where elevated walkways allow visitors to observe these tree-top dwellers at close range. Opposite here, a mini-golf course and fun park with an enormous three-dimensional maze are other ways to while away some time. In **Cowes** itself, the wide sheltered beach is good for bucket-and-spaders, while the alfresco eateries overlooking the harbour and lively Sunday **market** draw an older crowd. Cowes is where the words of "Waltzing Matilda", Australia's best known and much-loved national song, were penned.

French Island

Across from Phillip Island is the towering shape of **French Island**, named for the French scientific expedition, led by Nicholas Baudin, which visited in 1902. Previously, the first known European to sight the island was George Bass, who entered Westernport Bay in 1798 but mistook it for a promontory of the mainland. In 1802, it was named Western Island after Lieutenant John Murray spied it from the *Lady Nelson*. Subsequently inhabited by sealers, it became Victoria's own Alcatraz when it housed a prison farm from 1916 to 1975, but these days French Island is known for its raw natural beauty and rich wildlife. Over two-thirds of the island is a state park, whose inhabitants include a flourishing koala colony, sea eagles, mutton birds, pelicans and the rare potoroos. Not so rare are the mosquitoes – make sure you bring some repellent.

Salt marshes and mangroves ring the coastline, while the interior is mostly heathland with magnificent wildflower displays in spring. The island is largely unspoilt, supporting around six hundred plant species, as well as Australia's largest population of **koalas**, which can be seen throughout the island. Indeed, so abundant are the koalas that they are exported to zoos in Australia and around the world.

Largely flat, the island is a walker's paradise, and there are plenty of half- and full-day **walks** coiling inland and around the coastline, including a gentle 3km hike up to the Pinnacles, which affords good views over wetlands to the west, Westernport Bay and of Phillip Island. All walks start from Tankerton Foreshore Reserve, and guides to routes are available from the information board located next to Tankerton jetty. The **French Island Tourist Information Centre** on Bayview Road (℡5980 1241) also has information on local walks and activities. Despite the wet and sandy terrain, cycling and **mountain biking** are popular. You can bring your own bike or hire one from the French Island general store (℡5980 1209) or *Tortoise Head Guesthouse* (see overleaf).

The **McLeod Prison** and associated farm once housed over a hundred inmates serving the last periods of their sentences. From all reports the prison was quite comfortable – located amid extensive natural bushlands, inmates were consoled by a nine-hole golf course, basketball and tennis courts, and it was the first Australian prison to introduce television in the 1950s. Now the McLeod Eco-Farm and Historical Prison (℡5678 0155, @www.mcleodecofarm.com), it offers rooms in the old cells, a restaurant, guided tours of the prison facilities and bicycles for hire.

Practicalities

Access to French Island is via **ferry** ($8.50), although cars are not allowed on board. From Phillip Island, ferries depart Stony Point daily at 8.30am and 4.15pm, returning at 9.30am and 4.30pm, and from Cowes jetty daily at 9.10am, returning at 4.30pm. For more information, contact Inter Island Ferries (℡9585 5730; @www.interislandferries.com.au). You can also take a **bus tour**, which lasts about four hours and includes a history of the island and its flora and fauna, plus a visit to the McLeod Eco-Farm. French Island Bus Tours (℡5980 1241) depart at noon and French Island Eco-Tours (℡9770 1822) at 12.30pm, both from Stony Point.

For **accommodation**, the *McLeod Eco-Farm and Historical Prison*, on McLeod Road (℡5678 0155), has a range of basic (**❷**) and deluxe (**❹**) rooms in the former prison cells and officer's quarters. The rate includes three meals using produce organically grown on the farm, and transfer to and from the jetty

21km away. Another value-for-money option is the *Tortoise Head Guesthouse* (☎5980 1234 (❸)) on Tankerton Rd, plus there are three camping grounds on the island. Bring a gas stove as fires are not permitted, and it pays to also include fresh water which is also scarce on the island.

Wilsons Promontory National park

Forming the southernmost point of the Australian mainland, **Wilsons Promontory** (known locally as "The Prom") is one of Australia's best-loved national parks, renowned for bushland, granite mountain ranges, wetlands, mountain walks, and excellent surfing and swimming beaches. For most of the nineteenth century, this remote and relatively inaccessible location was only used by sealers, whalers and cattle-grazers, but by the 1880s, the park was a regular haunt of naturalists, who secured its position as a national park. Named in honour of prominent London businessman, Thomas Wilson, it became a commando training camp during World War II and is today an important refuge for a diverse range of native wildlife, with around half of all Victoria's bird species and a third of its mammals, including the threatened long-nosed potoroo and eastern pygmy possum, found there. Other fauna, such as wombats, emus, kangaroos and wallabies, are commonly sighted around visitor areas and near walking tracks. In recognition of its characteristic land forms, plants and animals, the park was designated a Biosphere Reserve by the United Nations Educational, Scientific and Cultural Organization (UNESCO) in 1982.

Tidal River, located thirty kilometres inside the park boundary by a small river on Norman Bay, is the park's only service area, and the chief focus for tourism and recreation. On the way in, it's possible to see large mobs of kangaroos, usually grazing or resting in the shade, and often emus and wombats. From here, you can get a closer view of the wildlife by exploring on foot, with myriad walking tracks zigzagging through the park's many ecosystems and habitats. The walk to the top of Mt Oberon, which looms over Norman Bay and Tidal River, has great views over the coast, offshore islands and Bass Strait. One of the best wildlife-viewing opportunities is the walk to Millers Landing on the southern shore of Corner Inlet, where you can see swamp wallabies and birdlife, including egrets and cormorants. Other popular walks include the **Lilly Pilly Gully Nature Walk** through heathland, eucalypt forest and rainforest, longer treks to Tongue Point and Sealers Cove, or numerous trails leading adventurous walkers to beachside campsites. You can also explore the northern part of the Prom, an officially designated wilderness, or take an overnight hike to one of the eleven outstation campsites (accessible only on foot). An obvious starting point, the **information centre** (daily 8.30am–4.30pm; ☎5680 9555) has audiovisual presentations, displays, maps and *Discovering the Prom on Foot* ($7.95), a handy reference if you're about to tackle one of the overnight walks.

Practicalities

Approximately 220km southeast of Melbourne, Wilsons Promontory National Park is a three-hour drive from Melbourne. You can reach it by following the South Gippsland Highway to Meeniyan, then turning right onto Route 189, which takes you all the way to the park entrance. Once you get into the park, it's 30km to Tidal River. There is no public transport directly to Wilsons Promontory.

An **entrance fee** is payable before entering The Prom at a large gate that marks the entrance to the park. A variety of passes are available: day pass for a car ($9); two-day pass for a car ($15); five-day pass for a car ($27); day pass for a motor bike ($2.50); two-day pass for a motorbike ($4); and two-day pass for a small bus ($44).

If you want **to stay** overnight, you have to arrange accommodation through the information centre, although it's virtually impossible to find a bed on spec during peak periods such as Christmas, weekends and public holidays, as places book up months in advance for Christmas. Accommodation is in basic motor huts ($51 for four beds). Capable of holding up to five hundred people, the camping site (❶) at Tidal River operates on a first-come, first-served basis and gets packed in summer, although plentiful walking tracks lead off to a number of bushcamping sites. Located just a few minutes from the entrance to The Prom at 770 Mill Road in Yanakie, *Prom Mill Huts* (☎5687 1375, ⓦwww .prommillhuts.net; ❺) offer a choice of standard one- or two-bedroom self-contained cottages, with private gardens.

The Dandenong Ranges

The peaceful and inviting hills of the **Dandenong Ranges**, 30km east of Melbourne, have been a popular weekend retreat for city dwellers for over a century. Modest in height (their most elevated point, Mount Dandenong, is only 633m), they are famous for their undulating woodland scenery, interesting fauna and excellent walking possibilities. There are also a few worthwhile tourist attractions: the historic **Puffing Billy** steam train; the lovely gardens and sculptures of the **William Ricketts Sanctuary**, and the towering mountain ash trees, varied wildlife and observation points of the **Dandenong Ranges National Park**.

Parts of the Dandenongs are easily accessible by **public transport**. Trains run from Flinders Street Station to Upper Ferntree Gully and Belgrave, from where buses go to many other destinations in the ranges, including the villages of Olinda, Emerald, Gembrook and Sassasfras – for more details contact the Met Information Centre (☎13 16 38). If you're travelling **by car**, a good route to take is the Burwood Highway to Upper Ferntree Gully, from where you're ideally placed to explore the area – the drive from Upper Ferntree Gully via the Mount Dandenong Tourist Road to the quaint villages of Sassasfras and Olinda and the Mount Dandenong Observatory is particularly good.

The best place for **tourist information** is the tourist office at 1211 Burwood Highway in Ferntree Gully (daily 9am–5pm; ☎9758 7522), which has walking guides and maps, and can help with a range of accommodation. If you're travelling by train, get off at the Upper Ferntree Gulley station; the office is a five-minute signposted walk from there.

Dandenong villages and gardens

The **Mount Dandenong Tourist Road** – stretching from Upper Ferntree Gully in the south to Montrose in the north – is lined with picturesque little villages, many with small cafes, galleries or craft shops. One of the most attractive villages on the road is **OLINDA** (ⓦwww.olindavillage.com.au). Here the vibrant **National Rhododendron Gardens** (daily 10pm–5pm; Sept, Oct & Nov $7, rest of year $5.40) boast more than 15,000 rhododendrons, as well as spectacular cherry and Japanese maple trees that are perfect for lazing under in spring when they flower. Another great garden around Olinda is the **R.J. Hamer Forest Arboretum** (open access 24hr; free), a vast expanse of woodland with over 150

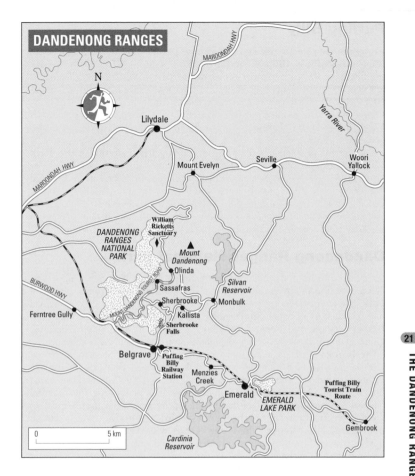

DANDENONG RANGES

species of native and exotic trees. After all that garden browsing, grab a quick lunch or a Devonshire tea (including fresh-baked scones) at *Pie in the Sky*, 43 Olinda–Monbulk Rd (Mon–Sat 10am–5pm, Sun 9.30am–5pm). For good old-fashioned sweets like gobstoppers, humbugs and some flavoursome Dutch liquorice, make a beeline for the *Olinda Sweet Co*, at 37 Monash Avenue.

Four kilometres south of Olinda, **SASSAFRAS** has a few more good options for afternoon tea: *Miss Marples Tearooms*, 382 Mount Dandenong Tourist Road (daily 10am–6pm; ⓦwww.missmarples.com.au), is decorated in homage to Agatha Christie's greatest female sleuth and doles out scones with lashings of cream and jam; *Tea Leaves* at no. 380 (ⓦwww.tealeaves.com.au) has over three hundred teas available for purchase; while the hospitable *Sassafras General Store* at no. 391 serves up coffee, cakes, Devonshire teas and handmade chocolates.

Just outside **SHERBROOKE**, the **Alfred Nicholas Memorial Gardens** (daily 10am–5pm; $6) was once Australia's finest private gardens and has been restored to some of its former glory by Parks Victoria. The ornamental lake makes a particularly nice spot to relax.

Puffing Billy

Perhaps the most enjoyable and comfortable introduction to the Dandenongs is by the **Puffing Billy** (2–6 daily; $28.50 return; T9754 6800, wwww .puffingbilly.com.au), a narrow-gauge steam railway which has run more or less continually since entering service in the early 1900s. The railway starts in **BELGRAVE**, 40km east of Melbourne, then winds the 24km through thick forests and lush fern-filled gullies to Gembrook, with other stops at Menzies Creek, Emerald and Lakeside. Special lunch and dinner packages are also available.

If you want to break up the two-hour round trip, **Emerald Lake Park** (daily: April–Sept 9am–4.40pm; Oct–March 9am–8pm; free, parking $2 per hour or $6 all day; wwww.emeraldlakepark.com.au), adjacent to Emerald station, has over 15km of bush walks, paddle boats for hire ($10 for 20min), a water slide and free swimming pool, and picnic and barbecue facilities, as well as a model railway (Tues–Sun 11.30am–4pm; $5.50). The park is a pleasant weekday escape, but it's rather clamorous at weekends.

Dandenong Ranges National Park

Stretching north of the railway line between Upper Ferntree Gulley and Gembrook, the mountain ash forests of the **Dandenong Ranges National Park** (wwww.parkweb.vic.gov.au) are well worth a visit. The park is divided into several areas, of which **Sherbrooke Forest** (a 15min signposted walk from Belgrave station) and **Ferntree Gulley** (a 5min walk from Upper Ferntree Gulley station) are the most accessible if you don't have your own transport.

Sherbrooke Falls is a popular destination within the Sherbrooke Forest section – an easy 2.5-kilometre return walk signposted from the Sherbrooke Picnic Ground, off Sherbrooke Road (reached from the Mount Dandenong Tourist Road). Alternatively, you can try your luck at spotting the beautiful lyrebird – named after the lyre-shaped tails of the male – on the magnificent seven-kilometre **Eastern Sherbrooke Lyrebird Loop** (2hr), which sets off from Grant's Picnic Ground; this is one of the few places in Victoria where you might get to see one of these elusive birds in the wild. The walk also takes in other colourful birdlife including rosellas, kookaburras and honeyeaters. For a shorter stroll, the **Hardy Gully Nature Loop Walk**, also leaving from Grant's Picnic Ground, takes you into the thick bush on a walk of less than an hour. Walking maps for all of the park's numerous trails are available from the kiosks at both picnic areas, or from the Dandenong tourist office in Ferntree Gully (see p.178).

Up in the Doongalla section of the park, the **Mount Dandenong Observatory** is one of the park's most popular destinations; the observatory itself has seen better days, but the spectacular views east across Melbourne make up for it. To get there, take the Mount Dandenong Tourist Road then turn left at Ridge Road.

William Ricketts Sanctuary

Just off the Mount Dandenong Tourist Road towards the north end of the park is the **William Ricketts Sanctuary** (daily 10am–4.30pm; $5.60). Ricketts, an eccentric sculptor, worked here for many years until his death in 1993 at the age of 94. Set within the moss-covered rocks and damp fern beds of the sanctuary are various kiln-fired clay figures, that controversially blend Christianity with indigenous characters, which he created based on his experience of living among Aboriginal people in central Australia.

22

The Yarra Valley

A n hour's drive northeast of the city, the **Yarra Valley** is Victoria's wine district. A patchwork of historic vineyards and rich farmland, this former backwater now boasts more than thirty of the state's best **wineries**. It's a major wine tourism destination, with most vineyards providing tastings and cellar-door sales, and many offering winery tours. More and more are opening their own gourmet restaurants, where you can marry mouthwatering local fare with fine homegrown wines.

If you can drag yourself away from the cellars, there are also plenty of non-alcoholic attractions, from scenic **Kinglake National Park**, north of the valley, to **Healesville Sanctuary**, an outstanding wildlife park to the south. In and around you'll find a healthy selection of walking and cycling tracks in the magnificent **Yarra Ranges National Park**.

The region's vibrant calendar of seasonal events includes the annual **Grape Grazing Festival** (☎5965 2100, ⓦwww.grapegrazing.com.au) in February, when over twenty wineries combine in a summer celebration of wine, food and music.

Getting there and information

The southwestern gateway to the Yarra Valley is the Melbourne outer suburb of Lilydale on the Maroondah Highway, and a one-hour **train** journey from Flinders Street Station on the Lilydale line. From Lilydale, **bus** #685 travels to the valley's two main townships: Yarra Glen (to the north) and Healesville (to the northeast). If you're coming by **car**, take the Eastern Freeway from Fitzroy to Springvale Road and turn right; the Maroondah Highway to Lilydale is about 3km south down Springvale Road.

Several companies offer **winery tours** of the region, starting from around $75 for a basic one-day tour: try Link Tours (☎9699 8422, ⓦwww.linktours .com.au), Victorian Winery Tours (☎9621 2089, ⓦwww.winetours.com.au) or Yarra Valley Winery Tours (☎5962 3870, ⓦwww.yarravalleywinerytours .com.au). Alternatively, for a fresh and exciting view of the pretty Yarra Glen countryside, you can take to the skies in a **hot-air balloon** before gently descending into a vineyard to enjoy a sparkling wine breakfast: contact Go Wild Ballooning (☎9890 0339, ⓦwww.gowildballooning.com.au) or Global Ballooning (☎1800 627 661, ⓦwww.globalballooning.com.au) for details – packages cost around $250 during the week and $285 at weekends.

For **tourist information**, pick up a copy of *The Yarra Valley Tourist Route Map & Locality Guide* from the Melbourne Visitor Information Centre in Federation Square (see p.14), or check out the website ⓦwww.yarravalleytourism.asn .au – in addition to a comprehensive map of the valley, it lists wineries,

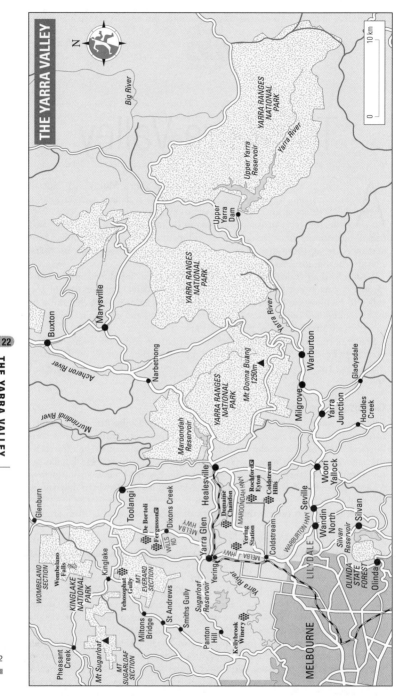

THE YARRA VALLEY

recreational activities, tours, festivals, attractions and places to eat. The *Yarra Valley Accommodation Guide* is also handy if you intend staying here. The area is fairly popular as a weekend break for Melbourne's urbanites, so **book ahead** if you're planning to visit over the weekend.

Yarra Valley wineries

The Yarra Valley's highest concentration of wineries is found in the triangle formed by Yarra Glen, Healesville and Dixon's Creek. Some recommended wineries are listed below.

Coldstream Hills 31 Maddens Lane, Coldstream ☎5964 9410, ⓦwww .coldstreamhills.com.au. Daily 10am–5pm. Cellar door tastings are on offer at this small winery; known for its Chardonnay and Pinots, it has garnered several awards in recent years.

De Bortoli Melba Highway ☎5965 2271 ⓦwww.debortoli.com.au. Daily 10am–5pm, tours daily at 11am & 3pm. With several wineries across Australia, the De Bortoli name is huge in Australian wine. The behind-the-vines tour here is followed by tastings. The restaurant (daily noon–3pm plus dinner on Sat) specializes in authentic Italian cuisine.

Domaine Chandon Green Point, Maroondah Highway ☎9739 1110, ⓦwww .domainechandon.com.au. Daily 10.30am–4.30pm. Owned by legendary bubbly makers, Möet et Chandon, this is one of Australia's premiere méthode champenoise sparkling wine makers. Sample a glass in the Green Point Room (tasting are $6–12 a glass with bread and cheese), or enjoy a platter of olives or antipasto looking out onto the gorgeous sprawling vineyard. Self-guided tours (in several languages) let visitors experience the wine-making process at their leisure.

Fergusson's Wills Road, off Melba Highway ☎5965 2237, ⓦwww.fergussonwinery .com.au, Daily 11am–5pm. First planted in 1968, this vineyard grows most of the major grape varieties. The attractive restaurant, with its use of native timber, blends in with the surrounding bush (open daily for lunch, morning and afternoon teas; dinner by appointment only).

Kellybrook Winery Fulford Road in Wonga Park ☎9722 1304, ⓦwww .kellybrookwinery.com.au. Mon–Sat 9am–6pm, Sun 11am–6pm. The sprawl of Lillydale has crept up to almost surround Kellybrook, the oldest licensed winery in the region, but it remains a good traditional place with old-fashioned cellar-door friendliness. Restaurant open lunch Sat & Sun, dinner Fri & Sat.

Rochford's Eyton Cnr of Maroondah Highway & Hill Road ☎5962 2119, ⓦwww .rochfordwines.com.au. Daily 10am–5pm. A cool, architect-designed winery with regular big-name concerts held in the surrounding gardens, and a large, airy restaurant that relies almost entirely on superb local produce. Mains start at around $30, but the lunch special – $25 for a two-course meal – represents excellent value.

Yering Station 38 Melba Hwy ☎9730 0100, ⓦwww.yering.com. Mon–Fri 10am–5pm, Sat & Sun 10am–6pm. Dominated by a sweeping wall hewn from local stone, this large complex has magnificent views along the Yarra Valley, wine-making facilities, a glass-walled restaurant, performance space and an amphitheatre. The cellar door operates from the original brick building and there's also a wine bar, an art gallery and modern Australian food from the restaurant. On the third Sunday of every month, the station's heritage-listed Old Barn hosts the Farmers' Market, which attracts food enthusiasts from Melbourne and elsewhere who stock up on a gobsmacking range of local produce. Next door is Yarra Valley's first vineyard, Chateau Yering, which was established in 1854 and re-established in 1996 as a magnificent luxury hotel – the Chateau Yering Historic House Hotel; here, you'll find the excellent Eleonore's Restaurant and Sweetwater Café.

Lilydale to Yarra Glen

The suburbs have expanded to swallow the tiny town that was once **LILYDALE** which is less than an hour's drive east of Melbourne's city centre. The only attraction of note is the **Museum of Lilydale** at 33 Castella St (Wed–Sun 11am–4pm; $3.20; ☏9739 7230), which has everything you might wish to know about famous Australian soprano Dame Nellie Melba, who, when she wasn't touring, spent much of her time in the small township of **Coldstream**, just north of Lilydale. Her former home, Coombe Cottage, is set behind a vast hedge at the junction of Melba and Maroondah highways, and is now privately owned.

Heading north along the Melba Highway, you'll come to the turn-off for the **Yarra Valley Dairy** (daily 10.30am–5pm; ☏9739 0023), a converted milking shed on McMeikans Road in **YERING**. There's a huge array of cheese on sale here, everything from washed rind to Persian feta and goat's cheeses. A few kilometres further up the highway, the township of **YARRA GLEN** lies in the centre of the Yarra Valley. On Bell Street, the main drag, you'll find the National Trust-classified *Yarra Glen Grand* (☏9730 1230, ⓦwww.yarraglengrand.com .au; ❼), a beautifully restored nineteenth-century hotel with boutique rooms and a café that does stylish pub grub. On the first Sunday of the month from October to June, the **Yarra Glen Craft Market** (9am–2pm) is held at the Yarra Glen Racecourse, 200m east of Bell Street.

Just north of Yarra Glen on the Melba Highway, the National Trust's **Gulf Station** (Wed–Sun & public holidays 10am–4pm; $6) is a large pastoral property which was once home to the Bell family, Scottish immigrants who settled here in 1854. The station contains ten hand-built farm buildings from the 1850s, representing the best-preserved slab-and-shingle complex in Victoria, and a glorious kitchen garden, while the avenue of quince trees leading to the cottage explodes with colour when in bloom in September and October.

Yarra Valley wineries

One of Australia's oldest grape-growing areas, the Yarra Valley is known as a cold-climate wine region, producing sleek Chardonnays, good Pinots and some solid bottles of Shiraz. Winemakers used to sell directly to the public at bargain prices using an outlet they called the **cellar door**, often little more than a cash register sitting beside maturing barrels of wine. Nowadays wineries have become more sophisticated, with handmade cheeses and olives on sale to accompany the best quaffs, and swanky restaurants on site. Others have live concerts among the vines or feature small art galleries with experimental works on display. Almost all wineries offer **tastings**, where you can sample the latest wines and buy in bulk. Unfortunately prices have risen with the more sophisticated surroundings, so prices may be only as good as your local bottle shop. But for many visitors a cellar door visit to the Yarra Valley remains a popular day-trip.

If you're planning on visiting a few wineries, be aware that local police are particularly active with the breathalyzer and will book **drivers** who exceed the blood alcohol limit of 0.05 (which usually equates to five 20ml tastes). You may be better off taking a tour (see p.181) and leaving the car at home.

Toolangi and the Kinglake National Park

North of Yarra Glen along the Melba Highway, the small timber town of **TOOLANGI** is where the Australian poet C.J. Dennis wrote "The Songs of a Sentimental Bloke" in 1915, a bawdy tale of larrikin Bill and his "ideal bit o'skirt", Doreen. In the same year, Dennis and his wife, Olive Herron, carved out of the Toolangi forest the pleasant **Singing Gardens of C.J. Dennis** (daily 10am–5pm; $2.50, free to those eating in the tearooms), at 1694 Main Road – right off the Melba Highway coming from Yarra Glen. After his death, the gardens were renamed after Dennis's last published work. They are filled with giant Australian mountain ash, European trees and flowers and are particularly spectacular in spring when the gardens blossom with azaleas, rhododendron, conifers and maples. Tours around the gardens include stories of "Den", his life and snatches of his poetry while Devonshire teas and lunches are available from the **tearooms** (daily 10am–5pm).

The **Toolangi Forest Discovery Centre** on the town's Main Road (daily 10am–5pm; free; ☎5962 9318) introduces visitors to the forest ecosystem, and has audiovisual displays and a Sculpture Trail – nine sculptures presented to the centre in 1996 after a UNESCO-sponsored event invited Asian-Pacific artists to represent their culture's relationship to the environment. Toolangi's **tourist office** is in the Old Courthouse on Harker Street (daily 9am–5pm; ☎5962 2600).

East of Toolangi lies the huge **Kinglake National Park**, an immense tract of eucalyptus forest and native bush with walking trails, picnic and barbecue spots, and lookouts. The park is divided into three distinct areas: the eastern Mount Everard section; the western Mount Sugarloaf section, beyond the township of Kinglake; and the northern Wombelano section. There are several signposted walking tracks across the park: two small waterfalls in the Mount Sugarloaf and Wombelano sections – Masons Falls and Wombelano Falls respectively – are noted for their views and platoons of native birds, while the Mount Everard section contains Jehosophat Gully, a small but beautiful picnicking area.

Healesville

The small town of **HEALESVILLE**, nestling beneath the forested slopes of the Great Dividing Range, was once a sleepy village, but today the main street is lined with tourist cafes and tea places. You can poke around the craft stores and junk and antique shops, and on Sundays and public holidays, the **Yarra Valley Tourist Railway** operates 25-minute rides on old trams on a scenic circuit around the town (every 30min 11am–4.30pm; $8; ☎5962 2490).

The town's main attraction, **Healesville Sanctuary**, 3km east of town on Badger Creek Road (daily 9am–5pm; $17.50; free guides 10am–3pm if booked in advance; ☎5957 2800, ⊛www.zoo.org.au), is one of Australia's outstanding conservation parks, and shouldn't be missed. Established in 1921 as a research institute for native fauna, the sanctuary takes advantage of its bushland setting to display the largest collection of Australian wildlife in the world. It also has a long and proud tradition of caring for injured and orphaned animals – over 1500 are received each year; some are returned to the wild, while those that are threatened or endangered join the park's education and breeding programmes. Visitors can experience close encounters with a number of native Australian fauna including platypuses, koalas, kangaroos and wombats, or go on meet-the-keeper sessions to learn more about the animals.

Across the road from the sanctuary car park, an informative Koori cultural centre and **restaurant**, *Bundjel*, 22 Glen Eadie Ave (daily 11am–4pm, Fri & Sat 4–10pm; ☎5962 1822, ⊛www.bundjel.com.au), uses traditional Koori ingredients in its modern Australian cuisine.

Yarra Ranges National Park

East of Healesville lie the spectacular mountain ash forests and fern gullies of the **Yarra Ranges National Park** (Ⓦwww.parkweb.vic.gov.au). Access to the park is limited, as it's an important catchment for Melbourne's water supply, but many areas remain open and accessible. At the southern end of the park, walking tracks fan out from **Mount Donna Buang**'s car park; one leads for 3km (1hr 30min) to the Rainforest Gallery, a spectacular walkway and observation platform at canopy height. This southern section of the park is easily reached by car, taking the Mount Donna Buang Road from the pretty town of **Warburton**, whose cool climate and hill-station atmosphere attracts droves of urban dwellers seeking respite from the city.

Macedon Ranges, Daylesford and Hepburn Springs

Sixty kilometres northwest of Melbourne, the Macedon Ranges feature pleasant townships like **Macedon** and **Woodend**, panoramic views and the spine-tinglingly eerie **Hanging Rock**, an austere lump of lava mythologized in book and film. Further west, **Daylesford** has a vibrant and easygoing alternative population, with gays and lesbians, greens, hippies and established migrant communities living side by side, while more wealthy types come to neighbouring **Hepburn Springs** to take in the waters at the Hepburn Spa Resort. Hundreds of natural mineral springs, each with their own distinctive flavour, flow through the surrounding hills – the reason why they are collectively known as the "Spa Centre of Australia". Each weekend, tourists flood the area to indulge in the languid comforts of the spas, but you'll also find fine food, galleries, antique and knick-knack shops, and kilometres of well-marked trails vectoring forests, national parks and waterfalls.

From Melbourne, the Macedon Ranges, Daylesford and Hepburn can be reached by **train** to either Woodend or Ballarat from Spencer Street Station. Arriving at either of these destinations, you can take a connecting **bus** to Daylesford. The combined train and bus fare is $14.60 one way, regardless of which route you take. There are regular trains to Woodend and Ballarat between Monday and Friday, although services at the weekend are extremely patchy; for further details, contact V/Line on ☎13 61 96. Alternatively, you can drive by taking the Western Highway towards Ballarat and turning off just beyond Ballan, from where Daylesford is only 30km away.

Woodend and Hanging Rock

The bucolic township of **WOODEND,** which seems to have somehow slipped under the mass-tourism radar, has some characterful old pubs and a good though rather expensive antiques gallery. Six kilometres northeast from here, the eerie, boulder-strewn **Hanging Rock** provided the setting for Joan Lindsay's novel *Picnic at Hanging Rock*, filmed by director Peter Weir in 1975,

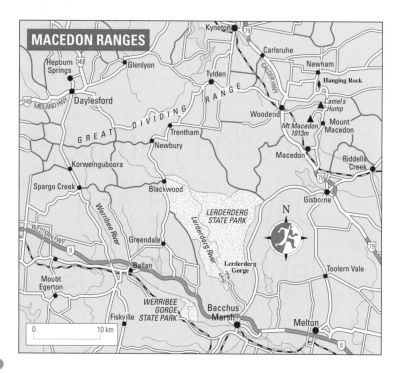

about the mysterious disappearance of two schoolgirls and a teacher. Created by a volcano eruption six million years ago, one of Victoria's most internationally famous sights was also the hideout of "Black Douglas", a notorious nineteenth century bushranger. Entry to the parking area at the base of the rock costs $8 per car. Also at the base, coin-operated electric and gas barbecues are available, while undercover facilities need to be reserved with the ranger.

Hanging Rock is the venue for two **horse-racing meetings**: one on New Year's Day, the other on Australia Day (January 26). Around February 20, it's the venue for the Harvest Picnic ($17 adults, children under 15 free), a hugely popular food-and-wine **festival** attracting dozens of small producers, performance artists, celebrity chefs and thousands of people eager to try the cheeses, boutique beers and preserves. Buses run from Melbourne ($25 return). For more information, call ☎13 28 86. In November several wineries band together for the Macedon **Budburst** (☎54220 0326, ⊛www.budburst.com .au), a celebration of local produce and wines.

There are microbreweries and more than a dozen **wineries** around Woodend and Hanging Rock. Lovers of cold-climate white wines (especially the Sauvignon Blanc and the sparkling) should head for Hanging Rock Winery 88 Jim Road, Newham (⊛www.hangingrock.com.au, ☎5427 0652, daily 10am-6pm for tastings) by taking the second turn-off to Woodend from the Western Highway. Another revered vineyard is Mount Macedon Winery at 433 Bawden Road, Woodend (☎5427 2735, ⊛www.mountmacedonwinery.com.au, open daily 10am-5pm for tastings), famous for producing Olivia Newton-John's Koala Blue range of wines..

Practicalities

For more information and maps, the **Woodend Tourist Office** (daily 9am–5pm; ☎5427 2033) is on the High Street, on the left as you drive out of town towards Hanging Rock.

If you haven't got your own **transport**, you can reach Hanging Rock by getting off the train at Woodend and walking 500m down the road to the Woodend Tourist Office, where you can fill up on water and maps, then trek the beautiful 6km to Hanging Rock. Alternatively, you could organize a cab (approximately $10) from Woodend Taxis (☎5427 2641).

As a small town, **places to stay** are limited. The *Seven Chimneys*, 45 High St (☎5427 1952) is a moderately priced B&B on Woodend's main street. Other B&Bs in the town include the pleasant *Colliers Cottage*, 9 Colliers Street (☎0411 644 627, ⓦwww.macedonranges.org.au-woodend) and the more opulent *Bentinck of Woodend* 8 Carlisle St (☎5427 2944,).

Eating in Woodend represents good old-fashioned country value. For a quick breakfast or lunch, try a quiche or a delicious dessert at *Maloa House Gourmet Delights*, 1/97 High St (☎5427 1608). Big kids can grab takeaway food or a selection of lollies at the *Mountain View Café and Milk Bar* at 77 High Street (☎5427 2470). For something more substantial, tuck into gourmet pies or creative risottos at *Holgate's Bar & Restaurant*, 79 High St (☎5427 2510).

Mount Macedon

Just east of Woodend lies **Mount Macedon**, an extinct thousand-metre-high volcano. In 1983 the Ash Wednesday bushfires swept through the area, killing seven people, scorching land and destroying a number of houses. Since then, homes have been rebuilt and the flora has grown back, although some scars remain. In autumn, Mount Macedon is particularly beautiful as the deciduous trees form spectacular russet avenues. Because of the abundance of pasture and water, snakes – some quite venomous – are found in the area.

On the summit of Mount Macedon, a huge **memorial cross** was erected by William Cameron in 1935 to commemorate his son and others killed in World War I. The steep walk (2km) from the car park and excellent **tearooms** is especially pretty, with gardens and forests lining the path. On a clear day there are great views across to Port Phillip Bay in the southeast, and Hanging Rock to the north. From here, you can set forth on a number of **walking tracks**, ranging in distance from one-to-two kilometres to a whopping 29km, grab a brochure from the visitors centre in Woodend or check out the Macedon Ranges section of the Visit Victoria website (ⓦwww.visitvictoria.com.au). On the easy drive to the summit, you pass sprawling homesteads and a number of plant nurseries, as well as a parking area and walking trail connecting you to **Camels Hump** (3 hours' walk from the car park), a lava outcrop popular with rockclimbers.

Daylesford

Forty-five kilometres west of Woodend, **DAYLESFORD** sports well-preserved Victorian and Edwardian streets and is a beacon for those who have left the rat-race behind: alternative lifestylers of every description call Daylesford home.

The **Daylesford Historical Museum** (Sat & Sun 1.30–4.30pm; free; ☎5348 1453), next door to the tourist office on the main Vincent Street, traces the town's origins in the 1850s goldrush. The museum's ramshackle collection of goldmining ephemera is housed in a former School of Mines, while the adjoining yard has numerous items of farm equipment and a tiny post office – once claimed to be the smallest in Victoria.

Down the hill from the museum is the picturesque **Lake Daylesford**. The sixteen-kilometre **Tipperary Walking Track** runs from here to Hepburn Mineral Springs Reserve (see opposite), passing through undulating open-forest country and several old gold-diggings. Also beginning from here is the 70km **Federation Track** to Ballarat (see p.192) across wooded hillsides, deserted mines, and burbling creeks and gullies. The walk, which usually takes around three days, has several camping areas if you want to pitch a tent; otherwise, basic accommodation in cottages, motels or dormitories can be arranged. Looking over the lake, the award-winning *Lake House* (℡5348 3329) is one of Australia's best restaurants, with a menu dominated by fresh local produce and a sublime wine list.

Wombat Hill rises above the town to the east. At the top, the **botanical gardens**, established in 1861, contain magnificent elms, conifers and oaks, and a lookout tower with views of the local countryside. The views are best seen on foot, although there's a pleasant circular driveway around the gardens. Just below the gardens, the **Convent Gallery** is on the corner of Daly and Hill streets (Mon–Fri 10am–5pm, Sat & Sun 10am–6pm; $3.50; ⓦwww.conventgallery.com.au). A former convent, religious retreat and gold commissioner's residence, it now has three levels of galleries selling arts, crafts and antiques, plus a café and gift shop at the front of the complex.

The old Daylesford **train station** is down the road from Wombat Hill, where the Midland Highway enters town. On Sundays the Central Highlands Tourist Railway runs from here through the Wombat State Forest to the nearby towns of Musk and Bullarto, a return journey of just under an hour (10am–3pm; $7 return to Bullarto). Also on Sundays, the station car park is the site of a lively **arts-and-crafts market** (9am–3pm).

Practicalities

On Vincent Street, the main drag, you'll find several good cafés, and a **tourist office** (daily 9am–5pm; ℡5348 1339) with information on accommodation, including a useful publication listing gay- and lesbian-run establishments. It also stocks pamphlets on local health practitioners, walking trails and mineral springs, and has a handy selection of maps. From here, **buses** travel around three times daily to neighbouring Hepburn Springs.

While accommodation in Daylesford is plentiful, the tourist boom has meant that prices are inflated. Wildwood YHA, 42 Main Rd in Hepburn Springs (℡5348 4438, ⓔdaylesford@yhavic.org.au; ❸), represents the best value, with dorm rooms and singles, some with views into the lush paddocks or bush out the back. The *Royal Hotel*, on the corner of Vincent & Albert streets (℡5348 2205; ❼), is a lovingly restored Victorian-era pub with heated rooms, some with spa facilities. For a decadent B&B-style room in town, *Town View Guesthouse* (℡5348 2095, ⓦwww.restindaylesford.com; ❺, ❼ at weekends), has well-appointed rooms in a restored Victorian house above a milk bar. For a real slice of the alternative lifestyle, Continental House, at 9 Lone Pine Ave, Hepburn Springs (℡5348 2005, ⓦwww.continentalhouse.com.au; ❸) offers a variety of rooms in a rambling house that includes yoga rooms and open fires, and a strictly vegan menu or self-catering kitchen.

The main street of Daylesford alone offers several good **eating** options with *Frangos & Frangos* and their sister café, *Koukla*, at 82 Vincent St (℡5348 2363), serving up an inventive range of pizzas, pastas and other mains. Alternatively, *Electric Sitar* at 4/27 Albert St (℡5348 1676) serves up groovy lip-smacking curries and *Sweet Decadence* at 87 Vincent St (☎5348 3202, ⊛www.sweetdecadence.com.au) offers coffee and all sorts of chocolate indulgence. The best table in town is at *The Lake House* on King Street (☎5348 3329, ⊛www.lakehouse.com.au) with a dynamic menu that samples Victoria's best regional food.

Hepburn Springs

Leaving Daylesford, Vincent Street heads on to **HEPBURN SPRINGS**, a few kilometres north. At the height of the 1848 revolution in Europe, many Italians and Swiss nationals settled around here, drawn by the lure of gold, the similar climate and the health-giving qualities of the natural mineral springs. For more than a century, Australia's only mineral spa resort has been a major destination for affluent tourists, although in recent years it has attracted more alternative types and some of the worst unemployment rates in Victoria.

As you enter the town, you'll pass the National Trust-listed **Old Macaroni Factory** on the left. Built in 1859, it was the first pasta factory in Australia; visitors can call ahead to arrange a tour of the frescoed interior ($3.30; ☎9457 7035). Further down the hill, on the corner of Tenth Street, **The Palais** is a lovingly restored 1920s theatre hosting everything from torch-song performances to gypsy swing bands, and has a good-value restaurant and bar.

At the bottom of Tenth Street, you'll pass through the Soldiers Memorial Park to the **Hepburn Mineral Springs Reserve**. There are four springs bubbling out in the immediate area, and a visit to any of them, taking with you a few empty containers, is a must. Old-fashioned hand pumps dispense the water, with each spring having a distinctive, effervescent taste. Most have a more robust flavour than the bland, filtered variety you can buy in shops, and all are better tasting than the local tap water which, ironically, tastes awful (the local council can't afford to upgrade the town's water-treatment facilities).

The renovated **Hepburn Spa Resort** (Mon–Thurs 10am–7pm, Fri 10am–8.15pm, Sat 9am–8.15pm, Sun 9am–7pm; ☎5348 2034), built in 1895, lies at the centre of the Hepburn Mineral Springs Reserve. Public facilities include a relaxation pool, spa and heavy mineral salt pool (Mon–Fri $10, Sat & Sun $15); there are also packages available using its extensive private facilities, including an aerospa bath, massage and flotation tanks. Prices range from $30 for an aerospa bath, $40 for a thirty-minute massage, $120 for two hours in a flotation tank to over $500 for a full-day deluxe package including pedicure, manicure, facial, full-body massage, and two-course lunch; book at least six weeks in advance.

Ballarat

J ust over 100km west of Melbourne, **Ballarat** (a combination of the Aboriginal words "Balla" and "Arat", meaning "to rest on one's elbow") holds a pivotal place in Australia's history. In the 1830s, white pastoralists fanning out from Port Phillip Bay were quick to appreciate the grazing potential of the lightly wooded hills and plains to the northwest. In August 1851, gold was discovered near Ballarat, which brought immense wealth to the town but also led to the country's only civil uprising – the bloody **Eureka Rebellion** (see p.195) – as put-upon prospectors revolted against the authorities. By the decade's end, Ballarat had grown into a prominent Australian city: gorgeous Victorian architecture lined its wide tree-lined avenues, and the city took on the airs and graces of a prosperous and conservative provincial centre.

With gold long gone – the last seam was exhausted in 1918 – tourism and information technology have now taken over as Ballarat's major sources of income (IBM has its Southeast Asian headquarters here), while a large student population from the excellent University of Ballarat has challenged the town's more insular inclinations.

Arrival and information

The Ballarat **tourist office** at 39 Sturt St (daily 9am–5pm; ☎5332 2694) is well stocked with maps, guides and tourist information; it also has a route map of the Eureka Trail (see p.194).

Trains run daily from Spencer Street Station to Ballarat, while V/Line **buses** depart Monday to Friday from Spencer Street Station, arriving at Ballarat Station, centrally located in Lydiard Street. Both bus and train take ninety minutes each way and cost $33 return. If you're **driving**, the quickest route is to take the Westgate Freeway out of Melbourne, then turn onto the Western Ring Road before taking the Western Highway to Ballarat; the trip takes just over an hour. A longer but more gentle drive is to approach from the south, via Geelong, on the Midland Highway. The Victorian government is planning to connect Ballarat to Melbourne via a Very Fast Train (VFT), which will dramatically cut travelling times between the two cities.

Accommodation

The well-preserved and often refurbished **hotels** of Ballarat are a great chance to experience Australian pub rooms with the bonus of a bit of luxury. Cheaper package deals for weekends are a good bet, though many hotels may require reservations of at least two nights.

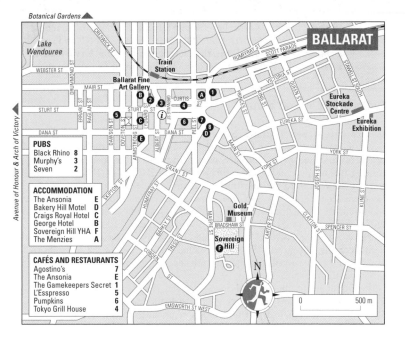

The Ansonia 32 Lydiard St ☎5332 4678, ⓦ**www.ballarat.com/Ansonia.htm.** This sprawling boutique hotel includes a first-class restaurant (see p.196) and attractive communal areas including a library and a guest lounge. The building's historic character has been fused with contemporary design and modern luxuries. ❼–❽

Bakery Hummfray St South ☎5333 1363, ⓕ5333 2335. Rooms are spacious and well appointed in this city-centre motel that is known for its friendly and helpful staff. ❺–❻

Craigs Royal Hotel 10 Lydiard St ☎5331 1377 or 1800 648 051, ⓕ5331 7103. Newly renovated suites and rooms are an indulgence in this Victorian-era hotel. The rooms are plush with own en-suites and much needed air-conditioning for the chilly nights. ❽–❾

George Hotel 27 Lydiard St ☎5333 4866, ⓕ5333 4818, ⓦ www.georgehotelballarat.com

.au. This quaintly terraced hotel was once a rallying point for police planning to lay siege to the Eureka Stockade. The rooms are a little cramped and cheaper ones have shared facilities. Shared bathrooms ❹, en-suites ❺

Sovereign Hill YHA Magpie St ☎5333 3409 or 1800 100 210, ⓕ5331 7103. This small hostel is set in the Sovereign Hill complex. Rooms are plain, but kitchen/common areas are roomy and good places to meet backpackers. Dorms ❶, double rooms ❸

The Menzies 5–7 Hummfray St ☎5331 3277 or 1800 100 210, ⓕ5332 3855, ⓦ www.ballarat .com/menzies. Aimed at business travellers, the Menzies has facilities like Internet dial-up and in-room fax machines. Decor is plain but the one-bedroom apartments include a well-equipped kitchen and lounge areas. Rooms ❼, one-bedroom apartments ❽

The Town

Reminders of Ballarat's glory days as a wealthy gold-mining centre can still be seen in elegant sandstone and Victorian buildings on and around

Lydiard Street. Further south lies Ballarat's most spectacular attraction, **Sovereign Hill**, a fabulous re-creation of the mining shafts, hotels and shops of the goldrush era. Beyond Ballarat, the tacky but endearing **Kryal Castle** warrants a visit, as does the Arch of Honour, a solemn memorial to those killed in arms.

Lydiard Street and around

The heart of Ballarat contains one of Australia's best-preserved nineteenth-century streetscapes, **Lydiard Street**. Running from the centre up past the train station, the street has several two-storey terraced shopfronts, with verandahs and decorative iron-lace work, mostly from the period 1862–89. Among the stately buildings, the former Mining Exchange (1888) has been recently renovated to its previous splendour, and the architecture of Her Majesty's Theatre (1875) also proclaims Ballarat's goldrush-era heyday. In addition there is a collection of fine hotels on Lydiard Street that once watered thirsty diggers, amongst them Craig's Royal Hotel at no. 10 and the George Hotel at no. 27, which are still an integral part of Ballarat's architectural heritage. Sadly, during the 1970s, the council forced most of the old pubs to pull down their verandahs on the grounds that they were unsafe, so very few survive in their original form.

The highlight of the street, however, is the superb **Ballarat Fine Art Gallery** at 40 Lydiard St North (daily 10.30am–5pm; $5). Established in 1884, this is Australia's largest and oldest regional gallery, home of one of Australia's greatest cultural icons – the original Eureka flag. For over a century, the flag was kept out of sight in a gallery cupboard, but it is now framed and displayed in a dimly lit, shrine-like room, the blue and white-starred fabric frayed but still impressive. Elsewhere, there is a fine collection of colonial and Heidelberg School paintings by artists such as Tom Roberts and Arthur Streeton, contemporary art and works by members of the talented Lindsay family, who lived in nearby Creswick. One room of the gallery is given over to a reconstruction of the Lindsay household's sitting room. The gallery's temporary exhibitions are usually first-rate.

A short distance west of Lydiard Street, the man-made **Lake Wendouree** was the site of the 1956 Olympics rowing events. Walking around the lake you'll see the austere Ex-Prisoners of War Memorial, a grim tribute to Australians captured during World War II. The **Ballarat Botanical Gardens**, situated on the western boundary, feature the striking Robert Clark Conservatory, which opened in 1995, with giant California redwoods, and a dazzling variety of flowers, shrubbery and gardens. Each year in March, the Begonia Festival (☎03 5320 5444, ⊛www.ballaratbegoniafestival.com) is held here, celebrating gardening and all things flower-related, in particular the humble begonia. Opposite the gardens, a terrific adventure playground, complete with a fortress-like cubbyhouse, makes for kiddie nirvana. On Wednesday afternoons, weekends and public holidays, visitors can take a ride around the lake on a tram along Wendouree Parade ($3.50).

The Eureka Trail and Centre

Starting at the post office on the corner of Lydiard and Sturt streets, the 3.5-kilometre **Eureka Trail**, opened in 1996, follows the path the troops took during their march to the Eureka Stockade (see box opposite). Starting on the site of the former government camp, the trail winds its way through the city along the Yarrowee River and through the city's older residential

The Eureka Rebellion

The **Eureka Rebellion** is one of the most celebrated events of Australian history, provoked by conditions in the goldfields where diggers had to pay exorbitantly for their right to prospect for gold without having any permanent right to the land they worked or the right to vote. Checks for licences were ruthless and brutal and corruption rife. The administration in Ballarat was particularly repressive, and in November 1854 local diggers formed the Ballarat Reform League and burnt their gold licences. Under the leadership of Peter Lalor, a group of two hundred miners barricaded themselves in a flimsy stockade, above which fluttered a blue flag featuring the Southern Cross.

Just before dawn on the morning of December 3, almost three hundred troops summoned from Melbourne slipped out of the government camp and made their way through the sleeping city. Upon reaching the stockade, they loaded muskets, fixed bayonets and charged. In less than fifteen minutes, more than thirty miners lay dead and 114 had been taken prisoner. Six troopers also died in the assault. Public opinion, however, sided firmly with the miners. Thirteen were charged with high treason but acquitted three months later, and within the year Peter Lalor was elected to the Victorian Parliament and the miners had earned the right to vote. When Mark Twain visited Ballarat he succinctly eulogized the uprising with "It was a revolution – small in size, but great politically; it was a strike for liberty, a struggle for a principle, a stand against injustice and oppression...It is another instance of a victory won by a lost battle."

suburbs before arriving at the **Eureka Stockade Centre** in Eureka Street (daily 9am–5pm; $8). Opened in 1998, the centre was built close to where the stockade is thought to have stood, and features a number of dull figures of soldiers and diggers, and multimedia galleries highlighting the main events behind the rebellion. Above, the huge **Eureka Sail** guarantees that the building can be seen for miles; inside, a fragment of the original flag has pride of place in the centre's central Contemplation Space. If you don't want to walk to the centre, take a Davis Bus Lines bus from Curtis Street just east of Lydiard Street ($3.50).

Sovereign Hill and around

Ballarat's undoubted highlight, **Sovereign Hill** (daily 10am–5.30pm; $29; ☎5331 1944, ⒲www.sovereignhill.com.au), is on Bradshaw Street just south of the city centre. To get there it's a 15min walk from Sturt Street, or take a Davis Bus Lines bus from Curtis Street ($3).

Open for over thirty years, this reconstruction of the goldmining township of Ballarat in the 1850s is complete with working mineshaft, over two hundred actors dressed in period costume, horse-drawn carriages and a Chinese Temple, and is well worth the admission price. Activities such as wheelwright demonstrations, riding in horse-drawn carriages, gold pourings, mine tours and music shows at the Victoria Theatre run throughout the day, while the evening sound-and-light show "Blood on the Southern Cross" (daily; $35; booking essential on ☎5331 1944) lavishly re-creates the Eureka Rebellion. On entry to Sovereign Hill, visitors are given a map and an itinerary of activities – it's worth spending a few minutes plotting your day before continuing. The site also has plenty of cafés, restaurants, picnic areas and hostel accommodation ($18.50 for multi-share room, $55 for twin room with en-suite).

Directly opposite here, the interesting **Gold Museum** (daily 9.30am–5pm; free with Sovereign Hill entry, $7 on its own) is crammed with coins, nuggets, alluvial deposits and temporary exhibitions.

Nearby, on the corner of Fussell and York streets, the award-winning **Ballarat Wildlife Park** (daily 9am–5.30pm; $14.50) has a large collection of koalas, wombats, goannas, saltwater and freshwater crocodiles, snakes and wallabies, some of which roam freely. Tours are free, and run daily 11am–noon.

Eating

Food options in Ballarat are better than many towns of this size in Australia due to the strong international community that stretches back to the days of the goldfield. You shouldn't need to stray too far from Lydiard St for a tasty meal.

Agostino's 8 Victoria St, ☏ 5333 3655. Good old-fashioned Italian cuisine is served up at this large multistorey café, including pastas, pizzas and risottos. Daily 11.30am–10.30pm. Inexpensive.

The Ansonia 32 Lydiard St, ☏ 5332 4678. Elegant dining in this hotel that features dishes like baked trout or roasted kangaroo with sweet potato gnocchi. Save room for the decadent desserts and perhaps a tipple of dessert wine. Breakfast daily, lunch Mon–Fri. Moderate.

Boatshed Restaurant 27A Wendouree Parade, ☏ 5333 5533. Relax with a sophisticated meal by scenic Lake Wendouree or enjoy a bottle of wine as swans and ducks float past.

The Gamekeepers Secret Cnr Mair & Humffray streets ☏ 5332 6000, ⓦ www.ballarat.com/gamekeeper. Safari in this fabulous African-themed restaurant for a menu thick with generous steaks and creative pastas.

Weekday lunches for $10 and delicious cake and coffee deals make for good value. Daily 11am–11pm. Inexpensive to moderate.

L'Esspresso 417 Sturt St ☏ 5333 1789. Suave waiting staff weave busily between tables at this popular coffee spot. Innovative breakfasts and lunches are worth checking out. Daily 7am–6pm, Thurs–Sun 6.30pm–midnight. Cheap to inexpensive.

Pumpkins 10 Little Bridge St, ☏ 5332 3638. Vegetarian and vegan heaven with inventive vegetarian curries, samosas and satay burgers to mention but a few. Grab a slice of cake as the perfect end to a lunch. Mon–Fri 9am–5pm. Cheap.

Tokyo Grill House 109 Bridge Mall ☏ 5333 3945. Head to this teppanyaki diner for a tasty dinner or lunchtime treat and the frenetic spectacle of having your food cooked whilst you watch. Open daily noon–11pm. Expensive.

Drinking

Clubs and **pubs** cluster around Lydiard and Sturt streets though there are a few good options to be found by wandering further out. The likeable Irish *Murphy's* 36 Sturt St (☏5331 4091) is a good Emerald Isle pub that is filled with regulars. A hip young crowd packs the stylish *Seven*, opposite the *George Hotel*, at 26 Lydiard St (☏5334 4022), a bar that also has a modest dance floor. The *Black Rhino*, on the corner of Humffray and Victoria streets (☏5331 5775), attracts the university students with pool tables and loads of drink specials. A modish middle-aged set frequent the *Gamekeeper Secret*, on the corner of Mair and Humffray streets (☏5332 6000), with a cosy bar area, decent wine list and over eight beers on tap. The cosy, but cool front bar of the *George Hotel*, at 27 Lydiard St (☏5333 4866), is a good spot for a drink to warm up for an evening out.

Around Ballarat

An unmistakeable sight on the Western Highway 8km east of Ballarat, **Kryal Castle**, on the slopes of Mount Warrenheip (Mon–Fri 10am–4pm, Sat & Sun 9am–5pm, $20; ☎5334 7388), is an ersatz castle-cum-medieval theme park whose mishmash of exhibits includes a gloriously tacky dungeon, torture chamber, cemetery and maze, and is where pretend whippings ("Whipping of the Wench") and hangings ("Hanging of the Town Villain") are conducted daily at 1.30pm. For a kooky night out, try their "Cocktails in the Graveyard" soirees ($45 for groups of ten, $50 for individuals) that boast a three-course meal, magic and comedy.

Five kilometres west of Ballarat on the Western Highway, the Arch of Victory heralds the entry to the 23-kilometre **Avenue of Honour**, a beautiful if sobering stretch of road. Flanking either side are over 3700 ash, elm, poplar, maple and plane trees dedicated to local soldiers who fought in World War I.

Geelong, the Bellarine Peninsula and around

Heading west from Melbourne the first real reason to make a stop is at **Werribee Park**, a glorious mansion and gardens, just beyond which lies **Werribee Open Range Zoo**, where you can roam safari-style among an interesting variety of animals. Continuing westward brings you to the small but rewarding **You Yangs Regional Park** and eventually, around 75km from Melbourne, **Geelong**, Victoria's second-largest city and gateway to the Bellarine Peninsula. Don't come looking for extraordinary natural landscapes or brilliant sunsets, however, because its attractions are predominantly man-made. Long the centre of Australia's wool industry, the city's main draws are its magnificent National Wool Museum and revitalized waterfront, but you'll also find a modicum of other sights like the town's excellent art gallery, botanic gardens and fine examples of colonial architecture. In addition, Deakin University and the Gordon Institute have attracted a younger population, and there's now a small arts community and healthy band scene (retro-rockers Jet hail from here), which lend a patina of hipness to the city. Beyond Geelong, the **Bellarine Peninsula**, a stubby finger of land pointing across Port Phillip Bay to Melbourne, has blossomed post-millennium, and offers the graceful beachfront town of **Queenscliff**, quaint fishing villages, some of Victoria's finest views, great food and wine, and activities such as swimming with dolphins and surfing.

West to Geelong

Beyond Melbourne the western outskirts lapse into drab suburbia until you approach Werribee. Here, stately **Werribee Park** adjoins the grassy plains of **Werribee Open Range Zoo**, while further west, the **You Yangs Regional Park** makes for a picturesque detour.

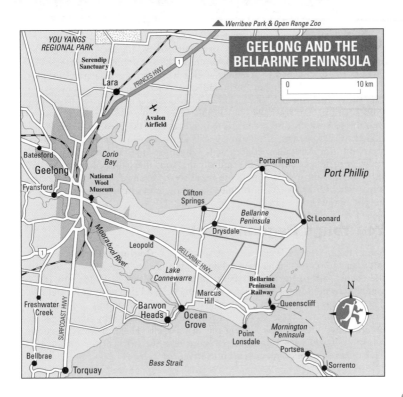

GEELONG AND THE
BELLARINE PENINSULA

YOU YANGS
REGIONAL PARK

Serendip
Sanctuary

Lara

PRINCES HWY

0   10 km

Avalon
Airfield

Batesford

Corio
Bay

Portarlington

Port Phillip

Geelong

National
Wool
Museum

Clifton
Springs

Fyansford

Bellarine
Peninsula

St Leonard

Drysdale

Moorabool River

Leopold

BELLARINE HWY

Lake
Connewarre

Bellarine
Peninsula
Railway

N

Freshwater
Creek

Marcus
Hill

Queenscliff

SURFCOAST HWY

Barwon
Heads

Ocean
Grove

Point
Lonsdale

Mornington
Peninsula

Bellbrae

Bass Strait

Portsea

Sorrento

Torquay

Werribee Park and around

Thirty kilometres west of Melbourne, **Werribee Park** (daily 10am–5pm; $11; ☎9741 2444; Werribee line train from Flinders Street Station, then bus #439), on K Road in Werribee, is an award-winning estate and Italianate mansion. Finished in 1877 by Scottish squatters Thomas and Andrew Chirnside, who struck it rich on the back of sheep, the sixty-room house is the largest private residence in Victoria. Guides in period costume show you inside the ornate homestead with impeccably restored bedrooms and reception rooms, and around the tranquil Victorian-era lawns and adjoining Victoria State Rose Garden, a splendid place to while away a sunny afternoon. Alternatively, free headsets providing a self-guiding commentary are available at the entrance. If you're interested in staying in the formal gardens *The Mansion Hotel* (☎9731 4000, ⊛www.mansiongroup.com.au), a former seminary, has boutique-style accommodation and a spa; you can also dine at *Joseph's* (☎9731 4000), an upmarket restaurant with a game-inspired menu and well-matched wine list. Close to the hotel you'll find the small **Shadowfax Winery**, an impressive box-like structure that offers cellar-door sales of Sauvignon Blanc, Chardonnay, Pinot and Shiraz (daily 11am–5pm; ⊛www.shadowfax.com.au), glimpses of the wine-making process and gourmet food from the deli. Also drawing the crowds are the jazz bands that play here every Sunday afternoon.

Beyond the mansion's gardens are the extensive grounds of **Werribee Open Range Zoo** (daily 9am–5pm; $15.80; ☎9731 9600, ⊛www.zoo.org.au).

Developed around the picturesque Werribee River, the zoo is home to Australian and African herbivores including rhinos, hippos, giraffes, zebras, monkeys, meerkats and other creatures. The magnificent savannah-like conditions are designed to resemble as closely as possible the natural habitats of the animals, which roam freely and can be seen on a fifty-minute safari **bus tour** (10.30am–3.40pm; included in entrance fee), conducted by trained guides. Visitors can also take the Volcanic Plains Walk which gives an insight into the re-creation of the endangered grasslands of the Western Basalt Plains (less than one percent of remnant grasslands remain in Victoria), and allows views into the Australian exhibit, with kangaroos, emus and wallabies. If you really want to get close to the animals the zoo offers the "Slumber Safari" ($160 per person; ☏9731 9600) with meals served in an African-inspired lodge kitted out with 1920s-style furnishings, and a night in a luxury canvas tent with king- and queen-sized beds.

You Yangs Regional Park

Some 15km west of Werribee, the **You Yangs Regional Park** is a small but rugged volcanic range with abundant birdlife and several walks around the central 348-metre Flinders Peak, climbed by Matthew Flinders in 1802; scramble to the top for fine views across the bay and down towards Geelong. The park was once used by the local Barrabool tribe as hunting grounds, and scattered here and there you'll find rock hollows enlarged by Aborigines to ensure water was available during the driest spells. The You Yangs are only accessible if you have your own transport: take the marked turn-off on the Melbourne–Geelong Freeway at Little River.

Geelong and around

Industrial **GEELONG** is not a particularly attractive city – the fact that the **National Wool Museum**, 26 Moorabool St (daily 9.30am–5pm; $7.30), is the main attraction will give you some idea of the place. Housed in an imposing bluestone building, the museum proves that Australia really did ride on the sheep's back. Inside, displays demonstrate the importance of the wool industry to the city, with life-like reconstructions of typical shearers' quarters, turn-of-the-twentieth-century looms (still in use), and evocative sound and image shows. On the corner of Gheringhap and Brougham streets, the **Ford Discovery Centre** (daily except Tues 10am–5pm; $7; ☻www.forddiscovery.com.au) looks behind the scenes of the car manufacture and design industry, with a huge car museum, and a good deal of marketing thrown in. Nearby another massive wool store has been converted into a campus for Deakin University.

Many of the town's best Victorian buildings are on **Little Malop Street**, three blocks south of the National Wool Museum in the city centre, including the elegant Geelong Art Gallery (Mon–Fri 10am–5pm, Sat & Sun 1–5pm; free), which has an extensive selection of works by nineteenth-century Australian artists such as Tom Roberts and Frederick McCubbin, plus contemporary Australian paintings and sculpture. Recent renovations have greatly enhanced this venerable building, creating larger exhibition spaces and allowing greater access to the works.

Geelong's waterfront

Neglected for many years, **Geelong's waterfront** from Rippleside Park to Eastern Beach has recently undergone a renaissance, with the shipping traffic and industrial skyline to the north now offset by stunning ocean views across green expanses. The promenades, rotunda, fountains and Art Deco-style swimming pool (on Eastern Beach, where swimming is also permitted inside an enclosure) have been renovated, as has a lovely nineteenth-century carousel featuring over thirty sculpted wooden horses.

Nestled among the lawns and trees are Geelong's historic **Botanic Gardens** (Mon–Fri 7.30am–5pm, Sat & Sun 7am–7pm; free). Begun in the late 1850s, they are the fourth oldest in Australia after those in Sydney, Melbourne and Hobart. The gardens have recently been expanded with a "twenty-first century" section showcasing local indigenous species, succulents and cactuses, an 1851 dragon tree and other plants that thrive in dry conditions. The new garden provides a stark contrast to the lush green lawns of the old, which boast rare and endangered plants, fountains, a geranium conservatory, sculptures and the *Tea House* (daily 11am–4pm), where you can enjoy refreshments with an excellent view of the garden.

The new-look waterfront has also seen the emergence of upmarket hotels, swanky apartments and eating places, notably the large restaurant complex at the end of **Cunningham Pier**, which really comes into its own at night. Built in the 1880s to load wool and gold onto ships, it's now host to more than a hundred brightly painted bollards, the work of local artist Jan Mitchell, depicting some of Geelong's historic characters, from footy players to old-fashioned bathers. Close to the pier, you can't miss the enormous "shark fins" carved from stone. A number of **bicycle** and **walking trails** head off from here along the western shore.

The bay is host to a number of sailing festivals and regattas, including January's **Skandia Geelong Week** (@www.geelongweek.com.au). Held since 1844 and recognized as the largest sailing regatta in Australia, it attracts more than 400 yachts of all shapes and sizes, and over 25,000 visitors. The four-day festival starts with racing in Melbourne, before the massive fleet – joined by visiting tall ships – heads for Corio Bay in the traditional Williamstown to Geelong race. As well as sailing, there are aerobatic displays, live music and a fireworks show.

Practicalities

Avalon **airport** (@www.avalonairport.com.au), Melbourne's newest domestic passenger terminal and home to Jetstar (☎13 15 38, @www.jetstar.com.au), Qantas's cut-price carrier, is 15km from Geelong and accessed via Avalon Airport Shuttle, which can drop you in various destinations around the Bellarine Peninsula (@www.avalonairportshuttle.com.au). The easiest way to get to Geelong from Melbourne is by **train** (hourly from Spencer Street Station; 1hr; $10.20 one-way). By **car**, it's an uneventful hour's drive southwest of Melbourne on the Princes Freeway.

As well as the **Victorian Visitor Information Centre** (daily 9am–5pm; ☎1800 620 888) in the museum – see opposite page – which provides lots of brochures and city and regional maps, there's a helpful staffed **tourist information stall** in the Market Square Shopping Centre at the corner of Moorabool and Malop streets (Mon–Sat 9am–5pm). For details of what's going on in the city and southwest Victoria, pick up a copy of the free magazine *Forte*, available from cafés, bookshops, record and CD stores, galleries and cinemas.

Accommodation

There's plenty of **accommodation** around Geelong, though rooms in summer can book up quickly. Also at this time some hotels and B&Bs may require a minimum booking of two nights at the weekends.

Mercure Geelong Cnr Gheringhap & Myer sts ☎5223 6200, ⓦwww.mercuregeelong.com.au. At the top of the hill, this hotel affords excellent bay views and a recent refit has created some modern rooms, though some areas still have a 1970s feel. Good deals including breakfast available and parking is free. ❻

Four Points Sheraton 10–14 Eastern Rd ☎5223 1377 ⓕ5223 3417. The best rooms in Geelong can be found at the *Sheraton's* luxury waterfront tower, and offer grand spa baths and large-screen TVs. Service is impeccable and there's also a decent restaurant and gym. ❾

Pevensey House Cnr of Malop St & Pevensey Crescent ☎5224 2810, ⓦwww.pevensey-house .com.au. A beautiful 1892 manor house where the hosts serve up huge cooked breakfasts (including smoked salmon and fresh juices) and just-baked biscuits. The rooms are characterful, and guests can relax in the downstairs sitting room or climb up to the Tower Room – a Moroccan-inspired space with views of the city and waterfront. Also has a small pool with Jacuzzi. ❻

Irish Murphy's 30 Aberdeen St ☎5221 4335, ⓦwww.irishmurphys.com. Cheerful pub offering basic six-bed dorm accomodation and also roomy twins. Noise levels can rise downstairs when players head here to celebrate after AFL games. ❶

Eating

There's a great range of popular dining options in Geelong, with restaurants to suit most budgets. Trendy Pakington Street has a number of good breakfast spots, including bright and bold *Relish One-3*, at no. 13/321 (☎5229 4466), and cosy *Newtown Provedore*, at no. 317A (☎5221 5654). For a caffeine fix, *Coffee Circle*, 83 Little Malop St (☎5229 0716), is a snug and snazzy spot on a bohemian street. Recently opened and moderately priced *Banc*, at the corner of Malop and Moorabool streets (☎5222 3155), is an upmarket dining room, successfully combining a vegetarian menu with modern Australian cuisine and an impressive wine list. Yarra Street is the place to head for just-off-the-boat seafood: for a French twist try *La Parisien*, 15 Eastern Beach Road (☎5229 3110), or in the same building, the *Wharf Shed Café* (☎5221 6645) serves huge burgers and gourmet pizzas, as well as more fishy delights.

Drinking

There are plenty of **pubs** in which to slake your thirst, but the *National Hotel*, 191 Moorabool St (☎5229 1211, ⓦwww.nationalhotel.com.au), also hosts local, and the odd international, rock, funk and hip-hop acts, while *The Barking Dog*, 126 Pakington St (☎5229 2889, ⓦwww.thebarkingdog.com.au) often has live folk or blues. *Tonic Lounge Bar and Restaurant*, 5 James St (☎5229 8899), has a laid-back club feel and also serves up delicious, affordable meals. If you just fancy a pint, including several Irish beers, and a male-dominated crowd, try *Irish Murphy's* (see above).

Around Geelong

Twenty kilometres north of Geelong is the little-visited **Serendip Sanctuary**, at 100 Windermere Rd in Lara (daily 10am–4pm; free but call in advance on ☎5282 2570; no public transport). A refuge for endangered Victorian birds, the sanctuary is renowned for its captive breeding programme of brolgas, magpie geese and Australian bustards. Kangaroos and other marsupials, including the rare pademelon wallaby, can also be viewed here in special enclosures.

Bellarine Peninsula

While it's not as exciting as the popular Mornington Peninsula (see p.169), which it faces across Port Phillip Bay, new development has invigorated the **Bellarine Peninsula** in the past couple of years, making it a popular escape from the city, as well as a sought-after residential area. Picturesque and palm-tree fringed, the peninsula has just enough sights to make a weekend trip worthwhile. The most obvious attraction is the quiet seaside resort of **Queenscliff**, with its historic buildings, fishermen's cottages and Victorian hotels, while nearby is an evocative lighthouse and a collection of interesting small coastal hamlets.

From Geelong, a **bus service** departs from Brougham Street (next to the National Wool Museum) for Ocean Grove and Barwon Heads, Point Lonsdale via Queenscliff, and St Leonards via Portarlington. Regular **ferries** link Queenscliff and Sorrento on the Mornington Peninsula – see p.171 for details.

Queenscliff

The Bellarine Highway runs 31km southeast from Geelong to **QUEENSCLIFF**, at the tip of the Bellarine Peninsula. From its humble beginnings as a sea pilot's station and fishing village, Queenscliff (named after Queen Victoria) became a fashionable resort in the 1880s before falling out of favour early in the 20th century. Since the 1990s, it has enjoyed a remarkable revival in popularity; quaint sailors' cottages and fine examples of Victorian-era buildings abound (such as the grand *Queenscliff*, *Ozone* and *Royal* hotels), while running down the centre, Hesse Street is home to a plethora of lifestyle stores and modish cafés, with even more poodles than Sorrento or Portsea.

Facing the fort at Point Nepean (see p.172), **Fort Queenscliff** demonstrates the town's strategic position near the narrow entrance to Port Phillip Bay. Planned during the Crimean War, but not completed until 1861, it was built in response to the perceived threat of a Russian invasion, and is now the home of the Australian Army Command and Staff College. Guided tours of the college (Sat & Sun 1pm & 3pm; school holidays daily 11am, 1pm & 3pm; 90min; $4.40) allow you to see tunnels built during the goldrush period, muzzle-loading cannons and the unusual "Black Lighthouse", the only one in Australia built of blackstone, which works in tandem with the Point Lonsdale lighthouse (see p.205). Further north on Weerona Parade, the **Queenscliff Maritime Museum** (Mon–Fri 10.30am–4.30pm, Sat & Sun 1.30pm–4.30pm; school holidays daily 10.30am–4.30pm; $5; ℡5258 3440) focuses on the many shipwrecks caused by "The Rip", a fierce current about 1km wide between Point Lonsdale and Point Nepean. The treacherous, churning stretch of water, with its strong currents and whirlpools, has accounted for numerous shipwrecks along the Victorian coastline. Follow signs from Point Lonsdale Road to the **Rip View Lookout** where you can watch container ships or cruise liners such as the *Queen Mary* make their entrance to Port Philip Bay (check the chalkboards in the main street in Point Lonsdale, see p.205, to find out when the next big ship will be passing through the heads).

Rail enthusiasts will want to take the steam-powered **Bellarine Peninsula Railway**, originally opened in 1879 as part of Australia's defences against a Russian invasion, which operates ninety-minute trips from the old Queenscliff Railway Station to Drysdale, 20km northwest (Sun 11.15am &

Bellarine Peninsula

2.30pm, more often during school holidays; $16 return; ☎5258 2069, ⓦwww .bpr.org.au), or to Laker's Siding, 5km from the station (Sun 1.30pm; 20min; $10 return). Four times a year – March, May, October and December – the railway hosts the Blues Train (booking through Ticketek ☎13 28 49, ⓦpremier .ticketek.com.au; $60 return and meal), a round trip with performances by Melbourne's leading blues and jazz musicians. The **Queenscliff Sunday Market** is held on the last Sunday of each month from August to May on Symonds Street, selling everything from household bric-a-brac to local jams and handicrafts.

Practicalities

Buses stop on Hesse Street, just a block before the excellent Victorian **Visitor Information Centre** at no. 55 (☎5258 4843), which offers plenty of advice on local sights and activities. The few good **accommodation** options in Queenscliff book up quickly. The elegant, stately *Queenscliff Hotel*, 16 Gellibrand St (☎5258 1899, ⓦwww.queenscliffhotel.com.au; ❼–❾), has good bed-and-breakfast packages, while the conveniently located, 10 Osprey Mews, actually at 23 Hesse Street (☎5258 3633, ⓦwww.ospreymews.com; ❽–❾), has spacious, modern units that are slightly cheaper in winter.

Around Queenscliff

With your own transport, you can head 3km west down the highway from Queenscliff to **Adventure Park** (Mon & Wed–Sun; $15.50, free for under-4s),

---

Activities in Queenscliff

Queenscliff offers a whole range of activities both in and out of the water. **Boat rides** can be organized through Swan Bay Boat Hire, 1195 Portarlington Road, with hourly and daily rates (from $14/$95; ☎5258 1780) that vary slightly, depending on the boat. It's also possible to rent a **kayak** from the marina on Larkin Parade ($24 for 2hr; ☎5258 2166).

For something more adventurous you can **swim with dolphins and seals** off the bay; Sea-All Dolphin Swims is a reliable tour operator with boats departing from the Queenscliff boat harbour near the car ferry (Oct–April daily 8am & 1pm weather permitting; $95 swimmers, $50 sightseers; bookings essential on ☎5258 3889, ⓦwww.dolphinswims.com.au). There's also great **scubadiving** available: Queenscliff Dive Centre ($125 for a one-day session; ☎5258 1188) offers trips to wrecks and Saltwater Adventures (☎5258 4888) leads dives that explore the South Channel Fort, a half-submerged island of underground passages and gun turrets that is also home to a colony of seals.

For something land-based, Queenscliff Historical Tours rent out a variety of **bicycles** (school holidays and summer; $15–20; ☎5258 3403), as well as providing a map of the town and a personal stereo so that you can do a sightseeing tour at your own pace. You can pick up the bike near the pier at the end of Symonds Road, or they will deliver it to your accommodation. If you follow the map, the ride takes a little under two hours. It's also possible to walk (maps available from the information centre) along the **Bellarine Rail Trail**, a fabulous track running 33km from Queenscliff to Geelong through farming and coastal countryside, and sharing some of the journey with the Bellarine Peninsula Railway (see previous page).

If you're after a rather less energetic activity, try the **Queenscliff Day Spa** in Hobson Street (call ☎5258 4233 for an appointment), where you can indulge in a range of facials, spas and body treatments, as well as a two-and-a-half-hour "Coast Experience" combining aromatherapy, body brushing, exfoliation, massage and hydrotherapy.

In 1803, during an exploration expedition around Queenscliff lead by Captain David Collins, an English convict, **William Buckley**, escaped. He was adopted by the local Wathaurong Aboriginal tribe, who lived around the Barwon River, and stayed with them for over thirty years. When the "wild white man" turned up at John Batman's camp at Indented Head, he was dressed in animal skins and could scarcely remember how to speak English; his survival has been immortalized in the phrase **"Buckley's chance"**.

In his day, there was huge reluctance on the part of the government to pardon Buckley, despite the fact that he later played an important role in building relations between Aborigines and white settlers. A committee was established in 2003 to promote the bicentenary of his escape, and educational resources on his story have been made available to schools in the Geelong region. A memorial for Buckley, further north at the more dramatic coastline of St Leonards, has also been proposed.

a big hit with kids. Spread over fifty acres of picturesque parkland, it provides everything from giant water slides to bouncy castles, go-karts, paddleboats and flying foxes. From Queenscliff it's about 5km west to peaceful **Point Lonsdale** (also just known as "Lonnie") and its 120-metre-high lighthouse (tours Sun 9.30am–1pm; approximately 45min; $5) at the edge of the foreshore reserve overlooking "The Rip". Built in 1902, it's visible for 30km out to sea and has sweeping views across to Point Nepean on the Mornington Peninsula. Beneath the lighthouse, on the edge of the bluff, "Buckley's Cave" is where the famous **William Buckley** reputedly made his home (see box above).

Fifteen kilometres west of Queenscliff, **Ocean Grove** and **Barwon Heads** face one another across the Barwon River – the former has one of Victoria's safest surf beaches, lookouts and a pleasant summer climate cooled by breezes blowing in from Bass Strait, while the latter (made popular as the fictional seaside backwater of "Pearl Bay" in *SeaChange*, a hit TV series made in the late 1990s) is a pretty town with a long sandy river foreshore, jetties, a collection of good eateries and bars, golf courses, heritage walks, delightful rock pools and a popular beach. Barwon Heads is also home to the **Jirrahlingha Koala and Wildlife Sanctuary** on Taits Road (daily 9am–5pm; ☎5254 2484; $10), where koalas, dingoes, wombats and other native fauna are found.

North of Queenscliff, **St Leonards** was founded in 1840 as a fishing base for Geelong. Formerly a haven for retirees, the town has glammed up, attracting a hipper and younger set of holidaymakers and city folk seeking a more relaxed lifestyle. Further north, at the hillside setting of **Portarlington,** there's the beautifully preserved, steam-powered **Portarlington Mill** at Turner Court (Sat & Sun noon–4pm; $2.50; call in advance to book tours ☎5259 3847). Four storeys of solid stone, this National Trust property was built in 1857 and is well worth visiting if you're interested in seeing how bluestone was once put to industrial use. Apart from a safe family beach and splendid views across the bay to the You Yangs Regional Park (see p.200), Portarlington is also within close proximity to some of Victoria's best **wineries**, including Kilgour Estate, 85 McAdams Lane (☎5251 2223), Scotchmans Hill, 190 Scotchmans Road, Drysdale (☎5251 3176, ⓦwww.scotchmanshill.com.au), and the glorious Spray Farm, 2275 Portarlington Road (☎5251 3176, ⓦwww.sprayfarm.com.au), with its heritage architecture and steep grounds leading down to Corio Bay. See ⓦwww.winegeelong.com.au for details of wineries further off the beaten track.

GEELONG AND AROUND | Bellarine Peninsula

The Great Ocean Road

The **Great Ocean Road** stretches from Torquay, 20km south of the major regional city of Geelong, all the way along the rugged Victorian coast to Warrnambool, almost 300km to the west. Regarded as one of the world's great coastal journeys, the road snakes past innumerable coves, cliffs, scenic lookouts, waterfalls, rainforests and shipwrecks, and there are plenty of opportunities en route for bushwalking, swimming, surfing, fishing and whale-watching. When construction began in 1919, the route was intended as a memorial to those who fell in World War I. As the Great Depression took hold it also became a source of much-needed work for thousands of unemployed ex-servicemen using little more than picks and shovels. After years of difficult and sometimes dangerous work, the Great Ocean Road was finally completed in 1932.

One of the most visited stretches of the route is the **Port Campbell National Park**. Buffeted by wild seas and fierce winds, the coastline here has been sculpted over millions of years to form a series of striking natural features. You can wander the boardwalks and paths at the **Twelve Apostles**, remarkable limestone rock stacks rising from the ocean, while further along, **London Bridge** is another amazing rock formation not to be missed.

Along with striking ocean views, the Great Ocean Road boasts a number of laid-back towns and villages on the water's edge: the resort town of **Torquay** is widely regarded as Australia's surfing capital; buzzing restaurants and cafés dot the picturesque beachfront towns of **Lorne** and **Apollo Bay**; **Warrnambool** is a prime whale-watching destination; and historic **Port Fairy** allows you to enjoy seafaring village life, with its fishing wharf, old pubs and beautifully preserved colonial buildings.

Getting around

Although it makes for exhilarating driving, the Great Ocean Road is best viewed from the passenger seat. From Melbourne, the Coast Link **bus** service goes along the coast to Geelong and Apollo Bay, then on to Warrnambool (departures every Friday at 8.48am, arriving in Warrnambool at 5pm; $41 one way; for further details, contact V/Line on ☎13 61 96). West Coast Railways (☎5221 8966) operate a **train** service between Melbourne and Warrnambool (Mon–Fri four departures daily; $57.60 one way), a journey of around three

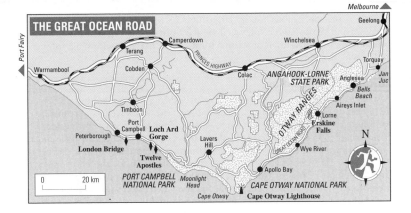

hours. In addition, a host of companies offer **tours** down the Great Ocean Road, either on its own or as part of a longer trip – contact the Melbourne Visitor Information Centre for details. A good resource for helping plan your itinerary is the website ⓦwww.greatoceanrd.org.au, which allows you to take a virtual tour.

From Torquay to Aireys Inlet

Gateway to the Great Ocean Road, **TORQUAY** is a nirvana for surf-seekers and those seeking a barefoot existence within reach of the beach. **Surfing** is big business here, which is hardly surprising given that some of the biggest surfing names had their beginnings in the southern coastal town. Teenage surfers from the 1960s, "hippy drop-outs" sick of braving the winter water, have grown up to become millionaire owners of locally based global wetsuit and surfwear brands like Rip Curl and Quicksilver (Billabong, Oakley and Reef are also on show here), while behind the ritzy shopfronts lining the Surfcoast Highway, newer surf and accessory labels are taking hold in the town's industrial estates. Business peaks in Torquay each Easter during the Rip Curl Pro surfing contest (ⓦwww.ripcurl.com) for boardriders, the world's longest-running professional surfing contest, which has been sponsored by Rip Curl since 1973.

If you don't know a point break from a reef break, the best place to start is the **Surfworld Museum** (daily 9am–5pm; $7.50) at the rear of the Surfcoast Plaza on the Surfcoast Highway. The world's largest surfing museum, it has a wave-making tank, interactive displays like paddling machines, and a collection of antique surfboards and Hawaiian shirts.

To check out the real thing, follow the signs to two of Victoria's best surf beaches: **Jan Juc** and **Bells Beach**. The former is the starting point for the 35-kilometre, two-day **Surf Coast Walk**, which follows the coastline along little-used roads, joining Anglesea all the way to Aireys Inlet; the latter – Australia's only official surfing reserve and site of the Rip Curl Pro contest – featured in the Patrick Swayze and Keanu Reeves movie *Point Break*, although the beach passed off as Bells was actually filmed in Canada.

Heading west along the coast, scenic **Point Addis** and the protected **Ironbark Basin Coastal Nature Reserve** have several marked walking trails and lookouts, while **Anglesea** is an appealing seaside resort of small shacks and more modern development popular with holidaying families and anglers;

its golf course is famous for its large mob of resident kangaroos. Leaving Anglesea and skirting the coast, you'll see the **Split Point Lighthouse** (1891) overlooking the small town of **Aireys Inlet**, which has fine swimming, fishing and beachcombing.

Torquay practicalities

A small tourist office within Torquay's Surfworld Museum (same hours; ☎5261 4219) hands out tidal reports and maps of local breaks, as well as information on where to rent boards and wet suits. If you want to cut your surfing teeth, there are plenty of **surf schools** along the Great Ocean Road, including Southern Exposure (☎5261 9170, ⊛www.southernexposure.com.au).

Thanks to the transient surf community who show up for the good waves, there are plenty of **places to stay** in or around Torquay. As you'd expect, prices are cheaper during winter when only the most dedicated surfers are braving the chilly waters. Easily found by its boldly coloured murals, *Bells Beach Lodge*, 51–53 Surfcoast Highway (☎5261 7070, ⊛www.bellsbeachbackpackers.com. au; dorms $19–23, doubles ❸), has helpful staff and hires out surf equipment. Pub-style rooms are on offer at the *Torquay Hotel*, 36 Bell St (☎5261 2001; ❺), which is located close to the waves and the town, or try the homely *Potters Inn*, 40 Bristol Rd (☎5261 4131; ❹–❺), with its crackling fires, lovely outdoor areas and pottery lessons from the potter-owner. *Zeally Bay Caravan Park* on the Esplanade (☎5261 2400) has on-site cabins, caravans and camping sites, some with great beach views.

For a sit-down **meal**, mosey into *Micha's Mexican Restaurant*, 23 The Esplanade (☎5261 2460), a longstanding favourite – book ahead on summer weekends. Alternatively, *Torquay Hotel* (see above) has hearty bistro fare, including a lip-smacking fish and chips, and is a good place for a few quiet drinks, except at weekends when it hosts live bands. Several takeaway joints line the main drag.

Lorne

Forty-five kilometres west of Torquay, surf culture rubs shoulders with café society at **LORNE**, the premier holiday town on Victoria's west coast. Lorne is also the home of the world's largest swimming race – the famous **Lorne Pier to Pub** ocean swim. This annual 1.2-kilometre event supposedly began in 1979 when a group of lifesavers dived off the Portsea pier and swam towards a nearby hotel – the last swimmer to reach the pub had to shout drinks for the rest. Taking place in early January, the race attracts several thousand competitors – for more information, visit ⊛www.lornesurfclub.com.au.

Inland of Lorne, many of the area's finest walking tracks crisscross the Lorne section of the **Angahook–Lorne State Park**, which takes in the lush eastern fringes of the Otway Ranges and the beaches around Aireys Inlet. One of the most accessible places to explore the park is from the **Blanket Leaf Picnic Area**, which is signposted from the town centre. From the picnic area there's a two-kilometre walk or drive to Erskine Falls, a stunning waterfall cascading over one of the largest drops in the Otways. For a longer hike, make for the **Sheoak Falls Trail** (signposted off the Great Ocean Road, about 5km out of Lorne), a three-hour scenic loop that follows a creek downstream to the ocean-side Swallow Cave, then back up to Castle Rock with awe-inspiring clifftop views. There's free **bush camping** at Wye River, Big Hill and a few other sites throughout the park. For more information on camping and trails visit the tourist office in Lorne (see p.210) or check out the Parks Victoria website ⊛www.parkweb.vic.gov.au.

△ Great Ocean Road

Practicalities

Lorne's well-stocked **tourist office** is upstairs at 144 Mountjoy Parade (daily 9am–5pm; ☎5289 1152). The best budget **rooms** are at the impressive *Great Ocean Road Backpackers YHA*, 10 Erskine Ave (☎5289 1809; dorm beds $20, rooms ➋–➌), which has timber verandahs to read on and spotless shared kitchens. There are also six-bed cottages available for groups (➏). The spectacular *Grand Pacific Hotel*, 268 Mountjoy Parade (☎5289 1609, ⊛www.grandpacific.com.au; ➎), is all opulence from the outside, but inside the rooms are simple motel-style affairs, though they do have stunning views. The hotel also has smarter apartments (➐) next door, some with spas, which are a better bet. The *Sandridge Motel*, 128 Mountjoy Parade (☎5289 2180, ☎5289 2722; ➎–➐), also has a range of rooms, the better-value ones with balconies looking out over the sea. Off the main drag yet still central with beach views, *Phoenix Apartments*, 60 Mountjoy Parade (☎5289 2000 or 0414 528 911, ☎5289 1298; ➒), has apartments with all the mod cons including TVs, videos (perfect for rainy days) and kitchens. Out of town in lush bush, the self-contained weatherboard units at *Lemonade Creek Cottages*, 690 Erskine Falls Road (☎& ☎5289 2600; ➏), are still within walking distance of the beach, and also have a heated pool and tennis court for the active.

There are no shortage of spots to grab a bite to **eat** in. *Kosta's* at 48 Mountjoy Parade (daily 9am–4pm, plus evenings Mon, Wed & Fri only; ☎5289 1883) is an unpretentious Greek staple that has been dishing up great breakfasts for decades. Another old favourite is *Mark's* at 124 Mountjoy Parade (daily: summer noon–3pm & 6pm–late; rest of year 6pm–late; closed in May; ☎5289 2787), with some of the best seafood on the Great Ocean Road, including hefty marlin steaks. For good bar meals, head for the *Lorne Hotel*, 176 Mountjoy Parade (☎5289 1409, ⊛www.lornehotel.com.au).

Apollo Bay

From Lorne the road twists and turns to **APOLLO BAY**, a less pretentious and more laid-back resort, with a lively alternative scene. A fishing port and former whaling station, its setting is one of the prettiest along the Great Ocean Road, with a crescent-shaped bay set beneath the rounded, sometimes foggy Otway Ranges. Gentle updraughts make these hills popular with hang-gliders, who can often be seen floating lazily above the town. The pier and breakwater are usually the province of anglers, and at the base of the pier the Fisherman's Co-op sells fresh seafood. In March, the town hosts the **Apollo Bay Music Festival** (⊛www.apollobaymusicfestival.com), featuring jazz, rock, blues and country. The **tourist office** at 100 Great Ocean Rd (daily 9am–5pm; ☎5237 6529) is a good resource for the area.

The Shipwreck Coast

Beyond Apollo Bay the Great Ocean Road heads inland, passing through the temperate rainforests and fern gullies of the **Cape Otway National Park**. In the late 1860s, loggers spread into the Otway Ranges and built a number of small townships that remain to this day, but nowadays tourism is the area's lifeblood. On the way to the hilltop town of Lavers Hill, you pass the turn-off to the **Cape Otway Lighthouse** (9am–5pm; $8). Erected in 1848 after the ship *Cataraqui* went down off the coast of King Island to the south, it is the oldest remaining lighthouse on the Australian mainland. Only nine of the 400 passengers survived – just one of many tragedies that gave the title Shipwreck Coast to the 130-kilometre stretch of coastline from nearby Moonlight Head to Port Fairy.

The eastern portion of the Shipwreck Coast is dominated by the narrow **Port Campbell National Park**. Windswept, heath-covered hills overlook Bass Strait and its sometimes awesome swells. There are several places to stop along this route, the most popular being the site overlooking the **Twelve Apostles** (now down to eight), which is just 80km after Lorne. At this lookout the waves of the Southern Ocean have worn the cliffs into a spectacular series of offshore limestone stacks.

A few kilometres further along is **Loch Ard Gorge**. In 1878 the clipper *Loch Ard* struck a reef near here and went down, taking 52 passengers with her – most of the passengers and crew are buried in the cemetery overlooking the gorge. For more information on the coast's maritime tragedies, visit the **Loch Ard Shipwreck Museum** (daily 9.30am–5.30pm; $2) in **PORT CAMPBELL**, a few kilometres to the west. Named after Captain Alexander Campbell, the manager of Port Fairy's whaling station, Port Campbell is a seriously incognito town of a couple of hundred regulars, with a pleasant beach and a jetty offering good fishing opportunities.

Just a few kilometres beyond Port Campbell is **London Bridge**, a rock formation whose two sections were formerly connected by a central span of rock – the "bridge". In 1990, this suddenly collapsed, leaving two rather startled people stranded on the outer section (they were eventually rescued by helicopter). Just beyond here, the **Grotto** – another amazing natural rock formation – has a path leading down to a rock pool beneath a limestone arch.

Warrnambool to Port Fairy

West of London Bridge, the Great Ocean Road passes through dairy country before ending just short of **WARRNAMBOOL**. Once home to sealers and whalers, it is now Victoria's pre-eminent destination for **whale-watching**: southern right whales can be sighted off Logans Beach, just east of town, between May and October. Warrnambool's excellent **Flagstaff Hill Maritime Village** on Merri Street (daily 9am–5pm; $14) is a re-created nineteenth-century fishing port, with the *Shipwrecked* sound-and-vision show telling the story of the sinking of the clipper *Loch Ard* in 1878, plus an impressive collection of shipwreck artefacts including the Loch Ard Peacock, an earthenware peacock washed ashore two days after the *Loch Ard* went down. On Liebig Street an excellent regional gallery, the **Warrnambool Art Gallery** (Mon–Fri 10am–5pm, Sat & Sun noon–5pm; $4), houses the paintings of Eugene Von Guerard (see below) and over six hundred contemporary works.

West of Warrnambool is the **Tower Hill Game Reserve** (sunrise–sunset; free). After years of logging, the area was replanted in the 1950s using an 1855 landscape painting by Eugene Von Guerard as a guide. More than 300,000 trees were introduced and the reserve now has an abundance of water birds, koalas, kangaroos and wallabies, as well as a Natural History Centre (daily 9.30am–12.30pm & 1.30–4.30pm; free) with geological and historical displays. There are several self-guided half-hour and hour-long walks (several are wheelchair accessible), as well as BBQs and picnic areas.

A few kilometres beyond Warrnambool, **PORT FAIRY** – initially called Belfast, but renamed in 1887 by Captain James Wishart after his cutter *Fairy* – is a quaint former whaling port that in the 1850s rivalled Sydney for its shipping business. Today it has numerous National Trust-listed buildings, interesting old pubs, and a historic wharf from where you can take **cruises** around the bay and trips to Julia Percy Island. Relaxed and low-key, with a peaceful fishing village atmosphere, it's home to a variety of musical festivals, most notably the **Port Fairy Folk Music Festival** (ⓦwww.portfairyfolkfestival.com), held every Labour Day over the long weekend in March. Port Fairy's **tourist office** is at Railway Place on Bank Street (daily 9am–5pm; ☎5568 2682).

Contexts

Contexts

History

The region surrounding the Melbourne that we know today has been inhabited for thousands of years, but the actual city itself has existed for only a fraction of that time. What follows is a concise account of the trials and tribulations of the first settlers, to the state of the city in the twenty-first century.

Melbourne's original owners

Melbourne and Victoria's original inhabitants were the **Kooris**, who have lived in the region for over 50,000 years. Semi-nomadic hunters and gatherers, they had a close relationship with the land, living a mostly comfortable life that was threatened only in times of scarcity. To protect themselves against the cold, Kooris built fires and turf huts, and donned great possum-skin cloaks. For leisure, they played a game where two competing teams attempted to catch a round ball made of possum skins that was kicked high into the air (a forerunner to Aussie Rules football).

Victoria's Aboriginal people also had a highly ordered social life, sophisticated traditional cultures, and around ten separate languages spoken by over thirty different dialect or sub-language groups. In the Port Phillip region, five different groups shared adjoining territories, a common language, and an integrated culture and belief system, forming a nation or confederacy known as the "Kulin". Periodically, groups from the Kulin would gather in areas around present-day Melbourne. But although the Aboriginal way of life had evolved over thousands of years, they were ill-prepared for Gubba (white) invasion.

Tentative beginnings

European involvement with Australia began in the early seventeenth century, when Portuguese, Spanish and Dutch expeditions mapped parts of the coastline, although the land's forbidding climate and seeming barrenness discouraged the Western powers from taking much of an interest in the country the Dutch called "New Holland". After the voyage of the British party under **Cook** in 1770, which claimed the eastern seaboard for King George III, in 1788 Europe's first settlement on Australian soil was established with the arrival of the **First Fleet** in Botany Bay, near present-day Sydney.

The first Briton to attempt to populate the Melbourne area, **Captain David Collins**, sailed from London, arriving in Port Phillip Bay in 1803 at the site of what is now Sorrento. Less than a year later, after declaring the location unsuitable due to its lack of fresh water, Collins abandoned the settlement and took his party of marines and convicts to Van Diemen's Land (now Tasmania). Around the same time, a party led by Charles Grimes, Surveyor-General of New South Wales, stumbled across the Yarra and had lunch on the present site of the city.

Across the Bass Strait, a number of Van Diemen's Land pastoralists, including John Batman and Thomas and John Henty, looking for favourable pasturage, had sought permission from authorities in London and Sydney to graze livestock on the mainland. Impetus was also spurred by the glowing reports of suitable land received from whalers active in the Bass Strait. However, the pastoralists' requests were consistently refused as the authorities in both London and Sydney believed it would prove too expensive. Tired of being bossed around, **Edward Henty** (Thomas's son) set out with his family and began squatting at Portland Bay on the southwest coast in 1834, thereby establishing the district's first permanent settlement.

Into the frontier

John Batman, a barrel-chested former bushranger, continued to harbour plans for a pastoral settlement in Victoria. In May 1835, together with a consortium of graziers, public servants and merchants, he set out to buy land from the local Aborigines. Leading a party on the sloop *Rebecca*, he reached Indented Head on the Bellarine Peninsula in Port Phillip Bay and proceeded to walk around Corio Bay, noting that the fertile countryside was "beyond my most sanguine expectations". After reaching the mouth of a river (later to be called the Yarra), he continued along one of its tributary streams until meeting a local Dugitalla tribe with whom, on June 6, 1835, a **treaty** of his own making was signed. Batman claimed to have procured 240,000 hectares (600,000 acres), which he paid for with £200 worth of goods (knives, tools and trinkets), promising similar payments each year. Today historians suggest that the Aborigines believed Batman was simply handing over gifts in return for visitation rights, but Batman thought he was actually buying the land.

Batman returned to Van Diemen's Land on June 9, leaving a small party at Indented Head to look after the land he had "bought". Days later, ensconced in the *Launceston Hotel*, Batman proclaimed he was "the greatest landowner in the world". His braggadocio was tempered, however, by the refusal of officials in Hobart and Sydney to recognize the settlement without permission from the British colonial authority. Until further instructions were received, those settling at Port Phillip (then part of New South Wales) were to be treated as trespassers.

Despite this setback, **plans for settlement** continued apace and by the end of June, Batman and his backers had formed a syndicate, called the Port Phillip Association, to send livestock to the mainland. However, it was another group led by the visionary **John Pascoe Fawkner** that played the major role in the establishment of Melbourne. The son of a convict and a member of Captain David Collins' party that landed in Sorrento, Fawkner had made his way in Van Diemen's Land as a baker, bookseller, newspaper owner (he would subsequently publish Melbourne's first newspaper, the *Melbourne Advertiser*) and publican of the *Launceston Hotel*. In April 1835, he bought the schooner *Enterprize* to ferry a new party of settlers to Port Phillip. The trip was planned for August 4 that year, but, having organized and financed a small group to accompany him, Fawkner was forced to disembark due to his own financial problems. The *Enterprize*, under the command of Captain John Lancey, continued without him, reaching the Yarra on August 29 and berthing at a natural rock barrier in the riverbed, near present-day William Street, where fresh water was guaranteed. Fawkner and his family arrived on October 11, with Batman – whose popularity as the city's traditional founder continues today – following on November 9.

Growing pains

In September 1836, orders arrived allowing settlement (although Batman's purchase was declared "invalid"), sparking a monumental **land grab** as increasing numbers of settlers from Van Diemen's Land, New South Wales and immigrants from Britain flocked to the new location. Sir Richard Bourke, governor general of New South Wales, visited in 1837, choosing the site for the city. He was accompanied by Surveyor-General **Robert Hoddle**, who famously mapped out the blueprint for Melbourne's spacious grid in a couple of hours, recording that, "in 1837, Governor Bourke entered my tent and gave me his list of names for the streets". Up until then, Melbourne had gone by a number of names – Dutti-Galla, Doutta Galla, Batmania, Bearbrass, Bearport, Barehup, Bareheep and Bareberp were all considered at one time or another – before it was decided in 1837 to name the town after William Lamb, second Viscount Melbourne and prime minister of Great Britain.

In 1839, **Charles La Trobe** arrived to administer the district, which one writer had called "unquestionably the most drunken region on the face of the earth". A precocious scholar and butterfly collector, La Trobe spent fifteen years in office, steering Victoria to self-government and establishing major public works such as the State Library of Victoria and other cultural institutions, intended to create a stable democracy and turn an uncouth frontier town into an urbane colonial city.

Under his guidance Melbourne rapidly began taking shape. The development was concentrated on the north bank of the river, as the south was an unstable floodplain – only since the 1970s have any buildings of consequence been built on this side. The city's population grew quickly, and such was the tumult on the streets that many people were gored or crushed to death by sundry drays, bullocks and horses. By 1840, the number of citizens had reached 10,000. **Aboriginal people** also began drifting into the settlement, as their land was taken and they became increasingly attracted to tobacco and alcohol. Largely seen as a degenerate people by the European populace, Aborigines did mostly menial work, trading goods such as feathers and skins, or acting as pastoral labourers. Although less violent than other settlements in Australia (predominantly due to John Batman's treaty and the Port Phillip Protectorate, which outlined laws to protect Aborigines), the massacres by white settlers, as well as poisoned waterholes and European diseases such as dysentery and measles, saw the Aboriginal population of Melbourne decline from around 15,000 in 1834 to 2000 in 1850. Alcohol abuse also reduced numbers, and by the mid-1850s there were few Aborigines left in the city.

In 1842, Melbourne was declared a town and, five years later, a city. The **Port Phillip District** separated from New South Wales (of which it was still part) in 1849 and, two years later, officially broke from the state when it was declared an independent colony, just nine days before gold was discovered.

The goldrush

The **discovery of gold** near Ballarat in 1851 irrevocably changed Melbourne's character. With its strongly rural atmosphere, the city had previously struggled to attract immigrants, but the goldrush saw hundreds of ships carrying fortune-seekers flooding in from around the world. Melbourne was transformed into a convulsing, sprawling and increasingly violent metropolis crammed with gaudy shops, brothels, flashy diggers, opportunists and no-hopers. Most migrants didn't stay long in the city but scurried off in search of gold; their desertion stripped Melbourne of much-needed labour, even forcing Governor La Trobe to feed and groom his own horses.

However, within a year, Melbourne's merchants were busy turning a profit from those returning from the goldfields. The city's population exploded, and Melbourne became the fastest-growing and richest port in the British Empire. Growth came at a price, though; with no infrastructure, city streets began accumulating filth at an astonishing rate, and it was not uncommon for citizens to walk ankle deep in mud or faeces in the downtown area. Sir Charles Hotham, who became Victoria's governor in 1854, wrote of the place before his death in office two years later: "It is a vile hole, and I shall never like it."

Among other things, the year 1854 also saw the first edition of *The Age* newspaper and the beginning of the Victorian rail network, with passenger and goods services between Flinders Street and Port Melbourne. It also heralded the miners' uprising in Ballarat. Known as the Eureka Rebellion, the stand of the miners represented a giant step in the march to liberty and democratic freedoms in the newly formed state.

Boom and bust

The 1860s to 1880s were years of great optimism and prosperity in "**Marvellous Melbourne**". The city, driven by gold and untramelled industry, took over from Sydney as Australia's financial centre. Rail lines and cable trams were introduced on Melbourne's streets, telephones were installed, and a night-time football match was played under electric lighting at the Melbourne Cricket Ground (MCG). Grandiose public developments such as the Royal Exhibition Building (built especially to stage the Melbourne International Exhibition of 1880–81) and the Melbourne Town Hall were constructed on goldrush profits, suburbs from St Kilda to Collingwood began to develop, and large tracts of the city centre were set aside as public parks and gardens. Always deferential towards the "Mother Country", Melbourne's well-to-do modelled themselves on middle-class English society, adopting the fashions, the furniture, and the carefully enunciated speech, while filling their gardens with imported shrubs and trees.

By the 1890s, however, Melbourne's star waned, as the city was rocked by a series of strikes, sparking a devastating depression and the beginning of the "**grey nineties**". Melbourne's earlier laissez-faire prosperity, fuelled by dubious financial speculation, had drawn manpower from the land, decreasing primary production. As land became unsaleable and wool and wheat prices slumped, companies were bankrupted and fortunes lost overnight.

The twentieth century

By the turn of the century Melbourne had recovered and financial stability returned. Following the unification of Australia's six colonies in 1901, the city became the country's political capital (the first session of the new Parliament was held in the Royal Exhibition Building) and remained so until the specially constructed capital city of Canberra was completed in 1927. Stability continued through World War I and beyond, until the city's prosperity was shattered by the Great Depression of the 1930s. With unemployment rife, many people were put to work building a series of public works, including St Kilda Road, the Shrine of Remembrance and the Great Ocean Road.

By the early 1930s, Melbourne had bounced back again and began a period of intense **industrial development**. Warehousing and manufacturing moved outwards from the city and into the suburbs, and families attached to these industries went to the outskirts for work and cheap housing. Following World War II, Melbourne continued its programme of development, beginning a huge **immigration push** that attracted waves of refugees and migrants from around the world – their arrival helped transform the city from a culturally suburban, stereotypically British backwater into a sophisticated international melting pot. As the inner suburbs became crowded and accommodation scarce, Melbourne built thousands of houses in the outer suburbs for low-income earners. The drift outwards continued until the 1960s, when new city-centre developments and the revitalization of inner-city suburbs such as Carlton and Fitzroy by Melbourne's growing band of bohemians, intellectuals and further waves of immigrants, helped reverse the trend.

The undoubted highlight of this era was the city's hosting of the **1956 Olympic Games**. After initial apprehension about Melbourne's ability to stage such an event (at the time, with a population of just 1.6 million, the city was considered rather provincial), the "friendly games" as they became known were a resounding success: not only did they lead to the Melbourne Cricket Ground (MCG) being transformed into Australia's largest and most famous stadium, but the event also put the city firmly on the world map.

Progress continued until the **1990s**, when Australia fell into recession. Melbourne, in particular, hit an all-time low as unemployment rose to record levels, factories closed, the property market collapsed and some of the city's largest financial institutions went under. The Labor government was unable to handle the state's finances, leading to a lack of trust among voters, who in 1992 elected a conservative Liberal/National party coalition under Jeff Kennett.

Kennett in power

Bold and occasionally boorish, Victoria's premier **Jeff Kennett** wielded almost complete control of parliament, and set about invigorating Melbourne by investing heavily in infrastructure. Dubbed the "Mitterrand of the South", he was keen to demonstrate that Melbourne was a "world-class" city, and new developments such as the Melbourne Museum and Federation Square sprung up all over town. To fund these works, the government oversaw savage budget cuts to health and education. Kennett also came under fire for Melbourne's gambling culture, as well as for harassing the media (he once shovelled sand over a group of reporters), and for making changes to the office of the auditor-general, which had previously investigated government officials' dubious tender processes and credit-card abuse. But despite Kennett's Thatcherite approach to the economy and propensity for antagonizing various sections of the community, his popularity as premier remained high, and he was widely recognized as Australia's most effective politician at both a state and federal level at the time. His activist government continued to celebrate the state's cultural, racial and religious diversity, and his lead against the fledgling One Nation Party – a new and xenophobic force in Australian politics – won him many admirers on both sides of the political fence.

The **Aboriginal population** in Melbourne had, since the 1850s steadily grown, with over 8000 Aborigines living in the city by the start of the new millennium. State-wide community organizations, schools and health and legal centres boosted Aboriginal esteem and provided widespread employment. In addition, Victorian and federal legislation have given control of some heritage and cultural sites to Aborigines. In 1998, the Melbourne City Council recognized the past suffering of Victorian Aborigines by issuing a formal apology during National Sorry Day.

A new millennium

In September 1999, arrogantly riding high in the polls and sporting a massive parliamentary majority, Kennett lost the "unloseable election" to rank outsider **Steve Bracks** of the Labor Party. Kennett's unexpected demise was largely due to his government's neglect of rural Victoria (he once memorably described Melbourne as the vital heart of the state and rural towns as the "toenails"). Bracks inherited a buoyant economy, efficient services, low unemployment and, unbeknown to Kennett, a massive budget surplus of $1.8 billion, which he proceeded to rapidly spend in rural and regional Victoria. At the same time he concentrated his party's efforts on improving the key areas of health and education. Bracks also continued the work of the former premier in encouraging **new developments** across the city, particularly along the river in the form of the Docklands project – set to transform the waterfront.

Re-elected in 2002, Bracks's government has had to struggle with an ailing economy, union unrest and a fall in immigration, but has succeeded in upgrading transport routes and pushing through environmental initiatives. Despite adopting, at times, a Kennett-style lack of concern for certain sections of the community, it looks, for the meantime, as if Melburnians want him to stay.

Books

Most of the following books are still in print, although some may be hard to find unless you visit a library, or secondhand or specialist bookshop. The Australian publisher is provided plus the UK and US publishers where available.

General introductions

Jim Davidson *The Sydney-Melbourne Book* (o/p). Entertaining and erudite collection of essays comparing the two cities. Topics range from politics, business, crime and education to cultural matters such as film, sport and religion.

W.H. Newnham *Melbourne – Biography of a City* (Hill of Content). The best and most detailed account of Melbourne's founding and subsequent growth, with a good sprinkling of photographs and illustrations.

History and culture

R. Barrett *The Inner Suburbs – The Evolution of an Industrial Area* (Melbourne University Press). The stuttering development of Collingwood and Richmond during the nineteenth century makes for a fascinating and grimy read, especially the warts-and-all picture of wealthy industrialists pouring noxious wastes into the Yarra.

C.P. Billot (ed) *Melbourne's Missing Chronicle – John Pascoe Fawkner* (Quartet). This private journal of John Pascoe Fawkner, the industrious former publican and early Melbourne settler, traces the city's formative years in 1835–36. Somewhat scrappy but disarmingly candid, it's an invaluable work for anyone interested in Melbourne's history and the life of one of the city's founders.

Michael Cannon *Old Melbourne Town* (Loch Haven). Interesting analysis of Melbourne life up until the discovery of gold. Cannon's sequel, *Melbourne After the Gold Rush* (Loch Haven), is equally good, concentrating on Melbourne's transformation from a small shantytown into a hectic and overcrowded metropolis.

Patricia Clancy and Jeanne Allen (ed) *The French Consul's Wife:*

Memoirs of Céleste de Chabrillan in Gold-Rush Australia (Melbourne University Press, Aus & UK). This racy memoir of the immigrant Céleste de Chabrillan (former Parisian courtesan, circus performer and dancer) and her encounter with mid-nineteenth-century Melbourne has insightful and deliciously impertinent descriptions of society during the goldrush era.

Jack Collins, Letizia Mondello, John Brehney and Tim Childs *Cosmopolitan Melbourne* (Big Box Publishing). Breezy lowdown on the city's migrant and indigenous populations combines history and cultural observances with local information on community groups, media, restaurants and bars.

Maree Coote *The Melbourne Book – A History of Now* (Hardie Grant). Writer and designer Maree Coote puts her professional knowledge to good use with this richly illustrated and well-researched tome, that combines interviews, photographs and anecdotes to give a unique view of the city. It gives background information on landmarks, personalities and everything that makes the city special.

Graeme Davidson *The Rise and Fall of Marvellous Melbourne* (o/p).

Scholarly and sometimes difficult to read, but worth persisting with to gain an idea of the "Marvellous Melbourne" era, during which the city became the wealthiest and most advanced in Australia.

Tim Flannery *The Birth of Melbourne* (Text Publishing). Handy look at early Melbourne through diary entries, newspaper clippings and letters from the likes of John Batman, Mathew Flinders, Rudyard Kipling and Alexandre Dumas. The material collated by naturalist and author Tim Flannery is often fun and entertaining, and conveys a city built on dispossession, ecological mismanagement and the greed of sleazy entrepreneurs.

Andrew Hoyne, Jason Loucas and Andrew Anastasios *St Kilda In Your Face* (Hoyne Design). This gorgeous volume of photographs and text romps around Melbourne's famous seaside suburb lovingly exploring its places and many characters.

Janet McCalman *Sex and Suffering: Women's Health and a Woman's Hospital* (Melbourne University Press, Aus & UK; Johns Hopkins University Press, US). A powerful and moving social history of the lives and suffering of Melbourne women since the 1850s, focusing on the nursing and medical staff at the Women's Hospital in Carlton.

Gary Presland *Aboriginal Melbourne: The Lost Land of the Kulin People* (o/p). Fascinating and readable short study of a vanished country and a remarkable way of life, with accounts of the Kulin lifestyle and the effects of white settlement on the Aboriginal population and culture.

⊡ **Jill and Jeff Sparrow** *Radical Melbourne 1 & 2* (Vulgar Press). These two volumes, covering the nineteenth and twentieth centuries respectively, examine political activism in Melbourne. Solid, sometimes secret, histories of the city, supported by rarely seen images from the archives of the State Library of Victoria.

Art and architecture

Maie Casey *Early Melbourne Architecture, 1840 to 1888* (Oxford University Press). Smallish but useful photographic representation (with brief notes) of the city's more architecturally interesting nineteenth-century buildings. Sadly, over one-third of the buildings included in the book have since been altered or demolished.

Leon van Shaik (ed) *Architectural Monographs No 50: Tom Kovac* (o/p). Nicely illustrated study of the Melbourne work of the enigmatic and provocative Tom Kovac, analysing nineteen completed and unfinished projects, including the Melbourne Museum and Federation Square. The results are witty and consistently entertaining.

Granville Wilson and Peter Sands *Building a City* (Oxford University Press). Meticulously researched and comprehensive general history of Melbourne's architecture.

Food and wine

⊡ **Stephanie Alexander** *The Cook's Companion* (Viking). Superb culinary collection of ingredients from one of Melbourne's finest chefs. Designed to be a gift from one generation of cooks to the next, this attractive (if very heavy) package is the "bible" in many Australian kitchens.

Max Allen *Sniff, Swirl, Slurp* (Mitchell Beazley). An abundance of helpful advice on how to get the most enjoyment out of drinking wine. Allen's skill lies in the fun way he describes the quaffing process, whether it be a bold red or crisp white.

Allan Campion and Michelle Curtis *The Foodies' Guide to Melbourne* (Hardie Grant). Released annually, this is one of the better food guides, spotlighting everything from delis and markets to Indian takeaways, picnic sites and late-night supper spots.

Stefano di Pieri *Gondola on the Murray* (o/p). Di Pieri, whose award-winning restaurant *Stefanos* is located in Mildura's *Grand Hotel*, distinguishes himself from other chefs turned authors by including fascinating stories that give glimpses into Italian country life. Featuring a rundown of the best Australian

produce, *Gondola on the Murray* is also available on CD and video.

Teague Ezard *Ezard* (Hardie Grant). This book traces how the style of Teague Ezard, known for his bold and imaginative Asian-inspired dishes, melded into the Melbourne food landscape. Apart from revelling in Ezard's enthusiasm for developing amazing flavours, you'll also be taken through the art of stir-frying, steaming and pasta making.

※ **Greg and Lucy Malouf** *Arabesque* (Hardie Grant). The Melbourne restaurateur couple's first foray into the publishing world is an award-winning and widely acclaimed book larded with the flavours of North Africa and the Middle East. Look out for their second offering, *Moorish: Flavours from Mecca to Marrakech*, which covers similar territory.

Fiction

Peter Carey *The True History of the Kelly Gang* (Alfred A Knopf). Ironically titled novel by Booker-prize winner Peter Carey about the Australian outlaw Ned Kelly masterfully combines several journals supposedly written by the man himself for his unborn daughter, in the process establishing a new and vivid mythology of Australia's most enduring legend.

J.R. Carroll *The Clan* (Pan Macmillan Australia). Admirable for its brutal, bare-knuckle approach, *The Clan* tells the story of the notoriously lawless Beattie clan, whose youngest son is killed by the police in a back alley. It's all here – epic family struggles, hold-ups, retribution and a Melbourne quite unlike any you imagined before.

Falkiner, Katie (ed.) *All Change Please* (Cardigan Press). The third and final instalment in this series of anthologies from new Melbourne writers (many students from RMIT). In a canny piece of marketing, stories

vary in word length to suit various tram journeys around the city.

Helen Garner *Monkey Grip* (McPhee Gribble, Aus). Prize-winning first novel set in Melbourne during the 1970s, about the passionate, volatile relationship between an inner-city artist type and a junkie. A meandering but worthwhile story, with much of it set in the skanky-bohemian areas of Fitzroy and Carlton, including key scenes at the Fitzroy Pool (see p.149). Made into a so-so film in 1982 that featured, interestingly, Garner's daughter Alice.

Frank Hardy *Power Without the Glory* (Mandarin). One of Australia's greatest and most controversial novels, *Power Without the Glory* is the semi-fictional account of the life of John Wren, a legendary criminal figure who lived in Collingwood in the 1930s. Hardy, who collected much of his material while working as a Melbourne journalist, had enormous difficulty in getting the work published, and was later sued (unsuccessfully) by Wren's wife for defamation.

Adele Lang *What Katya Did Next: The Katya Livingston Chronicles* (Vintage, Aus; Mainstream, UK). Self-absorbed member of the South Yarra Chardonnay set whines about her work (or lack of it), friends and sex life. The guffaw count is reasonably high, and there is plenty of name-dropping.

⊡ **Shane Maloney** *Stiff* (Text Publishing, Aus; Arcade, UK & US). Mixing a benighted central character (private detective and single parent Murray Whelan) with drugs, Turks and killer cars, *Stiff* is a fast and often funny thriller set in various Melbourne suburbs. First in a series that also includes *The Brush-Off* and *Nice Try*.

⊡ **Elliot Perlman** *Three Dollars* (Picador, Aus; Faber & Faber, UK; MacMurray & Beck, US). Stirring read that goes straight for the jugular in its depiction of economic rationalism and downsizing in modern Melbourne. Collected *The Age* Book of the Year award for 1998. His more recent endeavour *Seven Types of Ambiguity* and the award-winning short story collection *The Reason I Won't be Coming* are also both worth seeking out.

Adam Ford *Man Bites Dog* (Allen & Unwin). A laugh-out-loud funny novel for young adults that follows a local postman into Melbourne's subcultures of performance poetry and accidentally deceased pets.

Christos Tsiolkas *Loaded* (Vintage, Aus & UK). Convincingly maps out ideas on homosexuality, ethnicity, sex, drugs and music from the perspective of Ari, the unemployed son of Greek migrants. Think Jean Genet and William Burroughs with toothache and you're already halfway there. Made into the film *Head On* (see p.226).

Arthur Upfield *The Great Melbourne Cup Mystery* (ETT Imprint). A thriller about the Melbourne Cup might not sound like an intriguing prospect, yet Upfield has done a fine job in capturing Depression-era Melbourne, its seediness, corruption and underworld goings-on.

⊡ **Arnold Zable** *Café Scheherazade* (Text Publishing, Aus). Set around a famous Acland St cake shop (see p.91) this delicious, warm book explores Melbourne's Russian Jewish community. Zable's interest in the migrant experience c an also be seen in his more recent *Scraps of Heaven*.

Film

va Gardner's wrongly attributed words famously haunted Melbourne for years. "A great place to make a film about the end of the world," she reputedly quipped in 1959, during the shooting of Stanley Kramer's apocalyptic *On the Beach* (in fact, the remark was penned by a local journalist). At the time there was little film production in Melbourne, a far cry from the **beginning of the twentieth century**, when the city was pioneering the latest film technology. In 1900, over two thousand people packed the Melbourne Town Hall to watch *Soldiers of the Cross*, an evangelistic film made by the Salvation Army about early Christian martyrs. Six years later, John and Nevin Tait produced *The Story of the Kelly Gang*, one of the first feature-length fictional films in the world. But as the Hollywood silent era churned out miles of celluloid and "more stars than heaven" (as MGM claimed), Melbourne, like the rest of Australia, succumbed to the waves of overseas imports arriving on its shores.

The city's film culture was revived in the 1950s with the founding of the **Melbourne International Film Festival** (see p.141), which helped develop an interest in alternative cinema and fostered a modest "underground" of film-makers, who took their lead from the French New Wave. During the postwar years, Melbourne also became the engine room of Australian film studies. The National Film Theatre and the Australian Film Institute were founded in Melbourne, while **publications** such as *Lumiere* (now defunct) and *Cinema Papers*, Australia's premier film magazine, went into circulation. In addition, the first film studies department was instituted at La Trobe University, and the first film school introduced at Swinburne Institute of Technology (now at the Victoria College of the Arts). Melbourne and Australia's film renaissance was given a further boost in the 1970s, when state and federal government bodies started actively supporting the domestic film industry, a process that continues in fits and starts today.

By the early 1990s, however, Victoria's film business was in the doldrums. A welcome sign of improvement came in 1993, when Film Victoria established the **Melbourne Film Office** to entice film and television projects to the state. Production in Melbourne has since boomed, partly because the city sells its streets at a far lower price than Sydney, but also because of its "every-city" appeal. With the completion of the Central City film studios at Docklands, set to compete with Fox in Sydney and Warner Bros on the Gold Coast, it is hoped that scores more films will be made in the city.

The list of films that follow doesn't pretend to be exhaustive, but it should give you an idea of some of the films available with distinctive Melbourne qualities, or those that have their source in the city. Most can also be rented from video & DVD outlets around the city and suburbs.

Angel Baby (1995). Made with the help of the Australian Film Commission, *Angel Baby* sets out to unsettle, with a story of romance between two mentally disabled lovers. Starring a young Jacqueline McKenzie and John Lynch as the oddball couple, it's somewhat reminiscent of *Benny and Joon*, the Johnny Depp and Mary Stuart Masterton film.

Bad Eggs (2003). Low-budget comedy/thriller starring Melbourne funnyman Mick Molloy as a cop in a corrupt anti-crime unit. As you'd expect from a cast that features the slightly loopy talents of another local, Judith Lucy, and the writing skills of Tony Martin, a long-time collaborator of Molloy's, there's loads of sight gags and some truly inspired one-liners.

The Big Steal (1990). Director Nadia Tass's charming romantic comedy of a high-school boy's infatuation with a girl and Jaguar cars, and getting even with a shonky used-car dealer.

The Castle (1997). Salt-of-the-earth saga about the battling Kerrigan family taking on big business to save their home from an airport runway extension. The nods and winks at Aussie culture might not always make sense, but the more you know about Melbourne, the funnier it gets.

Chopper (2000). This semi-biopic of Mark "Chopper" Read, psychotic ex-crook and best-selling author, is a gem. Stylish, brutal and horribly funny, the film proved enormously popular in Australia, largely because of the masterly portrayal by one-time comedian Eric Bana, later of *Black Hawk Down*, *Hulk* and *Troy* fame. Filmed in a number of inner-city locations, the characters and action were so realistic that worried residents, not knowing what was going on, regularly called in the police.

The Club (1980). David Williamson's satirical play studies the intrigue and machismo within the ranks of Collingwood, the most famous AFL club in Australia. Perfectly adapted for film by director Bruce Beresford.

Crackerjack (2002). Mick Molloy again, this time playing Jack Simpson, who joins an inner-city bowling club facing closure to take advantage of the free parking. It's a cracking story, with Molloy naturally saving the day, not to mention popularizing the term "swear jar", and marijuana biscuits. Ever since, bowls clubs have become irresistible to the grunge crowd, who have now found a way to drink, smoke, wear thongs and get a bit of "sport" back into their lives.

Crackers (1998). Low-budget film tracing the humorous goings-on within the tightly knit Dredge family, a bunch of whackos who come together for Christmas festivities.

Death in Brunswick (1991). Directed by John Ruane and starring Sam Neill, this black comedy revolves around Neill's no-hoper cook who works at a nightclub in the multicultural melting pot of Brunswick. New Zealand-born, Melbourne-based comedian John Clarke is a scene-stealer at every turn.

Dogs in Space (1987). Unintentionally hilarious film about the punk-rock era of the late 1970s. Directed by Richard Lowenstein and starring the late Michael Hutchence, the film vainly attempts to capture glorious "youth" in all its waywardness. Over the years it's built up something of a cult, with ageing Melburnians in their Doc Martens still swearing by it.

Harvie Crumpet (2003). This charming claymation short won young Melbourne filmmaker Adam Elliot an Oscar, which is on display at ACMI (see p.66). As much for adults as for children, this story follows the adventures of Harvie and is narrated by Australian actor Geoffrey Rush.

Head On (1998). A raw and explicit story of a young "wog" (superbly played by hunky Alex Dimitriades) crashing through 24 hours of his life fuelled by vast quantities of sex, drugs and booze. Wonderfully photographed scenes of the seedier side of the city and deft insights into 1990s youth culture in multicultural Melbourne. Based on the cult Christos Tsiolkas novel *Loaded* (see p.226).

Hotel Sorrento (1994). Filmed on location at Sorrento, south of Melbourne, *Hotel Sorrento* comes over all deep and meaningful in its examination of the dysfunctional Moynihan family, particularly the rotten relationship between three sisters living very different lives. There's plenty to admire here – the performances, poisoned interactions and political musings on Australia's place in the world – but the final result is patchy and uneven, a film never quite sure of its own ambitions.

Love and Other Catastrophes (1996). Lightweight romantic comedy that follows the adventures of a group of students at a Melbourne university. Apart from the odd laugh and a reasonably good soundtrack, it's most notable for introducing a bunch of fresh-faced actors like Frances O'Connor, Radha Mitchell and Matt Day to the screen.

Love's Brother (2004). Starring the always watchable Giovanni Ribisi and Aussie ex-pat Adam Garcia, this is an old-fashioned romantic fable about two brothers from Italy, mixed identity and the first espresso machine in Australia. Set in Hepburn Springs, Victoria's glorious spa country, *Love's Brother* starts out with an inventive premise and some good insights into life in an Italian community in Australia in the 1950s, but unfortunately dissolves into caricature and tedium by the film's end.

Mad Max (1979). Where would Australian cinema be without George Miller's apocalyptic masterpiece? The story of a cop (Mel Gibson) who seeks revenge after witnessing the brutal deaths of his partner and family by gang leader Toecutter, it provided the template for road warrior movies ever since and struck a chord with audiences worldwide.

Malcolm (1986). Nadia Tass (see *The Big Steal* opposite) directed this delightful comedy about a social misfit inventor finding fulfilment as a criminal's offsider (assistant). Humorous, with great scenes of Melbourne and its rapidly disappearing W-class trams.

Mallboy (2000). Directed by local filmmaker Vincent Giarrusso and set in Melbourne's western suburbs, *Mallboy* is a gritty coming-of-age story in which a young tearaway aimlessly hangs out at the mall, thieving, smoking and generally playing up. Leaden at times, but excellent performances from the central characters.

Metal Skin (1994). Writer/director Geoffrey Wright's follow-up to the critically-acclaimed *Romper Stomper* (see overleaf) is an oppressive affair about a couple of "rev-heads" cruising the suburban streets of Melbourne. Violent, gloomy and filled with a collection of mostly unlikeable characters, it nonetheless features two remarkable performances from Aden Young and Ben Mendhelson and, if you can stick it out, a particularly gripping finale.

My First Wife (1984). Surprisingly engaging story of a tortured custody dispute amid calls for a reappraisal of the rights of the father in such cases. From Paul Cox, Melbourne's best-known author-director.

Ned Kelly (1970). Watchable "star" vehicle for Mick Jagger, who is ambitiously (and not altogether unsuccessfully) cast here by director Tony Richardson to play the totemic Australian outlaw Ned Kelly. Much emphasis is placed on the class conflict at the heart of Ned's story, and there are several good Irish ballads by Mick, Waylon Jennings and Kris Kristofferson among others. The story of Ned's short life was updated in 2003 again as *Ned Kelly* and filmed in Ballarat and the tiny Victorian country town of Clunes. This time, Heath Ledger plays the whiskery bushranger and Naomi Watts his love interest (Orlando Bloom also pops up as one of Ned's accomplices). Sentimental and dull, the film was pilloried for its mythologizing, and unsurprisingly sank without trace.

On the Beach (1959). Director Stanley Kramer's classic Cold War flick has Melbourne as the last place on earth that hasn't choked on the radioactive fallout of World War III. Gregory Peck, Ava Gardner, Anthony Perkins and Fred Astaire all give outstanding performances. Remade into a drab TV mini-series in 2001, starring Amande Assante, with the story set in 2006 after China's invasion of Taiwan triggers another world war.

One Perfect Day (2003). Promoted as the "techno answer to *Moulin Rouge*", *One Perfect Day* is an ambitious foray into Melbourne's dance culture. Tommy Matisse, played by Dan Spielman, is a gifted violinist who finds himself exploring clubland after a family tragedy. As with any fashionable scene, the club sequences already seem dated and despite great Aussie acting this film failed to impress at the box office.

Picnic at Hanging Rock (1975). Those who have seen this can never forget the haunting image of the virginal Miranda, immaculately dressed in white, spookily vanishing between the ageless boulders of Hanging Rock. Directed by Peter Weir, this is the pick of Australia's New Wave cinema – a classic turn-of-the-twentieth-century tale of vanishing schoolgirls, repressed sexuality and menacing landscapes.

Proof (1990). Jocelyn Moorehouse's quietly paced though chilling analysis of loveless sex, betrayal and broken marriages, with a blind photographer (Hugo Weaving) caught in the middle.

Romper Stomper (1992). Bleak and intense tale of neo-Nazis in Footscray and their running battles with the Vietnamese community. The film divided audiences on its release, with many railing against its random acts of pitiless violence.

Glossary of Melbourne terms

AFL Australian Football League, or "Aussie Rules", or simply "footy".

Ankle biter Small child.

Anzac Australia and New Zealand Army Corps; every town has a memorial to Anzac casualties from both world wars; Anzac Day is April 25.

Arvo Afternoon.

Barrack To cheer for (as in your favourite footy team).

Bathers Swimming costume (see "swimmers", "togs").

Beer o'clock Time to leave work.

Biffo A fight.

Bingle Mishap or car crash.

Blowies Blowflies.

Bludger Someone who doesn't pull their weight, or a scrounger – as in "dole bludger".

Blue A fight; also a red-haired person.

Bonzer Great, as in "we had a bonzer time".

Bottle shop Off-licence or liquor store.

Buckley's No chance; as in "hasn't got a Buckley's".

Budgie smugglers Speedos (swimming briefs).

BYO Bring Your Own; café or restaurant which allows you to bring your own alcohol.

Cactus Broken, useless, as in "the car's cactus".

Carked it Dead, died.

Chewy Chewing gum

Chuck a wobbly Have a temper tantrum.

Chrissie Christmas, which also involves "prezzies" or presents.

Chunder Vomit.

Connies Melbourne's late, lamented tram conductors, slowly being reintroduced.

Crap on Talk too much, often nonsense ("geez, you crap on sometimes").

Dag Friendly term for decidedly uncool person.

Dob in To tell on, to nominate someone for an unpleasant task.

Doing a Melba Reference to Dame Nellie Melba, famous Australian operatic soprano who retired, then made a series of comebacks.

Drongo An idiot, fool.

Dunny Toilet; usually an outside pit toilet.

Esky Portable, insulated box to keep food or beer cold.

Footy AFL.

The G Affectionate term for the Melbourne Cricket Ground (MCG).

G'day Hello, hi.

Grey Ghost A parking inspector.

Grog Alcohol.

Grommet Young surfer.

Gubba Europeans.

Gunzels Tram enthusiasts.

Gutless wonder Coward.

Hangy Hangover.

Harry Holt To "bolt", or leave unexpectedly (comes from ex-Australian prime minister Harry Holt, who disappeared, presumed drowned, while swimming off the Victorian coast).

Hip and shoulder Footy term for legal tackle.

Hook turn Driving manoeuvre (see p.24).

Hoon A yob, delinquent.

Icey-pole Ice lolly/popsicle.

Koori Collective name for Aboriginal people from southeastern Australia.

Loo Toilet.

Lay by Practice of putting a deposit on goods until they can be fully paid for.

Milk bar Corner shop, and often a small café.

More pull than a Collins Street dentist Often heard during the Spring Racing Carnival, and used to describe a tearaway racehorse.

Mulga The country.

Mystery bag Meat pie.

No worries That's OK; it doesn't matter; don't mention it.

Nuddie The nude.

Onya Good for you!

Op shop Short for "opportunity shop"; a charity shop or thrift store.

Pashing Kissing or snogging.

Pokies Poker machines, slot or fruit machines.

Pot 285ml or 10oz glass of beer.

Prang An accident, usually minor.

Rack of Go away, get out of here.

Rattler A train or tram.

Rego Vehicle registration document.

Root Vulgar term for sexual congress, often substituted with "pork".

Rooted To be very tired or to be beyond repair; as in "your car's rooted, mate".

Sangers Sandwiches.

Scull To down a drink (usually beer) quickly.

She'll be apples It will be okay.

Shirtfront Another footy term for a tackle.

Shonky Something or someone deceptive or unreliable.

Sickie Taking a day off work when you're not actually sick.

Silverhairs Retirees.

Slab 24-can carton of beer.

Smoko Tea break.

Snag Sausage usually cooked on a barbecue.

Snot block Vanilla slice.

Southerly buster Melbourne's much-welcomed cooling breeze.

Sticky-beak A closer look.

Swimmers Swimming costume.

Tanty Temper tantrum for children.

Thongs Flip-flops or sandals.

Tinnie Can of beer.

Togs Swimming costume.

Toorak tractor A 4WD used only for city driving.

Top drop An enjoyable drink, usually referring to alcohol.

Top shelf Really good person, as in "He's top shelf".

VB Victoria Bitter, the state's thirst-quenching lager.

Vegemite Blackish-brown yeast spread used on sandwiches. Aussie version of Marmite.

Wag To play truant.

Waxhead Surfer.

Weatherboard Wooden house.

White mice Football umpires, also known as "white maggots".

Wog Derogatory description for those of Mediterranean descent.

Write off A total loss.

Wuss To be weak, lacking commitment.

Zonked Tired, exhausted.

Rough Guides

advertiser

Rough Guides travel...

...music & reference

Trinidad & Tobago

Africa & Middle East
Cape Town
Egypt
The Gambia
Jordan
Kenya
Marrakesh
  DIRECTIONS
Morocco
South Africa, Lesotho
  & Swaziland
Syria
Tanzania
Tunisia
West Africa
Zanzibar
Zimbabwe

Travel Theme guides
First-Time Around the
  World
First-Time Asia
First-Time Europe
First-Time Latin
  America
Skiing & Snowboarding
  in North America
Travel Online
Travel Health
Walks in London & SE
  England
Women Travel

Restaurant guides
French Hotels &
  Restaurants
London
New York
San Francisco

Maps
Algarve
Amsterdam
Andalucia & Costa del Sol
Argentina

Athens
Australia
Baja California
Barcelona
Berlin
Boston
Brittany
Brussels
Chicago
Crete
Croatia
Cuba
Cyprus
Czech Republic
Dominican Republic
Dubai & UAE
Dublin
Egypt
Florence & Siena
Frankfurt
Greece
Guatemala & Belize
Iceland
Ireland
Kenya
Lisbon
London
Los Angeles
Madrid
Mexico
Miami & Key West
Morocco
New York City
New Zealand
Northern Spain
Paris
Peru
Portugal
Prague
Rome
San Francisco
Sicily
South Africa
South India
Sri Lanka
Tenerife
Thailand

Toronto
Trinidad & Tobago
Tuscany
Venice
Washington DC
Yucatán Peninsula

**Dictionary
Phrasebooks**
Czech
Dutch
Egyptian Arabic
EuropeanLanguages
  (Czech, French,
  German, Greek, Italian,
  Portuguese, Spanish)
French
German
Greek
Hindi & Urdu
Hungarian
Indonesian
Italian
Japanese
Mandarin Chinese
Mexican Spanish
Polish
Portuguese
Russian
Spanish
Swahili
Thai
Turkish
Vietnamese

Music Guides
The Beatles
Bob Dylan
Cult Pop
Classical Music
Country Music
Elvis
Hip Hop
House
Irish Music
Jazz
Music USA

Opera
Reggae
Rock
Techno
World Music (2 vols)

History Guides
China
Egypt
England
France
India
Islam
Italy
Spain
USA

Reference Guides
Books for Teenagers
Children's Books, 0–5
Children's Books, 5–11
Cult Fiction
Cult Football
Cult Movies
Cult TV
Ethical Shopping
Formula 1
The iPod, iTunes &
  Music Online
The Internet
Internet Radio
James Bond
Kids' Movies
Lord of the Rings
Muhammed Ali
Man Utd
Personal Computers
Pregnancy & Birth
Shakespeare
Superheroes
Unexplained
  Phenomena
The Universe
Videogaming
Weather
Website Directory

ROUGH GUIDES ADVERTISER

Also! More than 120 Rough Guide music CDs are available from all good book
and record stores. Listen in at www.worldmusic.net

Visit us online

roughguides.com

Information on over 25,000 destinations around the world

ROUGH GUIDES ADVERTISER

Don't bury your head in the sand!

Take cover!

with Rough Guide Travel Insurance

small print and

A Rough Guide to Rough Guides

In the summer of 1981, Mark Ellingham, a recent graduate from Bristol University, was travelling round Greece and couldn't find a guidebook that really met his needs. On the one hand there were the student guides, insistent on saving every last cent, and on the other the heavyweight cultural tomes whose authors seemed to have spent more time in a research library than lounging away the afternoon at a taverna or on the beach.

In a bid to avoid getting a job, Mark and a small group of writers set about creating their own guidebook. It was a guide to Greece that aimed to combine a journalistic approach to description with a thoroughly practical approach to travellers' needs – a guide that would incorporate culture, history and contemporary insights with a critical edge, together with up-to-date, value-for-money listings. Back in London, Mark and the team finished their Rough Guide, as they called it, and talked Routledge into publishing the book.

That first *Rough Guide to Greece*, published in 1982, was a student scheme that became a publishing phenomenon. The immediate success of the book – with numerous reprints and a Thomas Cook prize shortlisting – spawned a series that rapidly covered dozens of destinations. Rough Guides had a ready market among low-budget backpackers, but soon also acquired a much broader and older readership that relished Rough Guides' wit and inquisitiveness as much as their enthusiastic, critical approach. Everyone wants value for money, but not at any price.

Rough Guides soon began supplementing the "rougher" information about hostels and low-budget listings with the kind of detail on restaurants and quality hotels that independent-minded visitors on any budget might expect, whether on business in New York or trekking in Thailand.

These days the guides – distributed worldwide by the Penguin group – offer recommendations from shoestring to luxury and cover more than 200 destinations around the globe, including almost every country in the Americas and Europe, more than half of Africa and most of Asia and Australasia. Our ever-growing team of authors and photographers is spread all over the world, particularly in Europe, the USA and Australia.

In 1994, we published the *Rough Guide to World Music* and *Rough Guide to Classical Music*; and a year later the *Rough Guide to the Internet*. All three books have become benchmark titles in their fields – which encouraged us to expand into other areas of publishing, mainly around popular culture. Rough Guides now publish:

- Travel guides to more than 200 worldwide destinations
- Dictionary phrasebooks to 22 major languages
- History guides ranging from Ireland to Islam
- Maps printed on rip-proof and waterproof Polyart™ paper
- Music guides running the gamut from Opera to Elvis
- Restaurant guides to London, New York and San Francisco
- Reference books on topics as diverse as the Weather and Shakespeare
- Sports guides from Formula 1 to Man Utd
- Pop culture books from *Lord of the Rings* to Cult TV
- World Music CDs in association with World Music Network

Visit **www.roughguides.com** to see our latest publications.

Rough Guide credits

Text editors: Lucy Ratcliffe, Claire Saunders, Sally Schafer, Clifton Wilkinson
Layout: Jessica Subramanian
Cartography: Stratigraphics
Picture research: Harriet Mills
Proofreader: David Price
Editorial: **London** Martin Dunford, Kate Berens, Helena Smith, Claire Saunders, Geoff Howard, Ruth Blackmore, Gavin Thomas, Polly Thomas, Richard Lim, Clifton Wilkinson, Alison Murchie, Fran Sandham, Sally Schafer, Alexander Mark Rogers, Karoline Densley, Andy Turner, Ella O'Donnell, Keith Drew, Edward Aves, Andrew Lockett, Joe Staines, Duncan Clark, Peter Buckley, Matthew Milton, Daniel Crewe; **New York** Andrew Rosenberg, Richard Koss, Yuki Takagaki, Chris Barsanti, Steven Horak, AnneLise Sorenson, Amy Hegarty
Design & Pictures: London Simon Bracken, Dan May, Diana Jarvis, Mark Thomas, Jj Luck, Harriet Mills, Chloë Roberts; **Delhi** Madhulita Mohapatra, Umesh Aggarwal, Ajay Verma, Jessica Subramanian, Amit Verma

Production: Julia Bovis, Sophie Hewat, Katherine Owers
Cartography: **London** Maxine Repath, Ed Wright, Katie Lloyd-Jones, Miles Irving; **Delhi** Manish Chandra, Rajesh Chhibber, Jai Prakesh Mishra, Ashutosh Bharti, Rajesh Mishra, Animesh Pathak, Jasbir Sandhu, Karobi Gogoi
Online: **New York** Jennifer Gold, Cree Lawson, Suzanne Welles, Benjamin Ross; **Delhi** Manik Chauhan, Narender Kumar, Shekhar Jha, Rakesh Kumar
Marketing & Publicity: **London** Richard Trillo, Niki Hanmer, David Wearn, Chloë Roberts, Demelza Dallow, Kristina Pentland; **New York** Geoff Colquitt, Megan Kennedy
Custom publishing and foreign rights: Philippa Hopkins
Finance: Gary Singh
Manager India: Punita Singh
Series editor: Mark Ellingham
PA to Managing Director: Julie Sanderson
Managing Director: Kevin Fitzgerald

Publishing information

This third edition published April 2005 by **Rough Guides Ltd**,
80 Strand, London WC2R 0RL.
345 Hudson St, 4th Floor,
New York, NY 10014, USA.
Distributed by the Penguin Group
Penguin Books Ltd,
80 Strand, London WC2R 0RL
Penguin Putnam, Inc.
375 Hudson Street, NY 10014, USA
Penguin Group (Australia)
250 Camberwell Road, Camberwell
Victoria 3124, Australia
Penguin Books Canada Ltd,
10 Alcorn Avenue, Toronto, Ontario,
Canada M4V 1E4
Penguin Group (New Zealand)
Cnr Rosedale and Airborne Roads
Albany, Auckland, New Zealand
Typeset in Bembo and Helvetica to an original design by Henry Iles.

Printed and bound in China

© Rough Guides, 2005

No part of this book may be reproduced in any form without permission from the publisher except for the quotation of brief passages in reviews.

256pp includes index
A catalogue record for this book is available from the British Library

ISBN 1-84353-284-0

The publishers and authors have done their best to ensure the accuracy and currency of all the information in **The Rough Guide to Melbourne**, however, they can accept no responsibility for any loss, injury, or inconvenience sustained by any traveller as a result of information or advice contained in the guide.

1   3   5   7   9   8   6   4   2

Help us update

We've gone to a lot of effort to ensure that the third edition of **The Rough Guide to Melbourne** is accurate and up to date. However, things change – places get "discovered", opening hours are notoriously fickle, restaurants and rooms raise prices or lower standards. If you feel we've got it wrong or left something out, we'd like to know, and if you can remember the address, the price, the time, the phone number, so much the better.

We'll credit all contributions, and send a copy of the next edition (or any other Rough Guide if you prefer) for the best letters. Everyone who writes to us and isn't already a subscriber will receive a copy of our full-colour thrice-yearly newsletter. Please mark letters: "**Rough Guide Melbourne Update**" and send to: Rough Guides, 80 Strand, London WC2R 0RL, or Rough Guides, 4th Floor, 345 Hudson St, New York, NY 10014. Or send an email to **mail@roughguides.com**

Have your questions answered and tell others about your trip at **www.roughguides.atinfopop.com**

Photo credits

Index

Map entries are in colour.

Map symbols

maps are listed in the full index using coloured text

═══	Freeway	⋀⋀	Spring
═══	Main road	✈	Airport
═══	Minor road	✈	Airfield
───	Unpaved road	⸙	Lighthouse
▓▓	Pedestrianized street	♣	Vineyard
-----	Path	ⓘ	Information office
━━━	Railway	✉	Post office
── ──	Ferry route	▣	Restaurant
───	River	▬	Building
─ ─ ─	Chapter boundary	✚	Church/cathedral
▪	Point of interest	░	Beach
▲	Mountain peak	⊞	Cemetery
⸎	Gorge	▦	Park
⸙	Waterfall		

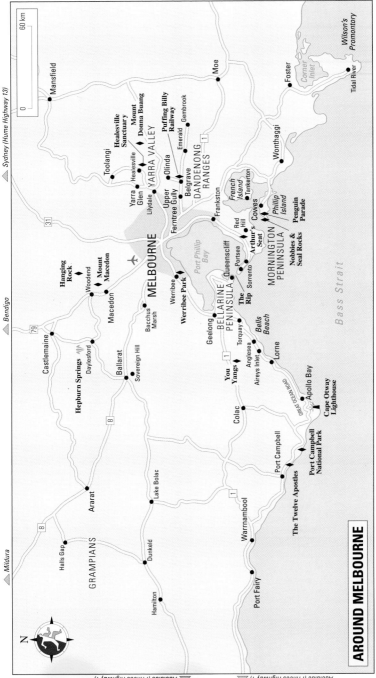

AROUND MELBOURNE

N

Wilson's Promontory

Corner Inlet

Tidal River

Foster

Wonthaggi

Moe

Gembrook
Emerald
Puffing Billy Railway
Mount Donna Buang
Healesville Sanctuary
YARRA VALLEY
Toolangi
Mansfield

Olinda
Belgrave
DANDENONG RANGES
Upper Ferntree Gully
Healesville
Yarra Glen
Lilydale

French Island
Tankerton
Cowes
Phillip Island
Penguin Parade
Nobbies & Seal Rocks
MORNINGTON PENINSULA

Red Hill
Arthur's Seat
Portsea
Sorrento
Queenscliff
The Rip
BELLARINE PENINSULA

Frankston

MELBOURNE

Port Phillip Bay

Werribee
Werribee Park

Bass Strait

Geelong
Torquay
Bells Beach
Anglesea
Aireys Inlet
Lorne

You Yangs

GREAT OCEAN ROAD

Apollo Bay
Cape Otway Lighthouse

Colac

Bacchus Marsh
Macedon
Woodend
Hanging Rock
Mount Macedon

Ballarat
Sovereign Hill
Daylesford
Hepburn Springs

Castlemaine

Lake Bolac

Ararat

Halls Gap
GRAMPIANS
Dunkeld

Hamilton

Port Fairy

Warrnambool

Port Campbell
Port Campbell National Park
The Twelve Apostles

60 km
0

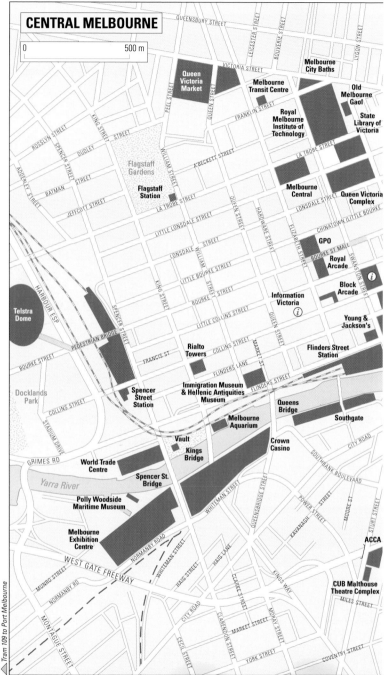

CENTRAL MELBOURNE

0   500 m

QUEENSBURY STREET
LEICESTER STREET
BOUVERIE STREET
LYGON STREET

VICTORIA STREET

Melbourne City Baths

Queen Victoria Market

Melbourne Transit Centre

Old Melbourne Gaol

FRANKLIN STREET

Royal Melbourne Institute of Technology

State Library of Victoria

PEEL STREET
QUEEN STREET

ROSSLYN STREET
SPENCER STREET
KING STREET
STREET

DUDLEY STREET

A'BECKETT STREET

LA TROBE STREET

WILLIAM STREET

Flagstaff Gardens

ADDERLEY STREET
BATMAN STREET

JEFFCOTT STREET

Flagstaff Station

LA TROBE STREET

Melbourne Central

Queen Victoria Complex

LONSDALE STREET

LITTLE LONSDALE STREET

QUEEN STREET
HARDWARE STREET

CHINATOWN (LITTLE BOURKE)

LONSDALE STREET

WILLIAM STREET
KING STREET

LITTLE BOURKE STREET

ELIZABETH STREET

GPO

BOURKE ST MALL

Royal Arcade

SWANSTON STREET

BOURKE STREET

LITTLE COLLINS STREET

Information Victoria ⓘ

Block Arcade

ⓘ

Telstra Dome

HARBOUR ESP

PEDESTRIAN BRIDGE

SPENCER STREET

Young & Jackson's

BOURKE STREET

LITTLE COLLINS STREET

Rialto Towers

COLLINS STREET

MARKET ST
QUEEN STREET

Flinders Street Station

FRANCIS ST

FLINDERS LANE

Docklands Park

COLLINS STREET

STADIUM DRIVE

Spencer Street Station

Immigration Museum & Hellenic Antiquities Museum

FLINDERS STREET
FLINDERS LANE

Queens Bridge

Southgate

GRIMES RD

Melbourne Aquarium

Vault

Kings Bridge

Crown Casino

CITY ROAD

SOUTHBANK BOULEVARD

World Trade Centre

Spencer St. Bridge

Yarra River

Polly Woodside Maritime Museum

WHITEMAN STREET

QUEENSBRIDGE STREET

POWER STREET

MOORE ST

STURT STREET

SOUTHBANK BOULEVARD

KAVANAGH STREET

Melbourne Exhibition Centre

NORMANBY ROAD

WEST GATE FREEWAY

WHITEMAN STREET

HAIG STREET

HAIG LANE

CLARKE STREET

KINGS WAY

ACCA

MUNRO STREET

NORMANBY RD

CITY ROAD

MORAY STREET

CUB Malthouse Theatre Complex

MILES STREET

MONTAGUE STREET

MARKET STREET

CLARENDON STREET

CECIL STREET

YORK STREET

COVENTRY STREET

◁ *Tram 109 to Port Melbourne*

▽ *Tram 96 to St Kilda*

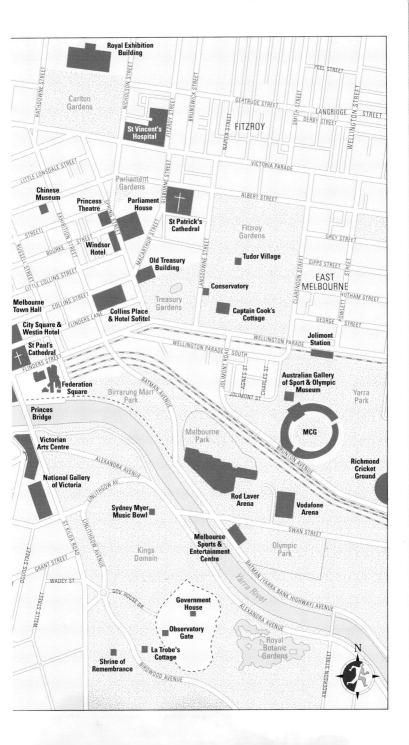

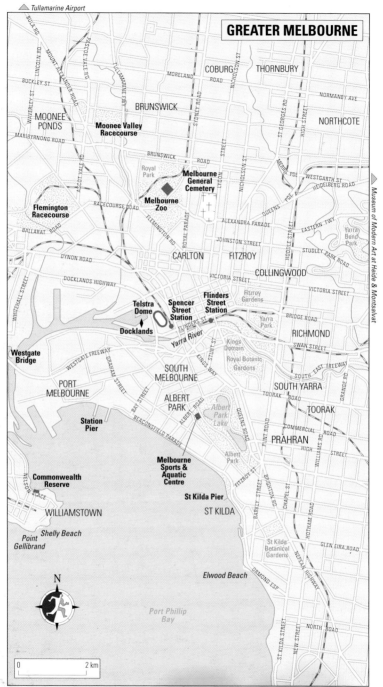

GREATER MELBOURNE

BULLA RD
LINCOLN RD
MOUNT ALEXANDER ROAD
PASCOE VALE RD
TULLAMARINE FWY
SYDNEY ROAD
NICHOLSON ST
COBURG
THORNBURY
MORELAND ROAD
NORMANBY AVE
BUCKLEY ST
ST GEORGES RD
HIGH STREET
WAVERLEY ST
QUEENS RD
BRUNSWICK
NORTHCOTE
MOONEE PONDS
Moonee Valley Racecourse
MARIBYRNONG ROAD
BRUNSWICK ROAD
LYGON ST
NICHOLSON ST
Royal Park
Melbourne General Cemetery
MERRI PDE
WESTGARTH ST
HEIDELBERG ROAD
ASCOT VALE RD
RACECOURSE ROAD
Melbourne Zoo
QUEENS PDE
EASTERN FWY
Yarra Bend Park
Flemington Racecourse
BALLARAT ROAD
FLEMINGTON RD
ROYAL PARADE
ALEXANDRA PARADE
HODDLE STREET
DYNON ROAD
JOHNSTON STREET
STUDLEY PARK ROAD
CARLTON
FITZROY
WHITEHALL STREET
DOCKLANDS HIGHWAY
VICTORIA STREET
COLLINGWOOD
VICTORIA STREET
Telstra Dome
Spencer Street Station
Flinders Street Station
Fitzroy Gardens
BRIDGE ROAD
RICHMOND
Docklands
FLINDERS ST
Yarra Park
Yarra River
Kings Domain
SWAN STREET
Westgate Bridge
WESTGATE FREEWAY
GRAHAM STREET
Royal Botanic Gardens
SOUTH EAST FREEWAY
GRANGE RD
SOUTH MELBOURNE
KINGS WAY
STURT ST
SOUTH YARRA
PORT MELBOURNE
BAY STREET
TOORAK ROAD
TOORAK
Station Pier
ALBERT PARK
ALBERT ROAD
Albert Park Lake
QUEENS ROAD
COMMERCIAL ROAD
WILLIAMS STREET
BEACONSFIELD PARADE
PRAHRAN
HIGH STREET
Melbourne Sports & Aquatic Centre
Albert Park
FITZROY ST
BRIGHTON RD
PUNT ROAD
CHAPEL ST
HOTHAM STREET
Commonwealth Reserve
St Kilda Pier
BARKLY STREET
NELSON PLACE
WILLIAMSTOWN
ST KILDA
St Kilda Botanical Gardens
GLEN EIRA ROAD
NEPEAN HIGHWAY
Point Gellibrand
Shelly Beach
Elwood Beach
ORMOND ESP
N
Port Phillip Bay
ST KILDA STREET
NEW STREET
NORTH ROAD

0   2 km